For Trisie
Hope you enjoy the
Tale

The Singer's Tale

from

Carol
2021

Gottahavebooks
16 Middle Street, Great Gransden
SG19 3AD
United Kingdom
sales@gottahavebooks.co.uk
www.gottahavebooks.co.uk

ISBN 978-0-9933781-6-4

Cover and page layout design by Bounford.com
Front cover photo reproduced with the kind permission of Bryan Wharton
Unless otherwise stated, all images are copyright of the author
or the credited photographer.

The Singer's Tale

Carol Grimes

Dedications

The *Singer's Tale* is dedicated to Terri Banks, Kasia Rose Hrybowicz, Sam Smart, Sasha Childers, Sarah Craig, Mark Jennet, Howard Lester, Pip Mayo, Maureen 'Beat' Beattie, Jane Gittens and her wonderful family. To Carol Paul and Llewellyn Gittens, and to Louis, Dee, Frank and John 'Hoppy' Hopkins – no longer here but always in my heart. And Jo Ann Kelly who back in the 1960s inspired me to get on with it. To Anne Brownell and dear Brian Blaine.

To oh so many wonderful musicians. To Annie Whitehead, Winston Clifford, Henry McCullough, Paul Carrack, Jennifer Maidman, Steve Lodder, Dorian Ford, Alastair Gavin, Neil Hubbard, Josefina Cupido, Mervyn Africa, Root Jackson, Donald 'Duck' Dunn and Willie Hall, Frederick Knight and The Memphis Horns, Maciek Hrybowicz Lol Coxhill, Alison Rayner, Harry Beckett, Gail Ann Dorsey and Mark Hewins, Elton Dean, Billy Jenkins, Steve and Phil Miller, Deirdre Cartwright, Neville Malcolm, John Meringue Jamieson, Sami El Salahi, Martin Stone, Freddie King, Linda Malone, Laka Daisical, Sammy 'Snazzy' Mitchell, Gasper Lawal, David Skinner, Stan Adler, Mac Gayden and Sam Kelly.

To the wonderful singers I've sung with and shared stages with. To Ian Shaw, Sarah Jane Morris, Linda Lewis and Madeline Bell, The Shout, Maggie Nichols, Julie Driscoll Tippetts, Najma Akhtar, Dyan Birch, Claire Martin, Jimmy Lindsay, and latterly Randolph Matthews, a fellow spirt.

To Dingwalls and The Vortex, Ronnie Scott's (when Ronnie was still in charge) – spiritual homes, and now the Lime Bar in Folkestone, Andi and Cath.

To my singing friends in the Bloomsbury Choir who inspire me so much. To Anne Brownell and the singers I've met in the Voice Movement Therapy world who dared to make that leap and sing for a living. It's no easy thing.

To the photographers and documentary makers who gave me the images for my life. Thank you Sheila Burnett, Julia Maloof Verderosa, Guy Cross, Barry J Gibb, Glen Davis, Bryan Wharton, Terry Seymour, Val Wilmer, Keith Morris and many others.

To Julie and Trevor Bounford of Gottahavebooks for putting my tale out there.

Finally, to Louis and Ella who live on in the delicious wildness of my cats – Louis and Ella.

Contents

Foreword

She is cracked teacups and old wind up toys.
A museum of treasured books
and memories in miniature -
shelves and shelves of ornaments
like a patchwork quilt,
a story in every square.
And baked potatoes
And buttered crumpets...

These are lines from a poem I wrote for Carol on her 50th birthday. It was 7 April 1994. Carol was doing a gig and celebrating with friends at the *Vortex Jazz Club*, on Stoke Newington Church Street, North London, before the club resituated to Gillett Square, Dalston. I saw her there performing with trombonist Annie Whitehead and drummer Winston Clifford only a few weeks ago in October 2017. Listening to Carol sing that night, and now reading her story, is for me like coming home.

I've known Carol since 1980, just at the point in the narrative that 'the girl' and her colourful array of voices, that tempestuous tapestry of personalities that chide, taunt, goad, fuel and support her in *The Singer's Tale*, leave off their extraordinary commentary. So, on a personal level, I'm hoping Carol is working on a second volume and that there will be many more 'verses' to come.

Not that the first doesn't take us on the most dazzling and dizzying spin through her life 'til then. A musical, political and social history spanning the 1940s and the war-torn London of Carol's birth, through schools, foster homes, teenage sex, cigarettes and listening to music on the jukebox in '50s seaside Britain. Sleazy studios and nefarious Nashville goings-on in recording studios in the '60s, from Nashville to Notting Hill, where roots reggae and reefers had become de rigueur against the backdrop of the rising punk era of the '70s. And all the while we occupy a ringside seat in our singer's imagined, and real, theatrical circus. It's a wild and unforgettable show.

In 1981 I moved to Tower Hamlets with my soon-to-be husband, pianist Alastair Gavin, into a flat in the Boundary Estate, just opposite Brick Lane in London's East

End. It was a vibrant and colourful area. Carol lived just up the road, at the other end of Bethnal Green. Alastair was in Carol's band, The Crocodiles, for a year or so, was on their 1979 single *Keys to the House*, and would eventually produce her 1986 album *Eyes Wide Open*.

We had moved from Archway, where I'd been squatting an unoccupied flat with a friend and Alastair was renting a room downstairs with the jazz singer Jan Ponsford. At 21, I was writing and performing my poetry, acting in plays with various fringe theatre groups and, like so many others, busily seeking any kind of paid work I could lay my hands on. I was just at the beginning of everything. Carol was 36 and, it seemed to me, had already lived more lives than I could imagine. She was wise, warm, quick-witted and quirky. Her home, which she shared with her son Sam, was a treasure trove of trinkets and smelled of cinnamon and baked apple. I loved her immediately.

Carol and I shared a love of poetry. She collected old books of it, like I did, and confessed she had written many poems, which she rarely dared showed to anyone. I would not be surprised if the writing of *The Singer's Tale* was well under way, even then. Over the next few years the two of us cooked up a plan to put together a show that combined poetry, music and song, and told a story. We staged the show in 1985 for five performances at *The Duke of Wellington* in Dalston, and called it *Starring the Wife*. I was an ingénue, six months pregnant with my first child and just married to Alastair. Carol was a grand dame, with a successful music career that had already crowned her a blues legend, and a teenage son, and one divorce behind her.

Our stage set was 'The Sunflower Seed Rainbow Rising Togetherness Teashop'. Carol was in charge of songs and the hat stand, while I dealt with words and nappies. Carol filled every crevice of the tiny back room of that pub with her passion, her voice, her humour and her poetry, and I will always cherish the memories of sharing the stage with her.

In early January 1986, when Carol and Alastair and the band were recording *Eyes Wide Open*, I lay with my eyes shut on a sofa in the *Livingston Studio*, soaking up the music. I was just a few weeks away from giving birth to my first child. Carol's voice and the lyrics to her songs *Your Blues*, *Mau-Mau*, *The Circus* and *Alexandria Dance* absorbed into my being, and the life of the child I was carrying inside me.

Much of *The Singer's Tale* addresses the idea of motherhood. The presence and absence of mothers. What it is to be one and what it is to be without one. The book,

in many ways, serves as a tender love letter to her children, Sam and Kasia.

The Singer's Tale, like Chaucer's prose that inspired its title, is highly original and complex in the way it employs different literary devices to achieve its end; the third person narrative which allows the writer to more closely examine her younger self, 'the girl'; the startling chorus of internal voices which Carol refers to in her introduction as 'the cast of others gathered in my innards'; and her invention of the bridge device which serves, much as it might in music, to link 'chorus' to 'verse', and to transport us to somewhere else.

The Singer's Tale is a confessional, an irreverent romp, bawdy and boisterous. It is a work of psychological astuteness offering an unflinching look at the terrible hurt, pain and sadness that we, as human beings, are capable of inflicting upon one another, and how we can learn from that. It is a celebration of life. Expect darkness and light, ugliness and beauty, comedy and tragedy.

Carol Grimes, when she sings, is a powerhouse, a spark, an electric current, a pulse that occupies the body and gets right to the soul of the listener. Carol Grimes, the writer, is all of these things and more. Her voice is honest, awe-inspiring, utterly unique and you will find it so, in all its authenticity, on every single page of this wonderful tale.

Cheryl Moskowitz,
November 2017

Preface

My name is Carol Grimes, the name under which I have sung since the late sixties. My name. I chose it. I call my story *The Singer's Tale* because of Geoffrey Chaucer who wrote his tales in his wanderings from Southwark to Canterbury. I have lived both north and south of the river Thames and now live on the coast in Kent near Canterbury. Chaucer wrote about cooks and friars, lawyers, nuns and millers but not about singers, so here's a singer's tale. He didn't write one, so I have. How presumptuous of me!

I was born in 1944 in southeast London, when bombs were falling from the skies. There were no bananas and radio was the music and the word. Not much song for me in those days, though in 1959 I fell in love with Ray Charles. It was Margie Hendricks roaring out the chorus of *Night Time is the Right Time* on a juke box on a pier in Lowestoft, Suffolk. It made me wanna holler, made me wanna sing. And the voice of Ella Fitzgerald singing *Every time we say goodbye* touched me deeply. Those early musical memories and the voices of women, the likes of which I'd never heard before. Strong, powerful and full of passion, giving me a life-long love of jazz and blues, melody, rhythm and improvisation.

My singing didn't start during childhood and adolescence but once I opened my mouth at the age of 19, I couldn't stop. I became addicted. Addicted to the feeling, the soaring and roaring feeling inside my belly. A release, a catharsis? Whatever it was, I loved it. Singing in the streets of London as a busker. First as a bottler for an accordion player called Paris Nat, and then along the south coast in the mid-1960s, working with assorted guitar and harmonica players until I joined my first band called the Race. *The Singer's Tale* weaves its stories, sometimes shady, mad and bad with music, song and London at its heart. From singing in the streets to *Ronnie Scott's Jazz Club* in Soho, and the concert halls of the South Bank. Recording in Nashville, Memphis, San Fransisco, Sweden, the Isle of Jura. Singing cotemporary opera in Japan, Europe and the USA, singing in Eastern Europe before the Berlin Wall came down. Always returning to London.

Written looking back from the millennium years to early days in the 1940s and '50s as a child in south east London, then always moving. From London to

Weymouth and back again. To Lowestoft, Norwich and Cambridge, Tunbridge Wells, then finally returning to London. My first 16 years, many schools, many moves, failing the 11 plus and off to secondary modern school, leaving just before my fifteenth birthday which fell during the Easter holiday in 1959.

From 1963, bedsits, shared flats and sofas in Earl's Court, Fulham, Chiswick, Chelsea, and then to The Grove in west London in 1966. The early days of the hippy invasion of the Balearic Islands in the Mediterranean, long before the rave and club scene it has since become. Living in a caravan in the Welsh countryside. A little shack on stilts on the banks of the Sacramento river in the Bay Area of northern California. In Texas and Tennessee. And an island north of Stockholm. Touring Poland, Estonia and East Germany. Before the USSR was dismantled and the big boot removed from its occupied eastern European countries. Living in 8a All Saints Road in North Kensington from the late 1960s, within the heart of the Caribbean community, seeing first hand the harassment they endured. By then, in my twenties, I had begun to understand that woman struggled more than man. She seemed to be considered *less* than. She had to work harder in order to be heard and endure unwelcome attention from men in the music business who appeared to be more interested in her breasts than her voice. If she had sex with these men there were no end of promises of a glittering career, money and fame.

I became an activist. The first musician to step up for *Rock against Racism* and then against sexism, reclaiming the night. I sang for the striking miners and the Brunswick women. I became angry, seeing injustice, poverty and cruelty all around. I was nicknamed 'Benefit Bertha' by some of my friends.

Married twice, first to Larry Smart, an artist and then to Maciek Hrybowicz, a musician. Both marriages gave me children. First a son, then 20 years later, a daughter. Coming from a background that was at best bleak, I had to learn to be a mother. Fortunately my love for them was immediate and strong.

My lack of a good and consistent education, leaving school at the age of 15 having attended many, made me realise that the uneducated woman has even more of a struggle to be taken seriously. I read ferociously, and wanted to write, but for many years my jottings were hidden in boxes or inside my head. In my early thirties I thought, 'Sod it,' and began to write for myself. Songs, poems, anything that needed to emerge, anything I needed to say. I loved the writing as much as the singing.

Carol and Sam in 113 St Stephen's Gardens, London 1968.
photo: Bryan Wharton

My story is of a child, an adolescent, mother, a singer and an observer of human kind. In my later years I've worked with people with neurological conditions, singing in choirs. I ran workshops for young people from disadvantaged backgrounds for *The Princes Trust* and rock school. I sang, toured and recorded for 12 years with a 16 piece contemporary opera choral group called The Shout.

I write about the music I love, from folk to blues, rock to jazz and even stories about the musicians I sang with, the adventures away from home, and recording in London, Nashville, Memphis, Stockholm... I've had an organic career. That's to say, mainly unguided and unmanaged. Sometimes dubious decisions were made but never regretted, although I often flew by the seat of my best *M&S* pants. I was often broke but singing gave me a life. Being a musician is not just the preserve of the educated. I can still sing and I do but I'm facing ageism in later life. Too old to sing? Not this old 'gal, not until I croak.

It was during the 1980s that I felt the compulsion to make sense of this life of mine. Thoughts came through into the lyrics I was singing, and I was asked to do two shows about my life, *Lipstick and Lights* followed by *Day Dreams and Danger*. These shows meant writing prose as well as verse. The audience at the *Drill Hall* loved them, and they were well reviewed. Suddenly, I felt a book starting to sing inside me. In spare moments the writing began to emerge. Not just about me and my world of music but also about the London I lived in and loved, and about how during the 1970s political activism and music joined forces.

Recently, other books have appeared about these times in which I played a part but all from a man's perspective. I was goaded into getting my book into shape and seeking a publisher.

Looking back at the child and the young woman I became is like looking back at a stranger. Throughout my life a cast of others has gathered in my innards. Voices with distinct roles. We're all aware of our various personalities, the work hat, the home hat and many more. I use these others to help speak my tale, from my birth to the millennium years. From the year 2000 I write with my own voice and attempt to tell the others to butt out; Procrastinating Patsy, Nasty Nellie, the Boss, Misery Ivy and Betty Blues Belter, a pale mouse called Frank and a few more. It was very busy inside my head on occasions. I put this *Singer's Tale* alongside my music because as I wrote it all down, it felt like a song. My song, with many verses. Each has music at its heart and I sing in my head as I write. A drum and a voice as I tap out my story.

Carol performing with the late Llew Gittens, 'Lipstick and Lights', Drill Hall Arts Centre, London in 1985.
photo: Sheila Burnett

Here's something I wrote in tribute to some of the musicians who inspired me. When beginning to sing a song you often have an intro, so here's mine.

I heard Ray Charles on a jukebox in 1959 *Night time is the right time.*
And oh, that sound was fine.
Miles Davis blew *Kind Of Blue.* A bitter and sweet refrain.
And I never heard a saxophone played as wild as John Coltrane.
When Ella sang *How Strange The Change From Major to Minor*
And Charlie was the 'Bird' who cried. I never heard a sound, mmm any finer.
It caught my heart inside.
Aretha soared and Otis roared and Bobby 'Big Blue' Bland could sing his song.
Before too long you know you understand the blues; your blues; my blues.
Now, Oscar Brown, he was cool, old school cool.
Like Mingus, *Ah Um* break the rules.
Betty Wright *Out 'a sight* 'Shoo rah, shoo rah.'
Gil Scott Heron, no music for fools.
And Joni sweet Joni, blue, like a river she flows: the blues; your blues; my blues.
Bold fingers, that's Mingus; no funk like Thelonius Monk.
The sound lingers, soul singers. Marvin Gaye, Sam and Dave,
Staple Singers, Sam Cooke, ooh I'm sunk.
When Bessie sang *Any Woman's Blues* she took my breath away.
Body and soul, I lost control at the sound of *Lady Day.*
A sensual moan, Nina Simone.
Stevie Wonder, the music's inside. 'No, no regrets' I'll never forget Edith Piaf.
She sang from inside: the blues; your blues; my blues.

Recorded in London on The CD *Eyes Wide Open* 1986

VERSE 1

The photograph

Who are you? Carol Grimes *Alive at Ronnie Scotts* 1996

2000: looking back. A snapshot from 1948, as the inner voices explode and a life story begins to unravel. Gathering the threads of singing for her supper. Of time in Estonia, the Balearic Islands, Memphis and Stax Studios with Donald 'Duck' Dunn, and more. A caravan, a barge, a wooden shack, a settee.

The photograph arrived in a small brown packet stamped NEW ZEALAND. The address was handwritten and the writing unfamiliar. It was a melancholy, misty February Monday morning, millennium year 2000. Not a year to forget. All the frazzle dazzle of the western world's New Year's Eve celebrations were only just beginning to wind down. A loud trumpeted leap into a new century, all the gunpowder whiz-bang, gallons of alcohol, bonhomie, and media delirium hadn't changed a thing. Still the same old world out there.

The morning promised another drizzle day, one that invites you to linger in bed, indulging in dreams and half-sleep for another hour or two, when there might be a small patch of blue in the sky, a suggestion of sunshine, a warmer light to dilute the dull slate skies of winter. With curiosity blurred by bleary early morning 'not enough sleep' eyes, I picked up the packet, sniffed it, shook it, and then stuffed it into a pocket in the blue kimono that was my dressing gown, moving on to the task of persuading my teenage daughter out of her warm bed. I was a late night singer of jazz songs and blues songs, songs that tell tales of lost love and mad, bad moments. Songs for after

Carol and sister, Jennifer, in Lewisham, London 1948.

14

midnight. So this moment was too early. I looked in the mirror in a dimly lit passage, all the better not to see the creases of sleep and age lines. All my mirrors are badly lit. I do my make-up by memory. In 2000 it was then a hit and miss 56. I shuddered, reflecting on the woman I was in my twenties and thirties. I looked back on a stranger. Like she wasn't the me that I am. She's in a half-light, half familiar.

* * *

She, that young woman, had dropped acid as she lay on pale silver sand hidden amongst hot rocks in the hazy heat of the Balearic Islands, watching golden lizards crawling on her naked belly. One midsummer's eve she sang on a beach in Estonia, underneath a pale northern night sky where a red midnight sun and a pale spectral moon stared across the universe at each other. Singing her songs to the moon, the sun and the pale silver stars. She'd been devilish high, whirling drunk in Memphis, Tennessee in 1974. Way in over her head and under the table, then wandering into the humid night looking for a cab to where she was staying. Trying to remember where she should be. He said, 'Ma'am, we don't hail cabs on the street here in Memphis, where y'all from?'

    PISS POT POLLY 'It's only me in here, a little bit tipsy and wanting a cab, a bed and a roof over my head.'

That was what she wanted to say, but of course she didn't. It was the one inside who drank to ease her nervousness. He got her to the right hotel anyway. So that was good. He could see she was a stranger in town. Could've been bad. Or so she was told the following morning as she balanced a worse than aching head on the top of her neck, and stared at a rapidly congealing *Holiday Inn* breakfast.

    She'd been in a bar with the 'Potter Monster', studio engineer and producer Bob Potter and some of his guys, hanging out before the recording of her new album began. The bar had an identical room each side of the entrance. Turn left or right, the rest rooms were in between the two identical doors. She'd gone to empty the several beers she'd downed (her bladder had never been strong) and she'd taken a wrong turning. Confused, she turned left. They'd gone. 'Bastards!' Then, she went out in the street to the cab driver who'd pulled into the curb beside her. She said, 'I want to go to the *Holiday Inn*, please.' 'Which one ma'am? We have two here in town?' 'Oh God, I don't know,' she said, trying to remember where she'd slept the night before. They, the men she had lost the previous evening, thought it was funny. Laughed like drains. Getting one up on. They said I was one of the boys, fair game. It wasn't the first time she'd been duped. They were still there and she was wrong. But they didn't look for her. They carried on drinking in the bar on the right, 'good 'ole boys' having fun.

Later, after a recording session in the *Stax Studios*, hanging out in bass man Donald 'Duck' Dunn's house outside the city, they were rolling skinny American grass joints, shaking the seeds free from the weed in the lids of studio tape boxes. She was with the guys who'd worked with Otis Redding and Booker T & The M.G's. She pinched herself. Yes, she felt the pinch.

Grooving in Donald 'Duck' Dunn's house, listening to old rehearsal and recording sessions on old 16-track tape. Hearing those slow southern voices, the well known banter between them all, and hearing Otis Redding's voice, years after his death, sounding so alive. She felt as if she'd been in the room with him, almost touched him, felt his breath as he sang *Respect*. Bass line slapping, snare drum whip cracking, guitar tight as a nutmeg skin with the swirl of the keys, making the sound fat and funky. She was in Memphis, down the road from Graceland, although she didn't get to go. Time was swallowed up in the madness of those recording days. Who'd have thought it? That girl, back in 1957 had fallen in love with Elvis, and then in the 1960s with Otis Redding, and Memphis had seemed like a golden music city.

Then later she had floated along on an endless river of highways with its stream of trucks and cars, passing by oil refineries and car lots, black rubber tyre mountains and mile after mile of big billboards, all spread out as high and far as an elephant's eye. All climbing clear up to the sky. Sometimes in a timeless drifting sort of day, trailing in the wake of other people's lives, she sat on high stools in dark and sunless bars on long crazy afternoons, or ate late lunches in neon chrome gleaming diners, drinking cheap coffee with stacks of fries piled high in red cardboard containers, tumbling out onto red formica counter tops. In America, she slept in motel rooms beside freeways that led to God knows where, in rooms that were always anonymous.

Looking out and down from behind a window, 14 or 19 floors high, amazed by the sight of the relentless rigid grid of American towns, feeling another universe away from home. Not a continent and an ocean's journey away, but living in a whole new galaxy. Neon signs flash, flashing, 'come and buy me, come and eat me.' Buy me at *Taco Bell*, *McDonald's* and *T. J. Friday's* or *Macy's* & *Penney's*. Lost and confused on a simple mission for toothpaste, cotton wool or lipstick in the maze of mammoth shopping malls; confusion, like saying she was pissed and they all thought she was angry, or the time she said fortnight. She might as well have been a mediaeval ghost, they laughed at her, some of those Americans. She had felt more at ease in European countries, where the language wasn't hers, but the land and the people, the smells and the labyrinthine old streets and squares were more familiar to her, alienated her less. The country she'd dreamed of since she was almost 12 years old wasn't for her. The vastness was terrifying. She didn't find her tribe although she met some fine people.

London was calling. In the old country she resumed the old life. Singing for her supper up and down the motorways of Britain, a long way from Route 66. The M1, M4 and the A1. The winding little B roads and lanes that take you off the main roads into the villages, leaving the urban orange glow of light pollution behind. Before settling into the van for the journey back to the 'Big Smoke', she would steal a moment to stand under a clear starry sky under the heavenly magic dust of the Milky Way. Holding it in her minds eye, taking it home to the city, secreted away to be relished, where there is no Milky Way to be seen. In this way, travelling with her friends and musicians in a transit van, pungent with the smell of socks, cigarette's, take-away chicken and chips, curries from Birmingham or Bradford, beer and sticky dark brown hashish joints, she sang and made a living.

* * *

Walking past a mirror in the corridor leading from the front door and the bathroom, on into the kitchen, I peered at myself, pushing the hair out of my eyes, 'Well, who are you?' Perhaps I shouldn't have emptied the bottle last night, stayed so long by the bar, not wanting the night to end or the people to leave.

PISS POT POLLY 'One for the road?'

THE BOSS 'Another hangover day. We've been there before. Come on, get the coffee down. That'll do the trick.'

NASTY NELLIE 'Your father, who was he? Where is he? Gone? Bumped his head running into a brick wall and forgot you'd ever been born? Anything but a life within a scrawny brat infant child of a slut, you're not nice at all.'

I recoiled from my own insane conversations, 'Ah shut up.' Out of my mouth and over my breath. I turned on the radio. John Humphrys was giving a posturing politician a hard time, 'Good, you go for him.' The man will not utter a simple 'yes' or 'no' to a fairly obvious question.

17

WICKED WILL O' MINA 'Wriggle, wriggle, poke him with a stick, John.'
I moved away from my face in the glass and the twisting words in my head. Forget the London rush hour, trying to squeeze your tired body onto a bus or a tube, in amongst other bodies, some forgetting their back packs, knocking folk flying in their wake. Some hanging around in clumps in the exits and entrances, maps in their hands, 'Excuse me, excuse me.' And as for around King's Cross and St Pancras Stations, and the labyrinthine underground tunnels, or any supermarket on a Saturday morning, or any high street anywhere, the weekend before Christmas. No, inside my bloody mind. That's where the pandemonium lies. 'Right.' Gathering my thoughts in a rubbing hands together, efficient sort of way

SENSIBLE MA SADIE 'Put the kettle on. Coffee, yes. Cut some bread for toast, maybe some scrambled eggs?'

Now, am I in a *Marmite* or a marmalade mood?

Wearing blue cotton pyjamas with a pattern of cartoon cats, my beloved daughter stared into the same mirror that had reflected my older face and complained about the curls in her hair, the shape of her mouth, a possible spot on her chin, the colour of her eyes. As if I can do anything about it. Wave a wand? Cast a spell? No, that would be far too peculiar. The ridiculous words of useless comfort remained silent behind my lips. Don't mention spells. Don't tell her that her curls are beautiful. Don't say, 'to me you are the loveliest girl in the whole wide world.' Not now, not in this moment. She will protest. She's 13 years old. Of course, she's far too old for sentimental mother stuff. Growing up, up and away. In this moment, she wants straight hair and another two hours in bed. The girl who's so beautiful shouldn't look too closely at she who is her mother.

NASTY NELLIE 'Now there's a deranged woman. She needs attending to. She has no sense of past or present. Lives in limbo, in an empty tin can. She hasn't got a heart, blood or tongue. And she has voices inside her that won't stop, running like human waste in the twisted pipes inside herself.'

The bathroom, an arched alcove under the steps leading up to the main front door at pavement level, was once a coal hole. I covered the walls and the low curve over the bath in shells and pebbles. A bathing grotto. Friends had contributed little patches, a mythical sea creature from Karen, a tree in shell and a seaweed garland created by my friend Didi Hopkins. With the steam rising from a bath and a candle burning, its soft glow flickering on the shells and tiny shards of beach smoothed

18

glass and pebbles, it was a magical place hidden from the street above and the people passing on the pavement overhead.

Kasia whistled as she splashed. Both mother and daughter had what their friends described as a 'builders whistle.' Locating a hairbrush from underneath a pile of paper beside the phone, I began to brush my long and rebellious hair, smiling as the whistling drew to its piercing conclusion. 'Mum!' she bellowed, 'Mum, where are my books? I had them last night, what've you done with them?' I continued to tug at the bird's nest mess that was my hair, 'on the kitchen table where you left them last night.' Picking up a blue and white spotted bandana in the mound of lipsticks, hair-clips and crumpled shopping lists, I pulled the unruly hank of hair back from my face and prepared myself for the next half hour or so of mild chaos, taking a peek in the mirror, tentatively touching my lip, checking for signs of a beard or moustache.

NASTY NELLIE 'If you see me with a dangling two foot whisker, shoot me.'

Why is it, that all my life I had pale red hair, had dyed it a bright henna red for many years, then as the white began to show, the darkest of dark black hairs appear upon my chin? Picking and plucking, sucking in my belly, pulling on a pair of jeans one size too small, 'I won't eat today,' I thought, 'or drink.'

PISS POT POLLY 'Just one more and then I really must get going.'

THE BOSS 'Oh yea?'

NASTY NELLIE 'Listen to me. Inside your body is at odds with your outside face. Inside that smiley clown face, cracking a joke, having a fucking laugh, lays the cavity that contains the bits of your shattered mind.'

Ah well, just another lunatic headfull after a dream fuelled night. I tried to think nice thoughts, turned up the radio and it's the eight o'clock news. She, the nasty one, fades in and out like the Cheshire Cat, leaving only her grinning spouting mouth, sitting just out of sight but well within my hearing.

NASTY NELLIE 'I said listen to me. That heart is full of old onions. Those veins are running with mercury. Drip dribble, slip slithering like manic globules of red spit. Oh yes, and inside your mouth, where a tongue should be, sits a bunch of thistles. Oh yes I can see you, old onion face.'

It's as if I've had a life-long running commentary or a thousand acts of some scary play. A constant self chastisement. I have poems that never see the light of day. Ideas and plans never realised. Up in the morning being mum, making breakfast, finding clothes and books, encouraging eating, teeth brushing and so on. This life held the joy in the knowing and being there for my eccentric and lovely child. And the necessity for order. For safety and knowing what the next few days will bring. It had taken a long while to find my way with that life. I try a bit of singing. I do this every day, always amazed that my voice is still there. I can sing for our supper one more time. Often in a small sweaty place, changing in a toilet, putting on make up in a half-light. I sing and I love it. It's my life.

You made me love you (I didn't wanna do it) and I didn't. 'Oh mum please don't sing,' said the daughter, 'Hey! Me no sing, you no eat.' I joke in a silly voice. She doesn't react. She doesn't think it's funny. Perhaps I should've found a nice normal man and lived in a village called Bell-Yew-Green, somewhere cosy in the home counties, and given birth to four chubby babies, shopping and lunching in town once a month with the girlfriends. And perhaps by now, a furtive and exciting affair. Lusty afternoons in a hotel room in West Kensington or Marylebone. What is a nice normal man anyway? Stir your stumps, woman. Make the coffee, dark and strong. Strong enough to shake the timbers and tickle an early morning mind into the day ahead. Shuffle the beloved daughter out of the house and on her way to school, which naturally she hates. 'It's all rubbish, can't I stay at home today?' 'No, you need to go to School.' 'Oh why? I'm nearly late, it won't be worth it. I've lost my english homework. I'll be in trouble, big trouble.' 'No! Here you are,' I said, producing a blue rain hat.

'I'm not going to wear that hat. I look stupid in hats and it's not pouring with rain. What umbrella? You know I hate school dinners. I didn't have the umbrella, mum! I'm late. I like the rain. My new jeans? I don't feel well.' On and on, the relentless rant of a pre-pubescent and reluctant schoolgirl. 'Your jeans are probably on the floor in your room and will remain there unwashed until you bring them to me. I'm not your maidservant, and please eat some breakfast.' I implore, and finally insist. Hooting with laughter, and hauling her school bag onto her shoulders, enormous on her tiny back, she allowed me to hug her just for a second before she wriggled her way out of my arms. Sometimes I hug her to me with a sort of hunger, as if she might disappear if I don't hold her. 'Stay,' I whispered 'Stay.' She leaves. Without the hat, the hood of her jacket barely covering her head, ready to be shaken off the moment she turns the corner. Out of sight, my sight. 'Love you more than a million universes,' I said, meaning it and more. She turns, halfway up the steps to the street, almost smiling in response to the familiar almost whispered words. Pleased, and then, a little accusingly, 'shush mum, someone will hear you.'

Kasia and Carol
in Primrose Hill,
London 2002.

The child and the young woman she's on the verge of becoming, alive in the one little body. Mother love moved inside me like a warm golden olive oil lubricating the thistles inside my mouth. Nuzzling the old onions in the hollow tin can.

It continued to rain and I stood there, the door open. I liked the smell. It was as if the deluge had washed the city clean. Leaning against the door frame, inhaling the air and listening to the water gushing in the gutter, slipping down the gnarled bark on the trunks of the old trees in the square, making them glisten in a silky dark wet way. A perfect moment of happiness. 'It's raining, it's pouring; the old man is snoring,' singing a little louder. The child has gone, she can't hear me now, and I won't embarrass her. Reluctant to leave the rain and the child I see in my mind, walking to school, in through the old Victorian school gates and on into the classroom. I stay a little longer. Two doors down the street a door opened and a woman complained. 'Oh hell, it's bloody pouring.' Chuckling at her indignation, I like a bit of contrary weather myself. I remembered the unopened packet. Not moving for a moment, enjoying the smell, the rain, the picture in my mind of my daughter, her face, her smile, her voice. I'm interrupted.

WICKED WILL O'MINA 'They sweat; they feign a faint; say they are suffocating and wish for the rain. The magnificent gods and arrangers of weather.'

The other voices have become more lenient, less accusatory. Venom is directed elsewhere. What a relief. I like that. That's good. Go on. Go on. I might write it all down, it could become a song. A man walked past, holding a newspaper over his head, the curve of his back declaring his dissatisfaction with the rain. He didn't notice me down in the basement, still wearing my kimono.

> WICKED WILLOW O'MINA 'Let's send down a lightning rod, see if you like that. Hissing and cackling with glee, you'll soon see how dreadful the weather can be. Let's boil up the sea and stir up the trees, whip off their leaves. The magnificent gods and arrangers of weather.'

I shake myself. I ought to get going, 'Now where did I put that letter?'

> WICKED WILL O'MINA 'Shiver their timbers and rip up their roots'

Oh no! What did the trees do to deserve such weatherly rage? I do love trees. Pondering upon the day ahead, there were beds to make, washing to wash, a living to earn, Phone calls, work to find.

> WICKED WILL O' MINA 'Watch this trick. A twisty wind on a city street and whoops a' daisy, see them fly, coat tails flapping wrapping their arms around a lamp-post.'

I agreed with my inner ramblings.

> WICKED WILL O'MINA 'They squeal and the weather gods laugh, dispatching a wet torrent, each raindrop as sharp as an elfin sword, piercing their soft skin and drowning their cats.'

A slender tendril of jasmine in a pot beside the door trailed along the ground. I twisted it gently around a nail in the wall beside the bathroom window. A stray orange plastic bag had wrapped itself around the railings near the bottom step. *Sainsbury's* blown up from Camden Town like dandelions on Wicked Will O'Mina's winds. Picking at some withered flower heads on a straggly pink geranium. I made a mental note to sweep the basement steps.

I was on a roll and spinning back to a northern island under a tin roof and a wild night sky. Tucked snug beneath a feather eiderdown, the hailstones pounding on the roof, beating an erratic rhythm complex enough to rival any virtuoso jazz drummer.

I can see that long ago girl in a flash of lightening on a wild and luminous sea, only two seconds and inky blackness. I see her eyes, blind in the impenetrable soft darkness and there it is again. The light, the water, the land, ghostly in a dramatic illumination, then disappeared again. The ship rolled and returned to port. She had witnessed the power of nature and the insignificance of herself. That woman who was the younger me, an almost forgotten ferry journey in 1982 before my daughter was born. My son still at home and living in Bethnal Green in the East End of London. The *Grand Union Housing Coop*. The longest time I ever lived anywhere.

All those places I have temporarily called home appeared as shadowy images in my mind's eye. London, south, east, west, north and east again. A caravan in a field in Carmarthenshire, a barge on the Thames, and several floors and settees when homeless. Crockett in California, living in a small wooden shack with my son, Sam, beside the railway tracks, supported on wooden stilts buried into the bed of the Sacramento river. Built for the factory workers in the *Tate and Lyle* sugar factory just down the track. Only three remained, spread out along the bank, like a few rotting brown teeth in ancient gums. The girl's shack was owned by a musician who was away working in Nashville.

Further down the track was an old black man who kept himself to himself, spending his days fishing in a silent way. He would nod 'hello' with a shy grin and murmur a greeting indecipherable to my English ears. The third one was empty, derelict and almost fallen into the river. Sliding down the bank, wet after the rain. Across the rail tracks watching out for the trains, heavy American engines that shook the shacks as they roared past on their way from the northwest into Oakland and San Francisco, 'Wo-oo, wo-oo, wo-oo, mystery train.' Living on corn flakes, bread and peanut butter. Listening to Gladys Knight and the Pips, *Midnight Train to Georgia*. I remembered I'd been home-sick and couldn't come home. There were no trains to London, England running along that track.

Singing at the *Fillmore West* where Janis had sung; where Aretha had roared out *Dr. Feel Good in the Morning*. Walking the streets that Jack Kerouac and Alan Ginsburg had walked, and always as if cowering in the basement of her own life. Looking out through guarded eyes, singing to a somebody who never ever was there, from a body that was in transit. She sang and got ripped off by unspeakable guys with contracts and promises. Rampant dicks and unwanted hands, with the morals of sewer rats and the devious, hard hearts of greedy businessmen, 'oh well. Nobody's life is a bed of lavender.' I see her in a wooden house on Vaxholm, a Swedish island north of Stockholm. Waking in the morning beside a frozen ocean, yellow piss holes in white snow underneath a window. The hairs on a red toothbrush, icicle hard in a cold white enamel sink.

I shook my head. It was all too many years ago. Back in the now, leaning against a north London front door, a wood pigeon called. I answered, 'caroo-caroo-coo.'

Returning from a head full of recollections, of huge seas and wild weather, I closed the door, 'Now where did I put that letter?' Pouring the third, and by now tepid cup of coffee, slathering another slice of toast with too much butter, and a good slick of *Dundee* thick cut marmalade, I sat down at the table. Inside was a postcard and a photograph of two children. A girl and a baby sitting on concrete steps that looked as if they led up to a house. The girl in the picture was about four years old. She had one arm around the baby's back and a thinly disguised sense of anxiety visible on her face as she squinted into the camera lens. The face was oddly familiar. Was it me?

NASTY NELLIE 'There's a thing. You assume we don't see you. Oh but we do, excuse me we do.'

Nastie Nellie is back and she's not going to stop. She turned the tide, from the weather back to me. Crazy words, pointing fingers in my mind. Each syllable dripping it would seem with slime. Are there more voices than I imagined?

THE BOSS 'Hell's teeth and dangling nostril hairs, get on with it.'

NASTY NELLIE 'I can see clear under your bones and inside your heart. I see right through you. You're transparent and it's quite apparent that you're murky, like a sewer, a drain, like foul acid rain. A cesspool of a woman with a rag and bone body and boils on your feet. A discarded meal infested with maggots.'

I almost remembered the girl in the photograph. Remembered her before she was a woman. Of course, look at the eyes, the mouth. 1948. Post war London. The baby was her sister, Jennifer Margaret. I hadn't seen her for 25 years or more. She lived in New Zealand. They'd been in touch by letter for a few years and had seen each other briefly when Jennifer Margaret was visiting London. I wondered if the mountains on the card were just outside the window as I sloshed away, doing the dishes at the kitchen sink. Until that moment I'd never seen myself as a child. Not with outside eyes.

Looking at my hands holding the picture, it was as if I'd never really considered them before. Working hands freckled with torn and dirty fingernails, a middle-aged woman's hands. Smelling, touching, tasting and desperate to see, to catch a glimpse of the girl I had once and certainly been. Long ago forgotten. Devouring the toast, the coffee and the photograph, it was as if I'd never existed as a daughter, not been any mother's child. Hands to photograph and photograph to hands. The eyes, the lips, the shape of the head. All so familiar and at the same time so utterly not. I picked up the card and scrutinised the landscape and the few words written on the back.

'You mentioned you had no photos of you as a child when I was in London,
so I had a copy made of this one. Hope you are well, all best, Jenny.'

Well, that's kind of her,' I said to myself, trying to remember what she looked like. It had been a long time of not knowing each other. I had experienced more intimate conversations with complete strangers at bus stops. Walking past the mirror in the passage and into my daughter's room, I looked out of the window at the black iron railings and a bicycle rusting in the rain. Here in this morning looking at the clock, I imagined that in New Zealand they're all asleep in their beds. Up here in the north we're drinking morning coffee or tea. When Jennifer Margaret awakes, it will be to an antipodean summer. Upside down and inside out. I had never seen that kitchen sink all those thousands of miles away.

The photo had unsettled me. I remembered a young woman busking in the London streets, wearing a red satin dress or a pair of *Levis* and a long black sweater. Walking in the moonlight on a Sussex beach with a big hairy bear of a man called Macca, a guitar slung onto his back and tied around his waist with an old leather belt. All the procrastination I could so skilfully indulge in, and all the voices inside my head could not remove what the picture of the two children on a London doorstep had bought forth into the present. To that rainy day in a London basement, north of the river. I was ranting with Procrastinating Patsy and Wicked Willow O'Mina, 'Oh praise the rain on a scorched dusty day, washing the air with a waterman's breath. Quenching the thirst of the tall plane trees beside a traffic choked street. The birds and the flowers drinking the drips to the very last drop.' Filling up with breath and more of the speech I proclaimed to an imaginary audience, 'Thank you, thank you gods of rain, for the brilliant sun shining in a blue sky. Unexpected on a mad March day. Scattering rainbows to curve down to the earth. Pots of gold and gems galore.'

A Bridge back to time present and past

Carefully pushing away the ancient cobweb pictures of the past, brushing them into the dusty files at the back of my head. I must not break the threads. The singer is easier to find. She's still singing. Sensible Ma Sadie is making the beds, then she'll wash the breakfast things and begin the day with Auntie *BBC* as her constant companion.

VERSE 2

Identity

Mother John Lennon 1970

2004: a possible murder and confusion as a clown appears, and the band gather to fight the battle. Carol who? Cecilie's secret.

'Wake up, wake up, wake up!' My eyes wouldn't open. The lids felt glued together. I stuck out an arm and felt blindly for the light beside my bed, knocking over a glass. It wasn't quite empty and water slopped onto the floor, making a cold puddle. It was a very small room and I'm a clumsy woman. Rubbing my eyes open, my bare feet met the grey before daylight chill, and the puddle. Shit, it was cold. Stumbling out of the tiny room in a basement flat in Chalcot Square, it barely held my double bed. Padding across the cold quarry tiled kitchen to the window in the room at the front. Dizzy with sleep I peered up and out into the orange glow of the street. It was eerily empty. No wait a moment, loud footsteps in the almost silence. The London hum was beginning to thrum. A man walked past the railings of the basement with his coat collar turned up over his ears against the dark early morning. Dawn over in the eastern sky was beginning to rise. A siren wailed in the near distance and beyond the trees in the square, a dog barked. Then it was quiet once more. I looked at the clock. Five-thirty. Where was he going? Words were spinning around in my head. Guilty Gertie tapped on the walls of my skull.

    GUILTY GERTIE 'I've murdered someone. I absolutely know I have but when, where and who was my victim?'

Shaking myself and muttering 'Where do I have to go today? What do I have to do?' I remembered. After the hours of water bladder-fullness I emptied myself and went back to bed. I had two hours left to snuggle underneath the still warm duvet and two pillows to comfort my guilty head. Switching on the radio, I drifted into sleep. An uneasy just below the surface sleep. At eight o'clock, still bleary eyed and wearing a large pair of blue and white striped pyjamas, I stared into the bathroom mirror.

    GUILTY GERTIE 'What have you done?'

The sensation of a crime committed, my crime, was still running through my blood, my head. And I felt a creeping dread.

GUILTY GERTIE 'Did you a murder a pale grey man?'

'Not guilty,' said I.

SENSIBLE MA SADIE 'Ignore it. Get dressed. Make coffee.'

'Not guilty,' I repeated.

GUILTY GERTIE 'Or was it your mother? Perhaps it was the night after the day you murdered your boyfriend. Or was it the afternoon? Hot and torrid when you lay stinking drunk and remembered you had murdered your brother?'

'No! I don't have brother. I don't have a brother. Do I?' I thought as I selected the tools for the mask of the day. It was just a dream, of course it was, 'Is red, very, very red lipstick too much for my mouth?' I ask myself, as I smeared black kohl around my eyelids and scarlet lipstick on my lips, 'Is this a look to leave behind?'

NASTY NELLIE 'Mutton? Lamb? Do me a favour. You're facile, narcissistic, as shallow as loose shit in a hospital bedpan.'

Squinting into the mirror I saw a woman. Young and voluptuous, a woman from the hills of Cadiz, a Flamenco singer. Yes that's me. Pastora Pavon, La Niña de los Peines, and the bathroom filled with my fantasy song. Moving closer to the glass in order to apply black mascara, a clown's face looked out at me, interrupting my song. I'll have to blow all of my breath into a mound of balloons. Red, yellow and blue, a never-ending pile of rubber in my clown's enormous garments. An elegant dancer's stance but my shoes were too big, my trousers too long. I kept the smile on my red mouth, upon red mouth, upon red mouth. I am....

CLARA THE CLOWN 'Hello, Hello. Ta dah!'

I leaned forward, squinting with the wand of mascara in my hand, 'Ole!' I said to my own reflection. The Spanish singer tossed her lustrous black hair over her shoulder and pinned it with gloriously decorated combs. A pale woman with henna red hair stared back at me through the mirror on the wall in the bathroom. The singer had lost her voice and the clown was left behind with a scarlet mouth.

CLARA THE CLOWN 'I'm a clown, a joker and a knave. There's no grave face on me. I'll smile my way to the grave.'

In fact it was to the job centre on the Euston Road by ten o'clock. April 2004, a decade past my half-century and in my hand was a copy of my birth certificate. It identified me as Carol Ann 'Higgs', a surname I've never used, not as far back as my ever.

Now I was in the new millennium. Sixty years old and as usual, short of cash. I wanted my pension, what there was of it. I hadn't paid enough into the government coffers for the full amount. I needed money but I didn't need 60.

> MISERY IVY 'Actually, she's a miserable fucker. She keeps her hat, those shoes and all the red mouths in a box, in a drawer underneath her bed.'

> CLARA THE CLOWN 'Look at me, look at me. One two, three, mother caught a flea... you can't catch me.'

It took several months to prove my existence. I tried. I really tried to convince the departments that deal with who you are. I spent hours on the phone. The conversations were ridiculous. The problem was my name, or rather names plural. Blip. Numbers 347, 348, 349. It was like waiting to be sentenced. Blip. Numbers 423, 424, 425, 'Shit, that's my number.' I gathered my stuff, dropped my glasses, flustered, picked them up, and couldn't find the case. So I shoved them into my bag where they would probably break. Quickly now, no time, no time. Hurry! Hurry!

> THE BOSS 'Stay cool and think very carefully before you speak. Don't blabber and bluster, mutter and stutter. And do not swear!'

My internal oh so bossy one had spoken. I rushed to my allocated cubicle. 'Yes, can I help you? Your name is?' Asked the woman behind the glass. 'Carol Grimes,' I said, pulling a big balloon blowing breath of air into my lungs. When faced with authority, bureaucracy and forms I panic, stutter, fluster and blabber

> THE BOSS 'Get a grip woman, what are you? A mouse?'

An explanation is given, tales of fruitless conversations with various departments are described. She said, 'Do you have your birth certificate?' 'Here it is.' 'So who is Carol Higgs?' I hesitate for a second or two. 'Me,' I said. 'I see. So Grimes is your married name?' she asked. 'No, but it's been my name since 1969.' She said, 'But you need your birth name on a birth certificate.' 'I am that person but I've never been known as that... I...' I trailed off, in some confusion. If I'm confused there's no hope for the woman behind the desk.

With a perplexed look the interrogator interrupted my feeble attempt at clarity. 'Do you have a marriage certificate?' 'Here it is, the first one. 1967. The second one, 1987.' 'It says "Freeman" here. "Freeman" married to "Smart", and "Smart" married to "Hrybowicz".' I gulped, swallowing my own saliva. Gathering myself and my spit, I said, 'yes, "Freeman" was my stepfather. I went to school with that name. I don't remember ever being called Carol Higgs at school.' 'Right, so I assume that

Carol.
photo: Julia Maloof Verderosa

Higgs was your father?' 'Actually, I don't know, I never met him, but my stepfather was "Freeman", as I said. My mother was with a man called Higgs before I was born, so his name is on it but I was told he wasn't my father and... I...'

My words were tumbling free fall, making no sense. 'Your adoption papers?' 'So why Carol Grimes?' 'I wanted my own name.' The woman sighed audibly and then sucked her teeth. 'Grimes by deed poll?' 'No but I've paid tax in that name, Grimes I mean, since 19... I mean I... well basically you see, it's like this. That's to say, I mean, my mother doesn't live here. She's British... but I... she's... erm... ' My voice becomes as tight as a soldiers snare drum. I feel like I'm being throttled. Tax details, work contracts and letters are shown to no avail. Confusion. We begin at the beginning. 'I'm afraid you must have a birth certificate in that name in order to receive your pension.' 'What name?' 'Grimes.' 'I don't have one. I just told you.' 'But your tax details are in the name of Grimes?' 'Yes.' 'So where's your father? Do you have an address?' 'No, I said no, I don't know I...'

Who is 'Carol Grimes'? Who is 'Carol Freeman'? Who is 'Carol Smart'? Who is 'Carol Hrybowicz'? Who is 'Carol Higgs'?' Round and round we go, ring around the benefit offices. Pop goes the weasel and my pension. A mad torrent of oaths lurking in-between my teeth and my tongue.

WICKED WILL O'MINA 'Go on I dare you, curse away. You want to, oh yes you do.'

My hands twitched in my lap. I wanted to smash the glass behind which sat the officials. The ones who ask you the questions and look at you as if you're the

29

lunatic escaped from the asylum. I sat on my hands and bit my lip, trapping my lily liver and my bold mouthed one. 'We will send all the papers to Newcastle and then somebody will be in touch with you.' She turned away. I was dismissed. Looking slightly pissed off, she shuffled the papers in her hand, and left. Out for a cup of tea, maybe even a fag outside where the smokers gathered. I imagined her saying as she sipped her tea out of a flowery mug stained with the drinking of many *PG Tips* and not enough elbow grease with the sponge and *Fairy Liquid*. 'Got a right one here, don't think she knows who she is.'

I ran out into the chaos and the traffic of the Euston Road. My thoughts were as confused as the papers that couldn't prove I'm the person I say I am. I needed a large drink, a very large drink. Walking quickly, dodging the crowds on the concourse of Euston Station, into the ladies, desperate to pee, and then out into Eversholt Street, planning to catch the No168 bus back to Chalk Farm. I pitched into the nearest pub, the *Royal George*, one I'd never been into before. 'What are your dry white wines?' I knew the answer, 'Red or white?' Bad and very bad, it wasn't a question, more a statement. A large glass of pub white wine, and I didn't care whether it was good, average or gut rot. It went down, straight down.

PISS POT POLLY 'Just one more.'

I ordered another. Halfway down the second, sitting in a corner at a small wooden table for two, I looked around. It was a very ordinary pub. Near a station sort of place, attracting travellers coming or going, filling a spare half hour. But of course the traveller doesn't see that this is a local to the locals, not just a pitstop for those passing through.

It was late morning, not yet lunch time and long past breakfast. A man sat at the bar and was in occasional conversation with the barman who wiped glasses and soaked up the wet slops with a small red towel. A few sad-eyed grey men sat silently sipping pints whilst watching a flat screen. A match of some sort. A crumpled copy of *The Sun* and money enough to nurse another pint, then back to the streets and estates or cheap bedsits, hostels and low-end hotels. This was an area once known as Somers Town or the red light district. A table of young men wearing suits, ties undone in that way young men do when out of the office, away from the boss's eye. The ubiquitous black case containing laptop and smart phone. Never really off duty. Ready for any call. The office, a meeting. 'Gotta go, go, go.' Ram a sandwich in the mouth, sink a drink. I finished my wine and wandered outside feeling somewhat blurred in the head. Sitting at a table was a young couple with backpacks beside them, looking at a map of London. The girl asked me the way to Camden Lock. They were from Munich.

A week later I'm on the phone to Newcastle-upon-Tyne. 'I'll put you through to pensions.' She had an annoying voice. It seemed to come from the inner recesses of her nose. 'They will help you with your query.' Half an hour later I pushed the phone violently back into its plastic holder. I would like to have broken it into tiny pieces, crushed it in my hand. I swore like a navvy on the piss. The expletive wasn't even delivered into the ear of my tormentor. No such luck. I tried again the following day. Into my left ear oozed a loathsome tinkling noise, mice on speed slaughtering Bach. 'Oh, yes, could you put me through to...' She who'd been so syrupy polite had long gone and the mice played on. I sat and sat. Occasionally a robot interrupted with a mantra. 'We are sorry to keep you waiting. You are in a queue and will be dealt with as soon as possible.' Back once more to the tinny sounds in my ear, 'Dealt with!' I shrieked to the walls, to nobody, to emptiness. 'What *are* you going to do? Hang me? Banish Me? Send me back? Where to?' I hung on because it's a queue, because what else could I do? On and bloody on as all the wrongs ever done to me gathered in my mind, as the minutes gathered as history. I was cut off again.

    Misery Ivy 'Oh God, it's not fair. Why can't they see me? Why don't people believe me?'

I was trying to find out what had happened to my papers, to my claim, to my very existence since the morning I'd spent in the Euston Road office. I rang again. Beep, beep and beep. I waited and simmered. And plotted. And remembered. I pictured Ms ever so smarmy voice, she who cut me off before I could say what I wanted. She'd be wearing a pale turquoise cardigan with a smart black skirt, tights and smart well polished shoes. I hissed. She had long pearly pinky painted fingernails. The phone was in my mouth. And she was so enormously obese, no office chair could contain her. I growled and softly rehearsed what I was about to say. They who lurked behind the numbers and the glass in the cubicles would be reduced to an apologetic obedience.

    The words were bubbling beautifully.

    Bandzerglob the Beast 'Now, you listen to me. Behind my eyes, my ordinary eyes, inside my bones, my ordinary bones, I'm a many-headed loathsome and terrifying woman'

'Oh yes,' I muttered, 'come on.'

    Bandzerglob the Beast 'Don't invite me. Don't tempt me to your feast. I'm a beast with a scaly tail and leaden wings. Claws capable of tearing flesh from bone. My strength is unknown, too violent to contemplate.'

I liked it. A vicious beast. That would get them moving. That would scare them. I redialed. I was ready for them. 'Hello can I help you?' A man's voice sounding faintly harassed. 'Oh, yes please. I was speaking with a Ms Harris in pensions and was cut off. I... ' He interrupted my flow. I hate that. 'This is not pensions, you need 084,' I howled with frustration. I didn't even register the number. 'I, I, I've been hanging on to speak to someone for almost t-two hours... I want you to put me through, I will not...' Gone, the phone was left purring in my left ear. I looked at my hands. Where were my claws, where was my savage heart, my bold growl? 'Oh, screw you then!' I howled. Nobody was listening but the cursing made me feel better. Then with rage simmering she cried, 'Mother, tell them who I am!'

She was dead, dead, dead. Died 14th April 2004 just one week after my birthday in the year that I became 60 and tried to prove I was me. Good timing mother. How did I feel? At first nothing and then anger, and then nothing again. And then one day as I was walking through Regents Park I danced a little jig. Nothing too fancy as people might laugh but a jig and a little song.

WICKED WILL O'MINA 'She's gone, gone, gone.'

My legs twitched. I imagined a child asking a parent. 'What's that funny woman doing?' The parent holds the child's hand a little tighter.

CLARA THE CLOWN 'I'm dancing on her grave. I'm singing a song, *Put on a happy face.*'

Her silent denial of me in life had been as loud as the traffic on the Euston Road on the morning I attempted to state my claim as a real person, a live human being, 'Take off the gloomy mask of tragedy, It's not your style.' The truths, all the unanswered questions died with her and she'll speak no longer. She was called Cecilie and she died in New Zealand. She had gone to the other side of the world when I was 17. I hadn't seen her more than twice since I was almost fifteen in 1959. Many years later I met my beautiful niece Sacha and then my half sisters, Jennifer and Lindsay, girls the last time I saw them.

I'll never know who my mother really was. She hadn't known me as a woman or a mother and barely as a child. I was left with trails of dust, the dust that she will become in the coffin in the cemetery in a country that I've never visited and probably never will. On the day of her funeral a large woman, a sister in law to Cecilie, heavily sweating and wiping her face with a cotton handkerchief approached my niece, Sacha. 'Hello, I don't think we've met have we? Who are you?' she asked, extending a sweaty hand. 'I'm Sacha, Cecilie's granddaughter.' 'My dear girl, that's complete nonsense, that's not possible.' Huffing, the woman was more than a little out of sorts. 'She had no children so how can you be her granddaughter?' Sacha replied, 'You see that woman over there?' Pointing to a slight, red haired woman 'She's my aunt Jennifer. And the two guys with her?' Sacha continued, although the woman was looking rather shocked, 'They're Cecilie's grandsons. She has a daughter in London, Carol, who has a son and a daughter. And my mother who lives in California. So you see she was a mother. She had three daughters and she has five grandchildren.' The woman backed away and gave Sacha sidelong glances for the next hour or so. Later on Sacha noticed the woman sitting with her aunt Jennifer in deep conversation, frantically fanning her face which appeared to be more boiled and lobster-like by the second. 'Oh my God,' thought Sacha, 'looks like she's gonna have a heart attack. A death at Cecilie's funeral.'

Cecilie had married in New Zealand and as she was over 20 years older than her man she may have lied about her age. Worried he would slip away, maybe. She lost touch with her daughters, all three. She told him she had none and of course as always, a big fat lie will be found out sooner or later. And it was to be so. He the new husband had promised not to tell his family or their friends. At the funeral her cover was blown. Oh dear, oh my, what a palaver. The woman who was born in Ash, Kent in 1918 at the tail end of another dreadful war and named after her own mother who had died a day later. Cecilie's secrets. Who was the first Cecile? (Cecile and Cecilie can be traced to the same name, Caecilia) Why was she alone in death, her infant beside her?

The secret of Cecilie's maternal grandparents who were never seen in Ash or anywhere else. And Percy, her father who's family were not spoken about. The secret of my father. Who was he? Perhaps I did have a brother. But did I murder him? A year later Sacha gathered in Cecile's photo album, scanned the pictures onto a disc, and there was my beautiful grandmother. Sacha's great-grandmother, my children's great-grandmother, the long lost and forgotten ancestor. She was beautiful. She'll always be 20 years old. A dark-eyed girl, long with thick hair worn in a plait, dark against a white lace dress. The book ends of my mother's life, from Ash, a village in England, to ashes and dust in Wellington, New Zealand. I'm filling in the middle years. I'm colouring in-between the lines.

THE BOSS 'Be careful not to smudge. Watch the lines.'

Eight months later in November, a very helpful person managed to negotiate the red, white and blue tape and I was allowed to claim my pension as Carol Grimes.

I exist! I had murdered Carol Higgs. That's all right then. I won't be up before the judge. Not yet.

Working for the theatre company *Welfare State*, a few years ago in Ulverston, in the south Lake District, the subject *Rites of Passage*, I met the American writer and academic Ronald L. Grimes. 'I've been looking forward to meeting a fellow Grimes,' he said, when we were introduced on the first day. Oh God, what do I say? Lie? Make up a life, invent a family? I told the truth. I said, 'I chose it.' At dinner on the second evening, 'I needed to find another name. Oh, that sounds bad. I'm not on the run. I mean I wasn't on the... Oh shit.' Coming to a halt, I was digging a hole.

> NASTY NELLIE 'For God's sake put her in a home for the bothered and bewildered. Her and her calamitous company blabbering away, day and bloody night. Chat, natter, squawk and moan. Lock the door and throw the key in the Thames, to be washed away in the mud and the tide. Hide her.'

'Ah,' he said. A very kind man was he. 'You're indeed even better than I imagined then. You're a chosen Grimes.' I felt like a cheat, an impostor, a thief, and a stealer of names. I had paid tax and insurance in the name Grimes for nearly 40 years. They took money from Grimes but would not give money to her. I felt like a no-one. Born to a mother who couldn't love me and a father who didn't know me.

1944 was a very sad year. Dried milk and bombs, bad teeth and powdered eggs. Thousands of children who never knew their fathers for one reason or another. Death, lost at sea, shot from a plane, gunned down in a desert or simply vanished in the chaos of post-war Britain. I had the one photo of me when I tried to prove who I was. A child aged four looking out at me from the photograph that had arrived that morning back in 2000. Who was she?

A Bridge looking back to 1944

It's difficult to see the 'me'. To see the girl in the photograph from long ago as my flesh. It's much easier to see her from a distance. With a distance, and a singing mouth, all the better to tell the tale. My writing of *The Singer's Tale* began because of that photograph, which plopped through my letterbox in the tiny hallway beside the shell bathroom under the pavement in Primrose Hill, north London in 2000. It took me back to wartime London.

VERSE 3

Family roots

Oh What a beautiful Morning from *Oklamoha* 1944

1944: songs in wartime London, another child, another air raid. A hissing lamps and smog place, dark damp and dank place. Grandfather Percy, another war and the story of Cecilie the first.

She was born 7th April 1944. It was the day before the end of the *Little Blitz*. She was given the surname of a man who wasn't her father. Higgs. It was Good Friday. And it was not a beautiful morning. It would not be a beautiful day. There was an absence of bright golden meadows and sunshine goodness in the world. It was a world at war and people danced whenever they could to the bands of Glen Miller, Lawrence Welk and Joe Loss. Louis Jordan sang *Ration Blues* and Frank Sinatra *Couldn't Sleep a Wink Last Night*. You could dance your troubles away, you could sing your dreams and pretend in those moments that your world wasn't hanging on a thread. And you could be dead tomorrow. Those who weren't buried or burned alive gathered in their aching bones and broken hearts and got on with their lives. In London people had expected to be gassed to death, a poisonous end. A 'time to live now, pay later' place. There may be neither time now nor later. Yes, oh yes, *Oh what a beautiful morning* and *Straighten up and fly right*.

People were flying and trying all right. And the bands played on in a city of rubble and stained sandbags, the soot-laced skeletons of burned out churches and the mournful craters in the ground where once homes had been. Vera Lynn, Bing Crosby, Judy Garland and Gracie Fields sang the songs of love and loss and longing for home. Finding love in a dark corner on a dark street. *I'm going to get lit up (when the lights go on in London)*. The lights may have been out in Piccadilly and Leicester Square but the moon and the stars were still in the sky.

Bombs do your worst by the light of the moon. The sun will rise again for another dawn. Wilfred Pickles and John Snagge were more familiar than your own dad. Dads, brothers and uncles were drowning as battle ships and destroyers were sunk in cold foreign seas, or burned alive in flaming planes as they crazy spiralled to the ground or into the ocean. For those with money there was *Lyons Corner House*, the *Gargoyle*

Club, the *Ritz Bar*, the *NAAFI*, the *Odeon* and the *ABC*. There was still food, films, drink, dancing and shows for those who had the money.

Women like Ruby, Gladys and Winnie queued for hours with ration books. There were no bananas or oranges. Eggs? Pass the powder. Children went to school with rubbery gas masks in brown cardboard boxes hanging on a strap alongside winter mittens on a string around their necks.

Her family? She wasn't plucked from a gooseberry bush or found fallen from a London plane tree. *She* had a grandfather, a Devonshire man called Percival Brimblecombe, the son of a grocer from Plymouth. Percival's father, a Plymouth Brethren, was tyrannical and brutal, and often beat his son. Percy had been apprenticed as a shipwright in the Royal Naval dockyards in Devonport. He had no choice in the matter. A clever young man, he was taken under the boss's wing and eventually sent to Durham University on a scholarship of £50 a year to study Newcastle's naval architecture. He ended up with the firm that built the Titanic at the Harland and Wolf Shipyard in Belfast. Out in the world, he would never return to his childhood home. One day when the Titanic sailed, Percy, along with thousands of others, was ill with the flu. So the ship sailed without him and he survived. The man that took his place did not. Without that flu epidemic, this *Singer's Tale* would not be sung. Turn right or left one day and your path can be changed for ever.

Percy was invalided out of the war in 1917, sailing home on the ship *Britannia*, which was then sunk by a submarine on its return voyage back to France, carrying his regiment. He had survived a bullying father, the trenches of

Carol's grandfather in WWI.

The cottage in Ash, Kent.

World War One and two sunken ships. Four lives? Five lives? He went to work in the secret port of Richborough on the marshlands flanking the banks of the river Stour, near Sandwich in Kent. He married the first Cecile and they lived in the village of Ash in Kent. The baby, called Cecilie, was born 22nd November 1918.

The young mother Cecile died a day later, alone with her baby beside her. Barely 20 years old, she was buried in St Nicholas Church in Ash. Percy sent the baby Cecilie away, to be looked after his cousin Kitty who was no kind of mother. It was said that she only took the infant because she wanted to

Carol's grandmother, Cecilie (Cecile).

marry Percy. It was also said that she had a temper and drank too much. Who knows? Percy met a woman called Beryl and Kitty didn't get her man. Nine years later Percy and Beryl married and Cecilie had a stepmother. There we are, grandfather, grandmother, mother and a half-sister, Gillian. Cecile the first disappeared into a time that is forever held in sepia. She was to reappear much later on a disc of photographs after my mother's death in New Zealand, her beautiful forever young face. Down all the years nothing was said about the first Cecile. It seemed such a cruel and lonely death and such a harsh dispatching of the motherless child but these were difficult times in a war weary

Left, Percival Brimblecombe in 1925 and *right*, Percival and Beryl's wedding in 1928.

country with a shocking death toll. A generation of young men had been obliterated in the mud and the blood of France and beyond.

Years later, Cecilie the second was 24 years old and living in yet another war. Her job was demonstrating gas cookers for the *Gas Board*, wearing an almost formal dress and full make-up. She was beautiful and she wanted to be an actress. She met a man called John Higgs. They rented a flat and John went off to war. Their flat was bombed in the raids of September 1940 and they lost everything they owned.

The dark places beside the river Thames, luminous with the pinpricks of white-hot bombs, bursting shells, balloons, flares and the ferocious grind of the engines. Boom boom as the thunder of the blitz tore the guts out of the city. Cecilie was living her young life in a war, like her mother before her. Good-bye Mr Higgs. Off to fight the war once more. Later Cecilie heard from Mr Higgs. He wanted a divorce. Cecilie did the thing that you did back then. A night in a hotel, a man, a camera, a divorce. In August 1943, a divorced Cecilie met a soldier on leave. She was out walking on a Welsh cliff top. The story was told much later by the stepmother, Beryl. Beryl was in Wales, escaping the London bombs with Cecilie's half-sister, Gillian. Percy was working at Woolwich Arsenal, working once more with the weapons of war.

Cecilie was devastated after the fire and the divorce. There was no room for her with the family in Wales, as cousins on Beryl's side were staying. So she was lodged in a nearby guest house. It was whispered much later that a young soldier on leave had watched her hovering close to the edge of the cliffs and he had talked her out of a possible leap. Who knows? It was whispered in corners over the years that *he* was my father. Who was he? Nine months later on that not very Good Friday in April, a baby was born. Higgs was the man on the birth certificate but he wasn't the father. The dates didn't tally. He was away fighting for his country.

On the subject of father, later down the years, the mother had said to the girl, 'He was a dreadful man. He made my life a misery. *You* are just like him. You're nothing like me. You don't even look like me.' And on another day she said, 'Actually, you're not John Higgs' daughter.' 'So who's my father?' and, 'Where is my father?' The answers were not forthcoming.

Beryl did her duty. She wouldn't allow the baby to be adopted, which was what Cecilie had wanted. In the first few weeks they lived with Beryl who, just before the birth, had returned from Wales and was living near Halstead in Kent. The question is, *Is you is or is you ain't (my baby)?* 'Mother, is I?'

Percy once cooked his first grandchild a duck egg for tea. She puked up the lot, splatter, splat over a rust coloured quarry tiled floor. She didn't cook, look at or eat a duck egg ever again. The duck egg and the grandfather are as one in her memory. One of very few memories. She didn't see him much and he died aged 61 before she was 10. His many lives had run their course.

Cecilie was small. Five feet two inches tall, delicately boned with dark lustrous hair and large violet eyes fringed by very dark lashes like her mother before her. Her eyes could flash with anger or amusement in quick succession but you sensed you were only at the surface of who she was and what she was really thinking behind those flirtatious smiles. She held you at arms length with a steeley strength. Men turned their heads as she passed them in the street. Her hands would dance as she spoke, vibrantly illustrating her words.

She was an actor by temperament and aspiration. She spoke with the cultivated accent of an urbane middle class young woman. Her voice held authority and superiority in the days when class was clear. You were one or the other. She gave birth in a time when there was no place for sentiment or sympathy for mere childbirth. 'Come along dear, push, push. Stop making such a fuss. You're only having a baby and there are men out there fighting the war for you. Push.' And, 'Not married?' 'What a scandal, shocking.' 'Shameful!' Cecilie may have said, 'my fiancé was killed in action, we were planning to marry.' A plausible explanation and who really knows? Who cares? Another day, another child, another air raid. An infant's first breath of earthly air fetid with the smoke and the sorrow of combat and chaos. Another tiny fist raised, another voice crying a first cry in the theatre of war. In a city with an uninterrupted jumble of roads, railways, archways, engine sheds, cathedrals, canals, markets, mausoleums and terrifying mayhem.

May 1944. The girl was four weeks old. A move for the mother and baby was arranged by Beryl, to a room in Winchester House, a place for unmarried women and their babies overlooking Blackheath railway station. A red brick Victorian gothic building with mullioned windows, towers and turrets. Barrage balloons and anti-aircraft gunfire boomed over the place where once Wat Tyler's peasants had gathered and highwaymen had lurked. Life was still dangerous. The war brought the doodlebug and the jitterbug, the bomb and the dance. Bring on the jitterbug. On 25th November in Deptford, just down the hill from Blackheath, people were queuing for one of 144 tin saucepans that had just arrived in *Woolworths*. It hit a bus, a pub and *Woolworths*. 'God rest ye merry Gentlemen let nothing you dismay!'

Oh my, my, what terrible dismay. Oh unhappy day. 'London's burning, London's burning, fetch the engines. Fire! Fire!' In 1944 the church bells were silent. No joyful ding dong peals for a wedding or a christening. Not even a funeral in a time when death was so frequent. Babies born in the city in that grey weary time were heralded by the baleful wail of air raid sirens and the shrill howling of fire engines and ambulances. What an appalling lullaby.

The late afternoon light was dissolving in a little room at the top of the huge house in Blackheath. A hint of the outside could be glimpsed through a narrow slit in a heavy dusty, almost black curtain hanging in the small window. A somber smudge, the inevitable weary light at the end of a foggy November afternoon. The softly hissing gas lamps hadn't yet been lit, and a small mound of dead soot, ash and grotesquely shaped clinkers were all that remained of a fire in the grate as the evening dusk gradually invaded every shadow and dark corner. Tugboats in the near distance hooted a muted river lullaby. Strangely soothing. A sound that reached the ears of the girl inside the cot in the house by the track. *Hush a bye Baby*. There were no lullabies, no good night story, not from the mother. How could she? Who had sung her to sleep? Tugboats and trains were the goodnight songs. Hoo hoo, a tug on the river and tackity-tack, soot and steam below the window as a train heaved into the station.

The tremble of steel and iron, thunderous upon the rails. Psssssst. Brakes screeching, smoke and steam belching from the engine's funnels, finding every crack and corner, up into the wooden roof of the ticket hall, squirming its way into the waiting room. A thick grey meandering mass twisted itself around the bodies of people waiting to board the train, sneaking into mouths, eyes and lungs. Finally it spiralled up through the dusty London plane trees. Up into the sky, blending with the early evening clouds. The guard waved his green flag and blew his piercing whistle. The heavy carriage doors slammed shut with a shuddering bang, bang, bang all along the length of the train as it heaved back into rhythm again.

'*Choo choo, choo choo, ch'boogie!*

Woo woo, ooh ooh, ch'boogie!

Choo choo, choo choo, ch'boogie!

Take me right back to the track, Jack!'

Cecilie was looking for work and needed to attend some interviews, so the baby was taken to Kent for a day. A doodlebug hovered overhead and with no time to reach a shelter, Beryl put the baby into a cupboard drawer, propped herself up against it and waited for the worst to happen. In the stillness that followed the explosion the baby mewed to be let out into the light and air. The house next door was flattened. Beryl lost her greenhouse.

A bridge called 'up to the river'

Up to London Bridge, Cannon Street or Charing Cross, trailing a sumptuously smoky tail past row upon row of little soot blackened London brick houses. Two up, two down. A lavatory in the back yard. Chuff, chuff up to Charing Cross past the *Peek Frean Biscuit Factory*, railway tracks dividing and expanding, carrying other trains and other people to different parts of the monumental metropolis. Past allotments with cabbages, potatoes, carrots and onions alongside bombed out buildings. Remnants of a once lived in family home, now exposed and broken. A fire place, a fragment of faded floral wallpaper, a splintered wardrobe lying on its back, dusty purple and yellow weeds occupying the place where once a suit, a dress and a shirt had hung, ironed and clean waiting to be worn. Rusty saucepans, a broken oven lying on its side occupied by a family of cats. A rag doll, a smashed bath, a set of dentures, a shoe, a toothbrush. Lives scattered on the ground.

From depots all over the city came battalions of red buses, trolleys and trams, swaying and clanking, moving like crimson blood through the veins of London. Transporting the workers to banks, brothels, breweries, bathhouses, shops, offices, churches, cinemas and synagogues. And to theatres, fire stations, schools and concert halls. Up to the cemeteries and hospitals, law courts, police stations, prisons and the Houses of Parliament. Out along the Strand, eastward to the slums and tenements of Bow and Bethnal Green, to Hackney, Wapping, Whitechapel and Stepney. 'Any more fares please? More room on top.'

A bridge called 'down to the river'

Down from the gentle green hills of Hampstead and Highgate, down into the West End, to Regent Street, Oxford Street, Tottenham Court Road and Park Lane, to Holborn and Bank, and south of the river. Wandsworth, Wimbledon, Camberwell, Clapham and Peckham. 'Hold very tight please. Ding, ding.' On the tube in from the west came people on the Central Line, or the District Line from Acton, Ealing or Shepherds Bush and Hammersmith. 'Move along the carraige please.' Down from the north on the Northern Line from Hampstead, Chalk Farm and Camden Town sliding underneath the sinuous river slick of liquid pewter that is the Thames.

Down to the Elephant and Castle, the convoys of red buses over the bridges. Solid arcs of intricate iron and stone connecting the north and south banks with Victorian sturdiness. To the east, hugging the river banks south and north, lay the sprawling steel forests of tall cranes. In docks that had once shipped coal, bananas, steel, tobacco, silk and spices, now scarred from the bombing and busy with the business of war. Squat grimy barges slip up and down stream under the constantly changing London skies and soot heavy rain. London cries alongside the sewage, gas and water pipes. Some of those millions from the little brick houses slept in the stations. Sheltering overnight from the bombs and the fires above ground. Asleep alongside the rats. Lying cheek by jowl with the nerves and muscles of the dark and serpentine underground. 'Mind the doors.' 'Mile End next stop, fares please.' 'Mind the gap.'

Above ground, keeping a silent watch, sat the somber statues. The nation's war heroes celebrating the capitalist nobles and the philanthropists of the Victorian age. The kings and queens and all those who have reigned over us, patriarchs of empire. 'Bomb us if you dare.' A thunderous voice, 'We are indestructible.' In the midst of this old and troubled city, the *BBC* declared a war, sung songs of hope and glory, raised a laugh and pretended to care. *Have A Go, Workers Playtime, Bandwagon* and *Much Binding in the Marsh*.

The railway and the radio, skeletons on which to hang a lifetime's memories. In my head I heard a cry. It sometimes comes to me in dreams. It was a cry from long ago. What's the point of crying now? What was the point of crying then? Best not to draw attention. Keep quiet and they'll forget you've been naughty or dirty; forget they're angry. Keeping quiet becomes a refuge, a hiding place and a noiseless mouth shaped into a perfect round and silent 'O'. And then?

MISERY IVY 'I don't want to go there.'

A half known and half forgotten place. A hissing lamps and smog place, dark damp and dank place. A linoleum and cabbage suffocating place. *Oh dear what can the matter be?* A baby struggling to stand, the train below had disturbed her sleep. Small cold hands gripped the bars of the cot. Swaying from side to side, she moved to a mysterious music, a dance to accompany the silent song. Her clothes were damp and hunger began to rise from a dark place inside the baby's belly. A hunger that wanted food, that craved unknowable needs and unfathomable desires. A bottomless and inexplicable lack of feelings she couldn't begin to understand. The dance and the voiceless song took place before an audience of shadows and obscure imaginings. In a winter moment the mist on a baby's breath was her existence and the disembodied sounds were the resonance and substance of life. Of otherness outside the mind of a child in a cot. On 6th August 1945, when she, the child of a mother who could not love, was 17 months old, the first atomic bomb was dropped by the Americans on the Japanese city of Hiroshima. A mushroom cloud of terror. The world would never return to the old ways of warfare. It had witnessed mass destruction on an unprecedented scale. That year Ella Fitzgerald sang *I'm making believe*. Well, hell yea. Might as well. That was the first two years for a war baby. Welcome to the brave new world.

Percy in Kalinova with a shell.

VERSE 4

Great heights

Who Know Where the Time Goes? Sandy Denny,
sung by Carol Grimes on *Mother* 2003

2005: a move to Deptford, a suicide, singing from a crane in Stuttgart, and the girl's first singing in Hastings in 1963. Or was it 1964?

On 5th January 2005, I moved from the basement flat in Primrose Hill. I had managed to prove I existed. I was officially Carol Grimes and drew my state pension. My passport still said Carol Hrybowicz, the name of my second husband. So there were still problems. I was very careful to inform airlines when buying tickets for travel.

I moved from green and oh so nicely pleasant hilly NW1. I loved the shops lit at dusk in winter. At night it was like peeping into magical jewel boxes. The sweets in gleaming wrappers, chocolate boxes as beautiful as the chocolates, all be-ribboned and gilded. A bath towel and a robe nestling next to a candle and soap, all in perfect arrangement and colour coordinated. A shabby chic chest of drawers, an exotic mirror. The perfect bathroom in *CP Hart. Ian Mankin* for fabrics, all stripes and deck chairs. Sea air and a case of Champagne in *Bibendium Wine* that once was a garage. *Richard Dare* where everything in the window said, 'You want me in your kitchen. Your kitchen is a dull kitchen without me. You can't cook unless you have me.' Interior emporiums for the wealthy who have no time to plan their own homes. Antiques and a carpet shop where the rugs were works of art. Pampering places, expensive fragrance washing the street for a moment through an open door. Luxurious promises of body perfection for the wealthy women in houses around NW1. Yoga and acupuncture in a small London village nestled against the hill.

Entering *Primrose Hill Books* made me feel like an illiterate, swept in by mistake. Mrs Welsh is no longer in her hardware store that was planted back in time. A much slower time, going for ant destroyer for the day when ants by the million raided my kitchen. A chat about this and that. An oasis of old fashioned calm in the rarified air of Primrose Hill.

I used to play a game. I imagined I had £10,000 and 20 minutes in which to spend it. The excitement of the game gave me goosebumps. A rug worth a thousand, a bath. Ooh hurry, hurry. A case of bubbly, blue and white striped linen, an enormous olive wood salad bowl. Oh!

WICKED WILL O'MINA 'Bong, too slow.'

All aboard the good ship shift, packing boxes. What to ditch. And as always, things are left. A basket of wooden boats, a jug in the garden, old tiles collected over years waiting for a 'forever home', so there they remain on the wall above the sink in the bathroom. Probably not. The new folks will renovate in their own style. The tiles would go in a skip, broken and gone. I moved south of the river, to Deptford High Street with a computer, a bed, a radio, one bag of clothes, a saucepan, a kettle, a towel, a toothbrush and my ghosts.

My boxes and furniture were in storage for three weeks. So this was minimalist living. I quite liked it at first. The flat was empty. The walls painted magnolia and it smelled of another life. I decided the man who had lived there before me liked the odd cigarette in the bathroom. It took months for the traces to disappear. I moved in on my own. My daughter Kasia, suddenly and without warning, had decided to leave school and had taken a live-in job in a bed and breakfast in Swiss Cottage. I missed her more than I can ever say. I had not lived alone for 38 years. My son was born in 1967.

On 9th January, the first weekend in my new home, and the day before his sixtieth birthday, my first husband Larry, the father of my first child Sam, hanged himself from the banisters with a scarf in a flat in Wood Green. He left his angry and confused son and German wife, Karin, to pick up the pieces. I felt I couldn't reach Sam, couldn't help him. He was so hurt. I felt as if my heart would break. The phone was on the floor of the soon-to-be-decorated front room. The echo of my voice in the empty space as I talked to my distraught son was deafening. Ricocheting off the walls and up from the floor of this suddenly more lonely than lonely place. I needed to sit down. There was only the floor. Sitting with my back against the wall next to a pot of chalky blue paint and a paint brush in a pot of water, I tried to calm my son. His sobs sliced through the thin flesh attached to my bones. I felt red raw. In the months that followed I didn't sleep for more than an hour or so at a time and when I did it was a bad sleep with bad dreams. Who teaches you how to be a mother? 'Larry, oh Larry what the fuck have you done?' I remembered the day in a pub in Blackheath when I met the young man who'd just finished art school. Blue eyes, a cute arse and a, 'come on over here, I like you' smile. And then we were a couple in Chelsea and then a three in The Grove. On that day in 2005, Sam was so hurt he went into raging madness. He had no one else to blame. So he blamed me.

In Primrose Hill I was in a basement and there were trees, beautiful trees. Up here I have sky. I can lie on my sofa and stare at Luke Howard's clouds. I spotted his name as I sat in the front seat on the top deck of the No149 bus from Bishopsgate to Wood Green. A blue plaque on the wall of a house beside the bus stop, 7 Bruce Grove.

'Luke Howard, namer of clouds, 1772 - 1864.'

How wonderful. As the bus rumbled on its way I say the names softly to myself. Better not let anyone hear me. Mad woman alert. *Cumulus, Stratus, Cirrus, Nimbus.* Sturdy names for such ephemeral forms. I imagined Luke staring up at the sky, dreaming names for the billowing shapes. 'Hello Luke.' I added him to the long list of ghosts that I've fallen in love with; Louis Armstrong, William Blake, Florence Mills, Fred Astaire, Bessie Smith, Umm Kalthum, Vesta Tilly, Albert Camus, Otis Redding, Mark Chagall, Memphis Minnie, Margot Fonteyn Oscar Brown Jnr and Paul Robeson. It's safe to love romantic and extraordinary ghosts. In this year my daughter took herself off to Hackney with the cat, Tiffany, to live with friends. It was her cat. I tried to persuade birds to visit my garden on the roof. I bought packets of peanuts, fat balls and birdseed. I worried about the people I loved most in the world. I bought too much food, not being used to cooking for one.

In June, six months after my move to Deptford and Larry's death, I found myself standing on another rooftop. The *Scholpp Crane* headquarters in Stuttgart, southwestern Germany. I stood, looking a long way down on a blazingly hot day. Looking out over the port on the river Neckar. I wanted to jump. It shivered my belly and startled my innards. Vertigo? Yes. Jump? No! I was looking forward to the next few days. Singing a theatre piece called the *Singing River* for Theatre de Welt, directed by the Swiss director, Tom Ryser, and Orlando Gough, who was to become the director and composer for The Shout, a composer that I spent 10 years of my life working for.

In 1996 she (that's me) met the composer Orlando Gough. He invited her to sing the part of a very drunk woman in his Opera *Hotel*. The libretto was written by Caryl Churchill and it was directed by Ian Spink from the theatre company, Second Stride. That was followed by a production called *The Shouting Fence*. Then after a visit one day in Primrose Hill from Orlando and the composer Richard Chew, the company called The Shout was born. She felt out of her depth in many ways, although the composers had said they wanted a diverse group from many disciplines. It didn't matter if you couldn't read music or hadn't been to music college. Or so they said. Of course all the other members had classical, jazz or theatre school training. On the first day of rehearsals when the scores were handed out she worked with her ears, flapping like a frantic bat, her heart thumping in her chest. Orlando said one day, 'You're off the score quickly.' Under her breath she muttered, 'I was never on it, mate.'

THE BOSS 'Shush, be quiet.'

Her voice rose up to a pitch that was so high her larynx disappeared through the top of her head. The opera took The Shout to Germany. She was singing without a microphone. Singing arrangements that were far removed from the verse, chorus, bridge formula. Time signatures far from four on the floor, they seemed to change every few bars. Harmonies were scrunchy. She loved the sound that many different voices could make together. The Shout will pop up as the tale gathers up the years.

The Singing River was devised for a river. A working dock including several cranes, mountains of broken glass, a very loud splash, a train, an engine shed, many choirs, an old piano, men, women and children, and boats. Little boats, huge barges, old boats, new boats, a raft, some diving fire fighters, a fleet of amphicars and four singers from The Shout; Jeremy Birchill, Manikam Yogaswarren, Wills Morgan and me.

Back on the roof and half believing I could leave all the troubles behind. Out of sight, maybe. Out of mind, hell no! But don't jump. It would be bloody messy. Some poor sod would have to scrape all that had been me from the ground below. Still, inside my bones and tickling in my entrails was a sense of unease. The world below seemed Lilliputian and removed. As if human kind, busying itself just out of my reach, was pulling me downwards. The great god of gravity and the whispering inside my head, wheeling and wanting.

NASTY NELLIE 'Do it, I dare you, do it. I dare you to do it.'

I had defied many dizzy demons to get up onto that roof. I don't like lifts. It's like being being shut up in a tin can or a lead coffin. Then a fairly solid iron stairway with no banisters. A sheer drop onto the concrete floor below, but manageable. Next a horizontal ladder, so straight it almost appeared to bend backwards as I climbed upwards on the unforgiving iron rungs in bare feet, holding onto my high heels. High heels! They give me some height and therefore a semblance of confidence. It helps ease the constant looking upwards into noses, talking to a chest instead of a face. I was always the short one. I was finally up through a trap door and out into the blazing light, ready for the sound test.

Going up was bad. I dreaded the return. Legs backwards into the groin trembling abyss. Down below me were the *Scholpp* cranes. Tall ones, yellow and red necks as long as digitally exaggerated giraffes. Short friendly stubby ones, busy and bustling, lifting, carrying and putting down. Old grey industrial sized riverside cranes, squatting in waiting for the heavy loads from the ships that bring the goods all the way up the Neckar, winding through rural and urban Germany. Grain, steel, soya beans and wood. Huge red trucks milling in and out like important and industrious tribes of red ants. All bustling and clamouring about their business in the dockyards.

NASTY NELLIE 'Jump, jump, go on.'

'Oh no please don't pester me, not now,' I pleaded, 'I'm working. Give me some bloody peace.' Surely it was merely a passing moment of lunacy, wanting a one way ticket to oblivion. Out there into the unknown, up over the hills and far away, gliding with the birds on the thermals. I had wanted to shout out loud to no one in particular and everyone all at the same time. I wanted so much to fly. Holding onto a pole with one hand, knuckles white with the effort of my grip, a megaphone in the other, I order my mind back into place.

I am, 'On the roof, it's peaceful as can be. And there the world below can't bother me. Let me tell you now,' sang The Drifters in 1962, and me to myself on a German roof in 2005. There's a song for every occasion. I was about to sing up on that concrete summit under a feverous sun, to sing an improvised calling duet with Jeremy who was standing on a crane ledge on the opposite bank of the river with a megaphone in his hand. Lifting the megaphone to my mouth I sing a birdcall song

Carol, 'The Singing River', Stuttgart, Germany.

across the *Scholpp* yard before going over the river to Jeremy. His huge bass voice bounced back at me and I smiled at the marvellous madness of it all.

Then down from the roof, running along the river bank, stepping down an iron ladder and into an amphicar to sing on the river. Past the stand where the audience will sit. Then clambering up the opposite bank beside the goods

48

railway track, along past the old piano and a children's choir. Up another ladder to join Jeremy on his crane for a final song.

Singing into the air, I felt that there was something both ethereal and separated. It was as if an unseen force was showing me that my song will always be distant and removed from the mainstream. The audience were to be seated on a large stand facing the opposite bank. I will sing behind their backs, across their heads over the river to the hills beyond, by which time my song will be a faint whisper on the wind, obscured by the hum of traffic on the motorway behind the docks. We bellow the calls back and forth, testing the sound. Where does the voice land, how does it carry? What shall I sing? I was meant to be the bird spirit of the river!

My disembodied voice skittered and bounced back at me from the high concrete walls behind Jeremy's crane. The calls end and in my ear piece Tom Ryser is telling me to hold it for a while. Walking away from the edge, looking beneath my feet rather than above my head, the surface was covered in plants. Densely growing stubby succulent mounds of red and gold, green and yellow; plum and ochre, nut brown and silvery green. Feathery, coarse, hairy plants, plants from Mars. Another secret garden in the sky.

Behind me more docks and cranes, and in the far distance, hills. Hazy in the summer heat, trembling as if about to burst into flame. Parcelled up into neat German fields. Row upon row of what could be vines. One huge crane loomed up and outwards, giving the impression it was about to scoop the whole panorama up into in its vast claw, carrying it all away. As if it's all a temporary stage set. Will I be scooped up and carried away? I found a skylight window and propped myself up against it. Sitting on the hot rosy stubble, swigging tepid water from a plastic bottle, waiting for the word that I should sing again. If I had envisaged how my life as a singer would be and where it would've taken me when I began as that tentative and insecure teenage singer, I would've laughed myself to death. No need to jump from a rooftop in Stuttgart.

There was a heat wave in May and June, and probably July come to that. Cats were lying around looking unsuitably dressed for the climate and I just wanted to be by the seaside beside the sea. Where the air is salty and fresh, the gorse velvet yellow and smelling coconut sweet, perhaps watching a black winged raven in a blue sky scattered with gentle white clouds and maybe a heavenly breeze. I might see a buzzard on a pole, waiting for a rabbit or a vole, and hear the bleat of sheep and the low-lowing of cows. All this in a blue mist distance, a sail away. Longing and belonging to a tide that flows into time and back again. Like my thoughts really. The long song with many verses.

Back from a heat wave in Germany to my own secret garden in the sky. The catholic school beside the railway station, Deptford market square, and the green dome of the planetarium. The trees and churches of Greenwich beyond the car park and the swimming pool. Deptford Creek and St Paul's Church, known as the jewel of Deptford. Its stately spire illuminated after dark until the clock strikes at noon or midnight. Bong.

THE BOSS 'Come on girl, get a move on.'

I was flapping like a pale butterfly, a Cabbage White at the end of a life, looking for an opening, a way out. I'm often afraid of the unknown not yet lived hours to come. I want to stay at home. I want to eat hot buttered toast and jam, drink wine, read a book, paint my toenails, play music, stare out of the window or do nothing. Changing my mind about what I should wear. Can't make my mind up.

PROCRASTINATING PATSY 'Check, re-check. Travel card, money, make-up, mobile, keys, mustn't forget the keys! Which coat or jacket? Which shoes to sing in? The high heeled black boots or the red wedges? If I wear the red, I need to change my earrings and make sure I have the red lipstick. Red for the mouth. Or should I go pale pink?'

I shook away my dithering thoughts, 'No, it must be red for Betty Blues Belter.' The last thing I do is put on my shoes. I was wearing black *Converse*, ankle high with long black laces. I struggled with the tying of the laces. Done. I was ready. I opened the door and got myself down the stairs, 42 of them to be precise. Picking up my bag, closing the door closed behind me. I was then standing on the platform at Deptford Station, waiting for the 16.39 train up to London Bridge. The skin on my head felt thin and taught around my skull. It was cold bone-shivering weather. Summer had gone, taking the heat with it. I should've worn a hat. All that fussing and fretting about earrings and lipstick and I didn't think to wear a hat or a scarf. It was after all December and the red winter sun, a big blood orange in the darkening sky, was setting fire to the glass and steel towers of Canary Wharf. A light winks on the grey pyramid perched on top of One Canada Square. Not a tomb for kings but a monument to money. Twenty-four hours, it never stops. Wink, wink, wink. A bizarre Christmas star calling shepherds to Mammon. A train was due in seven minutes.

My mobile phone rang in the depths of the full to the brim bag slung over my shoulder. Its insistent tinny tinkling annoyed me. 'Shut up, go away,' I said, under my breath. I wanted to look at the sky. I answered the phone as a bank of charcoal grey cloud floated languidly above my head. An unearthly red-bellied beast trailing streaks of colour and glittering shards of sunlight in its wake. 'Hello, is that Carol Grimes?' It was a telephone interview with a Hastings local paper, promoting a gig at a jazz club later in the month. He sounded young and in a hurry, 'So when did you first sing? Where was your first gig?'

It had all began by accident. I learned my trade out on the road, up and down the motorways, in and out of a battered transit van with a cargo of *Marshall* amps, guitars, drum kit and musicians. Travelling south, back to London from Birmingham or Newcastle, legs stiff and blurry eyed into the *Blue Boar* services on the M1 in the hours before dawn, wanting greasy egg, chips and beans, and a mug of stewed brown tea. Or nights, what was left of them, in bad B&Bs and cheap hotels. In rooms smelling of stale tobacco, *Old Spice*, other people's sweat and sex. Beds slippery with cheap nylon sheets, dusty with musty blankets. Bra and knickers washed in the tiny hand basin, draped and dripping over the radiator. Hope they're dry before the morning. On and off the ferries bound for the clubs of Hamburg, Berlin, Amsterdam and Stockholm. Singing two or three sets a night. Hours on foreign freeways. Eating strange food in strange café stops on the wrong side of the road. 'Drummer wanted: must own a van'.

'So, when?' I hesitated, 'Well, it must have been...' Now there's a question. When? How? What do I say? Of course I remembered, 'It was in Hastings, August 1963.' 'Really?,' he said. I imagined his thoughts. I could almost hear his brain ticking as he totted up the years. Was I spinning him a yarn? But no, it had been. And I imagined it to be more than his lifetime ago.

My young voice swam eerily and half forgotten into my head, and I caught a glimpse of the girl I'd left behind. Standing there in that long gone moment, in a pub by the sea. Her first performance, the first song she sang out to anyone within earshot and eye distance, was in a narrow alley in front of 15 or so folk and a couple of hungry excited dogs. The inebriated overspill from a pub in Hastings Old Town on the English Sussex coast. On that day just before noon she felt anxious. She always did when walking into crowded places alone, overwhelmed by the sheer volume of people, not able to take all the hubbub into her head.

I still know that feeling. Pushing my hands deeper into my pockets, walking up and down the platform at Deptford Station, trying to keep warm. The sun had set, leaving a cosmic red afterglow. The night had fallen and the air was even colder. Oh skittish mind taken back to the girl in Hastings. The day I remembered was hot with little white clouds in a blue sky. A sunshine and seaside day.

She had turned 19 in April that year although she didn't look it. There was the pub. Where were her friends? They were prone to changing plans on a whim or a change in the wind. Eyeing the crowd by the bar she fought the urge to turn and leave. Art students, folk singers, beatniks, bright-eyed bold young women, and young men with bohemian beards sitting incongruously on their youthful chins.

In the darkest corners of the public bar sat rheumy-eyed old fishermen nursing their pints of bitter. As if cast in old stone, these ancient sculptures were saturated in sea salt, old sweat and tobacco. Their faces were lined and rusty from the ravages of wind, sun and sea, and their eyes were almost hidden behind a network of folds and creases constructed over years of watching in all weathers.

PROCRASTINATING PATSY 'Where should I sit? What's the best place to wait? Will they see me?'

The whole bar was blue hazy with smoke and seemed dark at first in stark contrast to the sparkling sea sun brightness outside. She hovered for a moment just inside the door whilst her eyes adjusted to the sudden lack of light. She was wearing *Levi 501* blue denim jeans, a blue and white striped t-shirt and scuffed brown boots. A black beret partly covered her long pale reddish hair, which in turn partly obscured her pale face. It was a face of scattering freckles and delicate yet unremarkable features apart from her eyes. The colour of icicles, these were unerringly pale blue. She was almost five feet two inches and because of her habit of wearing clothes several sizes too big, she often resembled a disheveled elf. Some of the people she ran into called her 'Tiny' or 'Imp' or worse, 'Shrimp'. A Shrimp? Pale pink and invisible. One swallow and gone.

In the winter she wore big black jumpers over her jeans and a dark navy blue *Duffel* coat. Ex-services issue from *Laurence Corner*, the army surplus shop on the Hampstead Road in London. And on special days when she was brave enough to show her legs, to show more of herself, she wore 1930s and '20s dresses she'd found in junk shops or street markets. Hats and old jingly, dangly jewellery. Glittering remnants of another generation. And the boots. She loved her boots. They made her feel strong and firmly planted on the ground. She felt she could muster a confident swagger wearing those funky boots. She carried a *Duffel* bag everywhere. It was a home from home for all that she owned. The place where she dropped the shells and stones that became her treasures. And a toothbrush, a spare pair of knickers, a bra, another striped t-shirt, a cotton spotted bandana or two, a piece of old black velvet that could be a skirt, a scarf, a hat or a cover-all for wherever she found herself at night.

She always carried a book, a note pad, a black biro, and pair of socks or tights. A half-eaten bar of *Cadbury's* milk chocolate and sometimes a packet of *Roundtrees Fruit Pastilles* or gums. In a little blue plastic make-up bag she would have a safety pin or two, some hair grips, a handful of crumpled tissues, a small round blue tin of *Nivea* face cream, her indispensable *Woolworths* solid sooty black cake mascara (applied using copious amounts of spit on a little black brush), a pink *Outdoor Girl* lipstick, blue eye shadow and a black liquid eye liner that gave her a smudged not enough sleep look.

As she stood in a pool of apprehension near the door, a young woman appeared. They'd met a couple of times earlier in the year in *Finches* off Goodge Street. 'See you around,' she'd said, and here she was in Hastings with two young men in her wake. The taller of the two held a guitar in his hand. His black hair long and uncombed, he wore a fringed black leather jacket on his back and black biker boots on his feet. The second man, red-haired short and brawny, was wearing jeans and walked barefoot as if he'd come from the beach to the pub, leaving his shoes behind on the shingle shore. She noticed his feet were quite dirty and his toe nails curled downwards at the edges like horns. He wore a navy blue fisherman's cap and a red and white spotty kerchief around his neck. The woman, tall and broad-shouldered, had long dark brown hair and a great big-toothed smile, her green eyes brimming over with bravado and bonhomie, 'Hey, how you doin"?' 'Wanna a drink? We're getting them in.' Gathering the girl into the pub through the crowd, saying, 'Hi man, hey, cool. What's happening?' A question not needing an answer, she seemed to know everyone up towards the bar.

The dark-haired man ordered the drinks. 'Hey' he said, grinning widely and passing a glass of cider, 'Get that down you.' He had two crooked front teeth and a silver skull earring hanging from his left ear, giving him the air of a jaunty pirate. With a pint glass that felt almost too large for her small hands she began to relax. She felt warm in the circle of light near the girl with the green eyes. There was going to be a session. Her belly lurched with anticipation, music, sweet music and she wanted it. Wanted to be a part of it. But how?

Back in the summer of 1959, when she was nearly 15 and still a schoolgirl hanging around a jukebox on the *Claremont Pier* in a town called Lowestoft on the

Suffolk coast, she'd heard Ray Charles for the first time *Night Time Is the Right Time*. Margie Hendricks wailed out the chorus, 'Baby. Baby. You know the night-time is the right time to be with the one you love...' The raw passion in that voice had hit the girl with all the force of a northern sea. The same sea that had rolled underneath the wooden boards of that old pier. On the jukebox, more Ray Charles, Connie Francis and t he sweet harmonies of the Everly Brothers, Marvin Rainwater, and Elvis *All Shook Up*. Buddy Holly *That'll Be The Day*. And it was the day. The day she heard the music. Somewhere, who knows where. Probably *Radio Luxembourg* or *The American Forces Network*, she'd heard Ella Fitzgerald *Every time we say Good-bye*.

She had wanted that heart full velvet voice to sing into her ear, to sing her to sleep when she lay down at night. She wanted to love and be loved so that saying good-bye could be like that. Feel like that. Make you sing like that. She kept the voices that seemed to sing of what she felt coiled up next to her heart. In her mind she sang alongside them and the singing behind her lips was good.

An hour or so later in Hastings as the afternoon slipped away in that smoky blue haze, glasses were piled high in the sink behind the beer stained mahogany bar, the wooden floors were sticky with spilt booze, cigarette butts overflowed in tin ash trays, crisp packets and peanut shells spilled over the tables and onto the floor, and the guitar players and harmonica blowers drifted out to play in the side alley. A bold voice was lurking in her spleen, waiting to vent, waiting to holler. It was a voice that didn't always seem to be her own, urging her on in a husky whisper, a wild woman rising with red hair aflame, her mouth wide and her desire enormous.

> **BETTY BLUES BELTER** 'Go on, sing. You want to. I dare you. You can, you know you can. Sing. Sing. Go on.'

'I'd like to sing' she said, feeling brave and a little bit drunk.

'What do you know?' he said.

> **PROCRASTINATING PATSY** 'Oops a' daisy, what do you know?'

'Oh' she thought, 'I don't... my mind's gone blank.' The taller of the guitar players grinned at her as he took a long swig of the dark beer in his glass. '*The House of The Rising Sun*?' she said. Almost a question, the words rushed and breathless. Perhaps they'll say, 'No' The guitarist asked, 'In E?' Was there a choice? Did she even know what in E meant? No she didn't. Out of the blue sky nowhere she sang. She opened her mouth, let rip and sang the first song she had in her head. She had heard it on the *Bob Dylan* album that everyone was playing that summer (released March 1962). The bittersweet song of gamblers and lovers had touched her. She knew the words and liked the bluesy feel of it. Closing her eyes, clenching her fists into two tight little balls, dragging a long gulp of air down into her lungs, the sound emerged. Gurgling at first then up out of her chest, spinning free like the hollering of a deranged banshee, 'There is a house in New Orleans, they call the rising sun, and it's been the ruin of many a poor girl. Oh God, I know I am one.'

The words danced into her head, up out into the air. Musician? No. Singer? Hardly. She couldn't tell you what notes she was singing. Somewhere, deep down in her innards she found a sense of rhythm, her ears tuned to the pitch and the gut quaking, leg shaking energy needed to make that sound resonated through her whole body. It found her heart, her head and the marrow in her bones. A big yelp of a voice spewed up and out of her throat, wrapped itself around the song and that was that, 'With one foot on the platform, and the other foot on the train, I'm going back to New Orleans to wear that ball and chain.' The song was at an end. The last verse was sung. 'Hell's bloody bells,' she said to herself, 'Hells bloody bells. I did it.' People were smiling, not laughing.

The guitarist was called Big Mack. He owned a battered old *Martin* and played it with a manic energy, making the instrument ring as he thrashed out the chords. A tall hurly burly man with disheveled curly hair bleached by the sun, wearing several big silver rings on his fingers. Tattoos on his arms, one a dark blue and crimson snake just visible below his black and white checked shirt sleeves rolled up to the elbows, and a glinting gold tooth. He sang with a big bold raspy voice, strained and grainy with beer and tobacco. He was older than she was, in his late twenties she reckoned. He became a friend. Whenever she ran into him, it was great. He always gave her a big bear hug and seemed pleased she was there in the same place as he was. Was that a friend? He said, 'I didn't know you sang. What else do you know?' *Mystery Train.* She'd heard it on an Elvis record. She'd heard people talking about its roots. It was folk, it was Irish. Or was it Scottish? It went to America and came back the way he sang it. She loved it. With her eyes closed, her brow furrowed with concentration, she sang the song, 'Train, train, comin' on 'round, 'round the bend. Well it took my baby, but it never will again.'

Another scattering of applause from the little gathering and the girl with green eyes said, 'Wow, you can sing.' Big Mack winked at her. A dog barked and more drinks were called for. The players were off again and someone was blowing the hell out of a harmonica on Bukka White's *Fixin' to Die.* Overcome and a little embarrassed, she scuttled away to hide for a moment in the pub's Victorian bottle green tiled lavatory. Sitting on the lid of an old wooden toilet seat behind the safety of a bolted door, shaking a little and yet elated with what she'd just done. She wrapped her arms around her chest and squeezed herself. Then, before she knew what she was doing, her thumb went into her mouth.

NASTY NELLIE 'Good grief girl, still needing that suck.'

Ignoring the nasty one, she whispered to herself in case anyone should overhear, 'Oh my god, oh yes, oh yes I did it. I sang. I can.' Checking her face in the cracked and mottled glass of an old mirror above the sink advertising *Mackeson's Stout*, shouting in capital letters, 'LOOKS GOOD, TASTES GOOD AND, BY GOLLY, IT DOES YOU GOOD.' She washed her hands and wiped away the smudged black mascara from under her eyelashes. She applied more black eye liner, then lipstick, ran shaking fingers through her hair and pulled her beret back onto her head.

Singing out loud in front of other people was an unexpected explosion of all the unsung songs that had lain inside her. Whoosh, whirling out of her mouth and into the air. It felt good. No, not just good. It was mind blowingly, wonderfully good. It almost scared her, that rib busting voice. Out in the bar a man with a bushy grey beard and a large ruddy pockmarked nose stopped her as she was heading back out to the alley. He invited her to come to a folk night in another pub the following night, 'You could get up in the from the floor spot,' he said, 'you're not a bad little singer.'

He wasn't looking at her face. His eyes were on her breasts. He offered to buy her a drink and the men grouped around him laughed, cracking a couple of asides she didn't quite understand. She dare not refuse the drink for fear of appearing to be a girl in a woman's world, although her head was beginning to whirl. A hand briefly but surely touched her arse and lingered there for a moment. A squeeze then the hand was gone. She looked into his watery blue red-rimmed eyes as he smiled drunkenly at her, passed her a pint and then turned back to his mates, saying, 'See you tomorrow then.' As if she'd been dismissed. He was saving her for later. The moment was over. Outside, Big Mack was singing *Love, Oh Love, Oh Careless Love*.

The following day, she was sitting on the beach in the Old Town, throwing pebbles into the sea. The sun was high in the sky. Shading her eyes from the glare on the sea, she watched a swarm of seagulls circling over the fishing boats. She was in a twist and several knots, feeling slightly cider sick. With a sneer and a snigger.

NASTY NELLIE 'No, you can't sing, don't kid yourself. You can't do anything.'

WICKED WILL O'MINA 'Little Miss Tugboat Annie from old London.'

NASTY NELLIE 'A voice like a squeaky gate.'

She didn't go. She didn't sing. Betty had gone and wouldn't return for quite a while. Piss Pot Polly was waiting in the wings.

All this in a blue mist distance, a sail away. Longing, belonging to a tide that flows into time and back again, like my thoughts really. Mine's a strange song, a long song with many verses. The man on the phone in Hastings asked, 'When?' I said, 'Ah well, there's a tale, a long tale.' I gave him my answer, 'A pub in Hastings in 1963 or was it '64?'

The article appeared in the paper the week of the gig in Hastings.

'*Jazz singer goes back to her roots.*'

Roots? What roots? Where?'

VERSE 5

Gaslight and shadows

I Don't Know Enough About You Peggy Lee 1946

1945 to 1946: another move, monsters in the corner of the room, an accident on the stairs, an official visit and the outside world.

The war was over. Bomb sites remained like open wounds in London, a city of ten million people with a shortage of homes. Great Britain was about to begin the decline of its world power, the loss of empire, no longer top bulldog. Post-war government acts would promise security and care from 'Cradle to Grave', and the first launderette would open in Bayswater. The slums would be cleared to make way for council estates. Prefabricated tower blocks, the slums of the future.

In 1945 life resumed as 'normal' in the homes that were still standing. You could seek a moment of solitude in an outside lavatory, with torn squares of yesterdays newspaper pronged onto a nail on the wall. A good place for some fluttering thoughts and no one worried about the freezing bum and cold hands. Kids played out in the street, winter, spring, summer and autumn. They played with marbles and skipping ropes. *Knock down Ginger, He, Hopscotch, Statues, Jack's* or *Cats Cradle* played with string. Or kicked a ball about until the occasional *Austin 7* or delivery truck with bread, milk or *Royal Mail* trundled by at a stately speed. The call of the rag and bone man or the coal man, 'Coal'o!' Old horse drawn carts clip clop as Mr what's 'is name next door shovelled up the horse-shit for his allotment. And finally, as dusk fell and the lamps were lit, 'Come on in, it's teatime.' Or later, 'Get in here now, it's bedtime.'

In February 1946 mother and child moved to one of those terraced houses. Under the sloping roof, a kitchen doubled as a bathroom, the bath covered with a wooden top that served as a table. In the front was a sitting room. In the back a bedroom, a box room and a lavatory. It wasn't far from Lewisham Market, the clock tower and *Chiesmans Department Store*. Just up the hill was Blackheath Village. You could go across the Heath and then on down through Greenwich Park to the river. *Muffin The Mule* appeared on the television as GI brides left Britain for new lives. Leaving gas lights and linoleum, corned beef and condensed milk for oranges and maple syrup. Nylons and real eggs were just around the corner.

I remember that house as if it was a map imprinted onto the inner lining of my eyelids. The main front door was approached from the street by a short garden path and steep concrete steps. A quarry tiled entrance hall. A door for the ground floor flat and stairs up to the first and second floor flats, the top one under the eaves with sloping ceilings at the front. More stairs led down to a basement flat which opened onto a small concrete area in the front and a long rectangular garden at the rear.

This was my third home since birth if you don't count the drawer in Kent. In a small room at the back overlooking the gardens was the girl who'd jumped so often and so high in her cot, it had given way. Look, look, a way out. The door was open. The stairs a long and mysterious chasm snaking downwards, twisting out of sight into god knows where land. What was she to do? She stood for a brief moment, one hand poised in mid-air as if to test the unexplored space suspended before her, the other in her mouth. Fear and curiosity rippled into her throat. Curiosity won. Crouching down onto the slippery brown linoleum, she slid her bottom to the very edge of the stairs. Down towards the next step, and then another. And as nothing fearful was happening, no appearance of the one who was mother, no darkness, no monstrous being, step-by-step she descended. Bump, bump, bump.

A boy stood at the bottom of the first flight of stairs. He was David Ashford and he was six years old. His thin and angular face seemed unnecessarily charged with a strong and defiant jaw. Dark and defensive eyes dominated the pale skin stretched across bird like bones. 'Hallo?' It was more a question than a greeting, 'Hallo?'

Again and louder as if talking to an idiot, the 'H' over pronounced, as if his tongue didn't like the sound of it. He was taunting her. She sat silently on the bottom step with her mouth hanging open. She was uncertain and in awe. The boy loomed above her, his manner belligerent. He demanded a response, 'I said Hello! Can't you talk or what?' he sneered. The air was cold, the linoleum beneath her legs was cold, the moment was cold, and she could only stare up at the boy. Her thumb went into her mouth and she sucked with such intensity she made furious gulping sounds. The boy laughed, 'You're a baby,' he said, 'you're a little baby. Cry Baby Bunting.' His laugh wasn't very friendly. The small girl remained sitting, sucking and looking while the boy sneered and stared.

Suddenly he was gone and she felt the wetness trickling from inside her, dripping down the step she sat upon, slipping along the floor and snaking into a corner making a small puddle. She remained on the step sitting in her puddle and felt a chill draught playing on the back of her neck coming from an ill-fitting window above. She twisted her head to look up at the steps she'd descended. She sucked and she sat, and still the boy was gone.

The silent stairwell was then disturbed by a resounding crash, which shook the house as the impact of a door slammed into its frame far down below. Loud voices stung the air. Not her mother's voice but a man's. And then another. Higher pitched, sharp and angry. The deeper voice of the man was thunderous, coming up into the stairwell, violent and threatening as if torn out of the owner's throat. Two people appeared on the landing and were seemingly unaware of the child on the step as their argument raged. The boy appeared again and was pushed backwards by the man, back into the place he'd gone before.

The woman stood panting heavily from the efforts of verbal warfare and the long climb. Her angular thin face, so like the boy's, was thrust nervously forward. The small veins visible under the skin of her throat were like a community of angry pulsating worms. Most of her hair was hidden underneath a woollen scarf tied under her chin. Dressed in a nondescript and threadbare grey coat, the hem of which drooped around her thin calves, her legs were stockingless and very pale. She wore a pair of grey socks and brown shoes with small heels in need of a good cobbler. In one hand she held a large basket and hanging heavily from the other, a string bag which contained two onions, a few potatoes and a cabbage. She noticed the child on the stair.

'Shut up Frank, shut up! What's she doing down here on her own?' The man replied, 'Who?' He turned to look. The man was missing an arm, the empty sleeve pinned up onto the left hand shoulder of his jacket. As gaunt as his wife, his eyes and jaw were the mirror of the boy's except for a pronounced Adam's apple which jerked about in his scrawny throat like an anxious ferret. Attempting a smile, he said, ''allo then, where's your mum?' The boy appeared again, 'She can't talk and she's stupid. I asked her.' He glared, 'I asked her.' The boy insisted, his defensive eyes both ablaze and afraid. 'Where is she then?' asked the man, his one thumb jerking upwards indicating the space above his head, 'What's the matter, cat got your tongue?' He turned to the boy. 'I don't know, I never saw her. I just came out here and she was sitting on the step. She's stupid, I told you!' The boy urged nervously, his voice rising to a desperate squeal. 'All right, all right, I 'eard you the first time,' growled the man. He turned to the woman, 'Peg, you go up and see if she's in.' The woman said, 'I don't want to talk to her. You go. I got this lot to sort out, and your blasted dinner to get on the stove.' She turned away to look at her own child who was still staring nervously from father to mother, his nose running with snot, his cheeks startlingly red. 'You get into that kitchen and put the kettle on, now!' Then, directing her words towards her one-armed husband, 'Look at 'er poor little mite. She never takes 'er out you know. No wonder she looks so pasty, she don't see daylight.' At this remark the woman who was Peg turned and looked down. Then she saw it, the puddle. 'Oh my good god!' she shrieked, 'she's gone and wet 'erself. I only washed this passage yesterday. On my hands and knees. You dirty little girl.'

The dirty one remained sucking her thumb, silently sitting in the dirty wetness. The front door opened. High heels clip clipping on the linoleum, the rustle and swish of skirts and her mother climbed the stairs towards the group on the landing. 'It's 'er,' said Frank. Pushing the boy in front of him, he opened a door leading to a kitchen, went in and pulled it shut behind him. A radio was switched on. *Workers Playtime.* 'She thinks she's so lah-di-dah,' muttered Peg under her breath, moments before Cecilie appeared on the landing. 'She's wet herself, and on my floor. If you think I'm clearing it up, you've got another thing coming.' The child cowered. She knew she was dirty.

Cecilie picked her up and with a haughty glance at Peg continued on her way to the rooms at the top of the house. No further word passed between the two women and the girl closed her eyes, squeezing them tightly as she jammed her thumb into her mouth again. For comfort, as if to ward off her mother's anger she closed down into herself, tried to turn herself into an invisible ball of nothingness. Clothes were wrenched over her head, harsh words snapped and cracked in the air and then she was in the cot in the dark room. Her body was still chilled from the stairway. Her eyes were alert, piercing the air like glistening beads and her heart pumped under her skin. She carried on sucking her thumb, sucking, sucking. In her mind's eye was an image of the boy downstairs, the boy with the pale face and the dribbling nose. The voices became a distant murmur, a low spinning wall of sound. The water that had flowed from her own body rose ever higher, threatening to drown the world. Finally she slept.

It was a very cold December and it snowed heavily two weeks before Christmas. The soft whiteness could be felt up in the top of the house in Lee Park. In her cot was a blue eiderdown. It was life itself. She would hold onto a corner with one hand and pick at the feathers inside the satin. She would play, snap and tease and then move onto a fresh feather. The eiderdown corners became wet and limp, worn and friendly.

Cecilie's part-time job demonstrating gas cookers in a London show room gave her time to audition for the actress jobs she so dearly wanted. She *had* to sell the cooker. Big smile, chic hair, perfect in a smart pinafore, the bow tied around her waist over a dress. Red nails, red lips, big eyes. Who could resist. But oh dear, there was this bloody baby. How was she to deal with that *and* her career? It was ruined.

A day or so after the descent down the stairs into the unknown there was a knock on the door of the flat. 'Who's there?' Cecilie called. A familiar voice, a male voice answered, 'It's Dr Browne here.' She opened the door. The local doctor stood on the stair. Cecilie had seen him on several occasions. A woman wearing a belted and very sensible looking blue woollen coat followed him. Mrs Boyd, welfare worker, 'How is your daughter?' Cecilie walked to the small room and indicated the cot in the corner, 'See, she's in her cot.' The voices, looming above and around the girl seemed to emanate from three heads stuck out from three necks, like a group of gesticulating turtles. Talking about her and over her as if she were invisible. Sucking her thumb, the girl in the cot closed her eyes and turned her head.

There were tears, Cecilie's tears. Tears that were wet and wouldn't stop falling, 'I can't cope with her, she's impossible, and she whines constantly, and she won't do as she's told. She's impossible. I simply can't cope!' Cecilie's hands were turning a white cotton handkerchief over and over. Her eyes glittered tremulous sobs in waiting, just under the surface of her words. Mrs Boyd bent down to stare intently at the child in the cot. The child stared back at the woman's face. Disturbingly close, she saw pale grey watery eyes behind steel framed glasses. Eyelids slightly red and sore looking as if they'd been constantly rubbed. 'She's a little bit too big to be in a cot, don't you think. How old is she now? She must be nearly two.'

Angrily Cecilie cried through her tears, 'Well, who's going to provide the where with all to organise something else? I'm on my own you know.' 'And the marks on her legs and face?' asked Mrs Boyd, who wasn't as careful or courteous as the doctor. 'I told them at the hospital that I wanted the child adopted you know, right from the start, and I felt absolutely bloody lousy all through the pregnancy. I'm not strong you know. I simply can't go on like this!'

The doctor spoke, 'I do understand. Don't distress yourself. We have to respond when this sort of information comes to our attention. It's more than likely to be idle gossip, I'm sure but it's been mentioned by the cleaner at the surgery that the child has been left 'er... unattended.' He coughed, his hand placed politely over his mouth, 'Now, I know all children need a good smack now and then; naughty little blighters 'ey?' he added, smiling at Cecilie, almost apologetically, 'You are a patient of mine. I do feel we must attempt to sort this out in as discreet a way as possible.'

He took her arm and inclining his head towards the door he added, 'So let's just talk calmly about the situation. Come along my dear.' He led her gently out of the room. She talked, the doctor being careful, the welfare worker suspicious, the child in question watching and listening.

On a smog choking grey morning the following week, and just before the girl's third Christmas, she sat on the lap of Mrs Boyd in the back of a black car. Her bare legs on the woman's prickly dark blue wool coat, she looked up at a large nose with the beginnings of a boil on one nostril. The car moved slowly. A cold sleet rain lashed against the windows. Houses and shops were barely visible either side as she made out rows of ghostly grey shapes on the edges of her eyes. She had a feeling she was going somewhere she'd never been before. And that it was to do with a mother who didn't want her. A mother who was angry because she wasn't good. It was to do with wetting herself in the cot and on the stairs. It was because she was bad. And it was because her mother was unwell.

The interminable child hours that she'd spent in the room at the top of the house remained forever in her head. An obscure and befogged blur, lurking like a collection of confused images that floated in and out of her dreams and thoughts. Images culled from the remote chambers of charred remembrances. Filtering through these veiled impressions came the soft hiss of the gas lamps and the black and eerily mobile shadows on the ceiling when dusk fell and the door was closed. A whisper of air from the half-open window disturbed the darkness, fluttering the monsters that inhabited the secret corners of the room. The feeling of dark material near her mouth, near her eyes, over her nose. And then it was gone. She remembers a woman frustrated and more than angry saying, 'I don't want you. I wish you hadn't been born, so there.'

The hands of the motherless child who couldn't love her own child were often slap happy, vibrating with annoyance as she administered to the child's basic needs. Attending with no intimacy and the least possible time spent. Hurrying, her mind was elsewhere, all her feelings locked away in an inaccessible place. The proceedings were a chore, an irritating drudgery that had to be endured. The child accepted this disconnected attention, for what else did she know? Pushing her away, the mother would say, 'Be quiet!'

Red London buses crawled towards them like vermilion phantoms out of the ghostly gloom. The car smelled of petrol and leather, Mrs Boyd's wet tweed, mothballs and carbolic soap. Londoners shuffled about, muffled footsteps walking through endless thick yellow walls. Street lamps hung in the air as a dim glow, visible one-by-one, and everyone walked around with scarves over their mouths and noses. Who knows who was out there in the sulphuric gloom. Their breath hung like clouds of vapour suspended in the air. She could touch it with her fingers. It was going to get much colder.

Carol's mother, Cecilie, 1920s.

Sunshine

I'm Wishing Frank Churchill and Larry Morey
Snow White and the Seven Dwarfs 1937

1946 to 1947: a home with no mothers belonging to the children, a very cold winter, a summer holiday at the seaside with Snow White and the Seven Dwarfs, and a cow that ripped a hole in the tent.

The girl was taken to a room filled with paper-chains and the excited babble of children's voices. On a dark brown shelf stood a wireless, maybe it was *Children's Hour*. Or *Listen with Mother*. There were no mothers belonging to the children. The gas fire gave a comforting red glow from behind an old nursery fireguard with a polished brass rim. The smell of disinfectant, paper paste and cabbage hung in the air. The children, about a dozen or so, were licking strips of red, green, yellow and blue paper, and looping them into chains. The paper snakes lay in tangles on every surface.

The girl tried to hide behind Mrs Boyd's broad tweed back. 'Come along dear.' Mrs Boyd pulled her by the hand, 'Don't you want to join in and make paper chains? Don't be silly now.' She pushed her forward. 'No, I don't want to,' the girl said, with her left hand thumb still plugged into her mouth. 'We can't hear you dear. Take that silly thumb out of your mouth and speak clearly.' She wanted to. Just didn't know how. Her mouth wouldn't release the thumb. 'No!' There was always something about 'No' It gave her a sense of satisfaction. 'No!' She hung back, interested, almost tempted. And then Mrs Boyd was gone. The chains were finished and a man with a stepladder came and hung them from the ceiling. She thought they looked beautiful. That was the beginning of Christmas 1946.

A tree was to arrive the following day. There would be baubles and tarnished pre-war tinsel. It was magical. Tea, or supper, got the thumb out of her mouth. Well, she loved to eat and never seemed to put much fat on her skinny bones. They used to say, 'You must have worms.' Later she was tested for these worms and there were none. She was very pleased about that. The thought of worms in her tummy had scared her terribly. There were several dreams where she just knew they were there, wriggling around. And in the morning when she awoke she'd be sure the worms were in her bed, crawling in a glutinous mass. They never were.

Some kids called her 'greedy guts' or 'pig snout' but she carried on eating, packing it away for a hungry winter's day. Bread and jam, pink tinned ham, beetroot sliced into crimson vinegary circles, and a *Huntley and Palmer*'s biscuit. One each or a slab of dark fruitcake. A feast. This was the place for sweet stuff. Mugs of hot milk or *Ovaltine* followed, then a spoonful of the sweetest stickiest mouthful she'd ever tasted. Malt. 'Oh more of that please, give me more, more, more,' she begged. A young woman with very red lips, her blond hair pulled back into a roll at the nape of her neck, laughed as she distributed this glorious spoonful, 'More tomorrow, you'll have a spoonful every day.' The jar of malt was gone. The girl with blonde hair came back and moved to pick up the girl. 'No, no, put me down, put me down,' she said that a lot, little Miss Put Me Down.

She loved the food, though there never seemed to be enough. Corned beef, semolina pudding that wasn't really semolina, bread and dripping, battered cod deep fried in beef dripping, scrambled dehydrated egg, hot toast and cabbage. Always cabbage, boiled to a pale green pulp. Cod liver oil and nasty-tasting orange juice in a flat bottle. She refused nothing and the little voice inside began to speak more and more with each passing hour. Every day and every week the other girl would speak, 'Put me down.' Then quietly, 'But can I have more please?' 'And where is Mr Manners?' the grown ups would say.

At five-thirty the washing began in a bathroom the size of a large kitchen. A bathroom that echoed and seemed cold in spite of a huge radiator, with brown linoleum on the floor and black and green tiles on the walls. Ears, fingers, toes and knees were inspected. Slivers of soap were gathered and squashed together to create a new bar. It could be very slimy that soap. A long sleeved blue flannel nightdress sprigged with small red flowers was pulled over her head. It was too long and trailed behind her. When they suggested they find a smaller one she protested, 'I like this one.' It felt perfect, like a cuddle. She was put into a small bed in a room that contained five more identical beds, lined up on each side of the room. White stiff sheets were packed tightly around her, then a pink blanket and a coverlet decorated with tumbling white rabbits. The blanket cocoon smelled of the carbolic soap they'd been washed with. Like Mrs Boyd without the wet prickly tweed. The door wasn't locked and the room rustled with the movements of the other children. Two girls giggled and another with shorn hair, snored. A clock chimed somewhere downstairs and then there was sleep. The girl occasionally woke in the night with a smothering feeling, over her nose, her mouth and her whole head.

The first week in the London County Council home was meant to be a respite for Cecilie and time for the authorities to assess whether there had been wanton neglect or perhaps a nervous breakdown. The reality, as it turned out was that she wanted the child put up for adoption. In those days they didn't talk about post natal depression. Beryl had said, 'No, she's your responsibility. You must buckle down and care for the child. It's not done to shirk your duty.' That was the step-grandmother's law.

The time in the children's home was good, even when the icy blast of that very cold winter ran into January and beyond. The snow fell heavily, freezing the rail points so the trains couldn't pull the coal. It was so cold that *Big Ben* miss-bonged one day. It was so cold that people had icicles hanging from their noses. Snot ran and you couldn't feel it. It was so cold the sea was frozen at Margate. All the children coughed and spluttered. Their noses were dripping, crusty and sore. The girl wore an itchy woollen *Balaclava* and one day when they were gathered for a walk, she was zipped into a siren suit, so warm she wanted to live, eat and sleep in it. It was red and she's loved wearing red ever since. Everywhere people went to bed to keep warm. Lots of loving under the blankets with ice on the insides of windows. The post-war baby boom.

Summer came and with it a holiday in Kent. The children lined up in the hallway in their summer clothes and were given little boxes with sandwiches wrapped in greaseproof paper. All ready to leave and Matron checked faces, 'Let me see.' She knew what was coming. 'I thought so,' Matron said, 'tut, tut you're filthy. Here!' With a small smile lifting the corners of her mouth, she produced a white cotton handkerchief from the depths of one of her many pockets. Spit, spit and the wet and disgusting cotton cloth was rubbed over the offending cheek and mouth. Matron ruled. With an inside voice the girl said, 'Little Miss Put Me Down. Oh no, put me down. Your handkerchief stinks. And your face is wobbly.' Matron's cheeks shook like jellies when she walked and she had at least three chins.

Off to the seaside by train from London Bridge. On the very same trains she'd heard screeching and rumbling from the flat above Blackheath Station. The steel wheels on the tracks, ticket-tack. How she loved that sound. The countryside rushing by, leafy green. And then the Chalk Downs. Conical topped oast houses near the hop fields, cows in the pasture, poppies in the corn, and a farm house with wood smoke curling from the chimney. London was left behind. She didn't want to talk. She wanted to look out the window.

They stayed on a farm near the sea between Sandwich and Deal in Kent. There were sand dunes and sheep, sandy beaches and birds; seagulls, kittiwakes, lapwings and golden plovers. There were buckets and spades and little packs of paper flags to stick on the turret of a sand castle. The Union Jack and the Welsh Dragon, the red and white cross of St George and the blue and white of Scotland flapping in the sea breeze. One rainy day when grey clouds hung so low you couldn't see the sea beyond the pebbles on the beach, an orderly crocodile of children walked along the seafront in Deal.

There were damp hours sitting in a shelter facing the massive grey swell of the English Channel, her skinny white legs stuck out in front of her like two matchsticks. Waiting for the return of the watery sunshine, waiting until the clouds lifted. The possibility of taking off her white socks and sandals and dipping her feet into the water excited her. She wanted to swim so badly, to duck her head under the sea, to find what might be hidden from sight under the waves that were being whipped up in the wind. On another wet day they went to the pictures and saw *Snow White and The Seven Dwarfs*. The terror, the wonderful toe curling shivering and excitement. The princess' voice was so high, so sweet, like a bird, a bird too impossible to imagine. Adriana Mitchell Caselotti and her flock of white doves, or were they pigeons? The girl was that princess in her head. The first voice she committed to memory. *I'm wishing*. On warm days she wore a blue wool swimsuit, which became twice its weight with salt and sand when she dipped under the waves. It hung and dragged around her skinny body like a spare skin as the waves washed around her. She learned to cheat swim, pushing herself along the sandy shallows with one foot, a lot of splashing, paddling with her arms.

LYING LIZZIE 'Look at me, I'm swimming.'

And she believed it herself. Was that her very first lie?

Four small girls were sleeping in a tent. One evening when a gate had been accidentally left open, a cow wandered into the field and ripped a hole in the side of the tent with the girls cowering inside. When the tale was recounted in the following years, the humble cow had became a raging red-eyed bull and the girls were all in mortal danger. This wasn't the case at all. It was merely a curious cow with an itch and an effective pair of horns.

Field mushrooms the size of plates were picked at dawn and fried for breakfast. The farmer's wife took a small group of children into the cowshed to see a newborn calf wobbling on little legs, its fur wet and curly. One day a plane flew low over the sand dunes near Sandwich Bay and the boys yelled, half in play and maybe with a little bit of fear, 'It's the Germans. The Germans are coming. Hide! Hide! It's war! War!' And, 'Rat atat tat.' Holding two fingers in cowboy gun position so beloved of little boys, aiming up at the sky where the plane was fading into the distance. The girl's screamed. She covered her head with her arms then peeped up into the blueness. Of course there were no bombs, no Germans. The plane was on its way to France or maybe even America, over the sea and far away.

Later on in the afternoon, *Walls* ice creams for tea. Her first creamy drip, dripping cold ice cream. It was delicious. Almost as good as the malt on the spoon. Mushrooms and seaside, *Muffin The Mule*, *Walls* ice cream and cruel queens, a princess, a wild cow, rain drops on the sea, make believe air raids, liberty bodices, pebble beaches and the English Channel.

Somebody held a buttercup under her chin and said, 'Ooh, you do love butter.' She did. Bread and butter. But butter was a rare treat indeed. *Echo Margarine* was what went onto bread. Her freckles multiplied. She was a city child, pale where the sun hadn't found her skin underneath the socks, the sandals and the blue wool bathing suit. Her bones were warm and she'd been to the pictures and witnessed magic.

Rag-books and dolls, a spinning top and a tea set. That was how she remembered those days in Kent and the children's home in Lewisham. London and the summer was hot. The tar on the roads almost bubbled, sticky black and melting in the heat. Dusty purple Buddleia, parched and drooping over hot red brick walls. Dogs panting in the shade of a doorway. The air was stagnant and thick with the stillness that comes with not a puff of air or a hint of rain. It was hard to find a place to keep the milk from turning sour and the meat from rotting. The mother is faint here, a pale and distant image. It was then that the small girl began to understand. If you stay in the present you could pretend the past need not exist.

VERSE 7

Families

Round About Midnight Thelonious Monk 1944

1947 to 1951: a de-mobbed stepfather, a half-sister, the cabbage and the truth. Do you want a girl? A school, a window to her tummy, running away and being sent away.

She was back in the Lewisham flat with her mother and now a stepfather, Arthur. Cecilie had met him when she'd been invited to a student dance at the Slade School of Art in the early part of spring. He was de-mobbed from the Navy. The mother wore a long satin dress, pale pink with a paler pink net over a full skirt scattered with sequins and thin satin straps that showed off her shoulders and arms. He'd fallen in love with her. She was unmarried with a three-year-old child though he didn't know that in the moment of seeing her for the first time. He just looked at Cecilie and had decided, 'That's the girl for me.'

A wedding day in 1947.

Arthur was one of the lucky ones. He'd survived. He wore a sailor's beard, a naval issue *Duffel* coat and brown cord trousers. He smoked a pipe and probably thought he was Jack the Lad. Born in Bermondsey to Gladys and Harry, just off the Old Kent Road south of the river, Arthur was ready to live in a way he could never have dreamed of. Harry had been a railway man. A man whose support for the general strike in 1926 had cost him any climb up the ladder, keeping him in the lower ranks. Harry was a flag waver, a whistle blower and a train door slammer. Gladys had kept house for the family of five and took in washing to add a little more to the small family income.

Arthur had travelled beyond the limits of the poor but friendly London streets of his boyhood. Barely a grown man, he had gone to sea and was bombed on his ship in the Baltic in 1943. He almost drowned, floating about in the freezing waters through one long dark and terrifying night and was rescued when most of his shipmates had been lost. Not for him a menial job. No, not when you had nearly lost your life, had felt the icy breath of death, struggling to keep your head above the water. He would become an artist. He won a scholarship to the prestigious art college. There he mixed with the arty and bohemian elite. Cecilie was an actress and was out looking for a man. Looking for a father for the child she didn't want. She married Arthur and they honeymooned in the Lake District.

Carol, Lewisham, 1949.

Cecilie regretted marrying Arthur almost as soon as she had. She turned again to blaming the girl for all that was wrong. Because Arthur was so besotted with Cecilie, he took to blaming the girl too. Whatever Cecilie said, whatever she wanted, Arthur would comply. There was a white Christmas again that year and in Kent thunder rumbled on Christmas Day. In the girl's mind were the fading pictures of the Christmas past. The paper-chains, other children and a rabbit covered bedspread in a large room with a high white ceiling. Her half-sister Jennifer yowled her way into life on 14th February 1948.

When baby Jennifer cried Arthur took care of her. Cecilie seemed to be out a lot and Arthur's moods depended on her. Cecilie told Beryl that Arthur was peculiar, that the honeymoon had been a disaster and she hated him. She only married to provide a father for her daughter and now here she was with two daughters. Once more, she said she couldn't cope. Arthur was the one who prepared the meals and filled the bath. He told the girl stories, told her to finish her greens, or to drink her milk, to brush her teeth. And in the asking he probed the catacomb of loneliness that seemed to be the absolute quintessence of her. All the aloneness she'd endured without knowing what being alone was. Because there was nothing else.

He sat her on the edge of the 'bath cum table' whilst the kettle on the gas hob whistled and steamed the kitchen into a cave of misty dampness. The boiling of cabbage, the frying of fatty meat, the making of tea and the washing and splashing of water in the big white chipped butlers sink. Sometimes Arthur

Jennifer with big sister Carol, Lewisham, 1951.

would draw a picture with his forefinger in the vaporous wetness on the window or the brown shiny walls and she was drawn into life.

Arthur would sing, 'Hooray and up she rises, what shall we do with the drunken sailor?' And sometimes *Beautiful Dreamer*. Or *Daddy wouldn't buy me a Bow Wow*. In later years she would remember, 'Beautiful Screamer, lashed up in stones.' Because that's what she'd heard at the time.

Arthur bought a Victorian copper warming pan in a junk shop on Lee High Road and hung it on the wall in the front room. She can see it clearly, gleaming under the gas lights. He bought books from secondhand bookshops up the hill in Blackheath or down by the river in Greenwich. He wanted a better life and he wanted to please Cecilie but that was a lost cause.

There were the Saturdays out shopping with Jennifer in her pram. The girl hanging onto the side trying to keep up with Arthur's brisk walk. The *Home and Colonial Stores* or *The Co-op* for tins of broken biscuits, two rashers of bacon, one egg, a jar of *Bovril*, the ration of *Echo Margarine*, maybe some penny buns, condensed milk and a tin of *Spam*. Sometimes there was bread and jam or dripping for tea, an arrowroot biscuit or a pickled egg.

Frying, endless frying. Fatty chops, streaky bacon, bread fried in lard, lard, lard. A generation raised on dripping and lard. Padding on the skinny bones. And if it wasn't fried, it was boiled to death. All of this she saw as the brown *Bakelite* radio on the shelf above the kitchen cupboard sang the songs of those bleak early post war years. Clipped English voices would speak of world affairs. Others, friendlier voices from Manchester or Liverpool and the East End of London, told the jokes that made a nation laugh after a war that had changed everything.

At night the gas lamps were lit and she called them, 'anksssss' because they hissed just a little bit, scared her, just a little bit. So she gave them a name to make them friendly and she had a little song and dance, 'I'm not afraid of the y'anks I'm not afraid of the y'anks.' Which sounded like 'Yanks' as she strung the words together. Strange to anyone who heard, 'Yanks are friend not foe.' Every London girl loved a Yank and his nylons, lipstick, dollar bills, chocolate, chewing gum and fancy dance steps. 'What a strange little child she is to be sure, Cecilie,' the friend said, who'd popped in to see Cecilie and was momentarily interested. The girl would stick her thumb in her mouth, unsure of her dance and the song.

Friends would occasionally call in on a weekend or a Friday evening. Women with berry red lips and powdered noses, wearing sharp shouldered suits with knee-length skirts or full skirted wasp waist dresses. The new look from Paris. Glamour. They wanted glamour after the dark dangerous days of war. Men in de-mob suits and a natty way with a cravat, with a moustache and a cigarette held aloft in one hand, found their way up the stairs. A quick drink in the front room with the copper warming pan and then, 'Up to town to catch a show and a drink perhaps.' Or, 'Visit old so and so, haven't seen her in years.' With a bottle of sherry, glasses at the ready, 'Cheerio.' 'Down the hatch old thing.' This was a generation who had lived their teenage and early twenties years in a war. Lost fathers and brothers, boyfriends and lovers.

At night when Cecilie and Arthur were out with friends or whatever, feelings remain in the memory as shadows. Later, when the girl thought about these moments she had no words. Only a belly ache, a low fluttering pain that made her want to cry. There they all lived in chaos, in a war between the angry mother and the confused and damaged man who wanted to paint and be loved. But he wasn't able to love Cecilie, not how she wanted him to. His life had damaged him, angered him. And his fairytale woman in a pink dress scattered with sequins hated him. Cecilie also hated the girl who had made her marry a man she didn't love. And then another baby. Oh dear, oh dear what can the matter be, chuck the lot down the lavatory, that's the way to do it. Only she couldn't and there they were.

A little Bridge

Scared of the night the when the hissing lamps were turned on. Scared of the stairs snaking downwards to unknown places. Scared of the sound of angry voices. Scared of her mothers hands. Scared of shadows and strange noises, 'I don't want to go to that place. That half known and half forgotten place, hissing lamps and smog place. A dark grey, damp, and dank place, linoleum and cabbage, dark and suffocating.' What's the point of crying? What's the point of bringing on the scorching rebuke, the harsh words, the stinging hand that slaps the face or stings the bare bottom? Best not to draw attention. Keep quiet and they'll forget you've been naughty or dirty, forget they're angry. And again and again the words, 'It's all your fault.'

Four years old and she was sent to a nursery school, 'Ding, ding, ding. Ding, ding, ding.' 'Are you sitting comfortably?' There was a pause and the radio, having listened to all the children in the land, replied. 'Then we'll begin.' If you got lucky on a Saturday, thruppence would buy you some pear drops or pineapple chunks. Weighed and poured into a white paper bag. A farthing could still buy you a handful of sweets and for another thruppence, a packet of *Smiths Crisps* with a little blue bag of salt. She once found three in one packet and felt absurdly joyful, 'Look! Look! I've got three salts.' What did she do with all that salt? Maybe she stuck her tongue into the blue paper and licked it clean. Well, she'd won it. It was special. She'd long for chewy bars, gob stoppers, liquorice sticks and sherbet dabs, fizzing as her tongue turned yellow.

One day she was alone in the kitchen in the flat at the top of the house, sitting at the table that was also a bath, having been told to, 'Finish your greens.' Told, 'you'll sit there until you've eaten all your greens.' Yellow, soggy, smelly, stone cold, chewed and spat out again. She pushed them round and round the plate, trying to hide them in the gravy or underneath a half eaten potato, hoping if she moved them enough they would vanish. Time became endless. She would be there in that room at that table until the end of hours, until it was dark and the 'anks were lit and the hissing would begin,'I'm not afraid of the y'anks.'

She stared out the window to the gardens down below and the tiny figures of the children playing in the bombed out houses. To the streets beyond, a craggy cliff of red brick where it was said that rats as big as dogs lived in the rubble. At dusk the glass-less window frames were like open mouths, silently asking questions. It was a mysterious playground.

Back to the cabbage and reality. 'Thou shalt not leave the food on your plate.' 'Children are starving in Africa.' 'Waste not, want not.' The room was steamy as usual with strips of flypaper hanging under the light bulb, the flies stuck, dead or dying and buzzing on the sticky surface. A pot was boiling on the stove.

She felt sick. Not because of the flies. No, they were very interesting. She was sick at the thought of the chewing followed by the swallowing. She looked at the flies and watched the dance of death. Buzz, buzz, buzz. Wings flapping. Dead, dead and another one dead. Arthur opened a window. The baby was crying. He went out of the kitchen and this was her moment. She put the cabbage in her mouth, clambered up onto the chair by the window, spat the nasty mess into her hand and lobbed it out. It landed splat on the concrete beside the basement back door in the area down below. She returned to her seat at the table.

The wireless was on in the front room. Kathleen Ferrier was singing, *Blow The Wind Southerly*. Cecilie was singing along with Kathleen. The girl sat very still in the kitchen. What's going to happen now? She hoped her mother would carry on singing. She hoped the baby would carry on crying. She hoped they'd all forget her. Forget it had been dinner and forget that she had any cabbage left to eat.

There was a knock on the door and a voice, 'Where did this come from?' A woman with her hands on her hips stood on the top step when Arthur opened the door. It was Mrs Saltz from the basement flat. She sounded cross. She was invited into the kitchen and as they all piled in, Cecilie, Arthur and the woman. The girl shrank. Mrs Saltz didn't look as fierce as Cecilie. Cecilie's eyes were flashing, her rage barely concealed. Oh dear, here it comes. Duck, hide your head, watch your back, stuff your hands in your pockets. Don't let her catch your legs with that slap.

The cabbage had narrowly missed Mrs Saltz's head as she was outside putting rubbish into the dustbin. A severe telling off began to erupt. Cecilie shouted, then Arthur. The baby began to bawl and as the tears began to fall from the girl's eyes onto the almost empty dinner plate, Mrs Saltz softened and asked if she could take her downstairs to see her boys. And, 'Come on Mrs er... do let her, no harm done, it was only a little bit. I put it in the bin. She must've eaten most of it, didn't you dear?' The girl nodded and had a feeling it was going to be alright. 'Well, just for an hour,' Cecilie said. Arthur agreed. He always agreed with Cecilie, 'You behave yourself or there'll be trouble.'

Mrs Saltz took the girl's small hand in hers as they climbed down those stairs, past the rooms where the boy called David lived. The hallway and stairs smelt faintly of piss and cabbage overlaid with *Jeyes Cleaning Fluid*. Old Mrs Craddock in the flat below popped her head out the door, as she always did when she heard footsteps. ''Allo Ruby,' she said. ''Allo, Mrs. C.' ''Ow's that 'usband of yours doin?' said Mrs Saltz. 'Oh well, no change, the doctors got 'im on some pills, but...' And she shrugged. You hardly ever saw old man Craddock. He sat in a chair all day listening to the radio, poker faced and mute with grief. His only son was killed in Singapore in 1942. "'Ow's your 'Arry and the boys? I saw young Philip yesterday. A big lad now. Shot up, nearly as tall as 'is dad.' The two women chatted on the stair for a moment.

The girl stared as they talked and thought the old lady must be ancient, at least 100. Her lined face looked crumpled, her mouth was empty but for a few old yellow teeth and the scarf wrapped around her nodding head had strange little ridges. Mrs Saltz had told her they were curlers. The scarf came off on a Sunday to reveal orderly rows of tight white rolls, her scalp pink inbetween. The girl saw them the following week, was fascinated and wanted to touch them. The yellow teeth and the wrinkles scared her.

When Cecilie had her hair done it didn't look like that. She had a chignon at the nape of her neck and a soft roll on her forehead. Her hair was dark and shiny, her teeth white and even. She thought that Cecilie was beautiful. Except when her eyes glittered and her mouth became a thin line. Then she looked like the Wicked Queen in *Snow White*.

Mrs Saltz and the girl went down the slippery brown linoleum stairs to the ground floor and the door she'd never been through before. On that day, a very good day as it turned out, for the whole of the hot afternoon she played with those boys in the garden out the back. The garden was divided into three parts, one for each flat. A narrow rectangle, muddy in the rain or dusty in the sunshine, with a dirt path down one side. The Saltz's garden was given over to vegetable growing and the two trees still gave fruit; apples and pears. And there was a gooseberry bush or two. An urban garden is a wonderful place. A haven of green and growth in the rubble and sadness that was about in those post-war times. The fruit went into jams, pickles and pies and the rats enjoyed what ever fell onto the ground overnight.

The Ashfords, David's parents, had potatoes, carrots and cabbages but Mr Ashford's missing arm meant Mrs Ashford had to do the digging and the weeding. She also did the housework and a part-time job as a cleaner at the local doctors. And she shopped for mum down the road and took her washing in with her own. That patch was a little weary. Vegetables fighting a battle with weeds and sadness. Cecilie had never used her patch of earth.

At the end of the garden, backing onto a red brick wall, was a shed and a horse chestnut tree. The perfect climbing tree. It had become a wonderful place for a small gang of kids. A hide and seek and kiss chase heaven. To the right of the path were four prefabs and in one of them lived another boy. He had a broken leg in a white plaster cast covered with writing. She thought that was pretty amazing too. It lent him an air of romantic danger. She hadn't seen anyone with a broken limb before. He managed to hobble to the fence and hang out there, commenting on this and that, cracking jokes and wanting to play.

The big tree was possibly the reason for his broken leg as he'd been high up in the branches throwing down the glowing mahogany brown conkers. What is a boy to do when he has such magnificent climbing apparatus on his patch? Climb it, of course. They were her first friends. Phil had two squashed fingers on his right hand. The story was they'd been damaged at London Zoo, squashed under the feet of an elephant. She believed the tale, which was probably as tall as an elephant's trunk is long but it created an air of bravado and daring do.

David, the boy she'd visited on her excursion down the stairs when nearly two and a half, appeared later on that first day. He showed her his willy at the end of the garden behind the shed. It was like the worm that Laurie had pulled out of the ground and had held up for inspection, only smaller. There was a birthday party one day in that September of 1949, just before summer burned its way into autumn. The leaves on the plane trees in Lee Park were beginning to lose the lush dark green, with edges crinkling and becoming the texture of old greaseproof paper. The birthday boy is lost in time. Laurie? Phil?

Never forgotten though was the pink rabbit blancmange on a white plate. Later, many years later in 1970, she had her own kitchen and her own birthday boy. On the day he was three she made a strawberry jelly in the shape of a rabbit and put it on a white plate with green jelly chopped up to look as if the rabbit was in a green field. The birthday boy didn't want to eat it because, 'I can't eat the rabbit, it's cruel.' He would take no amount of gentle assurance that it was all pretend, a jelly creature. Sam, that little boy became a vegetarian. She'd made sandwiches, cutting them into bite sized triangles. *Marmite* and cucumber, peanut butter, ham and jam, and biscuits with pink and blue icing. There were bowls of *Smarties* and *Cadbury's Chocolate Buttons*. And she'd made a birthday cake. A chocolate sponge with blue and white icing and three candles. Her first ever cake. It was a bit flat and didn't resemble the lush and fluffy two-tiered chocolate delights she'd seen in the glossy magazines. The children gobbled it all up and asked for more. And on that day in late May 1970, she remembered the Saltz family and wondered what their lives had been like.

The birthday party in 1949 had pilchard sandwiches, *Crosse & Blackwell* sandwich spread, *Marmite* sandwiches, 'cream' cakes made with corn flour, and sausage rolls in butter-free pastry. There were blue candles on a cake. A blowing out and singing then the surprise. Television! It sat in a corner of the sitting room covered in a golden brown chenille cloth, keeping the dust off until it was television hour. This was the grand unveiling of a brown *Bush* with its tiny eight-inch screen set in a brown cabinet with two cream control knobs and the cathode-ray tube protruding six inches at the back. Who Was That Masked Man? It was *The Lone Ranger* and Tonto played by Jay Silverheels. After that there was a lot of running around, patting bums with one hand, imaginary reins in the other, making clip clop noises as they rode imaginary horses around the streets of Lewisham. 'Bang, bang you're dead.' And, 'Stick 'em up!' Who's the cowboy? Who's the indian?

A big ship docked at Tilbury. 'Come to the motherland.' To the promised jobs in a battered country that had said they'd be needed and welcome.

'REGRET NO COLOUREDS.' 'NO IRISH, NO DOGS, NO BLACKS.'
She'd never met anyone from Jamaica, Trinidad or Africa and she was unaware of the Bible. Religion would come with school. With school would also come the children of the people that arrived on the big ships.

'Neither fornicators, nor idolaters, nor adulterers, nor effeminate, nor abusers of themselves with mankind. Nor theives, nor covetous, nor drunkards, nor revilers, nor extortioners, shall inherit the Kingdom of God.'
'Let them lie in jail or burn in hell,' she heard someone say. 'The Jews downstairs.' 'What are Jews?' she had asked. She thought Jews might've been sweets, like penny chews. Mr Saltz often had a sweet or two hidden in a pocket somewhere. 'It's a religion.' She was told, still none the wiser. 'It's because of them we went to war.' She thought of Mrs Saltz's sheets. 'We want Muffin, Muffin the Mule, dear old Muffin, playing the fool. We want Muffin, everybody sing, we want Muffin the Mule!'

She lived alongside all this and had no idea about the big wide world outside of southeast London. She spent more and more time with Laurie and Phil and thought she should really live with this mum and dad. They laughed a lot and Mr Saltz would pat Mrs Saltz on the bottom. She'd chide him and giggle, threatening him with, 'a good old what for' as she brandished a wooden spoon. Her hands were always busy. At the stove, mopping the floor, telling a yarn to her boys at bedtime or knitting. Her needles click clicking or darning a sock on a brown *Bakelite* mushroom. Mr Saltz was a tailor with a black moustache. His shiny oiled black hair combed straight back off his face He took his jacket off when he came home from work, carefully hanging it on the back of his chair. He wore black braces over his shirt and the beginnings of small paunch. He rolled up his sleeves, took of his shoes, put on the old worn leather slippers that sat beside the door. On Sundays he helped Mrs Saltz with the washing up.

'Do you want a girl?' she once asked Mrs Saltz as she helped lay the table for tea one Sunday afternoon. 'You don't have one, you just got boys,' Mrs Saltz said, 'Now what do you think I should pay for you then? Thruppence? Sixpence?' In the basement on a Monday, the winter boiling wash of snotty handkerchiefs and washing with bars of *Sunlight* soap and *Reckitts Blue*. 'To take yellow out of white lace curtains.' Wrap the *Blue* in cloth. Stir whilst squeezing into the last rinsing water. Dip articles separately for a short time and keep them moving. Long wooden sticks in the kitchens and outhouses of the land kept them moving. Shirts, sheets, overalls, pinafores, towels, socks, blouses, knickers and vests. Wash, scrub, boil and mangle. Hang out to dry, hope the rain isn't sooty. Then start all over again. Red, raw washing hands. And there's the ironing day when the smell of freshly laundered shirts and pillow-cases filled the whole house with sweetness and warmth. This was when Mrs Saltz became the mother by which all mothers were judged. The girl always loved the smell of washing.

September 1949. Time for the girl to go to school. Cecilie took her on that first day. The smell of chalk, boiled cabbage and sweaty feet. The chatter of a hundred little voices. The classrooms with rows of desks. Paints, blackboards, blue sugar paper ready for the row of little pots to be filled with paint. Red, yellow, green and blue paint powder, mixed with water. A mat for sitting down crossed-legged at story time. It all looked familiar to her, this gathering of children and women in charge. Cecilie hung back, aware that other children were clinging on to a mother, a nan or an aunt. Cecilie was embarrassed and needed a display of tears from the small girl, giving her a moment to be seen as a loving mother. It was was not to be. The girl didn't give her that. She turned her back and was gone.

After the first day the girl travelled to school on her own. A walk down to the Lee High Road to catch the No75 Bus. She loved to sit upstairs in the front seat. When the bus came to a junction where it would turn left she held onto the chrome bar in front, gripping it until her knuckles were white with the effort, willing it not to turn right down a road she didn't know. The bus always behaved and took the proper turn. She thought the No1 bus that said Willesden to Lewisham was the first bus ever in the world. The No75 would be quite young by her reckoning, 74 buses younger.

The steel nit comb, the liberty bodice with rows of fiddly rubber buttons up the front, *Start-Rite* shoes, or *Clarks* sandals with the t-bar straps. Tucking dresses into big navy blue knickers when puddles were in the playground, splash, splash. She got herself to school but she couldn't tie her shoelaces. So on the days when the children had PE she was constantly struggling to hold her plimsolls onto her feet with laces that came undone as soon as she ran. There were queues in the morning for a third of a pint of milk. In the winter the dinner ladies put the crates near the radiators to thaw the bottles. Near-frozen milk that wouldn't suck-up through the straw. And in the summer they left them out in the playground, curdling until collected mid-morning. Disgusting warm milk. It made her feel sick but the milk had to be drunk. 'Oh dear what can the matter be? Smelly girl is stuck in the lavatory. She was there from Monday to Saturday. Nobody knew she was there.'

Winter slides in the frosty playground. A continuous line of squealing children. The slide, dark blue glass and scarily slippery. Miraculously the ice melted by the end of the school day. A boy sat in the art class one day had painted the 'red sky' with his tongue poking out the corner of his mouth. He was lost in the paint and many colours. At the end of the lesson the teacher held up the red streaked sheet of paper for ridicule, 'You have wasted precious paint and paper. What is this?' The girl saw tears of humiliation and shame in the boy's eyes and she hated that teacher. She'd seen his 'red sky' and she knew it was real.

School dinners at tupppence a day. She loved her dinners. Mashed potato served in ice-cream scoops. 'One potato, two potato, three potato more.' She gobbled. Down the hatch. She always wanted more. More potato, more. She asked for seconds whenever there was any to be had. In that winter, on the cusp of 1950, she caught a bad cold. Arthur called the doctor who said, 'She's a little underweight and she has a bad cough.' She was sent to hospital and tested for worms. Her lungs and chest were also tested. She didn't have worms. She was just a scrawny girl who ate a lot. Not only her own school dinners but all the food the other children didn't want. A habit she was to carry on. Just like at the children's home, throughout her school days she was called 'greedy guts' or 'pig snout.'

Standing outside in the cold. Standing in the queue until it was time to go into the hall, to a trestle table set for eight with cutlery, a metal jug of water and metal drinking tumblers. At the end of most tables sat a teacher. Grace was said and some of the kids mouthed under their breath, 'For what we're about to leave, may the pigs be truly thankful.' She said the words in case anyone noticed that she hadn't and she giggled with the rest of them. She pretended she hated school dinners but secretly she quivered with pleasure. The food was pre-cooked, delivered to the school in the early morning and kept warm in containers filled with warm water. It was dished out by dinner ladies wearing their cross-over floral overalls and scarves tied like turbans over hair-nets and curlers.

Splat, onto the plate. The brown meat that lay in rows in the tin tray like a pile of curling soles from brown shoes. Dollop, a spoonful of greens or carrots. Slosh went the gravy. Brown, thick and glutinous over and around mounds of potato, like an incoming brown tide around a sandcastle. She happily tucked and even learned to like cabbage. Some saw only cold lumpy mash potato and greasy stew full of gristle or spam fritters or shepherds pie. When everyone had finished the main course, the plates and dishes were stacked. The children then returned to the hatch, queuing for pudding. Afters, beloved afters. Chocolate sponge and custard, rice or lumpy semolina pudding with melted jam. Sometimes roly-poly pudding and custard. Jam tart served from huge tin trays. She hoped she'd get a juicy middle bit and not a corner which was often burnt. She never learned to love frogspawn, *Tapioca* pudding. Ah but that was good. Something she could pass on. And it might stop them calling her 'greedy guts.' Trouble was, nobody wanted her frogspawn.

After the pudding the tables were cleared, wiped down and re-set for the next sitting. They weren't allowed to touch the blade of the knife, the prongs of the fork or the bowl of the spoon. 'Be very careful, just touch the handles.' Manners were everything. Table manners, queues and, 'mind your Ps and Qs.' A beaker full of water, spilling as she bent over to scoop some stew from another girl's plate, a girl who hated stew. Water all over the table, an accident. Another mishap. She who seemed to have a middle name 'Miss-take', 'Miss-hap', 'Miss what a bloody mess.' 'Oh you silly girl, you messy girl.'

In morning assembly a hundred little voices, 'Good Morning, Mrs Whoever you are.' 'Good morning Mr I've forgotten your name.' And so on and so on until 'Stand up, stand up for Jesus.' Those small voices singing and she'd no idea what it all meant. Jesus? 'Sit up straight! Fold your arms. Speak when you're spoken to.' Oh yes, she understood what that meant. 'Lord, behold us with thy blessing. Once again assembled here.' 'Children! Children! Don't run down the corridor!' 'Lord, dismiss us with thy blessing.' In October, 'We plough the fields and scaa-tter.' Not much ploughing to be had in SE13.No one had told her about the Jews and the religion. She was still waiting.

Little boys wearing grey flannel short trousers and long grey socks all year round. Little girls in pinafore dresses and blouses. Voluminous navy blue knickers and hair ribbons which the girl never managed to keep in place for more than an hour. She learned to skip. She skipped until she fell down with her legs all tangled in the skipping rope, 'Hink minx! The old witch winks, The fat begins to fry.'

The three 'Rs' and learning to write with nib pens on wooden holders, dipped in inkwells on the desk. *Janet and John* and *Beacon Readers*. Sometimes a boy was caned or a girl rapped on the knuckles with a ruler. 'Once one is one, two twos are?' Dreading the double figures, how would she do that? The thought of it made her head swim. The numbers became a blur of incomprehensible digits. The girls would learn to knit while the boys made models with *Plasticine*. She loved the smell and the flat tramline shapes of different colours. She loved being given a packet for Christmas. Red, blue, green, yellow and perfect. She tried to keep the colours separate and new but they always ended up in a brown streaky lump. But a lump worth holding and squeezing until warm in her hands when the smell became even more *Plasticine* powerful. The girls were knitting blanket squares for 'our boys in Korea.' She dropped stitches and made the rows so tight she couldn't insert her needle. Hers was the only square in a mess. She felt ashamed like the boy with his red sky.

Coming home from school one afternoon she stepped off the bus and slipped on a wet pavement, falling against the flint wall beside the bus stop. She banged her head and grazed her face and knees. Someone fetched Arthur and took her home. She remembered the sensation of his damp wool *Duffel* coat against her head as he carried her over his shoulder. Remembered the blood on her cheeks, her legs and her tears and the *Foxes Glacier* mint he gave her to suck.

One day she felt pains in her belly but was sent to school. And the next day and the one after that. The pain was so bad she cried and she didn't like crying at school. They called an ambulance. Off she went to Lewisham Hospital and out came her appendix. She had a long red scar and a transparent plaster so the nurses could see how she was healing. She loved that scar and its plaster. She called it, 'the window to my tummy.' She felt very important.

They gave her ice cream on her second day in hospital. Ice cream that the tonsillitis children had to soothe their red raw throats. The nurse who gave her two scoops in a white bowl told her she was special because she'd been a 'brave girl.' She fell in love with a pretty nurse who had dimples in her cheeks when she giggled and who called her 'Ducky.' Her white and blue striped dress rustled.

The rolled-up sleeves hidden under white lacy armbands, a crisp white cap, black stockings and black shiny shoes.

The ward sister, her starched cap a miracle of white winged glory perched on her head like a bird about to fly. And matron, holy of holies who must be feared, wore a darker, plain blue dress. Although she seemed serious, her back straight, her face often stern, matron was always very nice to the small girl with her appendix scar. The girl wanted to stay in the ward forever. She would be a nurse. She would help and eat ice cream everyday. But it was not to be. Back to the flat in Lee Park.

One spring day the sun was weak but shining and there was no radio, no baby crying and no Arthur boiling in the kitchen. The girl went downstairs and still no sound. She went on down to the Saltz's flat and there was nobody at home. Her bottom lip jutted, her eyes filled and she went to the big front door. Yes, the handle was in reach. One turn and she went out, down the steps and onto the street. Down the road she knew from the school journey. Lee High Road. Turn right and head for Lewisham. Past the fruit and veg shop, the sweets and newspapers, a hardware store, on and on. She felt quite grown up, walking to *Chiesmans*, the department store where Arthur told her she had come from. 'Where did I come from?' 'You were bought in *Chiesmans*; sixpence you cost. Or was it only thruppence?' That's what Mrs Saltz had thought she should pay for a new daughter, so that must be what she was worth.

In *Chiesmans* there were toys in the basement and a donkey ride. And a round place where, if you paid a penny or two to a man with a glass eye, a limp and a black and white checkered cap, ping pong balls, red, yellow and green, would whoosh up like a fountain. If you caught some in a net you won a prize. Some bubbles or a spinning top. She hadn't gone far when a policeman with a very nice face stopped her. He had twinkling eyes that looked like brown raisins in a round bun, 'And where do you think you're going, young lady?' She looked up into his face, 'To *Chiesmans*. I'm going to ride the donkey and win a prize.'

And that was it. She was taken to the police station. A policeman sat her on a chair whilst he, 'made inquiries.' He gave her a flat tuppenny bar of *Cadburys* chocolate and asked her where she lived. She said nothing. She grinned and salivated, wanting the cholocate to last for ever. She was collected with it smeared all over her mouth and was put straight to bed. But the escape was worth it. The chocolate was worth it. She'd run away and she'd do it again.

On her fifth Birthday, 7th April 1949, *South Pacific* opened on Broadway. That year Miles Davis began recording the album *Birth of the Cool*, featuring Gil Evans, J.J. Johnson, Gerry Mulligan, and Max Roach, with tracks *Boplicity* and *Venus de Milo*. Charles Mingus was out there. Ella and Louis had invented scat. It all happened back then, before the 1950s were ready to roll. When Elvis was 14 years old, over there in Tupelo Mississippi and Chuck Berry was out of jail, playing the blues and revving up for *Maybellene*.

The girl would have never known all this. She was in a place of being five and then six, in a world where not much was said except on the glorious days in the garden with the boys downstairs. The *Lone Ranger* lived over there in America and not all indians were baddies because Mr Saltz had said this was so. Maybe Mr Saltz had felt he was, 'Not one of them.' He came from somewhere in Europe, his family escaping whatever it was they had to flee from. Keeping quiet becomes a refuge, a hiding place. A way of being.

It was then that the photograph was taken. On the front steps of the house when she was almost five years old. She held her little sister. The photo arrived in Primrose Hill in the year 2000. Opening the letter, seeing the small girl and the baby and remembering. A lifetime to untangle. What was what and why?

Shortly afterwards she once more got onto a bus to another town. This time to an aunt? Gone in the muddle of those days. 'A month,' the mother said, 'we've a lot on our plate and can't deal with you now.' The girl stayed a month or so in a country town in the West Country with Irene, who was a godmother not an aunt. Until the day she was picked up at the bus station in Stroud the girl had no memory of her. Another school playground to negotiate, another school hall for dinner. The month was longer than a month, possibly three times as long? And when she returned it was to another upheaval, another move.

Weymouth

Blues in the Night Harold Arlen and Johnny Mercer 1952

1951 to 1953: moving to Weymouth, another school, singing to a pirate, a king dies, a queen is crowned and another half-sister is born. Back to Lewisham then to Lowestoft. Goodbye Saltz family.

The *Festival Of Britain* and a trip with the school to the newly built Southbank Arts Centre. And to the *Dome of Discovery* down by the river. Flags and people in thousands. The most extraordinary sights the girl from Lewisham had ever seen. Well, not since the stay in Deal when she saw *Snow-white and the seven Dwarfs*, and then her appendix operation. London was looking on and up. London was celebrating itself. London had Knickerbocker Glories in *Lyons* corner houses and department store cafés. *Kenco* coffee shops were grinding beans in huge machines in the windows on the high streets.

Arthur graduated from the Slade and Cecilie wasn't going to wait for the artist to earn. June came and they were off to Weymouth. He would be stationed at Portland Bill, back to the Navy with a regular salary. They stayed in a guesthouse at first and then a rented somewhere. The girl was sent to Holy Trinity school in Commercial Road. She was the new girl with a funny accent. She was seven years old and spent a lot of time kicking at the bubble gum splats which pock marked the asphalt schoolyard, pink and then grey. She looked at a lot of unknown children playing and waiting for the school dinner bell. Surely they had custard and jam sponge in Weymouth!

Walking in a crocodile line to dinners one day, to a hall shared by two schools because one had been bombed, she smelled something foul. Behind her a boy had shat himself. It was dribbling down his leg from beneath his grey flannel short trousers, down into his grey woollen socks. He looked so ashamed. She said nothing but of course another kid noticed, 'Miss, Sir, he's poohed his pants.' Then louder, 'Sir, Miss! He's shit 'isself!' Children giggled, pointed and held their noses. She felt so bad, so ashamed, as if the shit was dribbling down her leg. Inside she wept for the boy who would be forever known as, 'Shit pants.' 'Ink pink, pen and ink, you go out because you stink.'

They moved to a house called Sandsfoot in a different part of Weymouth. The Weymouth to Portland branch line ran behind a hedge at the end of the small garden. There was a ruined castle nearby and a little beach at the end of the road. Her second seaside, the beach was sandy, unlike the shingle at Deal. The beach in the centre of Weymouth was a wonderland with sand sculptures, *Punch and Judy* and donkeys to ride. There was a brass band, the *Ritz Theatre*, the *Jubilee Clock* and the endless esplanade alongside the endless sea.

A walk and then a bus ride to the new school down Rodwell Road. To the harbour and a fire station near the roundabout. One day she climbed aboard the bus to go home at the end of a school day. She had no money and then she remembered, 'Oh no, I was meant to be at the school dentist.' In a panic her heart pounding, she leapt off the bus, down the hill and over the road. There was a screech of brakes and she was lying on the road. A car had clipped her head. A fireman carried her into the fire station. They said she must have a head like concrete because she had barely a scratch on her and the car had a dent in the bumper. So all was fine and she never forgot the fireman. The car she remembered as a 'back to front car' because to her it looked as if it was going not coming. It was the first car she'd seen with what looked like the boot on the front as well as the back.

A Christmas a party on Portland Bill was arranged for children connected to the Navel base. A grotto had been built. The men were dressed up as pirates and a tape recorder had been hidden behind a treasure chest. Each child was encouraged to sing. She sang *Frere Jacques* in a small tremulous voice whilst staring at her feet and the feet of the pirate who was a really a sailor in the Royal Navy.

The children left the grotto and on the way out Father Christmas sat on red and white throne, wearing a long white cotton wool beard. He had a sack full of who knows what, all wrapped up in red and green paper. She hoped it would be *Plasticine* or crayons. As their gift was handed out, the song they had just sung was played back to each child. The girl was both astonished and embarrassed. Was it magic? How had they stolen her voice? She didn't sound like Snow White, that's for sure. These pirates were truly clever. She knew it was her voice but she sounded like a squeaky mouse.

There was a party in Sandsfoot House. Some of the guests were Siamese Naval officers and they looked very handsome in their uniforms. Cecilie wore a cotton dress with a full skirt, nipped in waist, white gloves and a little hat with a flounce of net over her face, or perhaps a flower perched in her hair, just so. She pronounced the 'h' in 'white' and 'where' and walked with her head held slightly to one side as if always listening.

Cecilie's high heels clip clipped up the garden path or on the pavements when she went out shopping. The girl who often looked after her sister Jennifer whilst Arthur was on Portland Bill, doing whatever he did after the war had ended, always knew when her pregnant mother was home from whatever she did on her afternoons. The heels were the signal.

Yes, Cecilie was pregnant. The house became vociferously silent. Unspoken rage hung in the air. That was when the locking of doors began again. Only this time Arthur was the jailer. The girl wanted to run away. The reason she was locked in was to prevent the running as the arguments raged between the mother and stepfather.

Carol's mother, Cecilie, in Weymouth.

One year slipped into the next and in February 1952 at school one day during the morning assembly there was a dramatic announcement, 'The King is dead.' On every street and in every home the radio proclaimed in hushed and serious voices, 'This is the BBC Home Service. His Majesty, King George VI has died peacefully in his sleep at Sandringham House.' The King had died and she cried because everyone was crying. But who was he, this man who had died? Her mother said, 'You didn't know him, did you.' No, she didn't. She assumed everyone else did and that's why the whole of Weymouth were bawling and wringing their hands and twisting their handkerchiefs.

A baby was born, Lindsay. And the girl went to her third school in Weymouth, walking down the hill from Hilltop House. They'd moved when the baby was three months old to the other side of Weymouth, up the Dorchester Road and off to the right towards the sea. A large brown dog lived next door and both girls were afraid. The dog barked a lot and seemed to have many sharp teeth and a long lolling tongue. It was a game of suspense. To brave the walk out of the gate, inch past the dog house before making a run for it.

Jennifer was to start school in September. Hilltop House had a garden. The two girls built dens that summer and wished they were allowed to go to the beach

Cecilie with Arthur and friends at Portland Bill.

without adults. They had to wait so the dens became the summer's main activities. It remained an unhappy household. The new baby was beautiful and provided a distraction. They took it in turns to play with her. A sort of truce was in the air. No, they were leaving. Leaving Hilltop House and returning to the flat in Lewisham.

The Mau Mau Uprising in Kenya was in the news and on peoples lips. The girl was aware of it but had little understanding. Passing snatches of conversations, grown up talk. Many years later she remembered and she wrote a poem called *Mau Mau* which became a song. On 12th September 2015, the British government unveiled a Mau Mau memorial statue in Nairobi's Uhuru Park. It was a long overdue pardon for the carnage. Here's a extract from that poem.

> *When I was a child growing up in the '50's, I remember the Mau Mau.*
> *Portrayed in the news, I heard it on the radio.*
> *I saw it in the papers and on the newsreel screen. Savage hoards of cannibals.*
> *People who killed and plundered, raiding white peoples home and lands.*
> *Mau Mau was the bogey man! The dark reason for my fears in dreams.*
> *Flashing eyes and spears and deafening screams.*
> *They crashed through jungles and crept across the lands, silently in the night*
> *to find me in my bed.*
> *And I was afraid. Why did nobody tell me, who was Mau Mau and why?*

Thoughts gathered in a child-like recollection. There were many questions. It wasn't fair. Why? And yet more why? Human beings it would seem were not a friendly species.

A Bridge of memories and sighs

It felt like they'd been away in Weymouth for an eternity. A year is an eternity to a child. A toy theatre of the mind. Flat people hidden behind flat painted cardboard scenery, sliding them in and out of sight. Mouths with no voices, flat bodies with no hearts, no smell, no roundness of limb and belly. A uniform, pressed black trousers, braid, badges and naval caps. Women in summer dresses, red lipstick and powder compacts. Pirates and *Punch and Judy*. The death of a king, a mother heavy with baby, a ruined castle on a clifftop and the transient magical castles of sand on the beach, washed away with the tide. Schools with unknown children running silently like ants in the playground or sitting in rows at wooden desks. Faces with no features, no voices, no names. People in a far away land tortured and abused. Why?

All slipped away into a flat one dimensional memory. There was nothing left but the fireman who'd picked her up from the road outside the school, the fire station and a captured voice singing *Frere Jacques* in a pirates cave on Portland Bill.

Only the air and the sea remained constant. It was November and it was back to the school in Lewisham. The desks were closer together than before, the children had multiplied. There was an explosion of five year olds and the queue for school dinners was longer. She worried that there wouldn't be enough when she got to the ladies and their ladles.

The teachers were the same but she had changed. She no longer felt she belonged in London any more. It was as if she'd been away for 100 years. She had picked up a different way of talking. A bit of the Dorset buzz in her voice. She had learned to tie her shoelaces and boasted she could swim. She did still hate school milk.

London was very grey and smelly after the bright sea air of Weymouth. The girls wanted the seaside again and were filled with fear. When would the next move happen? Where would they live? Perhaps a month or so would pass and then quick, pack your case! Each girl had her own brown cardboard case. Pack it and come now. And they were in another bedroom, sitting at another desk in yet another strange school. The smog was bad that winter. It slipped through the cracks under the doors, through the windows into noses and eyes and hung, yellow and acrid in the air. A creeping disease in a dirty old town. Cecilie had a bad cough

The baby was fretful and the flat overcrowded. The three girls in one small room. The boys downstairs were older and boys will be boys. She was shy and they were elsewhere. Out with other boys in the streets, playing ball or tag, cowboys and indians, or up to no good on the bomb sites.

On 31st January 1953, the North Sea rose. The sea monster swept on to Felixstowe, Harwich, Maldon, Yarmouth, Lowestoft, Canvey Island and Tilbury. It surged onwards to the narrow streets of West Ham and the Docklands, flooding oil refineries, factories, cement works, gasworks and electricity generating stations, onto Sheerness and the Kent coast.

Arthur, it would seem, was no longer in the Navy and had found a job in a technical college in Lowestoft, a small fishing town on the Suffolk Coast. He left in the Easter holidays to set up a home and begin work. The second day of June

1953 saw the Orb, the Sceptre, the Rod of Mercy, and the royal ring of sapphire and rubies on show. There were street parties and sack races. People piled into sitting rooms around television sets and underneath a grey sky, three million lined the streets of London, hoping to see a beautiful princess in a golden coach. We heard *God save the Queen* and gun salutes as she was crowned, and millions pretended that all was well with the world. The girl was with the Saltz family. She saw the Queen crowned on the television in the corner of the room and wished that she was

Jennifer and Lindsay, with an unknown friend, beside the Romany van.

Princess Anne with curly blonde hair and a queen for a mother. Her own mother went off with Jennifer and the baby for the day. Where? That's all long gone and wasn't spoken of at the time.

From somewhere back in Arthur's past a wooden Romany van arrived outside the house one morning, towed by a small truck. Painted green and red, it had two bunk beds in the back and a little window beside the upper bed. It had a fold away table, a bench against a window on one side, cupboards and best of all, a black leaded cooking range just inside the door which opened in two halves. If you were tall enough you could lean on the lower door and stare out at the world. Steps were placed up against the van when it was stationary. Steps you could sit on, swing your legs and eat a cheese roll or a jam sandwich. It was a thing of great beauty to the girls, a den to end all dens.

The royal festivities were over and normal service was resumed in Lee Park. Though it wasn't about to be normal at all for Cecilie and the three girls. Mrs Saltz made sandwiches, wrapped them neatly in greaseproof paper and together with a handful of Kent grown apples and some packets of crisps, she gave them to the mother, 'You'll need something for the little ones on the journey... 'ere you are ducks, your favourite.' It was butter, yes, real butter and *Marmite*. The girl thought she would burst. She knew she'd never see the Saltz family again. This was the end. The flat was emptied and the furniture disappeared into a *Pickford's* removal van. A smaller truck towed the van. That was the end of London. Life in another seaside town was waiting.

A Bridge to East Anglia

From London To Lowestoft.
The London of her early childhood, coal bunkers,
Smog masks, bomb sites and red London buses.
Trolleys in the high street and little cardboard tickets, clip, clip, ding, ding.
Move along inside please.
Standard Evening News.
Coal O, Rags ... The cries of London, she was leaving once more.
Goodbye David, goodbye Laurie.
And goodbye Mr and Mrs Saltz. Goodbye,
Don't cry they called, don't cry

Lowestoft

One for My Baby (and One More for the Road)
Fred Astaire in *The Sky's the Limit* 1943
Frank Sinatra in *Young at Heart* 1954
Carol Grimes on *CDAWN* 2013

1953 to 1957: three more schools, the North Sea, ships and the silver darlings, and a Suffolk dialect. Meeting Bridget, hearing Elvis and black American music. Cecilie leaves for Norwich.

From London out to Gants Hill, past the little rows of red brick houses, red buses, corner shops and dusty plane trees. Out to the flat fields through Essex to Ipswich in Suffolk. The A12, a meandering lorry chocked artery running from London to Lowestoft, snaking on as London Road south over the bridge becoming London Road north and then the High Street to Belle View Park, and onwards to Yarmouth. The biting salty air of the North Sea seemed sharper on the tongue and harsher in the lungs than the air in Kent and Dorset. It was a blustery summer's day. Clouds raced overhead and holiday makers with goose bumps in the chill wind moved in packs wearing plastic macs, looking for shelter away from the wet sand and sea spray.

From southeast London and then as east as it gets to Lowestoft, the town of the rising sun, the smell of fish and the impenetrable Suffolk dialect, 'Blast it.' And on the weather, 'When thass calm like there's noo movement.' She didn't understand a word and the buses weren't red. They were cream and brown, or was it primrose and maroon? It was as if she'd landed in Siberia or deepest Azerbaijan. The fishing, shipbuilding and seaside visitors had been put on hold for the war. For military work in the shipyards and bombs on the docks. Now fish were being caught again. The boats were in and out of the harbour where the swing bridge split the town in two. Oulton Broad to the west, slipping into Lake Lothing on into the harbour and then out to sea.

At the end of its glory days of the herring, Lowestoft was living after the floods in post-war austerity and unemployment. *Jeckells Net Store* and the smoke houses on Love Road and Raglan Street were still doing business. In a penny arcade just before the bridge on the north side sat a *Laughing Policeman,* rocking in its box like an absurd and captive drunk, 'Ha, ha, ho, ho.' Menacing yet mesmerising to a child from London with a hot brown penny in her hand. Make him laugh, make him rock. Seaside towns with cockles and mussels, whelks, shrimps, crab, fish and chips, candy floss and ice cream. Pink sugar rock, pinball machines, fortune-tellers, shooting galleries and fun at the end of the pier.

Rationing was still in place and along the long thin road that was the spine of Lowestoft were the shops where women took their coupons. *Liptons* or *The International Stores* or *John Devereux & Sons* grocery store where loose sugar and tea were weighed in little blue paper 'pokes'. Split peas and pearl barley, or a bag of broken biscuits, pounds of sugar scooped from hundred weight sacks. Bacon sliced from the sides of pigs and cheese cut with a wire from huge roundels on sparkling white marble counters constantly wiped clean by grocers in white overalls, a pencil stub stuck behind one ear. Fresh fish from *Carlton Fish Shop.*

Mothers moved in and out of The *Army & Navy Stores,* purses tightly closed, eagle-eyed they scoured the offerings. Seeking the luxury of new clothes, taking a look around *Tuttles Bon Marche* department store opposite the station, or *Rogers Menswear, Lillian's Drapery* and *Hailey's* department store with a sad little zoo in the basement. Bills were paid in part ration book, part cash. A shop assistant tucked the payment into a metal canister and fired it along the cable to the cashier who sat on high in a little illuminated window. Then whoosh, back to the customer. *Camp Coffee, Bovril, HP Sauce,* tins of condensed milk, corned beef and peaches in syrup for Sunday tea, all stacked in neat rows on shelves behind polished mahogany counters where huge glass bells covered tea cakes or bread pudding. Loose sweets in jars stood to attention in tantalising and luminous order. *Sherbet Lemons, Humbugs, Foxes Glacier Mints.* Two ounces or a quarter in paper bags, white gritty sugar dropping to the bottom, a last hit of sweetness that almost burned your tongue. *Parrs* hobby shop for cowboy books and romances and *Birds* cycle shop with a side window full of guns.

On a shopping Saturday, the *Tudor Café* was a spot for a pot of tea and a cream horn. Or maybe a bottle of *Fanta* and a ham roll in the *Fisherman's Café* on Whaplode Road, and some bloaters or kippers for tea. *Woolworths,* smelling of rubber shoes, lipstick, stewed tea, shoelaces and sweets. The place for a quick dip. No one looking, quick, quick, fingers into the pick and mix. Girls jostling at the cosmetics counter wanting *Outdoor Girl* lipstick and pan stick foundation or a new bra, American tan nylons, the latest hot disc. Hope you get that home without it breaking, smash upon the pavement. Many a record was smashed before it got home to the radiogram. Doris Day singing about her *Secret Love* or Johnnie Ray of *Such a Night*. The man of the day and the housewives choice. Vera Lynn was still in the charts. The nation still had its sweetheart, one foot in the old days of war, the other looking to a new world.

Arthur had changed his name to John. Why? No one had told her. Why had they left Weymouth? Why had they not stayed in London? Cecilie and John, the girl, the sister and the little Weymouth baby moved into a flat on Kirkley Cliff. The van was parked in a field just outside the town, in a place called Kessingland which for a long time the girl thought was 'Kissing-land'. The first flat was opposite the Kensington Gardens boating lake. Electric boats and Japanese gardens, a café, a pond, two bowling greens, four tennis courts and a children's corner. She liked the boats and the huge black rubber boots of the man who worked them. He waded into the little lake when a boat engine spluttered and died, pushing it into the side. A flotilla of silent boats waiting to be fixed at the end of the day.

She arrived at another rubber shoes and cabbage smelling school built of Victorian red brick not unlike Weymouth or London. The smells maybe familiar but the people weren't. Dads, uncles and brothers worked on the dwindling trawler fleet or in the shipyards, *Brooke Marine* and *Richard's Ironworks*. The mums worked, maybe part-time, in the *Birds Eye* pea factory or on the tills in the shops or as dinner ladies in the schools.

Secretaries and teachers, opticians and dentists, doctors and shop owners. These were the Lowestoft middle classes. There was a very big divide between the fisherman and the doctor in 1953. The girl wished she could spend the days in Kensington Gardens. She ran away to sea. Well, at least as far as the boating lake. She did that at least three times. She walked to school or rather pretended to. Hovering a yard or two from home, running and looking this way and that, peering from behind a wall or a hedge, then into the gardens. Of course she was caught. In those days people noticed a lone child who should be at school. The evacuees had long since gone back to London.

The girl wore grey woollen socks that slipped down underneath the heels of her black lace-ups, wearing holes and rubbing her skin raw. The kids called them 'spuds', which meant your mum or gran didn't do the mending. The black clodhoppers were a terrible thing. Apart from being hideous they were too small and they pinched her feet. She tried to lose them, stuffing them down the girl's toilets in the corner of the school playground at the end of the day. School lavatories were the pits. They froze your bum in winter and stunk to high heaven in summer. Blue bottles buzzing, hard shiny paper and piss on the floor. That day she walked home in her plimsolls with no socks and told them she'd lost her black shoes. They were found and returned to her mother, to be worn again.

The girl hated the shoes, the school, the toilets and the teachers. She didn't understand them nor they her. She was told to sit at the back of the classroom. She didn't understand long division. What was that? Multiplication, what was that? Logarithms passed her by, as did everything to do with numerals. She was always behind. They told her she was stupid and the mother did too. She was. She must be. She was afraid to say too much for fear of hearing the words, 'stupid and silly.'

She spent a lot of time being angry in 1953, wanting to hide her head in the wooden desk or stare out the window, counting the moments until dinner time, then playtime and finally hometime. A dawdling walk home to Kirkley Cliff and hopefully a wander in the park near the lake with the boats.

A few weeks later she made friends with a girl called Joy who had a cloud of curly fair hair and a very round face. Joy told everyone, well the girl from London, that her dad was American and that he knew Elvis Presley. 'Elvis who?' She didn't ask that question out loud. She just put on an impressed face and said, 'Oh' or whatever the expression for impressed was back then aged nearly ten in Lowestoft. Of course Joy was a fibber. Her dad was at sea on the trawlers and her mum was a dinner lady at the grammar school.

East Anglia had American bases and the music was on the jukeboxes. It began to catch on, like American food. Sliced white bread turned into grey dough balls if you rubbed a big fat crumb between your finger and thumb. Cereals and peanut butter. And as television became the thing, along came TV dinners. Yarmouth launched *Birds Eye Fish Fingers* and everybody wanted a fridge, a freezer, a television and a car. Saturday afternoon on the High Street and, 'We bought a car on the never-never.' The nation was about to be told, 'You've never had it so good.'

In July 1954, they moved to a red brick late Victorian semi-detached house called Shrublands on The Avenue near the junction of London Road South. A red phone box stood on the corner beside a brick wall that surrounded a big house which looked like it belonged in a *Hammer Horror* film. Four pennies and press buttons A and B for a connection to London. Clunk clunk, who would she call? The Saltz family had a phone but she didn't have the number. The red box became a symbol for the other world. London, all the way back down the A12.

September came along and, with another house, there was another school. Jennifer went to the infants and the girl went to the juniors. Jennifer had a haircut that looked like the man on the posters promoting *Hastings*, a smooth helmet of red hair. The girl had a hank of hair on one side of her head pulled up as tight as a gnat's arse and tied with a ribbon. She lost the ribbon a hundred times and so eventually she too got the 'Battle of Hastings' haircut. Both girls wore a liberty bodice with rubber buttons and large navy blue knickers. She would twist the knicker elastic in her fingers until it snapped apart. Then she was called 'dangle pants' or worse. She still sucked her thumb and picked at the feathers in her eiderdown. New teachers, new children and new tarmac territory to negotiate. The games, the rules, the kids to avoid and the teachers to fear.

Cecilie would entertain her new friends in the front room, which she referred to as, 'The drawing room.' Opposite the drawing room was the dining room in which very little dining happened. A shiny walnut table and six matching chairs, a dinner service in a glass fronted cabinet. China that was rarely used. Dark red velvet curtains, a mantelpiece with a clock that needed winding, and the old copper warming pan from Lewisham on the wall. The girls weren't allowed in these rooms. They used the kitchen and the small parlour at the back. It was as if Cecilie had created a stage set for her world outside Shrublands, 'Don't touch this. Don't touch that. You'll break it. You're so clumsy.'

Upstairs were two big bedrooms to the front, two smaller in the back, a tiny bathroom and a separate lavatory. On the top floor in the attic there was a small self-contained flat without a bathroom, which was rented out in the summer season. John and Cecilie slept in separate rooms, he on the left and she on the right. Her door were always locked. When accidentally opened, the girls could see a glass topped kidney shaped dressing table with three mirrors in a bay window, so that Cecilie could see her head from every angle. On the bedside table, a pile of magazines, *Woman* and *Woman's Own*. There was a large wardrobe in which she kept her summer dresses and petticoats, cotton blouses with batwing sleeves and turned up collars. In a smaller wardrobe hung a collection of furs. A *Musquash* fur coat with a shawl collar and bracelet length sleeves, an evening stole and a fox, its feet and claws clipped together in the front and a dangling dead head with glass eyes too real to be bearable. The girls were terrified of it. A living fox stalked the rooms of dreams at night, eyes bright and claws sharp.

On Saturdays the older girls did the chores, pushing the *Ewebank* sweeper over the carpets and mopping the kitchen floor. Then washing up, drying and putting away, hanging the washing on the line and dusting the shiny wood in the cold dining room. The room that was never used.

En route to school they passed the bus terminus in Pakefield and the bakers, *Mathes* where iced buns could be had for a penny. There was a sweet shop and news-agent where she could buy a 2d bar of *Cadburys* chocolate or a penny chew, a liquorice stick or banana split, if she could only squeeze the money out of her mother's purse.

That first winter was fierce. Winds whistling down from the Arctic or from the Urals across the Great European Plain, finding the cracks inbetween coats and necks, biting at toes, red ears and frozen noses, icy cold fingers on skin. The furious weather churned up muddy sediment from the sea bed, making the surface brown, seagull grey, seaweed green and then inky black. Out where the fishing boats battled with the North Sea swell, men pitted against water and weather. Waves thrashed onto the beaches, frothy with wild white edges, stealing the land slowly but completely. The ravenous sea had already claimed land in some places. Churches once a good way inland sat perilously close to the edge of the east most side of Britain. It was said that bells could be heard on dark windy nights as the lost villages moaned in the deep, on the sea bed. It felt like the end of the world.

Gulls hovered in huge packs, screeching hysterically around the trawlers. Drifters bobbed in the harbour, *Suffolk Punch*, *Dauntless Star*, *Margaret Hide* and the *Filby Queen*. Out for the 'Silver Darlings', the herrings.

That first Lowestoft winter the girl developed a split in the middle of her lower lip that refused to heal. It bled and was very sore. It got so bad the school nurse said, 'You'll need stitches for that.' Stitched! She would look like a chicken trussed for the oven. She found it painful to eat and that was a disaster. She loved eating most in the world, together with daydreaming, thumb sucking and feather picking.

She became a thief, devising a cunning stunt which involved some silver wrapping saved from a chocolate bar. She twice managed to pull a sixpence from her mother's purse. Only, on the way to school.

TILLY TEA LEAF 'Ooh, look, what's that?'

Her planted silver paper lay on the ground. Jennifer, walking a little way ahead of her, stopped and came back. She knew. She was a quiet and clever girl and nothing much happened that she didn't file and remember. Tilly Tea leaf had dropped the piece of silver foil and the sixpence from her hand onto the grass verge. The deed was done. They had an iced penny bun and a tuppenny bar of chocolate that day. The girl played that trick once more. She opened the back door one afternoon at four, and before she had a chance to duck, her mother landed several stinging slaps on her face. Her stepfather found the back of her legs. She was sent to bed with more than a flea in her ear, her mother shouting as she climbed the stairs. Every step another angry word. Even after the bedroom door was closed the tirade continued. She knew she was wrong. She knew she was guilty. Her life of occasional petty crime had begun.

They were shown a film in the school hall about the concentration camps and the Jews. She became hot and cold at the same time. She could see the Saltz family sitting around the television watching the *Lone Ranger*. She could smell the baking, could feel the warmth of Mrs Saltz when she gave her a cuddle, with the boys playing tag in the London garden, finding worms in the earth and slugs under stones.

She made a friend called Martin Newson. He once showed her his first pubic hair. He was rather proud of it. It was the first sign of the manhood that was 'a coming'. That summer, they played at being spies on a scrubby piece of land on the cliff tops near All Saints and St Margaret's in Pakefield. A church so close to the cliff edge that most of the ancient stone graves had tumbled into the sea. They searched for skeletons at the bottom of the cliffs and at the very least hoped for a skull. They never did find one. Memories come. A smell, a fragment of music, a sound, a word, and then a girl with a sweet smile and a love of swimming. She was at the school and then she wasn't.

A teacher told them about an 'Iron lung' and Polio. The children didn't know what an iron lung was but it sounded somehow grave and dangerous, the stuff of bad dreams. Collections were made and gifts were sent to the hospital. It was very sad and made the girl cry. The tears were good. She remembered that feeling, crying for another. How the wetness of the tears on her cheek felt somehow melancholic and good at the same time. And then came the shocking day when another girl fell to her death from the top of a slide in the playground near to the school. That child had a dad who played the accordion, sometimes coming into the school to play for a special assembly. He was never seen in the school again, and it was said he put his accordion away. It remained in its box, bellows and keys silent.

In assembly they sang *Eternal Father, Strong to Save*. The hymn was sung too many times as fathers and sons, uncles and brothers went down to the bottom of the sea. In 1954 there was a total solar eclipse and all the children were corralled onto the school playing field to watch, holding a piece of smoked glass to protect their eyes from the glare.

The girls had very few clothes. One pair of pants, a vest or liberty bodice, the school clothes and the Sunday best. It was embarrassing. The dresses were too short, the cardigans too small but out they came on Sundays. And of course poor Jennifer had all the hand me downs, 'They're as good as new,' the mother would say when the girls protested, 'you've barely worn them. Don't make such a fuss.' In the summer they wore the new swimming costumes made from nylon bubbles. Little pockets that swelled in the water. The girls looked like they were wearing small eiderdowns. This was where she fell in love with the sea again. Long days on the beach in the short East Anglian summer. Dark cloud storms, then plump pillows of white clouds hung in blue and dove grey skies. Sandcastles, *Punch and Judy*, ice creams and day-glow orange lollipops.

After one year in the Pakefield School the girl sat the Eleven-Plus, which of course she failed. Martin went to the grammar school. She, the one who was told you have no brain, went to the secondary modern, *Alderman Woodrow* in Notley Road. A walk down The Avenue, passing near the Blackheath woods, turn right, a main road, a roundabout, and then in through the boys playground. Girls in one end, boys in another, with a white line marking out the great divide. That was where the back chat and flirting happened.

Carol (third from right in the front row) appearing as Will o' the Wisp at Alderman Woodrow School, Lowestoft.

She met Joy again but Joy had changed. A year, a lifetime in a child's mind, had passed. Joy was now with girls who talked about film stars and boys, 'in that way' and she laughed at the girl from London. The girl knew the laughing was at her, not with her. She winced but didn't mention Elvis.

In the house in The Avenue they all lived in separate bubbles of confusion, thoughts and desires. John taught at the local technical college and at weekends he dug the garden, grew vegetables and tended his lawns front and back. The van sat in its new resting place at the end of the garden under an apple tree. This was the best place in the world, a place to dream. When she behaved badly she was sent to bed down in the van as a punishment. Not for her. For her it was peace. There was a potty, a hurricane lantern and she didn't even mind the spiders.

There were twins at Notley Road who wore blue kerchiefs on their heads, no hair showing. They had cancer and were always together, as twinned halves of a lemon. Filling in the gaps of each other's sentences, they were different but only spoke to each other, as if they were one body not two, needing only each other.

Once a week the class swam in the pool at Nicholas Everett Park in Oulton Broad. A queue at the turnstile, a shower, then the swimming. Bobbing about in the shallow end with a rubber cap on your head which pulled at your hair when you tried to haul it off, like ripping a plaster off a scab. Into the communal showers trying to avoid the smelly carbolic soap floating in glutinous lumps in the water around their feet. Then out with small inadequate towels around the shivering shrivelled prune like bodies. Pulling wet swimming costumes down and struggling back into navy blue knickers, skirts and blouses. The *Brylcreem* machine, an old penny pushed in the slot, a big glob of the greasy white stuff for the boys and the men. The girl learned to swim properly and did her two width 'learners'. Then her three length 'improvers'. Her only successful achievement at *Alderman Woodrow*.

Cecilie wore her dark hair in an Elizabeth Taylor style. She had the violet eyes and hourglass figure that made it all work. Swishing skirts over petticoats with her curves enhanced by a girdle and an uplift bra. She joined the local amateur dramatic company and was hardly ever at home. When she was, she wasn't happy. Her voice became overly mannered the longer she stayed in Lowestoft, as she pursued her desire of being an actress and getting the hell out of there.

The girls in the back of the house were dying to see Cecilie's glamorous guests when they occasionally called by. The one who was almost 13 and beginning to bud under her gym-slip, was asked to bring in a tray of tea and coffee from the kitchen.

'And how old are you dear?' Asked a Major Gage. The girl dubbed him, 'Major Greengage'. He wore a tweed sports jacket, a maroon and white spotted cravat tucked into the neck of a white shirt, grey flannels and brown suede shoes. He had a gold signet ring on a plump hairy finger and a gold watch on his wrist. He had a sandy handlebar moustache above his red lips that were always slightly wet as if constantly wetting his appetite. And he was. The girl saw the looks between him and the mother. His hand on the mother's back, a proprietary and hairy hand, as if he owned her. He smoked a cigarette held aloft and away and tapped the silvery ash into a cut glass ashtray. He smiled with a lot of big teeth but there was no light or warmth in his eyes. He looked bored. Before the girl could say, 'I'm nearly 13,' her mother declared, 'she's 11 and hasn't she got piggy little eyes! She takes after her father you know, not me.' 'Haw, haw, haw,' chuckled Major Greengage.

A woman with bright yellow hair who kept a powder compact in her handbag, powdering her nose at regular intervals, looked at the girl and said, 'Oh I don't know Cec, she's not so bad, surely not.' The woman bent down from her great high-heeled height, as if to give the girl a sweet sherry flavoured kiss. The girl shrank from the kiss and the words. Cecilie gave her tinkling laugh, 'She's not terribly bright you know. I really don't know what will become of her.' The girl with piggy eyes slipped out of the room, red faced and furious. She wanted so badly to shout.

Misery Ivy 'I'm not. I'm 13 and I hate you all!'
It was to be a long, long time before all three girls realised the extent to which their mother would lie in order to lower their ages and then finally deny their very existence. One Saturday a television appeared, sitting alongside the radiogram. John, in spite of the constant claims of poverty had also acquired a fridge. Perhaps it was all on the never never. Just to keep up with the neighbours. Like Mr and Mrs Lerner next door, living in a newly built house. They owned a ladies dress shop in the High Street. All very respectable. Secrets locked away, net curtains at the window and early to bed. Mr that and Mrs this, and mind your manners.

Cecilie, if at home, would take a rest in the afternoon. She had headache or was feeling tired, she would say. She would lay on her bed flicking through magazines, no doubt dreaming of another life where she was a famous actress with a penthouse in Mayfair. The girls would watch their mother as she stood in the hall in front of the round mirror. Too short to see their own reflections, they watched her from a place halfway up the stairs in the half light, careful not to make a sound as their mother took a powder compact out of her handbag and patted her nose.

Cecilie as Principal Boy at the Arcadia Theatre in Lowestoft.

Then the lipstick would extend magically from a gold tube, pillar box red smeared on her lips. She shut the gold clasp on her red leather handbag with a loud snap. Then run her fingers through her dark hair, open the front door and set off down the path out to who knows where. Clicking her high heels down to the front garden gate and out down The Avenue.

The girls' beautiful mother had been preparing her amateur dramatics. She had singing lessons and shows at *The Sparrows Nest*, and pantomime at the *Arcadia Theatre* and *The Repertory Company*. She'd charmed Roy Barbour, the owner of the theatre who'd been on the music halls. Seeming as old as old could be, at 60 he wasn't really. The girl thought he looked at least 100 but then she thought her mother old and she'd only just turned 30. It was said that Roy was a friend of George Formby, Charles Simon, Nancy McDermott, Des O Connor, Russ Conway and Michael Caine. All had tea or whatever in Cecilie's drawing room.

Suddenly, for there was no goodbye, the mother, her dead fox and the fur coats were not at home. She was away in Norwich. Cecilie had left local pantomimes and amateur dramatics behind. The girl stood on the landing outside the room, breathing in the faint smell of *Estée Lauder Youth Dew*. One day the door was unlocked. The dressing table was still covered with the pale golden dust of the mother's *Yardley Freesia* face powder, an almost empty box with the embossed golden bee on the lid, and a lipstick that was down to the stub. The girl stuffed them into the pocket of her navy blue gym-slip.

John was now in sole charge. His beautiful wife gone, gone to be 'on the stage.' For a while there was Mrs Wilson the housekeeper, who lived in at the top of the house in the attic flat. She was stiff lipped and stiff backed, a disapproving authority. She appeared to have no bosom under her neat pastel twin sets. She wore pleated grey skirts with sensible brown shoes and her neat hair didn't seem to move, her permed waves like a steel hat. Where had she come from? Unlike anyone else the girls had ever known, she was a woman from a bygone age.

Mrs Wilson introduced hands and neck inspections before bed, and bedtime was at six o'clock sharp. No one went to bed at six, no one. One day John bought a whole tongue and Jennifer found it in the larder. She shrieked and was outraged, 'A tongue! Who's tongue?' Mrs Wilson would snort, in a delicate way of course, 'You're lucky to have good food, there are children starving...'

NASTY NELLIE 'In Africa, yes, yes, take it and give it to them.'

It was the cabbage scenario all over again. Jennifer wasn't going to put that dead tongue anywhere near her mouth if she could help it. 'Ox tongue,' said Mrs Wilson, 'it's very good for you.' She bustled about the kitchen cluck-clucking and tut-tutting. Jennifer sobbed and hid behind the curtain in the dining room the whole of Sunday afternoon. Dead animals, offal and other bits of head parts, it was a regular house of horrors. Jennifer became a vegetarian. John bought a blender and decided that putting in whole eggs would make a good omelette, 'If you have to crack the shells it's not a labour saving device is it,' he reasoned. It was like eating fine gravel with the flavour of salty toenails. John kept chickens next to the van at the end of the garden and coated the eggs with a thin brown glaze to preserve them.

The girl was alone at home on a Saturday with a list of chores. John had taken her sisters out shopping and Mrs Wilson was elsewhere. Good. She could daydream and play. First she set to making a sandwich. Two slices of white bread, on with the *Echo*. Not nice but over the yellow margarine she added a good slick of *Tate and Lyle Golden Syrup*. It was a sandwich made in heaven, 'I'm just an old fashioned girl with an old fashioned mind.' She sang this song, looking at her reflection in the kitchen window. She imagined she was Eartha Kitt. She had a sort of similar vibrato, which years later when she first recorded in a proper studio, she thought sounded more like *Larry The Lamb* on speed than Eartha Kitt, 'As they slurp, slurp, slurp into the barrels.' Although she couldn't roll her 'rrrs' very well at all.

If John was in the garden or out the girl would switch on Saturday morning radio or play a record she liked. She listened to Uncle Mac and wished that inbetween *The Three Billy Goats Gruff* and *The Runaway Train* they'd play a modern grown up song. Doris Day or Johnny Ray. In 1954 the balladeers and the crooners dominated the charts though there was still Winifred Atwell and then Russ Conway.

She met a girl called Bridget. Bridget was at the grammar school and lived five doors down in The Avenue. Her father was a loud and ebullient man with a little black moustache. His oily dark hair slicked back with a centre parting, gave him the look of a city spiv rather than the schoolteacher he actually was. He fancied himself as a bit of a Clark Gable man. He drove a large red second-hand *Jaguar* with leather seats and a walnut dashboard. Mrs Smith was timid and her husband ruled the roost in that 1950s male fashion as she kept house and tried to control Steven, Shaun and Bridget, her trio of unruly children. Steven was a wild boy who had left school at 15 and worked at *Brooke Marine*. He was the first boy the girl had ever met who wore drainpipe trousers like Elvis. She was terrified, in awe and a little bit in love with him. She went with Bridget to the *Claremont Pier*. Bridget would grow up to be a wild woman.

'Well, since my baby left me, I've found a new place to dwell. It's down at the end of lonely street. At Heartbreak Hotel.'

The world changed the day the girl heard Elvis, a voice of youth and rebellion, defiance and sex. All the girls lusted for Elvis or second best, a boy who could look like Elvis, walk like Elvis, sweep his hair back like Elvis. You had to wait hours to hear the music on the radio. You got Burl Ives and the lady who swallowed a fly and so much more, silly woman. You'd think she might have stopped swallowing after the spider or at the very least, the bird. Families listened to the *BBC Light Programme*, Jack Payne's *Say it with Music*, *Housewives Choice*, *Two Way Family Favourites* and *Pick of the Pops* with Franklin Engelmann. In between all these you heard the raw voices of the new rock and roll and maybe the odd snatch of Elvis or *Sixteen Tons*, 'And what do you get?' More was to be heard on 208 on the dial, *Radio Luxemburg*. Horace Batchelor's 'K-E-Y-N-S-H-A-M', the word that a nation learned to spell in its sleep.

Under the bedclothes a million young ears hoping to hear the record, the track that thrilled. Fading in and out, reception was often lost. Crackle pop. It was the place where dreams and teenage longings were made. Youth was having its new dawn around the radio and the jukebox, and in the listening booths at 'Woollies' on a Saturday afternoon. The man in the street, normal man, still wore the brutal haircuts of Her Majesties Armed Forces. Short back and sides, a side parting as sharp as a razor, slathered in *Brylcreem* and *Old Spice*. Splash it on. Stale sweat was no longer acceptable in the front rooms of the new age. Women, if they had the money, wore gloves, a good coat, decent court shoes, a hat in church on Sundays and corsets underneath everything. All trussed up.

For years young teens had been dressed like their mums and dads. This was all going to change. Up The Avenue, beside the Smith's house sat the Smith's caravan. A modern one with red *Formica* tops, white paintwork, shiny chrome handles and a radio on a shelf above the pull-out table. This became headquarters for the two girls on the cusp of young womanhood. They'd heard about the *Kit Kat Café* on the end of Waterloo Road, where the owner had murdered a woman. Appalled and yet somehow strangely excited, it was as if the big bad world had come to their door.

Bridget boasted one day that she'd 'come on' and showed off the bra and some lipstick she'd bought in *Woolworths*. The secondary mod girl hung on her every word and thought her as beautiful as Brigitte Bardot. Bridget Smith, bold and fearless, ended up in reform school and then prison for a while.

Marion was also at *Alderman Woodrow*. She lived on the Gunton Estate up in the north end of the town. Her family had a radiogram like the one they had in Shrublands but they had better records to play. The smell of warm *Bakerlite* and the plop of the new 12" and 7" *Shellac* as it dropped down onto the deck one by one, *His Masters Voice*, *Phonograph*, *Fontana*, *Brunswick* and *Decca*. They played The Platters and Little Richard, her dad's records. Marion's mum liked Pat Boone and Johnnie Ray. In love with Elvis and Buddy Holly, Marion was the coolest dancer. Circle skirt flying, petticoat flashing and feet snapping, she was the jive queen of Lowestoft. She wore slip on shoes to school as did her brother, and the girl was again embarrassed by her old black lace ups.

This was where the girl first heard the black American music that had changed a generation. In a small house on a council estate in a small out of the way seaside town. Marion's family had *Picture Show* and *Picturegoer* on a coffee table with a glass top. Very modern. They listened to *Radio Luxemburg* in the evening over a cup of tea, the dad with a bottle of stout maybe and the girls with a *Cola*. They were a very modern family.

The girl was sometimes invited for tea. If it was the weekend they had tinned peaches with evaporated milk and *Bourbon* biscuits or *Battenberg* cake. She called it 'window cake'. Occasionally they'd have *Wagon Wheels* or *Penguins*. Heaven. Marion's dad would go off to read the paper and smoke in the lavatory for half an hour. The women played records and talked about boys or the latest film. Just chit and chat, this and that. All so very different from life in Shrublands.

At school in the playground at break and walking home, the talk if not of boys or pop stars was of film stars, Marilyn Monroe, Rock Hudson, Doris Day, James Dean, Yul

Brynner and Gina Lollobrigida. Marion had photos pinned up over her bed in the room she shared with her little sister. With all this new information the girl from London could play the film star game in the playground without feeling so stupid.

In her second year there was a school play. Enter Betty Blues Belter, later to appear when she first dared to sing in the pub beside the sea. It was a non-speaking or singing role. She skipped about the stage on tiptoe, waving her hands. And sat cross legged in various scenes, looking elfish in grey tights and a tunic. She was longing to wear a dragons head and sport a fabulous tail.

In music lessons she wasn't picked to sing. The teacher's idea of modern music was *The Dam Buster's March*. She called the new rock and roll 'jungle music', declaring, 'That's not singing, that's just a horrible noise.' The girls would giggle behind her neat floral bloused back. A back that didn't invite a touch. A back that clearly had never swung to a dance band, grooved to rock and roll or melted into the arms of a love song. What did she know? She was old and past it. They were made to sing of *The Ash Grove*, lost maidens and *Green Grow the Rushes, O*, with the shrill soprano of the music teacher soaring above. She was the one who'd said, 'No, you can't sing, Miss Tug Boat Annie from London.'

Pink Socks, Rock 'n Roll and Heartbreak Hotel

Night Time is the Right Time Ray Charles 1958

1957 to 1959: fisher boys and drainpipes. Sex, cigarettes, lipstick, blue jeans and winkle pickers. Love Me Tender at The Odeon, Buddy Holly, Connie Francis and Ray Charles on a juke box.

The girls were to be christened. 'Do you reject the devil and all rebellion against God?' 'I reject them.' With Cecilie away John reverted to the Christian faith of his upbringing. These heathen girls must be christened. Cecilie was gone and her refusal to have them christened gone with her. Skip, skip and skip some more until she was dizzy. Accepted into the arms of the Lord? Standing there in a frock that was too small, next to Jennifer in an even smaller one. There were yowling babes in arms and the three girls, John holding Lindsay by the hand. She was five and wore a blue velvet dress with a darker velvet collar.

The girl sat in a ramrod straight church pew, her back against old wood, afraid of a rap on the hand or the wrath of the Lord himself, listening to a priest droning. She was on the edges of womanhood, with jeans and high heels on her mind and rock and roll in her heart, itching for the dance.

WICKED WILL O'MINA 'She's got ants in her pants, look at her twitch.'

She was a girl with songs hidden inside her mouth and a dance in her toes. How? When? Where?

LYING LIZZIE 'I've been invited out with Bridget's family.'

Bridget was the girl's alibi. She knew a boy who could bunk in through the back doors of the *Odeon*, so they did. All the girls were drooling over Elvis. Bridget snogged the boy who'd got them in. Pay back. But he was a nice looking lad, except for the nasty and angry spots around his neck and chin. Bridget loved to kiss. At 13 years old they heard girls talk of boys and what you did with boys, of rings and getting engaged. Girls in the third year began to boast of conquests and 'going all the way.' The girl held back, confused. The giggles and the talk made her stomach spin.

One really did get engaged and flashed a diamond ring to gaggles of envious girls. Then a few months later she was gone. It was whispered she was pregnant and had been sent away to an aunt in Norwich or somewhere away from Lowestoft. Joy got engaged in the third year to a fisher boy. Her life was to be like her mother's. By the time she was 18 she had two kids and then at 24 there would be nights out at the new bingo place that had been a cinema. She'd also look like her mother. That was how it was in those last years of the 1950s. A brief and glorious teenage interlude then the expected. A life mapped out as if there was no other way.

Out on the Saturday parade the girl watched those in summer frocks and petticoats, high heels with short white socks or pedal pushers with crisp cotton shirts and collars up around the ears. Bill Haley ripped up the joint and cinema seats in all the land with *Rock Around The Clock* and nothing would be the same anywhere again. Tommy Steele sang *Rock With The Caveman* and now he was wooing the mums with *A Handful Of Songs*. Fisher boys, home on leave with money in their pockets, wore teddy boy drape suits and blue or black suede brothel creepers shaped like bumper cars attached to the ends of legs in tight drainpipe trousers. Dockside dandies wore full drape double breasted jackets and 32 inch bottoms in suits of electric colours, red, blue, lime green and tartan. Sometimes shot through with silver lurex thread, the jackets were pleated at the back with a velvet collar here, a fancy cuff there. White socks, thick crepe soled shoes, open necked shirts with the collar pulled out and up, white t-shirts, hair greased back in an opulent 'DA'. Peacocks on dry land looking for a one-night stand, a girl to kiss in the back row and maybe more to come later.

You could meet boys as they jostled around the jukeboxes in the greasy spoon cafés, testosterone tossing. Or on a bank holiday fair ground around the edges of dance halls, or in the amusement arcades and on the piers. Boys were very good at standing around. They would stand around street corners and they would stand around shops, especially ones that had mirrors in the windows, with a flick of the comb and a sly look at the cut of their jacket. Crowding round a table at *Capaldi's Ice Cream Parlour* to the scream and steam of the coffee machine, drinking hot blackcurrant juice or *Cola* in a small tough town coming out of a tough time. Moving into another way of life without the war. Looking for more than what had just been.

The girl began to grow her hair. She wanted to jive, wear a circle skirt and petticoats, high heeled shoes and a ponytail. She'd seen the white stiletto winkle pickers in the *Co-op* window. The girls with the snowy white socks were wearing them. She was ready. Ready to rock and roll in high heeled shoes. The trouble was, she had to wear the black lace ups or brown *Clarks* sandals. School clothes in the week and cotton dresses with silly white peter pan collars at the weekend.

'Will ya shut ya fuckin' tatter-trap a minute boy, fuck'n roight!' Along the London Road South one hot day when you could smell the sugar beet from the fields, came a tramp called Puggy Uttin, 'Get out the way, fuck, fuck, fuck you fuckin' bastard.' He was a 'gabbin' on to no one in particular, 'Bugger, bugger, bugger.' Both fearful and fascinated by Puggy, the girl learned all her juiciest curses from his mouth. He spent his life collecting things, anything he could get into his cart whilst walking and swearing. She decided she wouldn't mind joining him on his life's work. She wanted to know who he was. The girl had heard 'damn and blast' and at worst 'bloody and bugger', and they were bad words. The new words were even more delicious. She knew the curses were as bad as bad and she whispered them to herself, 'Fuck, fuck, fuck.' She also knew that if she dared to utter these at home or in school there'd be hell to pay. This made them even more thrilling. She practiced on her own in the van at the bottom of the garden. 'Fuck, fuck, fuck. Shit! Bastard! Bastard!' It felt good and she'd no idea why. The girl and Bridget would swear together and giggle at the sound of the words and the knowing that they were forbidden.

Bridget had some money one day, and so to the *Odeon* Cinema. For 1s6d they watched *Pathe News*, *Pearl and Dean* advertisements, a cartoon, a B movie and then *Jailhouse Rock*. She was in love with a celluloid man with laughing eyes the colour of raven's wings and whose hips caused a fluttering in the belly.

'Can she come out to play?' asked Bridget. They giggled. Playing was the last thing on Bridget's mind. On a windy Saturday morning in the middle of May they found a tube of *Gordon Moore's Cosmetic Toothpaste* in the bathroom cabinet. It must have been Cecilie's. 'As Used by Hollywood Stars.' Bridget suggested they rub some on their lips, 'Red lipstick,' she said. She was wearing a pair of jeans and a red shirt with batwing sleeves and a turned up collar, 'Here, wear this.' She handed the girl a similar shirt in pale blue, 'My mum's. I took it out of the ironing basket, she won't miss it.' They set off to walk the walk down to the town. As they reached the cafés with the jukebox and a glass of hot blackcurrant for 5d, they became aware of the stares and giggles. The toothpaste was running down the corners of their mouths, making them resemble a pair of Bram Stoker's handmaidens. 'Blast boy, oi larfed moi hid orf,' said one of the boys when he caught sight of the girls from The Avenue.

Money was desperately needed and they had to find a Saturday job. Shoes had to be bought as well as jeans, florescent pink socks and proper lipstick, *Outdoor Girl* from *Woolworths*. Her first job was in a flower shop near the railway station. Half a dozen roses at 4d ha'penny a rose. Two bits of green, tuppence a bit. All of this adding up, shillings and pence. All numbers were as foreign to her as the Suffolk accents. She drowned in numbers with her chaotic attempts. She guessed a lot of the time and then the figures didn't add up.

She was then put into the back room to make up bunches. She pricked her fingers, dropped the flowers and used too much cellophane. She was useless and got the sack after just three weeks. Bridget came to the rescue, 'They need waitresses in the boating lake café down the front.' The two girls tottered along one Saturday morning, 'Come on, let's put make up on, wear my heels, you got to look older.'

It was June and soon the town was full of visitors. Old ladies dressed in floral frocks and pastel cardigans, with white canvas sandals and beige stockings. Old men in trousers and shirtsleeves, braces clipped to high waist bands, shoes and socks. Wanting a deck chair if only the wind would stop, 'I'll take my shoes off tomorrow,' said Mr to Mrs from Birmingham, 'the weather is set for fair, they say.' When it was fair the men's paper white hairy legs emerged from rolled up grey flannel trousers and hankies knotted in four corners were placed on heads to keep the sun from burning the skin under thinning hair. They sat in little groups or couples in the shelters on the front and in the cafés in the afternoon, taking tea and a rock cake or a cheese roll. The families would follow in late July when school ended for the summer.

Bridget swung the jobs. She was good. She could charm the drainpipes off the best looking boy in town. Next weekend there they were. It was hard work. They waited on tables, dispensing cream horns and sausage rolls, *Fanta* and stewed brown tea, cheese rolls, ham rolls, *Wall's Ice Cream* and tea cakes. They washed up endless piles of cups, saucers, teaspoons and dishes, teapots and milk jugs. They wiped tables and swept floors from nine until six, with a half hour lunch break. That summer, come the end of term, they worked five days a week, from Wednesday and all over the weekend, finishing at five on a Sunday.

They bought black rubber soled gladiator sandals with bright red, blue or green towelling on the uppers and long black laces tied all the way up to the knee. *Woolworths* sold them. Bliss.

London boys were on the front near the *Claremont Pier*. 'You kippers, you Lowestoft kippers, come over 'ere and lets sniff yer knickers.' They jostled around the girls, holding their noses, cracking up at the hilarity of their own wit. There were five of them, about 14 or 15 years old. Flash boys with London voices. She remembered David Ashford and wondered if they knew him but she said nothing. Bridget back chatted, tossed her hair, flashed her eyes and used the new words they'd learned from Puggy.

One Saturday, after the season had come to an end and holiday jobs were no more, Bridget gave a lesson on how to 'shop lift' in *Woolworths*. One minute they were looking at make up, the next they were out of the door, 'Come on, quickly... walk fast. Now!' Out of the doors, onto the street, duck and dodge in the crowds, a lipstick and a pair of nylons in their pockets. Oh how her heart did bump inside her ribcage.

The following week they had black eyeliner and white cotton circular stitched pointed bras. 'Look at our tits,' said Bridget, admiring herself in the mirror on the wardrobe in her parents' bedroom, 'fuck! I'm gonna show that cow Rowena,' she giggled. Bridget had a black pencil skirt and gave the girl a pair of itchy woollen black *Watch Tartan* trews. Clumsily with a needle and thread, she took them in so they hugged her legs with a little slit at the ankle end to allow the foot through the tiny opening. They were so tight she could barely bend her knees.

They'd sneak out on a Saturday afternoon and as they became more brave, they'd go at night when everyone thought they were in bed. They changed in the lavatory at the rec around the corner, smearing *Max Factor* pan cake on their faces in a dim mirror over a cracked sink, then stuffing the little girl clothes in a hole in the hedge by the Smith's garage.

Mr. Smith enrolled them in the youth club in Morton Road on Wednesday evenings, six 'til nine. Table tennis and dancing to records. Boys one side of the room with the girls always instigating the dance. The girls danced together, one leading as the man, handbags on the floor beside them, waiting for the useless boys to get in. Dance you fools, dance.

There was one boy the girl noticed, the 'Jive King', the best dancer in the club with his greased back DA, wearing tight blue jeans, black suede brothel creepers and a white shirt, the collar up beside his ears. All the girls would flutter their eye lashes and smile at him, wanting a dance, giggling as they huddled around the mirror in the lavatory smearing a fresh slick of *Outdoor Girl* pink to the lips and more sooty black mascara. She was asked to dance one night by this boy. He was small but wiry. He led with the solid confidence of his moves, his hand firm in hers, spinning her round and round. She twirled, her feet almost slipping on the wooden floor but she survived. She was exhilarated. It was like nothing she'd ever felt before. 'You're not bad,' he said, 'I like the girl to be small, you'll do.' He did fancy tricks like sliding her through his legs and lifting her up off the floor. Whooo, she loved it and danced with him every session.

He never really talked to her, it was just for the jive. But the jive had meant she was no longer on the edges, though she wasn't sure about being seen. She was ashamed of the flatness of her chest, the plainness of her face and the awkwardness of her limbs. But somehow, with the strong guiding hand of the boy, her limbs found the moves and with each dance she grew more confident, 'Dancing to the Jailhouse Rock'. When the slow records came on, *To Know Him Is To Love Him* with Phil Spector and The Teddy Bears or 'You send me, Darling you, send me, honest you do honest you,' with Sam Cook. When the couples were on the floor, arms around each other, she didn't dance. Her jive partner had vanished.

The girl managed to pull a pair of laddered nylons from the laundry basket in her mother's room one day when Mrs Wilson, who'd been dusting in there, had left the door unlocked and was downstairs making a pot of tea. It was eleven o'clock in the morning. The teatime break was timed to the second. The stolen stockings were pushed into the *Woolworths* white cotton conical bra. If she took the stockings out and you pushed the pointed cups, there would be a telltale indentation where her small round tits should've been. Oh the horror of it. A boy at the youth club, his name gone as it's too awful to remember him, noticed a sliver of nylon and leaning forward, pulled it out. The whole embarrassing truth of her pointy little tits were brandished as a prize. From then on, known as 'stocking tits', she didn't go back. She dare not face her dancing boy.

Bridget was bored with the youth club anway. She'd bigger fish to fry. She wanted more than a quick fumble, a boy's hand finding its way inside her bra during a two minute snog. She wanted the real thing. Sex, going all the way. Evvo and Huggo were two fisher boys. Bridget wanted Evvo, so poor old Huggo had the small girl who looked about 12 but was really 14 and had a stolen bra stuffed with nylon stockings. If Bridget's parents were out they'd sneak into the Smith's caravan. Bridget and Evvo would get into heavy petting, hands up sweaters and into knickers. Huggo would look bored but was probably embarrassed. His fisher boy suit and slick greased back hair concealed a shy boy. The worst that happened to the girl was the smell of smoke on her clothes and the nutty whiff of beer on her breath as she sucked at the bottle of *Brown* the boys had provided for the carnal caravan conquests.

The girl's birthday fell in Easter holidays. At 14 she had another job, this time as a weekend breakfast waitress at the *Harbour Hotel* right by the bridge and the South Pier. She took the No14 bus from the Pakefield Terminus at six o'clock in the morning on Saturday and Sunday. She changed in a tiny room as small as a cupboard, into a little black dress provided by the hotel, smelling of old sweat and bacon fat. She had a white apron and cap and was all ready for a six-thirty start. Ready to lay tables, turning white table cloths in order to hide the previous day's coffee stains. She polished plate silver and dusted shelves. She filled pepper pots and salt cellars. She carried pots of tea and coffee, and toast in little racks. Breakfast was served from seven.

The other waitresses were older and wore the uniform of the 1950s. The girl was easy prey. They laughed at her little flat chest, 'Oooh they're like a pair of little golf balls,' said a woman called Doreen, reaching out and giving them a sharp squeeze, 'Blast it's hooly hot in here,' she said over her shoulder to the girl, and then added, 'Now you listen to me my girl, all the tips go into the pot and we share them out at the end of the shift, do you understand?'

Doreen wore dark red lipstick which bled into the tiny creases around her mouth. Her hair was the colour of old brass, her skirt shiny with age and her hat, stained yellow and limp. She went off to smoke in the windowless staff room, pulling a *Park Drive* out of a packet she kept near at all times. She left the girl in the kitchen with a pile of cutlery, gravy boats, cruets and the silver polish. At the end of the shift the girl was handed 4d. Her tips. She wanted the silver bits, the two shillings, half crowns, the sixpences and the hexagonal golden three-penny bit. Two and six a day, plus tips, that's 25 bob a week or more. That's what the women were on in the season.

    Tɪʟʟʏ Tᴇᴀ Lᴇᴀғ 'Now that's not fair is it? Think girl, think.'

The girl thought and the bra came into its own. She noticed that salesmen with suits and brief cases, and the odd theatrical traveller, would flirt, wink and press half a crown into her hand if she smiled a lot over the tea pots and the *Robertson's Marmalade*. Into her *Woolworths* bra went every other coin. She knew the old girls were taking the mick. Why not? She was just a chit of a girl with a London voice and little tits. What did she know? She began to make it her business to know. The polishing would take over an hour and until the hotel manager noticed one day, she was alone with the blackened cleaning rags, coffee pots and knives and forks.

She struggled with the waitress hierarchy. She lasted four months from January during the slow season. The girl spent her ill-gotten tips on blue jeans, a pink shirt with a turned up collar and florescent pink socks, their bright glow reflecting in the puddles. She had *Outdoor Girl* pink lips, *Outdoor Girl* black cake mascara, a long ponytail and high heeled shoes. Those cheap white stilettos with very pointed toes from the *Co-op*. Wiggle, wiggle trying to balance. Those heels made a woman, not a girl. Clip, clip on the pavement after dark when she walked the streets, eyes wide, quick peep in a shop window as she passed.

    PROCRASTINATING PATSY 'Do I look alright?'

Ponytail swinging, Buddy Holly or Fats Domino singing on the juke box, skinny boys in tight blue jeans and blue suede shoes, flicked back greasy hair, hidden eyes and the flashing comb.

    MISERY IVY 'Has he noticed me?'

She sat and daydreamed whilst the Everly Brothers sang the teen dream songs, sweet, sweet harmony, sweet voices.

    MISERY IVY 'I want a boy with big brown eyes and big boy shoulders
    in a black leather jacket. He's the cool one, the loner. Sooner or later,
    he'll drift in with a beautiful girl who hasn't picked up her shoes
    from a hole in the hedge and put her lipstick on in the dim light of
    a public lavatory.'

The truth was, if such a boy had looked at her, she'd have died of nerves and confusion. So instead she pined and longed from the safe distance of several feet and miles of pain. Her first fag, quick! A *Woodbine*, tipped. She felt bad, she felt sick but she wanted to sit in cafés and bars with the cigarette smoke blowing moody clouds, curling around her sooty-caked eyelashes. Sultry? She would be alone, mysterious and aloof. It saved her from having to talk.

    MISERY IVY 'What would I say?'

Cough. Splutter. Smoke gets in her eyes. Where's the mirror? Her eyes were smudged and her hair was a mess. Her tits? Too small. 'Dre-e-e-eam, dream, dream, dream. When I want you, in my arms.'

    NASTY NELLIE 'They can tell you know. They can see. You're not nice
    at all.'

CLARA THE CLOWN 'She's having a funny turn, turn, turn.'

Autumn came and the girl went back to the nowhere-land that was her school. Jennifer would go on next year to the grammar school after passing the Eleven-Plus. Unlike the girl, she was saved by her brain. The girl wasn't planning to be a secretary, or a nurse. She wasn't doing the domestic science thing. She wasn't engaged with a flashy little ring on her finger, a boy at sea and a baby on the way. No. And she definitely wasn't doing the dressmaking thing. Elbows and thumbs, she wasn't allowed to, 'Ruin good materials.' Miss Harris, the needlework teacher had a prim bun, a prim mouth and a clucking voice. Cluck! Right by the girl's ear. It was so loud she always jumped, even though she knew it was coming, 'Hasn't your mother taught you anything?' The girl stuck up her hand and asked to be excused, 'Please Miss, may I be...' 'Oh I suppose so,' said Miss Harris, 'you're not much use here.' She turned to another girl.

That was the day she felt the stickiness between her legs. Was she on? She was. She worried. Would she smell? Toilet paper wasn't a good thing to line your knickers with. She would crunch and crackle and stink of *Jeyes Fluid* as she walked back into the class. She remembered the handkerchief stuffed in her gym-slip pocket, a present from Beryl, a small white cotton square with a flower motive in one corner. She smoothed it out, lined her pants and longed for the home time bell. She was now a woman and couldn't wait to tell Bridget.

The year was moving on and the winds whipped down the High Street and up and down the Scores, the narrow ancient pathways leading down to the sea; Martin's Score, Rant Score and Wilde Score. The girl was off to start another Saturday job, this time at *The International Stores* as an assistant on the cheese counter. Mr Bossy whoever he was, in a clean white coat and slick shiny black hair, was going chocks away for the manager's job. And he didn't like little London girl. She was knife drumming on the marble counter, rat-at-a-tat and he told her to stop it.

She'd learned from the *Harbour Hotel* posse and began to cheat. She'd tuck the odd sixpence here and there, not into the till but in her pocket and then her bra. Out the back in the storeroom was a wooden box, a room within a room. It was the toilet. She sat and scratched one day, then another day and another. Then, looking down at her hand, she saw something moving sideways. A crab. She had crabs and she was a thief.

NASTY NELLIE 'You're a crab infested thief.'

Far, very far ahead in time, Crown Score became home to the *Invasion of Crabs* sculpture, created by artist Paul Amey, suggesting that the crabs, having escaped the fishmonger's slab, were threatening an assault on the high street. This wasn't on the high street but in the back of a high street grocer and inevitably she was caught with a sixpence that wasn't hers. She was out of there with another flea in her ear, and crabs in her pubic hair. Oh how low she had sunk. Who would want her now? Her marble drumming days were over and boring Mr 'Would be a manager one day' was pleased as Mr Punch, 'That's the way to do it.' The words actually spoken were, 'she's out of control.' The police weren't called but threats were made; the police, the school and worse, her mother. She kept her head down, her mouth firmly shut and became almost invisible. She was either on the firing line, or forgotten about. Doors opened late at night. Foxes with beady dead eyes, red ox tongues from the fridge. She was sent to a hostel that housed girls and boys who were deemed to be unmanageable, not conforming to the rules. She remained in the hostel for a while, banned from everything. From the town, from Bridget, from watching television, from life itself.

After she was discharged, when it seemed as if all had been forgotten, Bridget came round, 'Lets go out.' They scurried into the toilets at the rec where Bridget put on a pair of red toreador pants with a white shirt and then, wobbling wildly on her white stilettos, with a red wool swing coat borrowed from her mother, the two girls went to Woodbridge on the bus.

The American base wasn't far away. There was music on the juke box and Bridget in the red pants made flirting eyes with the GIs. The girl wore her tight *Black Watch* tartan trews, a white blouse and her one and only bra, by now in need of mending. A safety pin held it all together and it could do with a wash. One of the guys bought her a *Pepsi*. She sat listening to the records as they plopped one by one, 45s on a new machine. It felt like a bright new world. Bridget was sitting on a lap, and then another, her giggle was everywhere. 'You-ooh Send Me. I know You Send Me. I know You Send Me. Honest you do.'

In her mind the girl was jiving and then slow dancing but the man's face was unseen. She couldn't find his face. She watched and she listened, looking at the crew cut hair and khaki pants. All their jaws were working hard chewing gum. Two black men came into the café, talking with American accents, 'Hi Man.' They slapped backs, jostled and laughed, pushed more money into the jukebox and seemed so very different to the boys in Lowestoft or anywhere else. Exotic men from another universe.

116

She wondered if he, the one with very long curly black eyelashes, sang like Nat King Cole. She thought he looked a bit like him. Marion's mother loved Nat King Cole. He smiled at her. She remembered the Siamese naval officers in Weymouth. The wild voices on the jukebox were singing for her. The more they sang, the more the voices inside would babble and she began to talk less, became tongue-tied. 'She's shy,' Bridget would say. But of course nobody heard that.

They were back by six. Bridget was on a curfew.

Walking to the bus stop one day, the girl felt as if nothing in the world could make her smile, make her feel happy. She'd been taken to see a welfare worker, a woman who looked into her eyes and tried to make her talk but she wouldn't. She could and she couldn't in equal measure. She was barely talking at school. All she wanted was to be left alone with a book at the back of the classroom.

Huggo appeared one day as she waited for the bus. He was on a motorbike, a *Triumph Bonneville*. He'd become a biker. 'Hop on,' he said, 'I'll give you a ride. Where you off to?' She nodded with a 'nowhere' sort of shrug. 'Ever done the ton?' he said. 'No' she whispered, thinking, 'What's the ton?' She had a feeling that whatever it was it would be good. She loved his bike. She loved his dark hair and his shoulders, broad under his leather, and the chunky boots on his feet. She loved his blue jeans worn tight around his thighs. She felt his muscles moving as he switched gears and took the corners, leaning over almost on the tarmac, a ton up on Ella Aerodrome. Her lips flapped loose in the wind, she closed her mouth. Her belly did flips. She clung onto Huggo with her arms wrapped around his waist, her head pressed hard on his leather clad back. Oh the thrill, 'Oh hell, this is scary, this is the ton. This is great.' It wasn't only the speed that thrilled her. It was the feel of the man, the smell of him, and she thought that was being in love. She wanted to do the ton forever, never ever stop. He took her to a café with a great jukebox. 'I'm real nervous 'cause it sure is fun. Come on baby, you drive me crazy. Goodness gracious great balls of fire.'

Back to The Avenue. It was late, way gone six o'clock. What the hell would she say? Where had she been? She'd been told to be home by five. It was worth the slap even though her head reeled as it fell from her neck, red faced and angry eyed.

MISERY IVY 'What will they to do now? Fuck. Bugger. Shit."

'Ouch,' said her head from the floor where it lay.

NASTY NELLIE 'Send her to bed with no head. Her ragged neck will bleed. Where will the blood go? What a mess in the bed. And if she bleeds to death?'

Will they be sorry? No but she had done the ton, felt the thrill of speed and had held a man in a leather jacket. She went to sleep holding her head, thankfully not bleeding to death. Huggo picked her up the following week in the place beside the phone box at the end of the road. She had played hooky from school. They were roaring along Kirkley Cliff and just before the convent, WHAM! He pulled out and she found herself laying on the road. A nun and then another looked anxiously down at her, their black tunics flapping, pale faces with kind eyes framed in virginal white habits. She remembered her christening and asked herself, 'Am I in hell? Are there nuns in hell?' Huggo limped over to her and an ambulance arrived followed by the police. She was off to the hospital. Once again, like the car in Weymouth outside the fire station, it was nothing. A bruise, a scratch, nothing really and she was fine.

They said she was a teenage tearaway. More troubles, more slaps, more locked doors from six at night until seven in the morning. She didn't see Huggo again. He disappeared from her life. She stopped talking completely. Her head became extremely busy but the words failed to reach the air outside her mouth.

Bridget came round one Saturday morning. John was out shopping with Jennifer and Lindsay. 'I know how we can get a looood of money.' She outlined a crazy plan. There was a girl at the grammar school called Rowena, one of the sharpest dressers in town. Her mother owned a hairdressing salon. Rowena wore pencil skirts, high heels and American tan ladderless stockings. She wore a diamond ring on her finger, had dark beautifully groomed hair and perfect nails painted a pretty shade of peach. She was engaged to a boy who owned his own car and worked in his parents hotel on the London Road South. It would be his hotel one day.

This was the plan. The mother was at the salon, the father at work, and Rowena was with her boyfriend. The girl, who was small, would wriggle into the family house, in through the downstairs window. She did it. The girl was a cat burglar. In she went and opened the back door for Bridget who knew where to find the money. Up the stairs, rustle, rustle, then quick, out the door and belt down the back alley and out into the road, on into town. Bridget couldn't stop laughing, 'Lets go down the front,' she said, 'to the shelter and you'll see what I got.' One hundred and fifty pounds. They were silent for a moment, looking at the enormous amount of money.

TILLY TEA LEAF 'Wow, that's a proper haul... oh what a lot of money.'

Bridget said, 'I'll keep this under the mattress in the caravan, and we'll go to Ipswich on the train next week.' The girl was shaking and her hands felt hot and sticky. Next week came, a week of worry and dizzy excitement, turn and turn about. 'It's ok,' Bridget said, 'we go to different schools, no one will connect us, don't worry.' And she laughed, 'you great lummox, trust me, no one knows.' She talked about what she would buy and said, 'I'll show that cow, Rowena'. 'Poison Ivy, Poison Ivy, well late at night when you're sleeping. Poison Ivy comes a creeping all around.'

At Lowestoft station the following Saturday morning Bridget bought two tickets to Ipswich. Her heart pounding, the apprentice burglar followed her friend to the waiting room where a small coal fire glimmered in a black iron grate. One or two people sat on the dark leather seats under a window. A rustle of newspaper, a woman searching for something in a large handbag, a child sniffing. Nobody took any notice of the two young, almost women. The man behind the newspaper looked up and grunted something unintelligible but they knew it wasn't nice. More laughter.

They changed clothes in the ladies lavatory, smearing on *Max Factor* pan stick foundation, the colour far too dark for the pale girl. It made a line under her chin where her neck began. Then black eyeliner, lashes like spiders legs sticky with blobs that made her squint. She dare not rub her eye, that would be a smudge. Finally, pink lipstick. Bridget was confident and full of chatter about the money they'd spend. On the train to Oulton Broad South, Beccles and last stop, Ipswich.

Oh hell, there he was. Mr Smith on the platform at the first stop. Then in the train carriage, 'Right,' he said, 'not a word. Follow me and I don't want any lip from you, Bridget.' That was that. He took each girl firmly by the arm. He took the money and the girl was banned from the Smith's house. No police appeared. Once more, a reprieve. Mr Smith had influence it would seem. His daughter was saved from enquiries and the girl went hungry for a few days. There was talk of her being sent to a family to work as a mother's help. Her mother, who'd returned briefly from Norwich, was as icily quiet and tight-lipped as the daughter. The girl tried to speak to the mother of the nights, the fears, the claws and the danger. Of foxes and hands. No words would come to her lips. Their eyes were cast away from each other, both knowing but not saying.

There had been strange people in the house, in the drawing room and the rooms the girls weren't allowed into. There were murmurings, 'She can't stay here' and then shattering silences. It was the Easter holidays. School was over and she was about to become 15. Her birthday was in two weeks time but she could read, so all was not lost.

A welfare officer arrived and the girl was driven to a house in north Lowestoft near the Sparrows Nest where a doctor and his wife lived. The woman had a sweet smile and was holding an 18 month old girl in her arms. She showed her the bathroom and kitchen, the upstairs and a small room with a bed, a chest of drawers and a sink in the corner. Now that was novel, a sink in a bedroom. This was to be home for a few months. The girl was alone with the woman and baby. 'Would you like to help me with dinner?' she said, 'We're having shepherd's pie and carrots. You could peel the carrots.' The doctor husband arrived home. A tall man with laughter wrinkles around his eyes, he wore a tweed jacket with brown leather patches on the elbows and smelled faintly of disinfectant. He took the baby, threw her up in the air and she gurgled and giggled. He said to the girl, 'Are you going to help put the baby to bed?' The family were kind and tried to make her feel at home. She was angry and wouldn't speak. At night there was the haunting nightmare, so vivid it seeped into her days.

A bridge of nightmares: part 1

The Slug Man, pale and grey with a rotting sourness about him, a demonic face and a rasping breath. Like a film on a loop, the horror would never cease. A huge ship was disintegrating in a cacophony of shrieking steel and iron. A crowd of charcoal figures appeared from the bowels, stooped in silent activity on a murky corner of the upper deck. The figures were tall and spiky as if under the light of evening shadows. But for shadow there has to be a sun, a light, and there was none. A flotilla of small dinghies launched into the churning water below and the wind wailed as if in mourning for the dying ship. Stumbling, she edged her way along a slippery passage towards the silent people. A man wearing a white turban and flowing white robes plucked two young children from the midst of the hushed crowd. Holding them tenderly, he climbed over the rail of the pitching ship, slipped into a dinghy and was gone.

FRANK THE PALE MOUSE 'I don't like it here. Wake up wake up.'
She opened her mouth and there was nothing. Her mouth moved but made no sound. The words were lost, whipped away by the wind. She tried to roar and less than a whisper came. Her heavy legs resisted her plea to walk.

A bridge of nightmares: part 2

She made her way along the deck, her heart beating a tattoo in her throat and shapes looming out of the gloom brushing against her face. She felt an inhuman caress from a cluster of cold fingers. A row of clothes hung on a rope across a wide passageway, sodden with icy water. The forgotten clothes of the departed. She looked down at herself, naked, skinless and raw. She tried to pull a greasy wet garment from the line. It slid from her grasp.

THE BOSS 'Wake up, wake up!'

Through an open door lit by the light of an otherworldly moon came a tall thin man in a luminous white suit that hung loosely on his skeletal frame. His skin, an anaemic clammy sheen creased with lines, was transparent and bloodless. He looked like a grotesque arctic slug awakening from a deep sleep of a thousand years.

THE BOSS 'A flick of the switch and I can turn you off. It's not you screaming, those are not your hands, those are not your feet walking. I can switch you off. You're in my dream.'

Opening and closing her eyes she turned to face the wall. Her hands locked around her knees, pulled right up to her chin as she shrank, trying to disappear. And in her mouth were the words she needed to say over and over. The bed was a tumble of damp sheets. She was finally awake and not in that dreadful place. Oh yes, she was awake! She looked out the window. The sky was blue, the birds sang and all sounds outside were the same as yesterday.

Her fifteenth birthday was spent in the new house. She pushed the baby out for walk once a day in the big old navy blue and cream second hand *Pedigree* pram, down to the dunes and the sea, through the gardens at the Sparrows Nest or down to the old High Street. Although she tried to avoid the *International Stores* side, she could see him in the window. White coat, whiter than white and hair oiled as always. Patting butter, slicing hams, wrapping sugar. She wondered if the crabs still lurked in the lavatory at the back of the shop.

Stinging ulcers erupted inside her mouth. On her tongue and then the inside of her cheeks, like piles of poisonous tiny volcanos. Talking and eating were painful as she carried on with her duties. Feeding, bath time and dusting, most of the time daydreaming her way though the days and half the nights until she escaped to the jukeboxes. She met Bridget whenever she could, in cafés and around *Claremont Pier*.

The last adventure with Huggo happened as a chance meeting when she walked into the town on an afternoon off. He was still a biker boy, a rocker on his beloved *Triumph*. It was a glorious afternoon and he said, as before, 'Come on, lets go.' She did, as far as Southend. To the funfair, Southend *Kursaal*, to see George 'Tornado'

Smith on the *Wall-of-Death* where the audience looked down on the riders. Bike exhausts roaring and popping, round and dizzying round the walls of the gargantuan wooden barrel. You could almost touch them, feel the air as they defied gravity. It was the most exciting thing she'd ever seen. Her brush with the world of speed, machines and magic. But once more she would soon be moving on.

Lowestoft was a small town and strangers were noticed. An unusual woman caught her eye. Tall and slim, the woman wore black jeans with a green coat, a wide tie belt, black boots and a leather bag slung casually over one shoulder. Her cropped blonde hair gave her an androgynous look, artfully casual. She was a Swedish au pair and no one else looked like her. The girl followed her down to the town one day and there in a café she watched as the Swedish woman greeted three people. Two men with long hair but not in the teddy boy style. No grease and not engineered in the same way. The other girl had black hair, smooth like a dark river falling down over her shoulders almost reaching her waist. She was dressed in black, wearing high suede boots the colour of damsons. They were art students.

The Doctor's wife had eczema and asthma and they were returning to her home county of Devonshire where her family lived. What about the girl? She was to go to a family in Norwich and would leave in two days time. Leaving Lowestoft and Bridget, the sea, the pier and the jukeboxes. The black and white years slipped into colour. The 1960s were around the next bend. With the world conflict 15 years behind them, the war babies wanted to look forward, not back. Lowestoft in her future mind would always be fisher boys, teddy boys, rock and roll, jukeboxes, Elvis and Buddy, Ray Charles and The Raelets. Forever in the 1950s. The smell of a hot valve radiogram, discs dropping one by one, of frying fat in a back street café. Circle skirts and petticoats, a first cigarette, an awkward kiss behind a bus shelter or under the pier, and Sam Cooke was singing.

'She was only sixteen, only sixteen
With eyes that would glow
But she was too young to fall in love
And I was too young to know
She was too young to fall in love
And I was too young to know'

Well, she was still only 15.

A bridge from childhood to womanhood

Goodbye to the last summer of the 1950s, to childhood and long gone innocence.

Bye-bye Huggo and Bridget.

Bye-bye to the mother who would never ever hear her sing, to the father she would
never meet.
To a hickey, red on a neck or just showing, down on the rise of a girlish breast.
To navy knickers, semolina, ink wells and wooden desks.

Bye-bye to the BBC *Light Programme* in a kitchen on a Saturday morning.
To the North Sea swirling underneath the *Claremont Pier*.

Bye-bye to those in peril on the sea, *Punch and Judy*, 'that's the way to do it.'
To sausages, sandcastles, the illustrated man.
To the three-eyed woman and the humpbacked man, the human dromedary.

The whirlybird, whirligig spinning top girl was on her way to the next place.

VERSE 11

Norwich

It Doesn't Matter Anymore Buddy Holly 1959

1959 to 1960: another town, another job and back again. Families two and three. The end of family and childhood. A bus to Cambridge and another family. Anyone waving goodbye? Etta James, another voice to seek out.

It was a humid day. The girl was hot and worried about where she was going next. A dark blue *Citroen* pulled up outside Norwich station. A short stocky man heaved himself out of the driver's seat. He wore a dark peaked cap and a navy blue blazer, made important looking with gilt buttons. He looked her up and down as she stood holding her bag. She was dressed in her best, a red and white gingham skirt, a white blouse and a red cardigan draped over her shoulders. She wobbled on the white stilettos that were a little worse for wear, curling up at the toes.

'You must be the new girl.' He nodded at the car, indicating she should sit in the back. The heat, the smell of warm leather and petrol and the motion of the low-slung car, together with the speed with which he took the first corner out of the station concourse, churned her guts.

'How old are you then?' he asked, looking at her in the mirror. She swallowed, keeping her eyes on the road as the bile rose in her throat, 'I'm 15,' she whispered. 'What? Can't hear you.' 'I'm 15,' slightly louder. The driver chuckled, 'Of course you are, if you say so,' he said, 'you look like you should be in school. Don't know what Mr and Mrs G are gonna make of you, my girl.' The girl simmered quietly as he began whistling and seemed to forget she was there. She wanted to open the door and leap out. Through the city centre she barely noticed the cathedral or the castle, solid and foursquare on its round hill.

NASTY NELLIE 'Why don't you throw up over neck of the man in the front with the bright buttons? He'll let you out of the car if you do. Then you can run.'

She took a deep breath and hoped for the best. She was so scared. Scared of a new job, a new room, a new boss and a new town but at least she didn't have to endure the playground of a new school.

THE BOSS 'No, no, you mustn't be sick. Breathe and keep your eye on the road'.

CLARA THE CLOWN 'Row, row your boat, gently does it. Don't rock the boat la, la, la.'

NASTY NELLIE 'You'll be in the stream. Life is not a dream, it's a bloody nightmare.'

Driving up a wide tree-lined road and turning left, the tires crunch on gravel in front of a mock Georgian house. With barely a tree to soften its immaculate newness, the house was marooned on a plot of land like a huge toy mansion. The G family had money (the staff always called them Mr and Mrs G). They had gravel pits and construction work, a fleet of trucks, three cars and another house by the sea. She was taken round the back. The big new front door remained shut. Through the back door and a woman who said she was the cleaner showed her to a room next to the children's nursery near a small kitchen, laundry room and playroom. Mr and Mrs G called it 'the nursery wing.' There were two children, a boy of nearly five and a girl aged two and a half. She was given a navy blue dress with a white collar and cardigan to match. A uniform. The dress almost came down to her ankles. She felt dowdy and utterly ridiculous. And worse, she had to wear the flat black lace up shoes presented by Mrs G. 'Those shoes,' said Mrs G, looking at the girl's white high heels, 'those shoes are not suitable for working in. And there will be no blue jeans or make-up.' She passed the black lace ups, 'These should be about your size.' Mrs G herself looked like a princess. Golden skin, long blond hair tied with a bow at the nape of her neck, long smooth legs and perfect pink nails, fingers and toes.

The girl was to be paid once a week and she vowed to buy herself a new top to go with her gingham skirt. She thought about the Swedish girl in Lowestoft, her look and her boots. Maybe she would buy some boots. It wasn't like the doctor's house. She ate her meals with the children during the day and alone in the small children's kitchen at night. She was a servant and was treated like one. They employed a nanny but she was away on leave. A family bereavement they said, and the girl was a temporary replacement. She would possibly be kept on as an assistant to the nanny, if she was good enough. So this was a trial.

Up between six-thirty and seven in the morning, she dressed and washed the children, and prepared breakfast. Woe betide her if any dirt was in evidence when the children were inspected. Hands, necks, ears, knees and feet were always inspected by the mother, never the father. After breakfast, while the mother had the children for an hour or so, the girl cleaned the kitchen, made the beds and tidied the playroom. If the children woke at night she had to deal with them. The father was out most of the time, making money to buy the things for the house that Jack built.

Norwich was a grand place with its ancient castle, magnificent cathedral, market square and busy streets, in stark contrast to scruffy little Lowestoft. She didn't know a soul outside the shiny new house on the treeless hill. Every morning at ten o'clock she took the children for a walk. The boy held her hand or the handle of the pushchair in which the little girl rode and they crunched down the bare drive. No messy nature to spoil the carefully raked gravel. The newly planted trees in their orderly rows must grow to a uniform and orderly height. The lawns, green grass perfect, could have been sprayed onto the ground.

The walk took them onto the big road and over a zebra crossing where she found a market garden. She'd been told how to get to the park but on her first day had got hopelessly lost and was afraid to ask because that would be an admission of her stupidity. When out, she hoisted the uniform dress up and secured it with a thin black belt, knotting the red cardigan around her waist to hide the evidence. This made a bit of difference. At least she didn't look as though she'd stepped out of the 1890s. She pushed the pram down a little path alongside an old brick wall and then past an open fence where she could see the gardeners at work with their wheelbarrows and spades, their skin the shade of copper and their faces creased by the sun. She carried on beside a field of allotments and past some greenhouses. It was a good walk. She could smell the roses, the tomatoes and gooseberries.

After a while, the gardeners began to notice her. They'd smile, wave and shout, 'Wotcha darlin. Those your kids?' she'd giggle. It helped her feel a little less lonely and she liked the idea that they thought the kids were hers. She felt grown up and connected to the rest of the world, the normal world. To have had kids meant she had a man, a family.

On her return one day just before noon she was ready to feed the children and there was Mrs G who helped with the lunch and then settled the children down for their afternoon nap. 'Now,' she said, patting the seat beside her on the blue settee in the playroom, 'come and sit down with me. I know you've not been going to the park but to the gardens, chatting up the men on the greenhouse site.' 'Oh,' the girl began, 'but I didn't...' Mrs G held up her hand, 'look,' she said, with the vowels of a Norfolk girl attempting to sound home counties. 'I know young girls need to meet boys. It's only natural. But Mr G will not like it. You do that on your afternoon off, do you understand? I won't tell him this time. We're supposed to look out for you, you know. So, you go to the park tomorrow, please.' She smiled with her sad princess eyes and the girl glimpsed her sorrow.

Mrs G's mother arrived two weeks later. Every summer the whole family went to the house by the sea. The Gs spent a week there before travelling abroad to France or Italy, leaving grandmother and the nanny to look after the children. The car was packed and there was no driver with gilt buttons this time. Mr G liked to drive when the family went away on holiday. Once again sitting in the back, she struggled not to throw up. This time all over Mr G's neck and down the back of his pastel blue golfing cashmere sweater. She stared out the window, her eyes on the road. If she kept still maybe she could swallow and stop her stomach from churning. Her eyes pricked with tears. The ulcers had returned and she had two on her tongue. The children wriggled and wanted to play. So she was told to read them a story. As she bent over the book, waves of nausea swept up to her mouth and she had no choice, 'Please, I need to stop, I'm going to be sick.'

Mr G complained to his wife who sat beside him with her bare honey skinned arms and green summer dress, 'She's more trouble than the kids and that's saying something. I'm not a charity you know. I don't know why I pay her.' He made a big issue out of changing gears, swerving to overtake another car and swearing under his breath, 'She's a liability, she's useless. Why doesn't she talk properly? She whispers and mumbles. I thought you said she came from a nice family.' On he went for miles, as if the girl was invisible.

They went down country lanes, past a golf course and pulled up outside a house surrounded by soft lawns and pine trees. Just beyond were sand dunes and the sea. There was a sailing club nearby with many boats. Red sails, blue sails, white sails, 'Red sails in the sunset, way out on the sea. Oh, carry my loved one home safely to me,' she thought the whole scene could be from an American film. The grass was green and the air sweet. Tab Hunter was singing. Any minute she would be in his arms and...? A man called Mike arrived to help. Bags were hauled in and there was a discussion with Mr G about the house, roof and garage. They were to build a conservatory and a second garage. And there was new planting to do in the garden. The two men walked around, Mr G gesticulating and Mike listening and taking notes, 'Yes sir no sir.'

NASTY NELLIE 'Three bags full sir?'

Tired, hot and excited children ran about the house looking for buckets and spades, beach balls and swimsuits. The girl's room was next to the kitchen, 'Put your bag in there.' The grandmother gathered the evening meal, 'come and help me dear. There's lots do. And then unpack the children's bags.' Mr and Mrs oh so rich and beautiful went off to the clubhouse for gin and tonic on the terrace, then dinner in the restaurant. Plans for golf or sailing the next day, talk of boats and rigging and the price of property, 'How's business?' Women eyed other women, who was wearing what, 'Did you see those nails? She's not been taking care of herself.' 'I hear so and so is seeing someone.' 'No.' 'Oh yes, his secretary I believe, and years younger.' 'We're getting a new yacht this year.' 'Oh how lovely, and are you still driving the *Rover*?' 'Another G&T, darling?' Clink of ice, tinkle of laughter, eyes always watching.

The girl was made to eat her lunches silently in the kitchen at the red *Formica* topped table, only yards from the family in the dining room, 'Bring in another jug of lemon squash, the children are very thirsty.'

WICKED WILL O'MINA 'Please and thank you wouldn't hurt you'.

She was up and down for this and that. It was utterly humiliating. Treated like she was ridden with the pox, she did break out in a rash all over her chin. The ulcers spread and a cold sore appeared on her lower lip. Two weeks later the parents were gone, leaving grandmother and the girl with the children.

One morning the girl found grandmother cutting the label out from the back of a *Marks and Spencer* dress. Strange. Was she ashamed of *M&S*? Proud of her daughters 'good' marriage to a rich and successful man, a self-made man, a man of charisma and substance, she'd become caught up in a world that hadn't been her own. Her daughter's beauty had moved them up to a society that didn't seem to approve of an *M&S* summer frock. She heard from the grandmother stories of the 'other child, a 'mongol'. The first born boy who'd been sent away to a home for the afflicted. Hidden from the prying and pitying eyes of neighbours, friends on the legal bench or in the council chamber, ladies in hats on a Sunday and people who didn't shop in *Woolworths* or *Marks and Spencer*.

Mr G was 'him almighty.' What he said was sacrosanct and the girl began to despise him. Her ulcers were getting worse and she barely spoke. It hurt to speak and it hurt to eat. Especially fruit and sharp spiky things like toast or *Kellogg's Cornflakes*. The ulcers seemed to join her mind in preventing her mouth from working. She'd decided that no matter what anyone said she wouldn't speak. When the Gs returned to spend the last week of summer in Norfolk, she had a distinct feeling that her days were numbered. And she was right. Saturday morning and there was the mother from Lowestoft in a green *Austin A40*, driven by the oily Major Greengage. Obviously back from Norwich then. 'We'll send her things on from Norwich,' the grandmother said. Mr and Mrs G were out on the sailing boat with friends and the children were having their afternoon nap.

The car journey to Lowestoft was tense, as though a rubber band had been pulled so tight, if it snapped the occupants would've been catapulted to Mars. 'You just can't help yourself, can you,' said the mother, tight-lipped in a blue cotton summer dress covered in little pink sea horses, 'you're determined to ruin my life. I had to leave Norwich because of you.' Not so, the girl would later discover. The mother's contract had ended at the *Theatre Royal*. Back in Lowestoft the mother had gone into the antiques business with the odorous major. 'Yes, because of you, my career is over.' What had she done? It must be her fault. After all, she was so bad that an impious spell had smitten her with ulcers and spots, rendering her speechless.

NASTY NELLIE 'You're infested with the pox. First the crabs and now the spots. And nasty little acid mounds in your mouth.'

In the week after Mrs G had spoken to the mother things had been arranged. The girl was to go to family number three. She was back in the town with two piers and jukeboxes but not to the house in The Avenue. She was to be employed by a Mr and Mrs Carp. Methodists. Devout and strong supporters of Methodist and Victorian values in 1950s Britain. The teenage delinquent girl was to be saved. As a live in home help she was locked in her bedroom at night, 'to save you from temptation and evil,' they said.

WICKED WILL O'MINA 'The Lord's my Shepherd, I shall not want. Want? Who's to provide?'

A chorus of voices proclaimed,

'Why, the Lord, the Lord God Almighty.'

NASTY NELLIE 'Come on then, Lord God, show me your face.'

The bedroom was little more than a box room, overlooking a garden with privet hedges, a neat rectangle of lawn and two flower beds, one each side in perfect symmetry. A monkey puzzle tree stood to attention at the end, next to the potting shed. The girl thought it a particularly boring garden. As orderly as the house it belonged to, it had no surprises. No rampant shrub or blowsy rose bush, no daisies in the grass or dog shit on the path.

The girl's room was furnished with a single bed covered with a pale blue and thinning candlewick bedspread, a wardrobe, a bedside table and a blue rug on the brown linoleum floor. Which was just as well as the floor in the early morning was freezing underneath her bare feet. The door was unlocked at six o'clock in the morning. At six-fifteen on the dot, Mr Carp knocked and threw it open, 'You may use the bathroom for ten minutes.' He was a man with thinning hair swept over his shining slightly pink dome of a head. He had thick pendulous ears, big hare's teeth and a very red nose. He was a banking man, a man of pinstriped suits and waistcoats. And don't you forget it.

The man and his important brief case went out the front door at eight in the morning and returned at five forty-five in the evening, five days a week. Greeting his wife with a peck on her powdered cheek, he carefully placed his jacket on the back of his chair and then washed his hands. He read his newspaper whilst listening to the six o'clock news on the radio and food was always on the table at the appointed time of six forty-five. Chops on Tuesday after Monday's cottage pie that had been made with minced Sunday beef, and fish on Friday. Hell's fire. If the routine wasn't followed it was the end of his orderly world. He once said he would never trust a man who wore suede shoes and that women should be in the home, not in the world of work.

The rubber plants that stood on the first floor landing and in the sitting room bay window were lovingly wiped leaf by leaf once a week with a cloth dipped in milk. The pristine white linen antimacassars on the backs of the settee and armchairs had little dark patches. Traces of where Mr Carp's head had rested as he nodded off over his *Daily Telegraph* in front of the fireplace. The girl doubted a fire had ever burned merrily there with its black grate and polished mantle piece gleaming and dust free. When not is use, the newspaper was kept folded crisply on the coffee table.

Mr Carp was a man who'd look down his nose at any speck of dust that offended his adherence to a spotless house and home, to order and attention to detail. In that sense Mr and Mr Carp were not so dissimilar to Mr and Mrs G, though the girl doubted Mr G would give the Lowestof banker the time of day in his semi-detached house on a main road. He would've mocked the floral wallpaper and the perfectly polished brasses.

The Carps had two children. Photos of a young man were displayed on the mantelpiece. He had a severe haircut, protruding teeth and large ears just like his father. An unfortunate combination. He was in the Midlands with relatives, working in a small hotel for the summer. 'He'll be gaining vital business experience,' Mr Carp said, rubbing his hands with satisfaction. The good son would back at the end of August. Cast in the mould of the good father, he was bred to be the head of a family, the man in charge who controlled all signs of female rebellion.

The daughter had finished school and was going to secretarial college in the autumn. She had neatly cut brown hair cut and a long thin nose that protruded over a thin lipped mouth. She wore the same sort of clothes as her mother. Neat nylon blouses with peter pan collars and neat skirts, all a respectable mid-calf length with sensible shoes. She had little heels for dates with the boyfriend and church on Sundays and flat slip-on shoes for everyday. The daughter gave the impression of a woman far older than her years. Almost the boy next door, the boyfriend also had the brutal Carp haircut. He wore his thick glasses, tweed jacket and grey slacks with an air of satisfaction, a celebration of normal-ness.

The parents could barely conceal their pride. Their children had done so well and a place in heaven was guaranteed. 'Of course, my daughter will not work for long once she's married.' Mr Carp smiled his big toothy smile, barely causing a ripple beyond his mouth, his face set in stone. 'These modern girls,' he said, attempting a jocular tone, 'they think they can live as men do but they soon see reason when they're pregnant. A working wife, ha. Working once married?' The very idea. A woman's place.

The girl began her work at seven in the morning precisely. She had half a day off a week and one weekend a month. She was chaperoned to the library and to the shop for personal purchases by her saintliness, Mrs Carp. Mummified with boredom, the girl read, waited, watched and wished for freedom. She felt she was in prison and would never escape. This was it. She felt herself getting smaller and smaller.

Nasty Nellie 'You're a pale grey mouse. All you can do is squeak, squeak. And you'll dust and clean until your whiskers refuse to twitch. There's nothing to twitch for. You'll die with a duster in one paw and a tea towel in the other. Forever the mouse in the hole down in the skirting board. Out of sight.'

One day when out shopping with Mrs Carp, carrying two string bags with vegetables and meat for the evening meal, they saw the girl's mother. So her mother had been just around the corner all the time she'd been living with Mr and Mrs Carp. She had no idea she was so close. She'd assumed her mother was living in Norwich. Wearing a full-skirted red dress covered in white polka dots, a white straw hat and white high heels with a matching handbag, her mother stood there and chatted about this and that. The weather and the lateness of the buses. Then that was it. She was gone, red skirts swishing. It was like she had no daughter and she was a passing acquaintance.

Mrs Carp, with her sensible grey skirt, pale lemon twinset, brown court shoes and brown hair permed once a fortnight at the hairdressers by the bus terminus, seemed drab beside the girl's mother. She felt a hesitant pride in her mother's bright beauty as she herself stood awkwardly blushing and shifting from foot to foot as they exchanged pleasantries.

Afterwards Mrs Carp said, 'Your mother is to be in the new production at the *Arcadia*, the pantomime.' Sniffing disdainfully, she ushered the girl on like a child. She obviously didn't approve of 'show business people' for they were ungodly. The girl felt a hot flush on her face as she dragged her feet back to the house, back to uninterrupted boredom and endless dusting.

MISERY IVY 'I'd rather be a tramp like Puggy Uttin in the rain and the wind. I don't care. I just want to be anywhere but here.'

She really had no idea where she'd like to be and retreated into books, imaginings and dreams. The ulcers healed but her heart did not. She'd wanted her mother to love her. She'd wanted her mother to care, to believe in her.

NASTY NELLIE 'Three blind mice. See how they run. Cut off your tail with a carving knife and pull out your squeak with a spoon.'

The wireless, 'Hey, you down there with the glasses, ta da da da dah. It's *The Billy Cotton Band Show*!'

NASTY NELLIE 'She's hiding in a subterranean lavatory. Pull the chain and wash her away.'

Christmas that year was spent with a family that prayed before and after meals and took life and discipline very seriously.

The time with the Carp family had come to an end. Now she would leave and not return for many years to the town, the smell of fish, the sea and the first sunrises in the land. The mother had contacted Beryl, whom the girl hadn't seen since the move to Lowestoft. The grandfather, Percy Brimblecombe had died and Beryl had given up being a school teacher. She was now a social worker and as such would know what to do with the girl, who was then sent to a small village outside Cambridge to again live in as a mothers help. This time it was with a fellow of Sidney Sussex College, his wife, their two sons aged four and two and a baby girl. They were relatives on Beryl's side.

'This is going to be weird,' she said to herself. These people had a family connection, though she barely remembered who they were and how they were connected. They'll be posh, she thought. And they'll be clever. He's a professor and I bet their kids are brainy too. So thought the girl whose own mother had an accent you could cut glass with and acted like the bloody queen.

WICKED WILL O'MINA 'Kiss my hand and curtsey, don't you know.'

It was January 1960 and in four months she would be 16, nobody's sweet 16. A new year, a new decade and a new town. Goodbye Lowestoft.

CLARA THE CLOWN 'Good bye Muddah. Goodbye Fadduh. We will not be in Cape Granada.'

She felt the tears welling up as the coach turned out of Lowestoft bus station and chugged down the main road. Out of town, past the cinema and the station, a last glimpse of the sea, over the bridge, boats bobbing in the harbour, the *Harbour Hotel* sitting square on the corner opposite the South Pier. And would she, the one who'd laughed at her tits, who stole her tips and who smoked so much her fingers turned the colour of old brass, would she be on the silver cleaning? Or was there another young girl rubbing the spoons, learning the ways of survival from an old hand? There were people on the street. Lowestoft faces she recognised even if they'd never spoken. They carried on with their day as usual, as she was leaving forever. She knew that. This was the end of family and childhood and she had no idea what she was going to.

She sat with her head pressed against the glass of the window. Would she see her mother wrapped up in her winter furs or her sister in her grammar school uniform? She swallowed, willing herself not to cry, angrily brushing away the tears that dripped down the sides of her nose. Who was she crying for? Certainly no one cried for her. No mother waving a handkerchief, no sisters hanging on to her arm, no father there to press a half crown into her hand. She was gone and good riddance as the coach disappeared in a cloud of black smoke.

It was as if she'd never lived there, never inhaled the north sea air into her London lungs, never talked with a Suffolk lilt or found her place beside a jukebox, digging the music. It was as if she'd never been part of it or them. Not had sisters or a mother or a place in this town. She'd leave with barely an imprint. It was as if the Lowestoft years were nothing but a very strange dream. A dream with a rock and roll heart, blue jeans and motor bikes, florescent pink socks and white stilettos. She heard Etta James sing *At Last* that year. Such a voice, another voice to seek out when she needed to feel, to dream, to pray. But who would she pray to?

'At last my love has come along
My lonely days are over and life is like a song...
I found a dream that I could speak to
A dream that I can call my own.'

The mouse went forth to Cambridge, her whiskers limp, her stringy tail behind her, 'Squeak.' Clara the Clown cackling, Misery Ivy blithering on whilst The Boss tried to get a word in edgeways, up-ways and down-ways with no luck at all. And Buddy Holly sang...

'Now you go your way Baby and I'll go mine.
Now and forever till the end of time.
And I'll find somebody new and baby we'll say we're through.
You won't matter anymore. You won't matter anymore.'

Cambridge

Lift to the Scaffold Miles Davis 1958

1960 to 1961: the head of Oliver Cromwell, Wimpy Bars, reefers and Miles Davis. A desire for funky boots and big black jumpers.

Suffolk span out past her eyes. From Framlingham on to Bury St. Edmunds, past old stone churches, Suffolk pink washed cottages and windmills. The *Sunrise Coast* and the *Broads* gave way to Newmarket and on into Cambridgeshire. Her Mouse whiskers rose to greet the new city. The coach pulled into the bus station next to a green called *Christ's Pieces*. The Carps were on her tail, their pious prayers still a sting in her ears as she found the right stop for the local bus out on to the Cambridge Road, passing through Barton, Little Eversden and finally to Great Eversden.

It was a strange place, not the Lowestoft or Weymouth of seaside and harbour, or the red brick chimney pots, red buses and swirling smog of London. This was a land of flat brown furrowed fields, stubby green hedges and trees, branches leaf-naked, moving gracefully like darkly beautiful dancers under the pale grey January skies. It looked like it was going to rain. She, the aunt who was not really an aunt, met her where the bus stopped beside a telephone box and a puddle at the end of a narrow lane.

The aunt was pushing a pram and wearing muddy wellington boots, a woollen green and brown checked scarf tied under her chin and a muddy waxed jacket. 'I'm so sorry not to have come into Cambridge to meet you,' she said, 'but the children, you know.' She continued talking as they walked, her voice a slow and nasal drawl. The girl could barely understand her. The aunt talked about her husband. And then about Beryl who was the aunt of the man who was to be called uncle. 'Who, as you know,' she said, 'isn't really your grandmother. So we're not really related. My husband is not actually your uncle.' The girl didn't know what her reply should be, so she peered into the grey and white pram and saw a pink baby wearing a pink and white knitted bonnet, quietly asleep and smelling of milk and baby talc. Half sisters, headless siblings, step grandmothers, uncles who are not uncles. The girl's head was spinning.

NASTY NELLIE 'I am the devil incarnate.'

She smiled sweetly at the sleeping baby as a beast rose up inside her, snarling and spitting flames. She had heard Mr Carp use the word 'incarnate.' It sounded weird she thought, weird and really bad.

NASTY NELLIE 'Yes, and I eat babies and sick up shit. So it's good that I'm not really a relative. Think how awful that would be. To be related to a shit spewing devil incarnate.'

She looked at the 'not really an aunt' from under her lashes. 'The boys will be home from school very soon, isn't that nice. We'll all have tea together.' The girl remembered the boy in Weymouth as he walked in the crocodile. She remembered the childrens' jeers ringing in his ears, the tears of shame on his cheeks as the shit ran down his leg.

NASTY NELLIE 'Yes, I'm the devil incarnate and I spew shit.'

FRANK THE PALE MOUSE 'You are? You do?'

NASTY NELLIE 'Yes, pathetic mouse. I'm the devil. Better a mouse than a pig with piggy little eyes!'

Her mother's laugh rang in her head. A head crowded with accusations and contradictions. And she could still feel the motion of the bus. It helped to walk and breath the fresh and damp earthy air. Her head cleared. They passed a congregational chapel with a small graveyard, hedges and ditches, a row of small cottages, one, two, three and a field with wet cows huddled under a tree. The family lived at the other end of the lane in a white house with a thatched roof, almost hidden behind two old beech trees. Snarled ivy crawled over the old brick walls bordering a garden that seemed to reach as far as the eye could see from a bedroom window. Moles lived under the lawn, making hillocks of freshly burrowed earth in the morning where rabbits played in the dew. Rooks gathered in the trees that swayed over the roof.

It was a house of books, nooks and crannies. There were papers on every surface, intricately patterned Turkish rugs, large comfortable and well used armchairs covered in rust and blue flowered chintz, old paintings in gilt frames on the walls, a well polished dark oak dining room table with six matching chairs, a low beamed kitchen, a kettle just under the boil on a kitchen range, steep stairs that creaked underfoot and bedrooms with floors that sloped gently as if you were on board a ship on a calm sea, on a calm day.

An extension had been built overlooking the garden. On the upper floor there was a small bathroom and a bedroom where the two boys slept. Just before the new rooms where the old end wall had been, there was a narrow staircase leading up to a small room with no door underneath the eaves and a casement window that looked onto the garden. This room contained a long shelf full of books above a bed covered with a dark blue satin eiderdown. Feathers! Oh yes, she could pick away up here, pick and pluck. Among the dusty brown, dark red and blue hardback covers, an Agatha Christie or two, a row of *The Famous Five*, *Down and Out In Paris and London*, a small pile of *Readers Digest*, some orange *Penguin* paper backs, five *Just William* stories, *The Outsider*, Camus, and an old well-thumbed dictionary.

In the boys room she found *The Wind in The Willows*, *Alice in Wonderland* and the *Eagle* and *Rupert the Bear* annuals. She dipped into the tranquil pre-war world of William and his sister Ethel and laughed loudly at Violet Elizabeth, Ginger, Henry and Douglas. Inside the fourth and fifth pages of *Down and Out in Paris and London* she found a dog-eared bookmark, a postcard of Leonardo da Vinci's *The Virgin of the Rocks*. She fell in love with the painting and vowed to find it, to see the real thing. She loved the Madonna's face and wanted to be in the picture, beyond the rocks where the sky was blue.

The girl decided 'The Road' was indeed a place to consider and as soon as possible she'd go to Paris or London. She also fell in love with Albert Camus and decided she'd become a writer or a poet or... Her head was full of the most glorious fantasies, all out of reach and away from the laughter of those who called her stupid. She'd never been to a gallery and there had been few books in the various homes she'd lived in, aside from those in the Lewisham children's home. Arthur, or was it John, had books about maths and a collection of art books from his days at the Slade. She was finally in a place of reflection after so many choatic years and though not entirely at ease, she felt peaceful.

She read about the Chinese taking Tibet. She read the *Penguin* paperbacks, *Tortilla Flat* and *The Outsider*, the Selected Verse of Baudelaire in French with English translations. And she disappeared into the world of *David Copperfield*, enjoying the references to Yarmouth and London. She'd read something familiar at school or rather listened to girls and boys stumbling over long words and speaking in that monosyllabic way children do when forced to read aloud. Then she thought it a boring tale but now in the little room under the eaves she found it enchanting. Finally, an education in a Cambridgeshire cottage.

The more she read, the more words she had in her head for her own voice. A voice that grew from a whisper to something audible. And the nasty little ulcers were gone. This was when her brain began to tick tock. What's out there, what's fair and what's not. She was in a place of reflection after 15 years of chaotic childhood and though not entirely at ease, she was peaceful. The rest of her life could wait until she caught up with wherever it may be. London seemed so far away now but it still seemed right to call it 'home.'

The first few weeks of her being with two people she'd been told she could call 'auntie and uncle' were strange. Here she was, employed, paid on Saturday morning after breakfast, yet neither kith nor kin, living in as a mother's help. The boys had pocket money. And the girl? She hadn't much more for the next nine months, with a free Wednesday afternoon and every other Saturday off. The days were spent in the by now familiar routine of dusting, cleaning, ironing and generally doing this and that until three in the afternoon when she collected the boys from the village school. The hours betwen then and seven were a blur of food and more food, homework, washing, inspecting ears and nails, *Horlicks* or chocolate and a bedtime story. All for the two little boys who weren't really her cousins.

The girl wanted to find friends but not in the village. There they looked at her strangely when she walked into the shop. They spoke with the local dialect or the superior vowels of the noble aunt. She did not. Her odd mix of London, Weymouth, Lowestoft and plain old middle class England didn't seem to belong anywhere she'd been so far. She was once more a stranger.

The people who said 'hello' to the aunt and the boys all appeared to be very old or married with children. University people living in the country just outside Cambridge. And there was a Mrs C who 'did for them' once a week a big laundry wash, the hoovering and the polishing. Mrs C was herself from the village and had the Cambridgeshire accent. She also had wobbly dentures and wore a flowery headscarf around her curlers from Monday 'til Thursday afternoon, when she had her hair done in the village. Her husband was retired from the local police force, her son worked at *Philips Electronics* and her daughter was married, living in a village not far away. Mrs C had a contagious laugh that made her ruddy country cheeks shake. It was like catching a cold. You couldn't help yourself.

The girl was off the leash and not in prison like she'd been at the Carp's house. The so-called aunt was actually very nice if you got past the posh voice. The boys were mostly well behaved and books were everywhere. But she must get to Cambridge, to young people and to life. Where was the music? And was the head of

Oliver Cromwell buried beneath the chapel floor in Sidney Sussex College? The talk in the white house at the end of the lane, in the village shop and presumably the pub was all of Oliver Cromwell. His head was in a wooden box. Did she see it in that house? It was all dramatically lodged in her mind. Perhaps she did.

The day the head was buried the uncle and aunt went off to the ceremony dressed in their very best. The girl and Mrs C stayed at home with the children. She'd dreamt about the head. Shrunken brown skin, warts, hairs and all, now resting somewhere at the college, unmarked with no body attached and in peace.

On Wednesday afternoons she would take the bus through the villages and fields to Cambridge where she would walk until she knew almost every inch of every pavement. Crossing roads, dodging bicycles, peering into coffee bars and interesting windows, maybe this would be the place. Trinity Street and King's Parade, Petty Cury, Rose Crescent and the Market Square. Along the *Backs* and over the bridges. The *Bridge of Sighs*, colleges, chapels, meadows and gardens. Looking, walking and thinking this must be the most beautiful city in the world. One day she dared to slip into *The Copper Kettle* on King's Parade and order tea with a slice of rich truffle cake. It made a dent in her wages but she wanted to taste the place and not just walk the streets looking in from the outside. She walked into *Heffers*, the book shop on Petty Cury, with her eyes open and nose twitching. It was a paradise and the books smelled delicious.

She was searching for who knows what. Where was she in all this? She was neither town nor gown in this city of wealth and ancient learning. She decided she'd become a *Beatnik*, walk barefoot, grow her hair and read poetry in cafés, in the hope that some interesting young man would talk with her.

In April she joined a dressmaking class in the community college and made a friend. A girl who took her to the *Young Liberals Club* one evening. That didn't feel right. She was looking for 'beats' and jazz. They went a jazz club in *The Anchor* pub where students wore big sweaters and college scarves, and girls had clear skin, good teeth, healthy hair and bright clever smiles. Kenny Ball and Acker Bilk, warm beer, flying arms and legs stomping. That's what they all did. She wanted to listen to Ray Charles. The best night was when The Monty Sunshine Band played with Beryl Bryden, singing *Dr Jazz*, strumming on a washboard with Jerry Salisbury playing the hell out of a tuba. She'd never heard a tuba. What a big fat warm plum of a sound. This was the first woman she'd seen singing and swinging her butt and that was good, so very, very good.

One day in the *Wimpy Bar* near the bus station a young man asked the girl if she was French. Afterwards she thought about this and decided that appearing so would make her more appealing, even exotic, like Brigitte Bardot and Jeanne Moreau. A black beret, a smooth sheet of hair down her back, she'd write poetry and be enigmatic. 'Ooh delicious,' she thought, as she sat in a coffee bar on Sidney Street with a book on her lap. A young man asked her to pass the sugar. She passed the bowl and he enquired, 'Where are you from, you don't look English?' 'I am from France,' she said, in a voice she imagined sounded French. 'Ah' he said, looking interested, as if being French meant immediate romance, 'where in France?' 'Paris,' she said as Lying Lizzie whispered in her ear. It was the only place she could think of. It hadn't occured to her that all these clever university people might speak the bloody language. In a rash moment of wanting to appear interesting, she'd not thought it through. Fool. She took flight and her attempt at being French was a disaster.

She returned on the bus to Great Eversden, to the children, the dusting and the books. In all the schools she'd attended she learned very little and certainly no other language but her own. As she'd arrived at each school they'd just done or had not got to this or that and were halfway through books. But she could read. She sat in the back of classes of 30 or more and let the proceedings pass her by. If quiet she could stay unnoticed, so busy were the teachers. Too many faces, too many names and new girls were an irritant, disturbing the daily flow and the all important routine.

One Wednesday evening in May, just after the Easter holidays, the girl and her new friend went to the *Modern Jazz Club* where a young sax player, Dick Heckstall-Smith was leading his university jazz band. The signature tune was Duke Ellington's *Satin Doll*. The pulse of the bass made her heart pump. Standing next to her whilst her friend had disappeared to the bar, was a guy with a beard, wearing a black polo neck and scarf. They all wore the scarf and she wondered if he was sweating. It was hot, really hot. Clicking his fingers and going with the beat, he grinned at her and said, 'hi.' She said, 'hi,' and grinned back.

She'd given up on the fake French accent for the time being. He seemed nice. He asked her about jazz and she wasn't sure whether to mention the other club where she'd seen Monty Sunshine and Beryl Bryden. It seemed the two clubs were in opposition, the cool modern jazz versus the trad stompers. Ah well, she told him how much she loved the singing and the tuba. After that she realised she knew nothing. She asked him if he liked Ray Charles. He seemed surprised, 'Yes,' he said, 'and what about?' He launched into a long oratory about music she'd never heard of, names that meant nothing to her. It all went over her head. He was nice though and asked her out. She said she lived in the country and could be in Cambridge the following Wednesday. And then she felt stupid, as if not in control of her own life. As if she were still at school. He had asked her out on a date. He said he was up at 'Emmanuel' and she assumed this was one of the colleges. 'Next Wednesday ok?' he asked, arranging to meet her in the *Wimpy Bar*. It was near the bus station.She liked the tomato soup and now and then, a burger and fries. Britain was in the grip of the new American style food. *Wimpy Bars* were cool.

He took her to his rooms in college. It was in the middle of the afternoon, a chaste time of day. She kept thinking they'd be stopped. Surely she wasn't allowed here. They went up a stone staircase and into his room. A desk, a bed, bookcases and books everywhere, an ashtray, mugs, a kettle, a record player and records piled on a table. He put on *Lift to The Scaffold* and rolled a cigarette. 'You smoke?' he asked, drawing deeply before passing it over to her. 'Thank you,' she said, sitting on a cushion on a floor cushion. She pulled the smoke into her lungs. It was her first reefer. Within moments she felt giddy and giggly. She oughed and couldn't stop, feeling stupid. She was worried she might wet herself. He simply sat and listened to Miles with a smile on his face. His eyes dipped low and he was gone. A hip cat.

The sound of the trumpet touched her, the muted tone like a cry or caress. A silvery moonlight tone whispering in her ear, brushing against her skin. She wanted to swallow it, to have it inside her, so she could regurgitate it, listen whenever she wanted. It made her want to cry. She didn't see the student again but he'd given her Miles Davis. She didn't have a record player and was determined she'd get one somehow, beg, borrow or steal.

In the big sitting room of the uncle and aunt was a radiogram. A talking, reading, walking sort of family, they hardly played music. Occasionally they switched on the radio for the news or a quiz show. It was a quiet, polite and bookish home.

On Saturday the girl went into Cambridge with her friend from the sewing class. They saw new Hitchcock film *Psycho*, had a coffee and got the bus home. Her friend alighted several stops before Great Eversden, leaving her as one of two passengers getting off at her stop. The other walked swiftly in the opposite direction. The bus hovered at the end of the lane, engine chugging and lights illuminating the lane as she walked towards the house. It was a friendly sound and a welcome light. The bus then turned to leave. As the front lights swept the trees and the chapel, the tail lights glowed red like devil's eyes. Turning left on the last journey of the night, the bus headed back to Cambridge. The engine noise grew fainter and fainter, and then silence. Darkness and silence.

The girl walked a few yards down the lane and, 'eeech, eeech, eeech', the screech of those *Psycho* fiddles, the violins and the stabbing. 'Oh God, oh help.' Walking past the chapel, the little cottages and open fields, she heard a rustle in the trees, a hooting owl, and a scuttle across the dark lane. Was it a rat, a fox or maybe a ghost? Or maybe a mad man with a knife, or a body-less head. This countryside wasn't as silent as she'd imagined. She ran, slowly at first and then like the clappers, her heart banging in her throat. In the gate, up the path, loose strands of ivy brushing her face, she opened the kitchen door and stood in a pool of fear. Thank you Alfred Hitchcock.

What to do with the girl now? She was to be dispatched to Beryl in Kent who had arranged a place in a *Dr Barnardos* home. If good enough she'd be trained as a nanny. A nanny?

WICKED WILL O'MINA 'What else are you going to do?'

Music. 'I love music, I want to sing.' But she'd have to wait a lot longer for that. She wasn't yet free, was still known as 'Freeman' and had no idea if a voice would actually emerge in a sonorous and musical way, even if a miracle did come along. Tug Boat Annie.

VERSE 13

The Knot Unravelled

Love me do The Beatles 1962

1961 to 1962: life as a 'blue' and meeting Jenny and Nina. Fred, CND, Thelonious Monk and Brubeck. Pleasing no one. A missile crisis. Onwards to the city, calling in at Hastings. 2005: performing STAND with The Shout, looking back to a march in Easter 1963. Ban the Bomb.

She arrived at *St Christopher's*, a *Dr Barnardos* home in Tunbridge Wells, Kent. The name 'Freeman' was still attached to her. Within the home was a training college for nursery nurses and nannies. If you were poor or had no one willing to pay the fees, you worked for a year as payment for the course, earning five pounds a month for essentials like toothpaste, sanitary towels, soap and maybe the odd record or a night at the pictures. You didn't get to the pictures very much. You wore a blue uniform. Those that could pay their fees wore pink.

Dressed in blue you waited on the staff, matron, the house mothers and all the girls in pink. For the pinks it was a two year or 18 month fast track course. It was the same for girls who'd previously taken a *Cordon Bleu* course or something similar. The course was regarded as good training for the daughters of the home counties, girls who weren't academic. It was preparation for marriage to a nice young man. Maybe a doctor, a dentist, or someone with a promising career in the city. Those girls would make good little wives, skilled in the arts of homemaking and raising a family.

The blues slept three or four to a room in converted *Nissan* huts close to the main house. The pinks had single or double rooms in a large Victorian house in the wooded grounds. The blues did the dirty jobs and the night shifts, with less time off for visits to home or for a social life. Not that the girl could go home. This was now her home. The blues washed floors, cleaned lavatories and worked in the sluice rooms and the laundry where mounds of terry towelling and muslin nappies were washed and disinfected. Young hands became crinkled like old parchment. The blues were first up, rising at five-thirty and in the kitchens for six, preparing and serving breakfast at seven-thirty for rows of girls in the pink, with their white starched collars, cuffs and caps.

The blues then bent over the sinks, washing up. Huge wire draining trays stacked full of clean crockery and cutlery were lowered into hot water for rinsing and then stacked onto shelves, ready for the next meal. Hair clung to foreheads in the steam and sweat dripped down their bodies under the uniform. When the first year was done the blues continued doing the worst jobs along with the training. The girls in pink talked of fiancés and holidays, mummies and daddies. They had brothers and sisters who wrote to them. They had bank accounts and an allowance. They had piano or violin grades and spent holidays abroad. They were pink flamingos with diamond rings in their sights, fluttering in their starched collars and cuffs that were always somehow more snowy white and crisp than the girls in blue. The girl who'd come via London, Weymouth, London again, Lowestoft, Norwich and Cambridge, liked to think about *Down and Out in Paris and London.*

'*A French cook will spit in the soup, that is if he is not going to drink it himself. He is an artist, but his art is not cleanliness.*'

WICKED WILL O'MINA 'Spit in the soup, go on, I dare you.'

NASTY NELLIE 'Go on, you're running around like blue-arsed fly. Why? Spit in it, gob in the soup.'

THE BOSS 'I beg to differ. Gird your loins girl, get on with it.'

FRANK THE PALE MOUSE 'Oh no, mustn't do that. That's awful.'

The girl was secretly in awe of the girls in pink, they were somehow made holy.

NASTY NELLIE 'You need to take few tips from Mighty Mouse. Even Micky's got more guts than you.'

Her head was elsewhere for a moment, enjoying her own little drama. Whoops she dropped a plate. She'd better pay attention. She didn't spit in the porridge, although she'd dearly like to.

The infants were housed in a nursery in the main house. The children grouped in smaller houses in the grounds under the rule of a housemother and her team of blues and pinks. A day in the kitchen peeling mountains of carrots and potatoes was a good shift with Mrs M from Plymouth. As round as her steam puddings, she waddled across her kitchen kingdom, treating blues and pinks almost alike, having a thinly disguised affection for the blues. Childless herself, her love was bottomless. She would've been a lovely mother. 'Come on my lover, lets 'ave them apples, watch me closely now.' She crumbled flour, butter and sugar with her plump dimpled hands in a massive mixing bowl. *Marmite* slices for breakfast on Thursdays. Oh, how the girl loved Thursdays. Whip up many eggs with a very big whisk, slop, slap, slop, then spread margarine followed by *Marmite* onto slices of bread. Make into sandwiches, cut into halves, dip into the egg mix and fry. Scrumptious. She could easily eat three or four rounds in one sitting. *Marmite* was on her best things to eat list, and *Cadburys* chocolate. The pinks on their sessions with Mrs M would order the blues to, 'Pass me that spoon, wash that dish and sweep up the broken plate.'

NASTY NELLIE 'You broke it bitch, you sweep it up.'

'Hurry up, I'm waiting for that spoon.'

WICKED WILL O'MINA 'Yea, yea, yea, here it is. Catch it. Whoops, dropped it on your foot, so sorry.'

She handed over the spoon which didn't really drop. With a sweet smile and wicked thoughts. Oops.

WICKED WILL O'MINA 'I'll sweep up the broken crockery and then I'll poke your eyes out with the broom handle.'

FRANK THE PALE MOUSE 'Oh so, so sorry. So sorry.'

In spite of the Nasty one, and the Wicked one, her default opinion was that the pinks 'are better than I'. More worthy, more clever, more beautiful, deserving and infinitely more superior. Therefore, they are to be obeyed. Mrs M winked and rolled her eyes. She knew. She had eyes, ears and a big heart. Could she read the girl's mind? She wondered. No, not possible.

Once a blue, always a blue. It stuck to you like a bad odour. It was the early 1960s and life was still not a good place for a young woman considered pretty worthless. The girl felt attached to an invisible rope, forever tethered to an invisible master. Pulled here and there with never a discussion about what she wanted to do with her life. She was a prisoner, seemingly with no feelings because the questions, 'How do you feel?' And, 'What would you like to do?' Were never asked of her.

A girl called Jenny arrived six months later from a *Dr Barnardos* home in North Wales and things looked up. She was dark eyed, dark haired and had an indecipherable accent. She was Jenny from everywhere and nowhere. Then the extraordinary Nina arrived in the second year. A pink but not like the other pinks. She was a Jewish girl with alabaster skin, dark curly hair which she always wore short, and an outrageous laugh. She had full lips, laughing red lipstick and was never seen without it despite being repeatedly told by the matron to remove it. Nina rebelled. The lipstick was wiped off and around the next corner it was on again. Red lipped and defiant. The girl looked on and was impressed. Nina had the pizzazz of Bridget from Lowestoft.

Nina told the girl one day, while hanging out after the other pinks and staff had left the dining room, that she'd been raised in Canada, at least for a few years. Her parents, German Jews, had died and Nina was dispatched in the early 1950s to an Aunt and Uncle in Surrey, who did their duty, rather like Beryl did with Cecilie and then the girl. Nina was without a mother or father in the great world and with only her Jewish-ness serving her identity. With that and the red lips, the red flag of Nina-ness, she seemed to be fuelled by some sort of invisible restless energy and intransigent spirit. She usually didn't notice the pink and the blue, and when she did, she cared not at all. Her aunt and uncle kept a strict kosher house. What to do with the parent-less girl from Canada? Nina cared not a fig for religion.

'Do you want to come to London with me on your half day off?' she asked the girl in blue one day. The girl explained the system. The next week on her half-day they went into Tunbridge Wells and sat in a café and talked. Nina really wanted a friend to scuttle up to London with. Hungry for more than sedate Tunbridge Wells, she wanted the excitement of the big city. Fearless, she'd go out onto the road and stick out her thumb, hitching a lift to the West End, to Soho and the clubs. She went alone if no one else would go with her. 'Are you coming? No? I'm off, bye.' In the clubs she'd dance her strange dance and men loved her. Nina, the girl with luscious red lips and gurgling giggles.

Whenever she could the girl would spend an hour or two in the town sitting in a coffee bar. She'd watch the art students with their black clothes, long hair and paint stained hands and fingernails. It was like watching a tribe. A tribe she wasn't related to but would like to be. What was it, she wondered. Why were they so enthralling?

One day, as she worked in one of the family houses, she watched in horror the housemother beating a child on his bare bottom as he stood in the bath. Terrified of the brutal hair washing tactics, water cascading down his face, the child's little chest heaved as he sobbed. The more he sobbed the more she struck him. The girl screamed. It was the loudest sound she'd made in many years, 'Stop, stop that, you stop it. I'll... I'll.' She held up a walking stick, the one leaning against the wall by the front door. What she'd actually do with it she didn't know.

Suddenly there were other people in the house. The two pinks must've raised the alarm. The boy, wrapped in a blanket and the girl, still holding the stick, were ushered away. She didn't hear the words and was once again silent. Her silence was mistaken for sullenness and the girl thought that would be that. Thought she'd be sent away in disgrace once more. But it wasn't to be. She'd threatened the woman but there was no punishment.

Questioned the next day, she whispered of what she'd seen. That the woman was cruel and unkind, even to the smallest children. The whispers spread around all the houses, in and out of dining rooms, the nurseries and the dormitories. And the offending woman was gone. The girl remained on kitchen duty for the rest of the week with the lovely Mrs M and her crumbles, sausages and mounds of mashed potatoes. Her voice remained lowered once more to a near whisper.

The girl was now a student and had a single room the size of a shoebox in the *Nissan* huts with a single bed and a small cupboard. The showers and lavatories were down a long corridor. One day in the coffee bar near the station in Tunbridge Wells, a man with a red beard and unruly red hair approached her, 'Anyone sitting here?' he asked, pulling out the chair opposite the girl, 'Cat got yer tongue?' He chuckled heartily and his eyes smiled, 'What are you thinking, sitting here on your own so long? Every time I see you, you sit and say nothing. Why? Don't you like the human race? Can't say I blame you.' That was the beginning of having a socialist boyfriend. He belonged to CND and had dropped out of art school. 'Got no time for the bourgeoisie,' he said, 'art is dead. Long live the proletariat.' The girl had no idea what he was talking about. 'Want to come to my place? Don't worry,' he said, 'I live with me dad. He's got cancer. Mum left and I take care of business.'

Fred was a paid up member of the *Communist Party*. She'd only a vague idea what a communist was, although she thought George Orwell was probably one. One evening they listened to *Roots* on the radio, his father nodding in a large flowery armchair beside the fire. Pale and thin, the father's skin was translucent, like tissue paper. The girl had never heard of Arnold Wesker or indeed of others Fred's friends talked about. He used words she'd not heard before and she realised she'd had very few conversations with adults, meaningful or otherwise.

Fred said her thighs were beautiful and she blushed. She'd never thought about her thighs before, never contemplated their attractiveness. She felt fat, well at least plump, and wanted a girdle. All women wore girdles. She'd watched the struggle to pull them up, aided by copious amounts of talcum powder. Wriggle, puff, pant and there it was. A smooth line and a flat tummy. But at what cost? How would they get the bloody thing off?

Fred liked jazz and thought the Beatles were shallow, 'for the kids.' He bought her singles. Thelonious Monk, *Blue Monk*, and Brubeck's *Take Five* with *Blue Rondo*

A teenage Carol with friends.

a La Turk on the B side. She didn't like to say she had no record player. Sheila and Angela, living in the room at the end of the corridor, had one. They played records after evening supper if they weren't on a night shift. Angela hated jazz but Sheila liked it. At least, she said she was learning to enjoy it. Her boyfriend liked it and had taken her to a jazz club.

With money from her pay the girl bought a black jumper and a red and white spotted cotton bandana. The first of many, in every colour always covered in spots. On a day trip to London with Nina they wandered into Drury Lane and she found her way to *Anello & Davide's*, supplier of footwear for the theatre. In a back room there were rows of secondhand boots. Who had danced on the boards of a West End stage in these boots? She didn't know at the time that they'd been the makers of Dorothy's unforgettable red slippers in *The Wizard of Oz*. She bought herself size four brown leather boots. They reached her knees and she loved them. Her own funky boots at last.

Fred took her to evening meetings once a week when she could get out. Things were more lenient in the second year, as if you'd earned your adulthood. The rope was ever so slightly slackened. Even so, some girls crawled out their windows after ten at night for clandestine meetings. Fred said one night as he walked her back to the home, 'I've got some condoms. I want to sleep with you. I love you.' She blushed. She wanted the sex and was scared. It was a strange place to be when all around her the place heaved with young lust and testosterone.

Maybe he went because she wouldn't give him what he wanted. The girl knew it was her fault. She'd frozen him out.

A few months later a man asked her out. He was handsome and had been the lover of a pink and glamorous blonde from Bristol. The girl was flattered. He seemed grown up. He chatted her up one day in a café near the *Pantiles* as she sat with Nina on her afternoon off. He bought them coffee and cake and flirted. The following week on her half day off the girl slid awkwardly into the low slung seat of his sports car for, as he said, a drive into the countryside. She'd never been in such a car and at such speed or indeed to such places. Green fringed lanes, thatched houses, lawns like velvet carpets, oak beamed pubs and duck ponds on picture postcard village greens.

Just before night fall, they parked on a rocky hill overlooking Tunbridge Wells, wth its lights twinkling down below. He took her hand and there it was, standing tall in his crotch. 'Rub this,' he said as he pulled her head down. She jerked away. He shrugged, muttered something about stupid young girls, buttoned himself away and dropped her off a mile or so from *St Christopher's*. She ran and could hear his laughter as he did a tyre screeching three point turn. He was gone. The ex-girlfriend, the blonde from Bristol, told her he was a travelling salesman, selling his wears in pubs here and there. Wine or beer? Garden furniture? Who knows. Gone, long gone.

There was the laundry, the kitchen, the nursery, the playroom, the walking of children in *Dunorlan Park*. The washing of little faces, one two three, the faces of unwanted children, four, five, six, seven. There was the making of beds, the dusting of furniture, the cleaning of cupboards. They left you alone to mop, wash, dust and dream.

PROCRASTINATING PATSY 'She loves me, she loves me not. Pick me up, put me down. Do I please you?'

'Come on, come on, come on, come on. Please, please me, like I please you.'

The Beatles sang, and she had not pleased Fred or the travelling salesman. She had not pleased the Lowestoft family, or the Norwich family or the dreadful Carps. And her own family were far away, barely acknowledging her existence. She hadn't pleased anyone, so she may as well please herself.

NASTY NELLIE 'One for you, one for me and one for the flea in your ear. Put that in yer pipe and smoke it.'

THE BOSS 'Oh my lady what are we going to do with you? What's your name, where are you going and why? Make up your own mind. If you can sort it out, please do.'

Sheila and Angela had a new record player, a birthday gift for Angela. So the girl was offered a loan of the old one. She played the jazz records Fred had given her.

She liked the music and danced to it in her head without trying to analyse what it was. Simply seductive. The music of Thelonious Monk, piano keys pounded with passionate hands and beating heart, exciting and dangerous, the notes clinging together precariously like birds on high cliff tops. *Blue Monk*, *Monks Dream* and *Round Midnight*.

CLARA THE CLOWN 'Monk, I doff my cap to your pork pie hat. Sir, you're a magical man, playing the piano-orgasmic blues for me.'

One afternoon in October 1962, when the autumn weather couldn't make up its mind, the girl walked into the café by the station. She'd heard a fragment of *Beautiful Dreamer* that morning on the radio, and felt unsettled. What was it? She was 18 years old, and as a war baby had heard war talk before. On that day, the world seemed poised before a storm as Russian nuclear missiles, 90 miles off the Florida coast, generated a global crisis so alarming that people talked of nothing else. Voices filled the streets, the pubs, offices, factories and the coffee bar where she sat on that long afternoon. She felt in her coat pocket for the bar of *Cadburys* milk chocolate she always liked to have at hand. Stuffing two squares into her mouth, she remembered the time she'd run away and the policeman who picked her up, sat her on the high wooden counter in Lewisham Police Station and gave her a square of chocolate, her first. Oh bliss and that was that. In times of trouble when all was not well in her heart, she ate chocolate. Fred was gone. His dad had died and Fred had gone to fight the system, and find a girl who would give him some loving.

The talk ranged from a cacophony to a murmur and back again. It climbed the walls, dropped from the ceiling, sneaked across the floor and crawled up into her head. Phrases she hadn't heard before like 'nuclear war', 'missile crisis', 'atomic age', 'pollution and radioactive danger', 'world war three', 'committee of 100' and 'Ban the bomb'. She sat at her table, as if witnessing a grotesque and terrifying drama playing out in slow motion. The world was about to be blown to smithereens. Thoughts crept under her skin and into her veins like a disease. She ate more chocolate and ordered another cup of coffee. In the background the radio was tuned to the BBC Home Service. Oxbridge voices, serious and solemn. The *Gaggia* gurgled and hissed, making cups of frothy coffee and the cutlery rattled. The door continuously opened and closed. Chairs were scraped across the wooden floor as people arrived and joined friends at already crowded tables.

The jazz and folk music that usually flowed from the *Dansette* record player sitting on a shelf behind the counter was silent. No Miles Davis, or Woody Guthrie, Bob Dylan or Joan Baez. Posters for jazz and poetry events were pinned to the walls alongside leaflets for political meetings. Musical instruments sat upon shelves and hung from the ceiling; guitars, mandolins, violins, a tuba, a banjo and an old French horn. All silent as if waiting for a musician to stroll in, pick one at random and begin to play. Books were stacked in dusty corners. There were green bottles with candles and wax droppings as thick as clotted cream. She picked at the wax until she had a little wax mountain on the table, and then swept it all into her bag.

It was raining hard and a dank smell mingled with the coffee and tea, cheese on toasts, egg and chips. Rain wet wool dried in the steamy heat as the hats, *Duffel* coats and scarves lay draped over chair backs with puddles gathering beneath. Umbrellas stood in a stand by the door and blue cigarette smoke filled the café more densely than usual. Marooned in her corner fenced in by chairs and tables, she watched and waited. For what she didn't know. A sign that this was a bad dream or a reached out hand to bring her into company. But the tables were full of people who knew each other, their heads close, an arm around a shoulder here, a hand held there. So she stayed at the corner table with an empty cup and the crumbs of a currant bun scattered on the one empty chair. 'Excuse me, is that chair taken?' And, 'Hi there, is there anyone sitting on that chair?'

NASTY NELLIE 'Do you see a person on this chair? Do you?'

She nodded a little too enthusiastically.

MISERY IVY 'I'm dying here; hey I'm dying here.'

She shivered. Was someone stomping on her grave?

MISERY IVY 'The bomb will drop any minute. Duck under the table. Do you think they hear you? Do you think they care? You've been kicked by a mule and kissed by a fool and now it's all over.'

THE BOSS 'Take a deep breath, it's not happened. Yet.'

FRANK PALE MOUSE 'Yet! Yet! Oh help, oh shit, oh save me.'

CLARA THE CLOWN 'Row, row your boat gently, down the stream. That does it. Don't rock the boat.'

WICKED WILL O'MINA 'You'll be in the stream. Life's not a dream, it's a bloody nightmare.'

Two hours passed, people began to drift away and the girl remained in her corner. Condensation streamed down the windows obscuring the shadowy figures outside. It felt like the whole world was crying. Tears dripping and drowning the world as it sinks towards oblivion. She couldn't summon the willpower get up and walk out into the street. Someone had drawn a face in the condensation and it slid downwards, the smile slipping. The sun suddenly appeared from behind a cloud and the raindrops glistened. The puddles outside shone with petrol rainbow brilliance. The man behind the counter said gently, as he draped a tea towel over the coffee maker and stacked chairs on tables, 'We're closing soon.'

The sky then darkened. Someone had switched off all the lights in the world. A battle raged inside her stomach. She picked up her bag, coat and hat, and ran without looking back. He didn't take her money. An unbearable sense of fear took hold and she knew with absolute certainty that if the world was about to an end, she had nowhere and no one to run to.

> NASTY NELLIE 'Yes it can and the world *will* burn and fry you alive. Your skin will peel away from your bones and you'll melt into a pool of hot fat.'
> MISERY IVY 'And who will be at your graveside? Who will weep for you?'

The girl felt the tears tumbling down her cheeks and angrily wiped them away.

> MISERY IVY 'No one.'
> NASTY NELLIE 'Oh come on, you're standing on your own two feet aren't you? You're not ill. Not starving.'

Bombs didn't drop. She didn't die. She didn't fry. She lived to scrub yet more pots, wash more nappies and mop more floors.

On one of those silent café days someone did attempt to draw her in, asking if she'd like to join them. She'd fallen into one of her 'can't speak, won't speak' silences. She smiled and shook her head. It was a 'no' with a 'yes' lurking behind her lips. They left her alone. She often thought she'd smiled but perhaps she hadn't. Maybe the smile was only on the inside. Inside the girl was full of contradictions. Monstrous and benign, hating and loving, desiring and regretting. She managed to occupy the past, present and future, rearranging the past, surviving the present and playing out that which may never happen. In a month or so London and the southeast would be in the grip of a very cold winter and like 1947, the sea would freeze. She remembered that time. Mrs Boyd and her very red nose, the matron and her spit laden hanky and all the runny noses and chapped lips. The girl's best friend that winter was *Vaseline*. In the Easter of 1963, the girl marched to London and Trafalgar Square. The world hadn't ended on that day in the coffee bar. Nina was away on holiday with her aunt and uncle. Jenny was out with the latest boyfriend. She tended to become unavailable when in love.

It was her second Christmas at *St Christopher's* and she was entitled to a four day break. A friend of Fred's invited her to spend it with his brother in Suffolk. He wasn't a boyfriend. His brother worked for a bird sanctuary and lived there in a cottage with his wife and the wildlife. The girl would've spent the break in the room in Tunbridge Wells, listening to Monk, Brubeck Fitzgerald, Holiday and the Beatles. This alternative would be an adventure. Laying at night in her single bed, knees drawn up to her chin, she felt a shaking low down in her insides. Suffolk? Lowestoft? The plan was to hitch up to London, then across and out of the suburbs from Gants Hill. They were going on the road with their thumbs out, on the road she'd taken from London to Lowestoft in 1956. London was successfully negotiated and then, 'I've been here before.' She remembered that unhappy journey from Lewisham.

The whole country froze. There were drifts as high as small hills at the roadsides, the sea froze over four miles out from Dunkirk and along the Kent coast. Stormy winds reached gale force eight. It was a dramatic winter indeed. Almost immediately after London they got a lift to beyond Ipswich and then another. They had a wait as the rain began to fall on Saxmundham and then a short lift to just past Southwold. They were doing well. It was nearing nine o'clock in the evening and raining hard. It was very cold and they had another 40 miles to go. As they approached the London Road South he said, 'Didn't you say your parents live here?' The old ache jerked into life in the pit of her stomach. She went into the phone box at the end of The Avenue and called the house. Jenny answered.

They were at the front door, ringing the bell. There was John, or was it Arthur? He stood in the hall with his hand on the door and both sisters hovered behind him. 'Your mother says no,' he said. She could hear footsteps at the top of the stairs. 'I'm sorry,' he said, 'but your mother says no.' He repeated the words in a mechanical fashion and didn't look her in the eye. The sisters scuttled back into the kitchen and the front door was firmly shut. She turned to look at the young man, his pack on his back, the rain dripping down his neck. He looked confused, took her by the hand and she stumbled beside him down to the London Road, thumbs out. Two days before Christmas eve at one in the morning, cold, wet and hungry, they finally reached their destination.

His brother, a wonderful man, was angry when he heard the story. 'That's it,' thought the girl, 'I'll never go there again.'

Nasty Nellie 'Like you have a choice. They don't want you. They don't care.'

A knot in the rope had unravelled. Three years had passed and Lowestoft was becoming a distant memory in the back of her mind, a house of dark corners and cold shadows. Routine took over as all her activity was mapped out for her. She became an expert in cleaning with a bumper, wielding the long wooden pole with a heavy metal ball on the end of it. Place the ball in the hole in the wooden square, then bumping the floors, up and down. Wash, polish and bump.

The following year in a world that hadn't ended, and she would soon sing and make a friend. One who would be there for life. Then everything would change though power still lay in the hands of men who dealt in politicking and war mongering. The girl had marched the 52 miles from a field in Aldermaston to Trafalgar Square, alongside hundreds and more. She was 19 years old and she would be part of this growing community that seemed to care. She wore her black and white CND badge with pride.

She was a Londoner, born in the year before the end of a war. Perhaps on that day when she thought the world was coming to an end she had shadows in her mind of the war that was then. She looked for her family and found it had never really existed. Not in the real 'I love you' kind of way. Not in the hugging and the tucking up in bed, feeling safe and knowing love kind of way, 'Sometimes I feel Like a motherless child, long way from home.' Though she wasn't a motherless child. Problem was she had a mother but the mother was gone. Gone and unable to love.

Onwards to the city. During the second year of training, the girls were sent to a hospital to work for three months in a maternity unit. The pinks were sent to *St.Thomas'* in London and the blues either to the *Pembury Hospital* in Tunbridge Wells, or to Beckenham. She wanted Beckenham and oh yes, she got it. She had a single room once again and was nearer to London. She had a radio and her record player, and would take the train up to the city on her days off, wandering the streets, acquainting herself with central London. She walked around Soho and Chelsea, to Hyde Park and down by the river, revisiting the scene where she'd seen the *Festival of Britain*, travelling everywhere where the names caught her imagination. She was taking in the city of her birth and going wherever she wanted. She had to be back in the hostel by nine in the evening when the door was locked.

They were not, and never would be, nurses. Lowest of the low, they did many more dirty jobs. One day the girl saw a dead baby, so small and blue. She couldn't sleep for many nights after that. The image wouldn't leave her, along with the smell of the wards, of disinfectant, the kitchen and the blood. The sheets became the biggest chore of all. Everyday making beds. Hospital corners were tricky for a small girl. She passed all her written exams, she did it all. When the head talked of jobs in America and the south of France and asked, 'Which one of you girls would like to apply for that?' The girl put her hand in the air. 'I would love that,' she thought, 'I could speak French and go to Paris and see where Miles Davis played.' The woman laughed, 'I hardly think so dear, it's not for you.' Being a blue was a ticket to the bottom of the pile.

NASTY NELLIE 'Oh I say, getting above our station are we.'
The Boss was absent. Out on a tea break or making friends with Bandzerglob the Beast. The girl flushed and that was that. She would aim to please these people no more and packed her bag. In Tunbridge Wells she met the friend she'd hitched to Suffolk with. He was going down to Hastings the next day. A scene was going on and she would go. She was ready and London could wait a little longer. She'd found the perfect context in which to place the words she'd heard from the mouth of Puggy Uttin on the London Road South. 'Fuck you,' she said as she walked through the gates of *St Christopher's* for the last time, 'fuck you all.' She heard the others inside echo her in mutual agreement, even The Boss who had returned.

'*This morning I was born again I was born again complete.*
I stood up above my troubles and I stand on my two feet
My hand it feels unlimited, my body feels like the sky
I feel at home in the universe where yonder planets fly'
Thank you Woody Guthrie.

They were off to the pub in Hastings where she'd begin to sing, sing, sing. She was called once more to the sea. One more time seduced by the tide, in and out like her breath. Her lungs wanted the sea air though she knew she'd eventually head back to London. Back to her city of birth.

BETTY BLUES BELTER 'Go on, sing. You want to. I dare you. You can, you know you can. Sing, sing. Go on.'

Her first song as told earlier, *The House of The Rising Sun* on a sunny day in Hastings in 1963. She would sing in London if she really wished and wanted it enough.

CLARA THE CLOWN 'I'm wishing, I'm wishing.'

* * *

On Sunday 14th August 2005, I stood on the steps in front of the *National Gallery* waiting to sing with The Shout. We were performing *Stand* written by Orlando Gough and Mike Henry as part of a London festival celebrating 700 years of free speech. *Nelson* posed ponderously tall on his column while the fountains spouted London water and the pigeons waddled, pecked and shat. We hoped it wouldn't rain before we finished. Dark clouds loomed behind *Canada House* and the gallery. *Big Ben* and the *Houses of Parliament* were just visible through the humid heat haze of that August summer day as tourists photographed friends and relatives.

I see my young self again, a young girl singing *The House of The Rising Sun* in an alley beside a pub in Hastings Old Town. I see her again on that Easter march of 1963, a girl asleep on her jacket underneath *Nelson*.

She'd marched through Southall, Slough and Reading, in through the western suburbs, catching the measles on route. She felt rough, smelt rough, her feet ached,

"SOMETHING TO SHOUT ABOUT" THE EVENING STANDARD

The Drill Hall presents

The Shout
sing Tall Stories

The Drill Hall

her head ached and she was being pushed aside to make way for clean people. Tall, loud and confident people who'd enjoyed the luxury of a night's sleep and a bath. All barging to get to the front, to be in on the action. Laying on her jacket on the ground, someone trod on the girl's foot. The speeches were about to begin and the crowd sang, 'We shall overcome, we shall overcome some day...'

She was overcome and fed up. Off she went to find a café, a warm place to sit. World war three hadn't erupted and the world was still turning. The girl felt like shit and needed a day, a night and more of sleep. Peering into the *Lyons Corner House* at Charing Cross, she thought it wasn't for her and wandered off to Villiers Street where she found what she was looking for. She ordered herself a cheese omelette and a cuppa. It came with two slices of bread and butter. She was very, very hungry. For the moment banning the bomb could wait. She had five bob in her pocket and that was enough to fill her belly.

A Ghostly Bridge

Looking at the Square, waiting to sing, watching people swimming silently in and out of my mind like ghostly fishes, darting here and there. I took a deep breath and then we sang. After the performance of I walked down the endless inner tunnels and subways, dragging my bags of memories, my mind on the ghosts of my past and that long afternoon in a café. I always see them as I wait for a train or a plane, wait to sing or for a phone call. As I wait to know whether the sings will come in and food will be on the table that week, next week, any week. At three in the morning in those body tired, mind flying, eyes not blinking, can't sleep but want to sleep moments. Call it what you will, the memories hover and wait to return in that weirdly odd way. Forever entwined, my young and my old mind, the voices inside me that chatter and chide, encourage and rage, as I look both outwards and in with the curiosity of a benign yet wary stranger.

Marilyn Monroe had died in 1962 and apartheid was mad and alive in the southern states of America. In Spring 1963, a Buddhist monk burned himself to death in Saigon. The world was angry and burning in 1963, when Martin Luther King declared, 'Let us not wallow in the valley of despair, I say to you today, my friends.' The girl tried not to wallow but that Nasty Nellie would get in the way sometimes. 'Ban the Bomb' and 'Out. Out. Out,' 'Don't want no war no more.' 'When will we ever learn?'

VERSE 14

Earl's Court

Detour Ahead Herb Ellis, John Frigo and Lou Carter 1947

1963 to 1964: London life. Drugs, singing and sinning. The Café des Artistes. The court of PJ Proby. First visit to the Marquee Club, and more. Blues at the Richmond Imperial. Lord John, April Ashley and John Dennis 'Biffo' Bindon. Goodbye, this time for good. Working for 'Paris Nat' Schaffer. The girl can sing.

The summer on the Sussex coast was over. The girl was 20 years old and had sung beside the seaside. With the bus fare up to London in her purse, a small bag containing the few belongings she'd acquired and with her mind tick ticking and dizzy, her London life could begin. Could she sing? Find some musicians maybe? How? She took the tube from Victoria Coach Station, rattled along the District Line to Earl's Court and emerged from the tunnels around Gloucester Road. She saw the backs of sooty brick houses, a red geranium balanced precariously on a window sill, red petals defying the city grime, and the underbelly of a road straddling the track. Weeds sprouted miraculously from the crevices, with yellow and purple heads. This was the city as seen from underneath. The girl was back where she'd been born but this time north of the river.

Still, the air was familiar with the aroma of coffee beans grinding in *Kenco* coffee shops. Of eggs frying in cafés, of chip fat and drains. She caught a waft of beer and tobacco as a pub door opened and of the traffic fumes, from the banging, clanging, horn hooting streets. She gave herself an inside hug to both reassure and to contain her excitement. Going out of the station, she turned left up the Earl's Court Road and stood at the bottom of four concrete steps which led to the door of a ground floor flat on the West Cromwell Road, close to the junction of Warwick Road. A 24 hour highway, a never ending flow of trucks, buses, cars and taxis belching fumes. Coaches and trucks rumbling out to Fulham, Hammersmith, Putney or Barnes, Chiswick and then onwards to Heathrow Airport and the West Country, Bristol and onwards to south Wales.

In those days young men and women came to the city from small towns and villages, from Scotland, Ireland, Wales and beyond. Women worked as secretaries or assistants in department stores, young men in banks and city firms. Clerks, nurses, mechanics, teachers, waiters and washer-uppers. Students in university colleges, art schools, drama, dance and fashion academies. All with dreams of love, fame and fortune.

In the early 1960s you could rent a room or share a flat in the peeling white Stucco buildings of Kensington, Paddington, Gloucester Road, around the Chelsea Squares towards World's End, Battersea and the leafy reaches of Hammersmith and Fulham. Bedsits in ram-shackled houses, basement flats in Queensway or Notting Hill. Nina and Jenny from *St. Christopher's* were set up with a furnished flat while the girl had been hanging out with the Beats in Hastings. She then moved in with them, her bed in the sitting room on the ground floor. A single bed that doubled as sofa during the day. Last to sleep and first to wake. The street was just a few feet away behind dusty glass windows and net curtains, pale grey with the London dirt. The carpet, worn threadbare in the centre, was gruesome with a garish pattern of red, orange, green and god knows what else. The colour of sick, hangover nausea sick.

There was a cheap table covered in a red gingham cloth, three chairs, a mantle piece covered in mugs of half-finished tea and overflowing ashtrays. She loved it. The fire in the grate had been replaced by a gas fire, the gas paid with money in a hall meter beside the front door, electricity in the same way. Big brown pennies, a sixpence, half crowns and a shilling. Old money, heavy money gobbled by the meters. This was her first real home in the city and there were no demons lurking in corners under dim gaslights. Nina and Jenny slept in two small rooms in the back, once one room now with thin partition walls and overstuffed with dark brown furniture, beds and cupboards. The place resembled a dumping ground for the unwanted possessions of the dead and buried. There was a bathroom with an enormous *Ascot* gas boiler that wheezed and groaned at the turn of the large tap, water spitting and spluttering into a stained and cracked bathtub. The boiler roared in disapprovingly when fired up. She called it Angry Norman.

Opposite the bathroom in a tiny space under the stairs was a windowless lavatory. The small kitchen had faded red linoleum floors, an ancient *New World* gas cooker probably installed before the First World War, and a butler's sink which showed no mercy to cups, plates, dishes and saucers, all chipped or broken. And as for glasses. There were never any glasses. The girls collected jam jars and ate bread and jam when the cupboard was bare. *Robertson's* Strawberry Jam on sliced white bread.

There was no fridge. The kitchen window sill was used as a place to keep things cool, a narrow sill almost permanently in the shade. The odd bottle of milk could last a day as long as it didn't end up in the basement below or pecked at by birds in a frenzy of starvation. There was no room to eat in the kitchen. Breakfast was taken on the run. Tea and toast, cornflakes or shredded wheat. The girls ate standing up and waited to get into the bathroom, sometimes hopping from foot to foot and yelling, 'Hurry up, I'm bursting for a wee!' Ready to start the day, they then rushed out the front door and into the world.

Their jobs varied as they worked as waitresses, barmaids, cleaners, or mother's helps for rich young families in Kensington and Chelsea. In the evening on a pay day, they sometimes lit a candle in a saucer and drank a bottle of *Mateus Rosé* or *Blue Nun*. They liked a take-away chinese from the Earl's Court Road or made their own spaghetti bolognese, very exotic with garlic and tinned tomatoes. Let the party begin. The girl was in heaven. She had no thoughts about the next month, week or even the next day. And she had the freedom to eat whatever, whenever. *Wall's* pork pies, *Heinz* spaghetti on toast, *Lyons* individual fruit pies.

She hadn't really seen this London before, the Africans, Chinese and Australians. The aroma of foreign food wafted up from basement kitchens. Women with make-up thickly caked onto pale white skin at nine in the morning. Ladies in furs in Knightsbridge and Sloane Square. Men in smart suits, carrying tightly furled umbrellas, a newspaper tucked under an arm on the way from the West to the city or Temple, to offices in the new glass and concrete castles.

Almost every day she walked from Earl's Court to Kensington. On some days she also walked into Piccadilly, through Knightsbridge, past *Harrods* and Hyde Park, the length of Oxford Street and on to Regent Street, then Soho and Covent Garden to Trafalgar Square and on to the Strand. She wandered into the *National Gallery* and found her painting *The Virgin of the Rocks*. She bought a postcard and slipped it into her bag. Back in the flat she put it on the mantle-piece, a move towards making a place that would be her own. A home.

The girl found a job in the *Evening Standard*. She was broke. 'Lady needs a companion. Light domestic duties, Gloucester Road. Five days a week, nine until six, lunch provided. Must be of a pleasant disposition and clean. References required. £10 a week, payable on a Friday with two weeks in hand.' 'Shit,' thought the girl, 'two weeks and no money. What do I do?'

The lady was a small bird-like woman from somewhere in Central Europe who wore vertiginously high heels, a floral shirt underneath a navy blue two-piece suit with gold braid around the jacket, and a pleated skirt. With high cheek bones and a wide jaw, she was maybe aged 50, it's hard to tell a person's age when you're young. The lady had hard brown eyes that had seen a few things, a frizzy red halo of henna dyed hair and a red mouth. She was pungently perfumed and had a smoker's rasp. Clearly a chain smoker. She held a small fluffy yapping dog in her arms that appeared to have a blocked nose as it dribbled and snuffled. It had small brown eyes, just like its owner. 'Come in come in, don't stand zere, I fant to cloze zee door. Arh ! Now zit zere,' said the brown-eyed woman, pointing to a chair beside a small table covered in newspapers, bottles of red nail varnish, an empty cup and an ashtray full to overflowing with red lipstick stained butts, all half a cigarette long. Foreign cigarettes in long blue packets sat in a box on another table.

> TILLY TEA LEAF 'Well, I'll take those. They look posh. Pop them into a
> tissue. What a waste. There must be three half-finished fags in that
> ash tray.'

The interview, as the woman called it, took half an hour. She barked questions, barely waiting for the answers and then gave the girl a tour of the flat. It reeked of her perfume, stale tobacco, her dog and underneath it all, the brandy she liked to sip in the evening in front of the television. The smell was in the carpet, the curtains, the clothes and even the towels that hung in the bathroom. The lady rattled out her instructions and the duties to be undertaken. The girl pulled her *St Christopher's* certificate out of her bag. The lady was impressed, even surprised. She nodded, 'ja. I vill giffe you zee chob.' 'Oh,' thought the girl, 'what have I done?' Then out loud, 'when do you want me to start?'

> WICKED WILLOW O' MINA 'Don't do it. You won't want this life. This life
> of being a servant because that's what it is. They get you and then
> they shit on you. Know your place. They say you're nothing, only fit
> to serve and be silent.'

'Monday morning,' came the reply, 'nine o'clock and I do not tolerate mein staff being late. Zis fill be a one month trial, to zee vether I like you to vork fiz me.'

The girl took the job. Her rent was due. The landlord collected every Saturday morning at ten o'clock on the dot. He always came with another man, large of chest and mean of mouth. The girl bought a pad of pale blue *Basildon Bond* paper and matching envelopes. She felt like a grown up in the grown up world. She had a flat and a job. She wrote to Beryl and received a reply, short and to the point.

'What is point of training to be a nanny if you are not going to use it?'
Beryl had a point.

161

MISERY IVY 'But I don't want to be a nanny. I don't want...I didn't choose. I want to be a... what do I want?'

The girl had no answer so she put Beryl's letter aside and forgot all about it. In her new job she had to wear her *St Christopher's* uniform. Her employer insisted. In the morning at nine on the dot, tip toeing as instructed, she took a list from the hall table and shopped in the Gloucester Road for bread, milk, fruit, salami sausage and the Daily Mail. She'd never seen salami before and watched as the man in the delicatessen sliced it on a gleaming steel machine with a blade that could sever a leg or an arm.

WICKED WILL O'MINA 'His arm slipped under the blade. There were little puffs of red at first and then a crimson river flowed from his fingerless hand. The shop keeper turned pale grey as his fingers rolled across the tiled shop floor.'

A little mound of the thinnest cut meat on a piece of greaseproof paper, a strange creamy white cheese and a packet of *Earl Grey* tea. She took these from the shopkeeper, all his fingers intact. She collected the dry cleaning. Two suits like the one the lady wore at the interview, dark red and black. She collected shoes from the cobbler, freshly heeled and soled, wrapped in a brown paper bag. She liked the smell of the cobblers.

Back at the flat that the lady insisted should be called an 'apartment', the girl prepared the food. She opened a can of meat and jelly for the dog, slopped it into a dish and retched. She cut a grapefruit in half, loosened the segments and gave them a sprinkle of castor sugar. And she set out a small bowl of flakes, a slice of toast cut to a certain thickness, a piece of cheese and a few rounds of salami. The lady would snort, sniff and yell, 'Don't you know how to prepare a decent breakfast? I cannot eat toast zat is zo zickly cut!' The dog yapped and smiling, the girl nodded, watched and learned.

NASTY NELLIE 'Yes miss, no miss, how many fucking bags full miss?'

The breakfast was placed on a tray with a clean white cloth, the creases ironed out and replaced everyday. The girl hand washed the tea towels, along with the silky underwear she found laying on the bedroom floor beside the dressing table. The lady didn't dress until after her bath which she took at nine-thirty. She then sat at an oval oak table in her sitting room, wearing a peach or a pale pink negligee and listening to the radio with the dog on her lap, snuffling and drooling. She fed the dog with bits of toast or salami from her plate and the girl felt sick at the sight of this horrid 'tete a tete.' Why did she have to be so squeamish?

Then there was the dusting. This was a complicated affair given the place was stuffed with knicknacks and framed photographs. Books in a mahogany book case, together with ornaments and paper flowers in flowery vases. A dusty spider plant in the sitting room alcove, another in the bathroom and one in the lobby. Piles of letters, papers, magazines, bottles of pills, dog collars, dog jackets, dog leads, chewed toys, soggy with sloppy dog saliva. Overflowing glass ash trays. A locked drinks cabinet, a radiogram with records of the shows and some light classical. Well, she was told it was classical. 'I am a very cultured person,' said the lady, 'my family fas fery important people, you know. I fent to a fery excluziffe school.' After every utterance, every over pronounced 'fery', the lady sniffed.

The girl winced. Each sniff was so disdainful, the lady and dog together. Sniff, sniff. The lady inspected the furniture, poking fingers looking for dust, picking up an ornament as if she expected it to be broken in some way. She talked incessantly, the girl nodding, agreeing and making sympathetic noises. A tirade of complaints. The lady's delicate temperament slighted by this person or that, by her indignation at the world at large. Nothing was as it should be. The girl wasn't invited to reply suspected that whatever she said would be of no interest anyway to the lady, who seemed only interested in herself.

After lunch on the fourth afternoon, the lady announced she was going out. She would return before five and by then the whole apartment had to be cleaned. 'I fant zee cupboards in sa kitchen turned out and all zurfaces cleaned properly, no corners can be cut.' On and on she demanded, 'and fill you make zure zat fen you answer my telephone, you take ze mezage down. Don't forget. And za toilet must be cleaned fiss ze blue cloth not fiss the cloth in za kitchen.'

WICKED WILL O'MINA 'Yes, yes and yes madam. No madam, up your arse madam. You smell madam. You stink, stink, stink, madam. Take the stupid dog madam, or I'll boil it's yapping head, madam. And watch your back, madam. I have a dagger in my hand.'

Piles of clothes spilled out of the very large oak wardrobe and two chests of drawers in her bedroom. The dressing room table, kidney shaped with a glass top like the girls mother's in Lowestoft, had a scattering of powder which had to be dusted daily. The lady's bottles of *Jean Patou Joy*, lipsticks coloured gothic purple and pillar box red, powder compacts and some gold jewellery in a carved wooden box, silky bits of negligee. Housecoats and nightdresses draped over every chair and on the floor, hats and fur coats. The tobacco, perfume, and dead animal skin smell was suffocating.

Week one came to an end. Thank you. If there is a God, thank you God for Saturday and Sunday. But ho hum, this was a job. And she had a free meal, and got to go out and shop, away from the voice, the sickly smell and the foul little dog. One morning after the usual jobs, the shopping and making breakfast, she heard a call from the bathroom, 'I vant you to vash my back.'

The girl flinched. The lady put out a red nailed hand. It was a claw, in the girls eyes, a grasping claw. 'Help me out of my bath,' she said, 'I am not vell today. I feel veak. You will haffe to help me dress.' The girl averted her eyes and handed over a large white towel as the lady stood in her bath. 'Tsk tsk, come nearer girl, I cannot do zis vith you standing a mile away. Help me viz za towel.'

> WICKED WILL O'MINA 'Stop jabbing, your arm is a spear, your red fingernails need cutting. You'll draw my blood with your incessant pointing.'

The next morning the lady wanted wanted her hair that brushed. And then she needed the girl to do up her brassiere. Each day she demanded more. She wanted her small body, a body with a rounded belly, low-slung heavy breasts and stick like arms and legs, to be fondled, and seemed to want her purple red puckered mouth kissed. She wanted a young woman to give her the touch she hadn't felt for many years. She'd never spoken about a husband and appeared to be childless. The photographs in the frames were of a place she called home and the people were from another time. Parents? Siblings? Who knows. The girl got out on week four. Friday wages. 'Thank you very much. Yes, I'll see you on Monday.' She almost tripped over her own feet, so anxious was she to be leaving that claustrophobic apartment. Run, run down the Gloucester Road onto the bus.

> CLARA THE CLOWN 'Hippy hop, don't stop. Don't ever go there again.'

The girl phoned the lady on Saturday morning, 'I'm so sorry, I'm leaving London, so sorry, I can't come again.'

> THE BOSS 'Look sharp, keep a wary eye and watch your back. Who knows who is hiding in the dark corners?'

Back to Earl's Court and the room on the ground floor that was home. In the hallway was a dark haired brown-eyed girl chatting to Jenny as she fed the hungry gas meter. They wandered into the sitting room. The girl was called Maureen and looked like a cross between Nina Simone and Buffy Sainte-Marie. She'd been raised in the same *Dr Barnado* home in North Wales as Jenny.

Maureen and her friends Velma and Diana had lived for a while in a halfway to freedom house in Ealing before moving to the hostel in Earl's Court. There they met Nina and the girl, and were reunited with Jenny, all not yet 20.

Maureen and Velma who shared a room were dark girls, called 'half-caste' or worse in those ill informed and bigoted days. Born just after the war to a young Irish girl and a black GI, Maureen had never met her father and had lost touch with her mother. Diana was small and blonde with the face of a life-weary angel. She styled herself on Brigitte Bardot and became one of the first *Penthouse Pets*, hanging out with Bob Guccione and the louche London crowd on the edge of sleaze. Her angel face would soon be bruised.

At first Maureen took no notice of the small girl wearing the blue cotton uniform. It was Nina, crashing into the flat half an hour later, who'd caught Maureen's attention with her bright red lipstick and extraordinary smile. She'd been out for days and was bursting to talk about her nights on the town and her new man from Italy. Nina would walk out onto the West Cromwell Road and hitch a lift into the West End, to *Le Kilt* or some other club. She often went alone and would almost always pick up a young man. Once or twice she had short lived affairs with Nigerians, one a lovely student at King's College with a gentle hesitant smile and eyes like deep dark lakes. That didn't last long. It was all very 'in the moment' with Nina and many a young man's heart was broken.

The girl pulled herself out of the blue uniform, stuffed it into the dustbin and that was that. A new life, her life, could begin. Jenny had a new man and Nina was always on the hunt. So the girl began to hang out with Maureen and Velma, mostly at the *Café des Artistes*, a basement club on the corner of Redcliffe Gardens and the Fulham Road. They were both hot dancers and at first the girl was a little intimidated. They looked so wild, as if the dance was life and life the dance. The girl called Maureen 'Beat' and a beat she was. They became inseparable. One night they watched a band with four guys fronted by the young Freddie Mercury. Blazing, he flashed and crackled, rehearsing his future trademark voice and moves.

The dark candlelit arches and the bar accommodated all manner of young men who believed themselves to be on the cusp of world superstardom. Who grew their hair long, rejected suits and ties and talked about bands they were in or about to join, planning and plotting. Young men on the make. To be a Mick, a Keith or an Eric. To have an *E type Jag* and a model girlfriend. These were working class boys with big dreams. *Got My Mojo Working*. The white boys were playing the black music of America and making big money. *Crawling King Snake*. Art Students from Surrey singing the blues.

The manager of the *Café des Artistes* paraded around his domain. Such power, chatting to this girl and that, flattering her with a drink and a cigarette. Then, a week or so later, he'd bang on her window saying she was his one true love. She wanted to believe him but there was never a date, a dinner for two or a film up West. Only the late night knock on her window. The city was full of gamblers and losers, pariahs and liars.

The girl met a man in the Chinese takeaway one evening. He asked her what she'd ordered and they chatted while they waited. He invited her to dinner, said he would do a steak. Promised it wouldn't be a takeaway. She'd never eaten steak before. It sounded sophisticated and very expensive. He lived just off the Warwick Road. On the night she dressed as well as she could with a black skirt, a white shirt, a black belt around her tiny waist, black boots and her red velvet beret which matched her red lipstick. She washed her hair and dabbed the pink sweet gloop that was *Coty L'Aimant* behind each ear, with a smear on her wrists. She had an idea that this would be a grown up date, a proper meal with a man.

He opened the door and she followed him up a flight of stairs to his first floor room. There was no smell of cooking. He offered her a brandy and she retched at the first sip. It reminded her of Gloucester Road and the red haired woman. He lit a cigarette, inhaled deeply, stood with his arms folded across his chest, stared at her and smiled. It wasn't a pleasant smile. 'Why are you dressed up?' he asked. He poured her another drink. She was nervous. Something was wrong. She couldn't relax. She wanted a cigarette but was afraid to ask. He began to laugh. Why? There'd been no joke. They weren't drunk although she would be if she had more brandy and no food. Perhaps she'd made a mistake. Perhaps they were eating out. She smiled back.

He put on a record. 'Too loud,' she thought. She was nervous and couldn't understand why. 'Hey, come here, baby,' he said, 'relax, don't you want to dance?' She nodded hesitantly. 'You like me, don't you?' He suddenly grabbed her around the waist and whirled her round so fast she almost fell against a chair wedged between the bed and a washbasin. She struggled to free herself. He firmed his grip and she said, 'Won't your neighbours mind?' She blushed. She'd sounded so uncool and was so nervous she nearly wet herself. Clamping her legs together and pulling up from her insides, she prayed she wouldn't the embarrassing thing and piss herself in front of this man. She had to get out of there.

'You're a tart,' he said, 'you're all tarts. Why do you wear that belt? To show off your waist and your tits? Your skirt's too short. You look like a slut. What are you? Yes, you're a slut, a tart.' She took backward steps to his door, knowing people

166

would be in the other rooms. She tried to scream but the scream wouldn't come. And the music was too loud. She managed to turn the door handle behind her back.

THE BOSS 'Get your backside out of there and catch your collar on the way. Don't let go until you're safely away. There are men out there who'll discard you as fast as an old banana skin and toss you into the gutter.'

The man laughed and hit her across the face. He wiped his hand across her mouth and smeared her lipstick across her face, blood red like the blood ringing in her ears. She heard the welcome sound of voices from downstairs. Thank God. The music stopped and she opened the door. He laughed, 'Go on, go,' he said, 'go. You're just a dirty little bitch. I wouldn't touch you anyway, I might get the clap.' She flew down the stairs and out main door, stumbling in her high heels shoes, sobs lodging in her throat.

They were all out when she got back. Shaking, she crawled into her bed, her pants damp with her own urine but she barely noticed or cared. She heard the door open and Jenny came in with her boyfriend. They opened her door and she stayed still and quiet. They closed the door. Then, later, a tap at the window. She ignored it. It was the man from the *Café des Artist*, 'Hey, let me in, it's me. I got a smoke. Come on, it's a great bit of draw.' She lay there immobile and unblinking. She thought he could surely hear her heart beating, so thunderous did it sound in her chest. He gave up. She heard him leave, cursing all women and her particularly. Then all she could hear was the sound of the all night traffic.

In November President John F. Kennedy was shot in the head and the shocked western world inhaled a collective breath. And the girl avoided men.

Christmas came and the girls cooked a meal together in West Cromwell Road. Chicken and potatoes, carrots with lumpy *Bisto* gravy, washed down with bottles of *Blue Nun* and lots of cigarettes. It all seemed rather wonderful in the scruffy flat on the busy road out to the airport and the west. Nina invited what felt like hundreds back for New Year's Eve. Young men slept wherever they could. A floor, a chair, feet up on an occupied bed. Even the bath was used for a fitful sleep, the dawn light seeping in through the ragged net curtains.

Beat may have lived in the hostel but she stayed at West Cromwell Road most of the time. It was the place for all the lost girls. The place to hang out when you couldn't afford the pub or the club or the gig. Jenny met an American singer called PJ Proby at a party and became his girlfriend. He wore suits of velvet in vivid colours, with skin-tight trousers and garish shirts, one for each day of the week. Velma was going out with a Rolling Stones roadie, one step nearer to Mick Jagger, her true desire. Beat and the girl secretly laughed at PJ and his ponytail. They laughed at his throne in his flat. How he sat there surrounded by the many girls he collected. A king and his court in Earl's Court. Jenny didn't last long. The neighbours spoke and after many words the landlord and his henchman appeared and they were out. It had to be the parties.

One cold January day Jenny moved to a flat in Redcliffe Gardens with a guy called Fergie. Beat and the girl were off to bedsit land. Two rooms in a house near Redcliffe Gardens, round the corner from *Café des Artistes*. Her room was tiny. Open the door and it hit the bed. Lay on the bed and you could touch the sink, the door, the wardrobe and the window, which was only half a window. The other half was in the room on the other side of the thin dividing wall. A bedside table was wedged between the bed and the window. You couldn't swing a mouse, let alone a cat. It was a roof and a bed. You could sit on the bed.

She wrote to Beryl, told her she'd moved and gave her the new address. She made no mention of anything to do with work. It was a letter with meaningless words, saying little. There was no reply.

One Friday night they went to the *Marquee Club* in Wardour Street. There they could see Sonny Boy Williamson, Long John Baldry and the Hoochie Coochie Men and The Yardbirds, all on one night. The girl saw the striped circus backdrop on the stage for the first time. The first ever published magazine photograph of herself was only a year or two away. A picture of her singing on that very same stage in front of the stripes.

London was hot with live music. The *100 Club, Ricky Tick, Blue Moon, Fender Club, The Crawdaddy* and *Klooks Kleek*, watching bands like Zoot Money's Big Roll Band, Chris Farlowe and the Thunderbirds, Georgie Fame and the Blue Flames, Herbie Goins and the Nightimers, Geno Washington and the Ram-Jam band, John Mayall and the Bluesbreakers and The Graham Bond Organisation. At *The Flamingo* all nighters, John Gunnell, one of the two brothers, took your cash. Five shillings, normally paid with a ten bob note with change left for a beer or two.

Entering the club was like walking into a wall of cheap perfume, roll on deodorant, smoke, sweat and dancing bodies, all accompanied by a throbbing R&B soundtrack. Up at the front were three rows of old cinema seats facing a small stage, a *Hammond Organ*, drums and amplifiers, all set up and ready to roll. Maybe

Georgie Fame singing Mose Allison's *Parchment Farm*, or Graham Bond rocking the roof with *Wade in The Water*.

Up all night, dancing in a fog of reefer smoke. Coming out in the early morning, eyes dry-wide, wandering down to Covent Garden where the pubs were open for the market porters. Eating doorstep bacon sandwiches with a smear of brown sauce and a mug of tea to wash it all down. Standing beside the milk machine in Berwick Street, the prostitutes selling their services for thirty shillings to any man who passed by. Spring was springing. Longer days and lighter nights.

The girl and Beat went off to Richmond one night, thumbs out on the Warwick Road. They went further west than they'd ever been to a pub called the *Imperial*. Ding, ding, seconds out. The pot man had been a boxer in his youth. Now punch drunk, the old till behind the bar would ring on every transaction. Ring, ring and for a second or two he'd be back in the boxing ring, hands up in front of his face, boxing the air, puffing out his breath. Booff, booff, right, left, just a moment. Then he resumed the collecting of glasses, a hundred times every night. Left, right jab, duck, dodge and jab.

Thumbs out at least twice weekly. They made friends. Ginger and his mates, guitars and harmonicas, the pub was a haunt of local beatniks, art students and emerging musicians all playing blues or folk music. They went to the *Richmond Jazz Festival*. Their first festival. And to gigs on *Eel Pie Island*. They loved crossing over the rickety bridge, making the place special, as if removed from the mainland. An island with music in its heart, the river Thames rippling alongside.

Too drunk or tired to face the hitchhike home back to Earl's Court, the girls sometimes stayed over at Ginger's or anyone who had floor space. At the *Crawdaddy Club* and at the *Station Hotel* they saw the Stones and the Yardbirds with Eric Clapton. Dave Brock and Davy Johnson, Johnny Silvo and Gerry Lockran, all guys heading for the gigs, the bands and the life.

Sitting in *Les Macabre*, a Soho coffe bar in Meard Street, at a table shaped like a coffin downstairs in the gloom, candles flickering inside skulls, she noticed a poster for the *Roundhouse* pub, where Alexis Korner and Cyril Davies ran a skiffle club. They went to *Les Cousins* and watched Alex Campbell, Noel Murphy, Davy Graham, Bert Jansch, Doris Henderson and John Renbourn. Old Meg would wander into *Les Cousins* to sing a song before making her way to someplace else with her carrier bags.

The girl watched Jo Ann Kelly singing blues and John Renbourn with Beverley Martyn. 'Wow,' she thought, 'that's what I want. To sing like Jo Ann.' The young women were often pill-eyed high and needed to satisfy early morning munchies at the *Golden Egg* in Leicester Square.

CLARA THE CLOWN 'We are gathered together in order to praise the *Golden Egg* in Oxford Street.'

If you were a blues fan, it had to be acoustic. The African Americans were loud and amplified in Chicago but in Britain, if you were into the blues, you weren't a real folk fan. And as for admitting you listened to the Beatles. Forget it. Then there was *Trad* versus *Modern*, Miles Davis versus Chris Barber. 'I love it all,' the girl said, 'why can't I love it all?'

One evening in the Richmond *Imperial* she noticed a guy wearing black leather but it wasn't the biker ton up boy look she'd known in Lowestoft. He was older and arty. The leathers hung on him differently. He sauntered over and sat with young women. He was an artist and lived above a bakery up on the hill. He spoke in a laconic kind of way and seemed unruffled by anything or anyone. Surprising for a painter, his nails were clean and well manicured. He must spend hours in the bathroom. And on his breath hung the faint smell of peppermint. He wore a subtle but expensive watch and on the other wrist, just visible beyond the cuff, an exotic band of intricately carved silver set with dark red stones. 'My one little family heirloom,' he would say, when anyone asked to see this piece of jewellery. It was the sort of object you'd expect a woman to wear, not a single man in his thirties. 'Isn't it lovely?'

He invited her to visit him the next weekend. He didn't seem to want to get her into bed so she began to relax. He wasn't on the make but he did have an air of danger. He persuaded her to have an urchin haircut. She wore her jeans and boots, and loved his *Harley Davidson* bike. He joked with her and called her 'Little Harry'. She turned up a little earlier than they'd arranged one evening and he was still eating. So she sat on a chair. He offered her nothing and she watched him eat. She suddenly felt an overwhelming sense of being in the wrong place with the wrong man. He was playing with her, like a cat with a mouse. He was laughing at her, not with her. He took her to a pub near the river in Twickenham. They had a few drinks and then she left. He was never going to be a boyfriend. That was that and the dreams of a haven above a bakery with an artist came to an end.

Beat and the girl were picked up one night as they hitched back to Earl's Court by a man in a large car who said his name was Lord John.

CLARA THE CLOWN 'Oh yeah?'

Tall and slender, with an aroma of sandalwood and shoe polish, Lord John dressed in a faultlessly elegant style, wearing a sober but exquisitely cut suit with a silk lining in Indian hot pink. The dark cloth of his jacket contrasted with an audaciously patterned tie, a swagger of a hat and a flash of jewel coloured socks. The young women wore black and purple, imagining they were bohemian, and he drove them to his house tucked away down a mews in Kensington. They discovered that he loved to entertain and to have pretty young girls about the place. Not for him but for show.

The people at his house were unlike any the young women had met before. People with loud and confident voices who wore very expensive clothes, drank martinis or whiskey, smoked cigarettes in holders and reefers as if absolutely normal. Soho was the place where you could buy garlic and listen to jazz, folk and blues. This was Bohemian Soho, with men of dubious reputations from Bethnal Green and Poplar, in their flash suits with gold tiepins, and debutant girls seeking a bit of rough in the after hours clubs and private watering holes. Aristocrats, villains, prostitutes, lawyers, politicians, gamblers and artists. Rock stars and photographers. Martinis, cocaine, sex and ill-gotten riches. All in the mix.

The young women met a man at a party in Chelsea thrown by April Ashley and John Dennis 'Biffo' Bindon, who it was said had the biggest dick in London. Servicing the gentry on the party circuit? Bindon was also an actor, playing a violent mobster alongside Mick Jagger in *Performance* (1970). Serious type casting. Whispered behind hands and over the telephone, were rampant rumours about Bindon and Princess Margaret at her home on *Mustique* in the Caribbean. East End bad boys had their hands in security and protection rackets. The Kray twins, the Richardson Gang and Jack The Hat McVitie. Corruption and obscenity, bent coppers and bent lawyers. All in each others pockets and worse.

THE BOSS 'It was always so.'

A snort of derision.

NASTY NELLIE 'A plague of worms, toads and cockroaches upon their heads.'

THE BOSS 'Above the law, entitled by rank, blood, land and privilege. The law itself, entitled by uniform connections, violence and control.'

NASTY NELLIE 'Toffs, I hate 'em.'

A haughty stare.

A woman drenched in *Chanel No 5*, with a red cashmere draped casually over her shoulders like she wasn't staying. Another party? A date? Her perfectly manicured hands, red nails like her jacket, held a slim glass with ice and vodka or gin. This Lord John seemed to have a bottomless supply of alcohol. Though there was no *Blue Nun*.

He collected them the following weekend in his dark maroon *Mercedes*. 'A party,' he said, 'a Sunday lunch party, do come.' The young women from Earl's Court had never tasted garlic on crisp warm French bread. They'd never seen olives, glistening black and green in olive oil. They'd never seen olive oil outside the chemist. There was the smell of cigarette smoke and Italian coffee, and a bubbling lasagna in a huge brown earthenware dish, with a crisp green salad in a large wooden bowl, dressed with oil, herbs and garlic. There was a wooden board with cheeses. Blue vein cheese, soft white cheese, golden and red cheese. And little round crackers, olives on sticks with little cubes of cheese, bowls of crisps and mounds of chocolates. A woman arrived dressed in furs over a little black dress, spilling out of her chauffeur driven car. Her appearance said, 'This is not cheap, I am not cheap.'

White powders were being sniffed up nostrils. This wasn't speed. This was grade A cocaine. The talk became insane and nobody appeared to listen. It was manic. They spoke fast and loud, all at once. The girl took a tentative sniff. It burned her nose, made her afraid and then paranoid. She slid out the room. Where was Beat? She searched the bedrooms, the bathroom and the stairs. Beat was nowhere to be seen. The girl began to sweat. No one noticed her and she started grinding her teeth. She found Beat eating in the kitchen and stuffed bread and little cubes of cheese into her mouth, trying to find a way back to normal. They left and walked home, not daring to take a bus or the tube, and smoked until the dawn light slid through the crack between the two dusty curtains. They then slept, curled up on the small bed.

When the girl awoke it was almost noon and Beat was gone. She lay in the clothes she'd worn the day before, staring at the ceiling following the map of cracks. Turning her head she noticed a spider's web between the bed and bedside table. Her finger disturbed the thin and delicate strands and a tiny spider scuttled to safety. She brought the finger to her face to inspect the debris and she cried. She'd broken the web, banished the spider and almost enjoyed it. She hated herself.

Invited on a date or two by Lord John, the girl knew she was out of her depth. His crowd talked in a language that whisked past her ears and over her head before she could grasp the meaning. He had many girls and she wasn't in love. Merely curious and scared of the white powder.

Out of the blue the girl received letter from Beryl. The Lowestoft family was moving to New Zealand. She rang Beryl who sounded irritated and announced in a cursory manner that she should meet her at Waterloo Station the following week where they would see the family off to the other side of the world.

At the station the sisters were clearly stiff with apprehension. Jennifer's lips were locked tight. The younger barely knew the girl who'd been away for more than five years. A long time in a very young life. The stepfather was busy organising bags and tickets. He didn't look at the girl. The mother closed her eyes as she sat on a brown suitcase and complained of a headache. Why, why, why was the mother going to the other side of the world with a man she claimed to hate? The train pulled out, bound for Southampton. The girl lifted her arm that weighed a ton and waved. No one waved back.

'What *exactly* are you doing with your life?' Asked Beryl. The girl replied, 'Ah well, I'm looking for another job.' Beryl looked impatient, 'I've done my best. It's up to you now to make something of it.'

Beryl disappeared down into the hot mouth of the underground station, bound for Charing Cross or London Bridge and on back to Sevenoaks. And the family was gone. Would the girl ever see them again? She stood for a moment watching other people leaving, arriving, buying newspapers and a cuppa. She felt stuck to the ground, as if her feet had been glued to the concourse, for ever and ever amen.

The girl received a card from Bridget and the old life she'd left behind was suddenly in sharp focus. She must've traced her through Beryl, though she couldn't figure out how. Bridget asked the girl to meet her off a coach at Victoria Station. She and Beat duly arrived half an hour early, and Bridget was walking down the steps from a coach that had come from Cheltenham.

What a shock. Gone was the Brigitte Bardot ponytail, the pale pink lipstick and the sexy crooked smile. Instead was a head on which sat a brittle blond candy-floss helmet and glasses with butterfly paste diamond wings. In a tight black skirt, her skinny legs wobbling on high heels, Bridget stood two suitcases on the ground, clearly meaning to stay and not just for a weekend. The girl made a bed on the floor of her tiny room. It didn't take long to work out that the interim years had moulded a very different Bridget. Her foray into crime hadn't stopped at the house of Rowena in Lowestoft all those years ago, and she'd ended up in a detention centre in Cheltenham. After her time was up she stayed put and found work in a casino, quickly locating the moneyed lads with dubious ways and means in that part of the world.

Within a week Bridget turned up her nose at the jazz and blues dives that Beat and the girl frequented, the scruffy down at heel musicians and would be poets and painters, writers and dreamers, ragamuffins all. She found herself a man of the turf, the owner of a string of bookies and within another week she was off. That was the last the girl ever heard from Bridget.

The girl found another job. Five days a week as an assistant at a nursery in Paddington on Westbourne Park Road, a No31 bus ride from Earl's Court to Chepstow Road. She discovered a new London area and liked it. The exotic food stores on Queensway and the Portobello Road. She loved the secondhand clothes, 1920s, '40s, even '50s dresses, feather boas and strange little velvet hats. Most other girls wanted new, new, new after a childhood of wearing 'hand me downs'.

She didn't like the new job though she did love the children. It felt like the old ropes that bound her were back. The cleaning, the matron and the other staff who didn't seem to accept her. Or was it she who couldn't connect? Normal life seemed shut off from her. She left before she was sacked after three months.

Summer 1964 in the city. It was a Thursday and the girl began to long for the salty sea-air. 'Let's go,' she said to Beat, 'let's go to Hastings.' Saturday morning before ten they took a tube down to the Oval in Kennington, then thumbs out. It took several lifts to get out of the southeast London sprawl, then on the outskirts of Bromley. They hopped into a truck bound for Tonbridge, then another two hops and they rode into Hastings in a van delivering carpets. It took them the best part of a day but they were outside the pub where she'd first sung, by five o'clock. They ate fish and chips wrapped in newspaper while sitting on the shingle, backs against a boat, and a little while later they were in the bar. Mack was there by eight and then some other faces she'd met before. It was a Saturday session, she was three ciders down and ready for it. She sang *Cocaine*. She knew how it worked on the brain, how it had driven her momentarily insane, and could sing it from the memory of a clenched jaw. The rush of nervous energy, the paranoia and despair came the following day.

The murder of the spider in its web. 'Rock me Baby, rock me all night long.' As she sang, she knew the sex she'd known was for sure no love sex. The song became a song of regret and need in an awful wave of confusion. 'Rock me baby

174

in your big brass bed... Rock me all night long.' Pop a pill, drink another drink, get wasted, that's the thing to do. Don't look behind the walls. Turn your back on all that. When she got up to sing, Beat was worried, assuming the girl would be a terrible embarrassment. Beat said afterwards that the hairs on the back of her neck bristled but oh, 'She can sing, oh my God, she wasn't bull-shitting.'

They slept up under the lea of a boat near the tall black fishing huts on the beach in the Old Town, using jackets as blankets and duffle bags as pillows. It was past dawn and the rising sun hinted at the warm day to come. They were stiff. Shingle is unforgiving but their bones were young and they woke refreshed by the sound of the sea lapping the shore, gulls screeching and the scrunch of shingle. As the fishermen gathered, the young women with salt on thier lips wandered off to find egg and chips, bread and butter. And tea, glorious tea. Hot, brown and sweet.

Back in Earl's Court, things were beginning to slide. The girl had no job and no money. And she was hooked on music and Methedrine. This demonic pair drove her through the nights and to hell with the days that were spent in bed where her sheets remained unwashed for weeks. She slept in that harsh way when you come down from a speedball high. An uncomfortable sleep with eyes feeling encrusted with grit and needles. Then she couldn't pay the rent. 'The rent today or you leave by the morning.' She did a moonlight flit and left to live in a house on the Fulham Road near the football ground. It was a house of madness. A time that became an empty memory. A dark time when possessions were worthless and anything you owned was stolen for somebody else's next fix. A way of life. What's yours is mine. She even momentarily lost Beat.

Nasty Nellie 'Oh, you'll end up a palsied old woman down Ragamuffin Road without a doorbell to call your own.'

The girl met 'Paris Nat' Schaffer in *Finches* pub just off Goodge Street. His loquacious talk was of gossip from the streets and he had a thorough yet strangely indefinable knowledge of politics. Nat held court. A small crowd of young men and very pretty girls hovered around him at the bar. Seemingly in his late thirties or early forties, he was a man with a charismatic and sometimes menacing energy. Dark eyed, he had thick black curly hair greying at the temples and always tucked under a black hat. He walked with a slight limp which he would at various times attribute to a war wound, a car accident or a fight. He hated all politicians and skilfully avoided giving away any details about his life.

It was hard to dislike him. His flirtatious and tantalising gossip amused. With an airy wave of his long fingered hand, with the fingers that so deftly played his accordion, with a dramatic yet comical sigh, with a rise of his dark bushy eyebrows, he would enquire, 'And you, what are *you* doing?'

NASTY NELLIE 'Oh my lady, what are we going to do with you? What's your name? How do you do? Where are you going and why?'

CLARA THE CLOWN 'I'll catch the moon tonight, watch me,'

Handing round a hat for Nat, the girl became his bottler. Flattered to be chosen but afraid of him at the same time, it seemed to be a feather in the cap in the busker's world to have bottled for Nat. He worked cinema and theatre queues, and the busy tube stations, Oxford Street and Tottenham Court Road, Bond Street, Charing Cross Road, Piccadilly, Leicester Square and Hyde Park Corner. She handed round the hat, smiling for money in the reeking traffic fumes. And she followed him as he dodged in and out of putrid pissy alleys, taking short cuts to this place or that, winding his way around central London. He knew all the back ways and how to avoid the law as if nothing in the world mattered except the next busking session, a few bob and a drink.

One day, in a lull whilst working a cinema queue, when the punters had all shuffled in to see *Carry On Jack*, or *This Sporting Life*, Nat asked the girl if she could sing and she dared to say yes. He put her out there and she had to find that big voice again. 'Sing up girlie.' He would bark like a rusty chain on a traction engine, 'we're not going to get any money with you whispering like that. Sing up!' She sang up. She'd rehearse in her head every waking hour and even in her dreams, imagining herself as a sanguine and fearless woman. He taught her a raggedy ragbag of songs. *Bye,Bye Blackbird*, *I Love Paris*, *Downtown* or *Roses of Picardy*.

She often sang *The House of the Rising Sun* wearing a black beret, an old red satin dress and a pair of red high heels, all of which she'd picked up in the London flea markets. She thought perhaps she'd look French, chic, older, taller. As if. London had moved into the 'Swinging '60s', with mini skirts and *Mary Quant*, *Vidal Sassoon* haircuts and carefully placed eyelashes. But the girl still hovered in the near dimly lit past.

Nat gave the girl her first gig, taught her to sing up, to sing out loud and for that, in her heart, she thanked him. She'd taken her second singing steps and her notes were out on the wind. She mused, 'I sing. I sing and who'd have thought it. Not the ones who wouldn't let me join the school choir or sing in the play in school in Lowestoft.'

NASTY NELLIE 'Hey I'm looking at you in your second hand clothes, working a cinema queue. Call that singing?'

WICKED WILL O'MINA 'Oh come now, you can do better than singing a song for sixpence.'

BETTY BLUES BELTER 'They *Call it Stormy Monday*.'

The old T-Bone Walker blues song, she loved it.

BETTY BLUES BELTER 'But Tuesday is just as bad'

One of the first blues players to take blues into the electric domain.

BETTY BLUES BELTER 'The eagle flies on Friday and Saturday, I go out to play, yeah, the eagle flies on Friday and Saturday, I go out to play...'

THE BOSS 'You need more than an eagle my dear, you need a whole gang, a convocation.'

NASTY NELLIE 'Ah quit withering on. Witter and whinge, you're highly unhinged. That voice is like an old gate in need of WD40.'

BETTY BLUES BELTER 'Sunday I go to church and I kneel down and pray. And this is what I say, baby. Lord have mercy. Lord have mercy on me. You know I cried. Lord have mercy, Lord have mercy on me.'

'Well, we've been there before, asking the Lord,' she thought, remembering Lowestoft and the water at the font. The dreadful Carp Family. Who, where and what was The Lord?

NERVY NORA 'Please. Pretend you never ever saw her, just ignore her. Let her shake and let her shiver, that's what she wants. So go on, give her the ammunition to help her wallow in self pity. Let her follow her nose. She knows you know. She's small and plain, her thoughts are mundane, all rolling interminably around in her brain.'

CLARA THE CLOWN 'I'm a clown, a knave, no grave face on me. The masquerade is here. I'm a jester with a joke on my lips. Listen, a serenade in your ear.'

THE BOSS 'Shut up.'

VERSE 15

The Race

Stormy Monday Bobby Blue Band, 1962

1964 to 1966: agony and below rock bottom. Joining Shades of Grey. Hilton Valentine and The Race. Playing at the Marquee, at Klooks Kleek and the 100 Club. Her first review. Meeting Larry Smart. Meeting Jimi Hendrix. The International Times launch at the Roundhouse. A quickening and a bridge towards motherhood.

In November she bumped into Beat in Earl's Court Road. She'd hoped she would. No longer in Redcliffe Gardens, Beat was staying in Velma's room. This wasn't ideal as Velma had a boyfriend. Two in a bed, one on a settee. They found a flat above a shop, opposite the *Brompton Cemetery* in Old Brompton Road, between Kempsford Gardens and Kramer Mews. The *Troubadour* was only a minute walk away.

The living room, on the first floor at the front, had a real fireplace and a mantle piece. The settee was covered in an Indian bedspread. Best not to look underneath. The table came with two mismatched wooden chairs. In the back there was a kitchen with a terrifying old gas cooker, an ancient chipped sink with an equally ancient *Ascot* boiler above it, a greasy wooden draining board and no fridge or table. There was a bath in the corner with a cotton curtain on a wire to give the bather privacy. A small window next to the cooker afforded a view of the back yard. A space with no flowers, only the overspill from the shop downstairs, old boxes, crates, bottles and mounds of 'could be anything'.

The lavatory was on the half-landing and upstairs there was a room on the second floor front with a double bed in each corner, an enormous wardrobe with one door missing, and a chest of drawers you couldn't open properly. If you danced a jig you'd crack your legs on the furniture. The walls were covered in a faded floral print, long ago reduced to a smudge. It was cheap. It was home. The girl could hear the voice of Mr and Mrs Carp declaring, 'It's a pig sty.'

NASTY NELLIE 'It's where you belong.'

A week's rent in advance and they were in. In the mews around the nearest corner was a coffin maker. This made sense with the cemetery so close by. The young women could collect offcuts from the coffin man. A tall black man with stooping shoulders from the many hours spent bending over his workbench and a woollen

178

hat clamped on the back of his head. His voice, deep and fruity, was never far from a laugh, his lilting Jamaican island accent a song on his lips. He took to the two girls, especially Beat. He flirted but never pushed it too far. A good man.

Winter in the new home across the road from the dead and they were as warm as they'd ever been in front of the spitting fire. They bought a fireguard in the market in North End Road and a clock for the mantle piece. The girl began to thaw as the speed and the fear melted away in the firelight.

The shop downstairs was run by a man from India who sat on a stool the whole day long, smoking, reading the paper and occasionally selling something. Dusty, the shop smelled of rancid butter and old fruit. The floors and shelves were covered in cracked linoleum and the faded wallpaper kept in situ by the glue of greasy muck and luck.

He sold tins of this and that and had a freezer full of peas and fish fingers. He sold newspapers, sweets, cigarettes and boxes of bananas, which looked like they'd turned rotten on the boats before docking at Tilbury. The young women took in a girl they'd met, homeless with a small child in tow. Who was she? Long gone. She only stayed a month and then moved on. One day he sold the homeless girl a *Cadburys* flake full of maggots and the maggots fell from the child's lips. They didn't much use the shop after that. The child lived.

A gang of prisoners worked in the cemetery, weeding, repairing, painting and doing whatever needs doing around the tombstones. They asked the girls to buy them five or ten *Weights* or *Park Drive*, thrusting coppers through the iron railings. At night it was one of London's weirdest cruising grounds. Illicit love amongst the Victorian dead.

The rent was due. It was always due. They met a young actress in the pub one night who told them about a cleaning agency where out of work actors, artists and the like could get paid work by the hour. Ironing, washing, dusting. Simple. The girl knew very well how to clean. If she could just be left alone to daydream and go home at the end of the days work. As long as the boss was pleasant and didn't treat the cleaner like the dirt she was removing. They enrolled with the agency the next day and had work within a week.

The girl cleaned in Chelsea for April Ashley, the first transsexual she'd met knowingly. April was charming. Her home, filled with vases of flowers on polished wooden tables, was beautiful and clean.

The girl did piles and piles of ironing for a busy lawyer in Fulham, a mother of two with a husband in the city.

The girl dusted and polished a dolls house studio in Glebe Place for a glamorous woman who painted portraits and adored Annigoni, talking of him endlessly.

The girl cleaned one day for a Canadian artist in a studio just off the Fulham Road. 'Why don't you model for me?' he said, 'I'll pay you the going rate.' 'Well, who'd have imagined that?' she thought.

The following week she found herself laying on a couch for two longs hours, with a red velvet shawl barely concealing her nakedness. 'Don't move,' he said, when she twitched, 'keep still.' That's what she was paid for, to be young, naked and still. One day a guitarist was there. 'Do you mind if he stays?' said the artist. The artist's friend, John Williams, played his guitar beautifully. The artist was gay and she was naked but safe. Were all artists gay, she wondered? 'I'm a queer dear, a queer,' he'd said when he first asked her to take off her clothes.

It was early March with an unexpected run of sunny days. The girl hated her lily white legs so went into *Boots* for a tube of *Tanfastic*. The result? Smeared patchy orange skin, especially on her knees, hands, feet and toes. She'd gone all rusty. He said, 'What have you done to your skin? The colour is all wrong. You had such a lovely skin tone and now you look blotchy.' She was embarrassed. Not so much by the reference to her pale white skin but by the compliment. She promised to resist future desires for suntanned limbs.

With money in their pockets, the young women went to *Biba* in Abingdon Road where Barbara Hulanicki made dresses with tight cut skinny sleeves that would only fit young skinny arms. Earthy colours. Plum, amber, dark blue. Hats and wide leg trousers, little striped tops and canvas boots, purple, red and black. They loved the look and strutted their threads with pride. The girl was beginning to own things. Her one bag was now three. She had a shawl, her clothes, a clock, a picture and some old china picked up on the Portobello Road. And a cushion, a blanket and one or two records.

She found another job. Three days a week as a receptionist for a dental surgery in an elegant early Victorian town house in Upper Brooke Street near Grosvenor Square. She took a bus down the Brompton Road to Knightsbridge and up Park Lane, around Marble Arch to Oxford Street. Her first task was to make *Nescafe* coffee and two rounds of toast in a little kitchen, and by nine o'clock the first patient would arrive. She had to show them into the waiting room, resplendent with dark oil paintings in heavy gilt frames and glossy magazines, *The Lady Vogue* and *Country Life*, on a highly polished oval table surrounded by comfortable armchairs.

A bell would ring and she'd show the patients to the surgery on the first floor. She was given luncheon vouchers and on the dot of one-fifteen sat in a café in Binney Street, ordering a cheese omelette and chips or a bowl of tomato soup, or perhaps a spaghetti bolognese. She hadn't eaten so well for a long time. In her little room next to the waiting room she read, daydreamed and wondered whether her days of strange and short lived jobs would ever be over so she could sing for her supper. With the job in the surgery, the cleaning and modelling, the rent was paid and more. She bought a new record, Howlin' Wolf *Moanin' in the Moonlight*. The scruffy flat on the Old Brompton Road began to smell of young women, perfume, talcum powder, scrambled eggs, toast and tea.

The girl met a man from Leeds in the folk club above a pub in Seagrave Road just around the corner. He was a student at one of the art schools in London and he was nice. She spent some time at his place with his flatmate, a cartoonist who was an amputee and drove a blue invalid car. The cartoonist made her laugh a lot, saying how he liked to freak people out by removing his legs in inappropriate places. He took them off before going to bed and sometimes in the evening when friends were around. 'They chafe my skin,' he said, 'where they fit onto my hips.' In the 1960s prosthetic limbs were uncomfortable and clumsy.

The girl felt easy with him, maybe because he seemed so comfortable with his legs, or rather the lack of them. He could move around the place on his stumps as nimbly as anyone she'd ever seen. In and out of the bedroom, the bathroom, and into the tiny kitchen, his strong arms hoisting his small body off and on chairs and beds. He had no self-pity and wanted no help unless it was absolutely necessary. She could've learned so much from this man.

The boyfriend from Leeds went off to visit his family seven weeks after they'd met, so the cartoonist and the girl hung out together. If they went to a pub that involved a journey, she'd squat down on the floor, curled up beside his metal limbs and they giggled their way to where ever it was they were going, especially at traffic lights when a car might pulled up and the driver peered in, seeing her there crouched beside his tin legs.

The art student boyfriend had invited her to visit his family that Christmas but cancelled at the last minute. His family didn't want this stranger in their home. They drifted apart and she moved on. Years later she regretted not staying in touch with the cartoonist. He'd gone by the time she'd plucked up courage to visit.

Beat and the girl spent many nights going to folk clubs. The *Troubadour* or the Seagrave Road pub, out to Richmond or to Soho. The guitarist John Renbourn fancied Beat. He'd sometimes come back to the flat, sit in a corner and play. They met two young men, Richard and Tony, when building a circle of friends. One evening in the *Roundhouse* they watched Dorris Henderson, the first black face they'd seen on the folk circuit apart from Davey Graham who was mixed race. They'd see her at the *Troubadour*, playing Appalachian ballads on her autoharp and hooking up with John Renbourn for a while. She was a wonder to the girls. It was said her grandfather was pure Blackfoot Indian.

London was beginning to buzz, shedding the war years like an old skin. The Rolling Stones, the Animals and the Beatles were the bands to be seen with. Models, photographers, actors, writers. London was swinging and things for the girl were steadying. She took the bus ride to Park Lane three days a week and the lunched in the café near *Selfridges* One night, in the *Goat in Boots* pub on the Fulham Road, they met Wally and Robin, two aspiring folk singers from South Wales who soon moved in on the young women. Wally took the girl and Robin, Beat. The flat began to smell of beer and men. The girl was in love, or so she imagined.

Wally was a gregarious man, quick to laugh and quick to anger. He made her feel like a queen, called her red because of the auburn lights in her hair. She started buying *Harmony*, a wash-in shampoo to 'bring out the red head in you.' He heard her sing one night in a pub after hours. He took her to meet his family in Llanelli, South Wales. They were a pious Chapel family and she slept in the spare room. She ate *Lava Bread* for breakfast and thought it salty and delicious despite looking like a cow pat. She did notice that no women were allowed in the public bar.

Out in Richmond the girl and Beat took the Welsh boys to the *Imperial*, the place with the punch drunk pot man, Ginger and the lads. Wally got jealous that night and punched her hard on the side of her head for, as he told her, looking at men. She was his and he made her feel she was the heart of his life. No one had ever made her feel that before. Wally was jealous of Richard and Tony, though they weren't, and never had been, lovers. He was jealous of anyone who looked at her when he was drunk, or simply in a bad mood.

With black eyes or a sore mouth she began to miss a day here and there at the dental surgery. She rang one day and said she was so sorry, she had to go away, 'My mother is ill.' Everyone has a mother. Sometimes they're ill and daughters have to rush home to help. They weren't to know that her mother was thousands of miles away, and that she was the last person she'd have called. In fact, the girl had no address or telephone number. Her family may as well have moved to Mars.

One night after a session at the *Goat In Boots*, back at the flat, he held her backwards over the bath, his hands around her neck. She thought she was going to die. The door suddenly crashed shut downstairs. Beat and Robin were in the kitchen and his hands fell away. He left, cursing his way down the stairs. Robin wandered off the next day and the young women were alone again in the place that hadn't felt like home for a while. The first thing she did was spring clean. Mops, buckets, brooms, polish, dusters, water, disinfectant. Wash, wash, wash, that's what she wanted to do.

A few weeks later and oh God, she knew she was pregnant. For the moment she kept it to herself. If the words remained unsaid then perhaps it wasn't true. It was her 21st birthday 7th April 1965. The young women were in *Finches* in the Fulham Road and someone said, 'It's her birthday, 21 today.' Before she could say, 'I'm pregnant!' Drinks were poured. She had wine, she had gin, she had cider and then she was back in the flat with no idea how she got there. She threw up, leaning over the bath where he'd tried to strangle her, the bruise still on her neck. These were desperate times but there came a miracle. In May she heard about another job as a live-in mother's help in Lyndhurst Gardens. Two children, a basement flat provided with her own entrance, possibly two sharing, and a small rent deducted from her wages. The family were desperate as the last help departed rather suddenly.

The young women went to the pretty pink cherry tree lined road off Kensington Church Street for the girl's interview. She took her *St Christopher's* papers but they didn't even ask for a reference. She appeared to be a nice girl and it all seemed perfect. In the kitchen there was a huge Welsh dresser, a vast and wonderful pine table, a bench against the wall and chairs enough for six people to eat at once. In the flat there was one small bedroom which Beat had and a pull out bed in the sitting room, which the girl took. The bathroom, with a slipper bath, was underneath the street where the coal cellar had once been. At the back was a sheltered courtyard full of shrubs with a bench seat, roses and a clematis, all outside the sitting cum bedroom.

It was a perfect place. A place that was to remain a vision of how she'd like a home to be. Friends gathered around a kitchen table, laden with plates and glasses. A meal in the oven and a secret garden, lush with plants. The world out there was beyond a solid front door. There for the taking and then you'd be home again, safe and sound.

NASTY NELLIE 'This isn't your home. You'll be gone, and sooner than you think.'

The voices were at it again.

CLARA THE CLOWN 'That's the way to do it.'

WICKED WILL O'MINA 'Here's the fire. Put your fingers in it. That's right, burn, burn, burn.'

She did seem to be inviting disaster. She'd parted company with her thinking feeling self back in in Lowestoft, or maybe who she'd been back in the flat under the eaves in Blackheath, in the days of bombs and the blackout with a mother who was unable to love.

Wally and Robin got hold of their address and came to visit on the same day as a friend from the girl's days in *St Christopher's*. Halina was a Polish girl, born in a displaced persons camp in France. At the end of the war Halina was brought to England by the *Ockendon Venture* to a country house on the outskirts of Woking in Surrey.

It was their first weekend in the flat. They made tea and bustled around the kitchen, playing house. The boys had beer and she wondered if the smile on her face betrayed the presence of the foetus in her belly. She said nothing and watched as Wally flirted with Halina. They all left for the pub at eight. She didn't join them and as the door closed she wept into her new pillow, face down on her new bed in the basement flat in cherry tree heaven.

THE BOSS 'Oh dear, what have you done. What a kerfuffle. You fool, you fool, you fool.'

The family wanted her to go with them to their house in Burnham on Crouch near the river. Yachts and club houses again. The girl played with the children, made lunches, cleaned the holiday home until every tap shone, and smiled despite feeling rough with sore breasts, morning sickness and heartache.

It was arranged that she'd return to London on the last weekend of the holiday, do a family shop, a little sorting in children's rooms and then they'd return mid-week. Desperate measures had to be taken. An abortion was lined up. She couldn't cope with a baby. She could barely cope with herself.

NASTY NELLIE 'Oh my, oh my. Just you see, that girl will cry.'

Richard had a friend who knew somebody. After telephone calls and cash in hand, the girl who was three months gone already, found herself with a woman and a tub of soapy water. Douche, and the job was done, the woman gone. 'Go to bed,' she said, 'take some aspirin, and make sure your friend is with you. It will all happen in a few hours.' Later that night the girl was in extreme pain. In belly gripping agony. Richard and Beat got her across to the Fulham Road Hospital where she waited in the outpatients and then darkness. In a bed, alone and frightened. What had she done? What was she doing? 'It was a boy.' The nurse who did little to hide her contempt, showed her the mess in the basin. A foetus in cold aluminium.

NASTY NELLIE 'You're a murderer and you're vile, vile, vile.'

She felt sick and threw up all over herself. Back in Lyndhurst Gardens, the job was up and with it the flat. It had lasted barely three months. She was sick in mind and body. Where would she go? A friend from the Richmond days offered a floor in his basement flat in Chiswick. In a room where the curtains were never opened because it could be seen from the street. The friend was a night prowler and a hashish dealer.

Losing large clots of blood, she shrank from being a small girl to a skeletal girl. She was weak and scared. Ginger and Beat tried to persuade her to go to the Labour Exchange to sign on. She was sick and she had no job and no home. National Assistance? She'd no idea what it all meant. Was she eligible? 'What do I say?' she said. 'They'll think I've had an abortion if I tell them what's happening. It's against the law and they'll put me in prison.' She went anyway and gave the address in Chiswick. Later in the week, with a few pounds in her pocket, she could eat, though she wasn't hungry most of the time.

Beat spiralled into a depression and both were at rock bottom. Ginger found them another place through a friend with a house boat on the river at Isleworth. The owner was away for a month and they would boat-sit. Their bags of cushions and clothes and bits of this and that made a home wherever they were.

Weaving across the wooden walkways, past the bobbing boats, drunk as skunks some nights and sinking into gently swaying beds that made them feel seasick. Muddy waters, deep in the shit they were, deep in the muddy shit. It was August, there was a hot sun over the river and the boat owner was returning. Where would they go?

Nina had a new flat and offered Beat a room. The girl was once more on the loose. She went back to the Fulham house, the house of pills and the ongoing drugs and sex that seemed to be the long party in the mid '60s. Spencer Davis *Keep on Running*. She'd run if only she knew where to run to. There was a Dr Robert in Chelsea, dispenser of drugs. *Methadone* and *Mandrax* to a Rolling Stone, to the bands and all the lost boys. Dr Robert didn't much like the girls. Boys were his toys.

She was now below rock bottom. The ropes she bound herself with were as tight as ever. Her brain was turning to liquid, her limbs stick thin but heavy and she could barely support her body. She mapped her path that had begun in Lewisham and she lost the line somewhere between London and Cambridge. Or was it elsewhere? The wall of death, speeding, 80, 90, 100 miles an hour. A grey pale man, a lined face, a slug man.

Richard asked her to sing with his new band, Shades of Grey. Was this a life line? Her first band? He played the guitar. There was a bongo player and another guitarist, David Circuit. They played in little club in Gloucester Road to an audience of five friends and several Australians. It was a start. She thought of the woman with the slobbering dog and wondered who was now buying the salami, picking up the silky clothes and washing her back.

After a month of rehearsals Shades Of Grey played a gig in a basement club off the King's Road. Richard had the rock star look. He was a thin, high cheek boned, dark haired, snake hipped, Keith Richard kind of guy and he would hang out with the guitarist Jimmy Page, the hot session player of the times. Jimmy took them into *Regent Sound Studios* in Denmark Street. Her first studio. It was a small room with the two track *Revox* recorder and egg cartons as soundproofing. The Stones had recorded there and she was a little star struck, as if they were all in the same studio at the same time. She was at least singing alongside the spirit of Mick Jagger. The engineer said, 'You have a good recording voice.'

They would often go to the *Gioconda Café* for egg and chips, and cups of tea or coffee. Her hands wrapped around the warm cup. Crisp chips, eggs with soft yellow yolks and frothy coffee.

> GUILTY GERTIE 'I'm afraid. I'm beneath contempt. I'm inadequate. I'm exempt. You assault me with a shocking tongue and I cower and break. You shatter me. I want to lie in a million shards of glass and bleed my last blood.'
>
> THE BOSS 'Oh God, do stop. What do you want? Redemption? Forgiveness?'

Things were looking better. She was singing in a band but the voices were still in her head, those insistent bloody voices. Spinning yarns, ordering her to do this or that, blaming, wheedling, and on a good day approving. Some days passed with just a mild chastisement or a little faint praise. Good grief.

Richard's girlfriend, Babette had pre-Raphaelite golden hair and wore 1920s velvet, floral frocks and lace. She made beautiful necklaces using glass beads. Richard said, 'Tony and Peta his chick, are leaving. Let's try and get in there. She's a crazy landlady but she's got a room. Lets go.' Once more the girl and her bags were on the move. She'd already lost the record player along the way. Down the New King's Road, turn right into Oakley Street and there they were, outside number 16. Tony and Peta, with their bags in hand, had had some sort of altercation. They were off and the girl was ushered in through the door. She was in and they were out.

Peta was a blonde model with the new *Vidal Sassoon* haircut and the long legged coltish look of the 'Chelsea Girl.' Tony and Peta wandered off in the direction of the King's Road. Like two halves of a lemon, the girl thought, they looked remarkably similar. 'Don't worry,' they'd said, 'we got a place in South Ken. See you later in the *Chelsea Potter*.'

Richard told Sheila the landlady, that the girl was a singer, so she called her Edith after her favourite, Piaf. The girl was worried in case Sheila asked her to sing and she'd be found out to be anything but a Piaf.

The girl wanted a room in the house. She wanted to put down her bags in a place where the curtains could be open in the daytime, where the electricity worked and the bath ran hot water. She longed for a place where no trip wires were hidden in a perfect meadow of a million blades of green grass, daisies and buttercups. She'd been homeless for almost a year and was exhausted.

She was taken to the first floor to a little room at the back overlooking Margaretta Terrace. The room was green. As green as the trees outside the window would become, with faded green velvet curtains, a green cover on the bed and pale green walls. There was a single brass bed, a tiny black fire grate, a little chair beside the fire, and a bookcase. Was this a refuge?

In the past Sheila had been admitted to hospitals for being peculiar. Forcibly taken in for her own good. Her penalty was a frontal lobotomy. She'd known Richard Wright, had moved in illustrious circles, had been married and had a daughter. Now she was all alone in a tall Chelsea house, drinking *Pernod* and collecting stray people. She shopped in the King's Road, often drunk and limping with her gammy foot and a basket balanced on her head.

'House rules,' she said to the girl, 'you must always use the *Badedas* when you bathe. Don't use soap, it makes the bath dirty.' The girl had a bath that night with a squeeze of the luminous yellow. The aroma was divine as she wallowed up to her neck in bubbles until her skin was crinkled. More rules. 'Always leave a light on in the hall for the unexpected visitor and when I need the butler. Make sure the bell is there,' Sheila said, picking up a silver bell from the hall table and ringing it. The girl tried not to laugh. 'And never wash the salad bowl. It's not good for the wood. Wipe it with a cloth. The oil keeps it in perfect condition.' Avocado pears, green and slimy in a green salad, tossed with lemon and olive oil in the wooden bowl. She'd had never eaten such a thing. Her mouth was expecting the sweet taste of a fruit. She was in sophisticated territory. A good meal for the girl was pie and chips, anything with chips, egg, bacon or sausage. She thought about Lord John and the party food in his mews home. Food not properly savoured, so greedy were his guests. Jabber, jabber, sniff, snort.

Butler? Paul Templeman was the Japanese butler. With a 'come on' grin on his very English face he said, 'Hello, I'm the Japanese butler and I have the front first floor room, next to yours.'

Robert lived on the second floor. An Adonis, Robert was tall and muscle bound with pecs popping and broad shoulders inside his snowy white t-shirt. He wore a clean one every day. He had blue eyes, short curly blonde hair and wore tight blue jeans. His clothes barely contained his bursting health and strong body. 'And this is Robert. Isn't he handsome?' Sheila grinned coyly up at Robert from her tiny five feet one, fluttering her eyelashes, a drink in one hand, a cigarette in the other. He was of course gay, and both he and Sheila played the game. Middle-aged woman and gay man. He knew exactly what to do and it suited them both. The rent wasn't extortionate at Number 16 but certain roles were played out.

In the basement rooms next to the kitchen lived Sue Burman and Ted. Both Australian and mad about tennis. Sue was a big woman with a big laugh and glossy black hair. Ted was the second gay man in the house but unlike Robert, he was slim and very camp. Sue and Ted hung out together, an Australian club of two. 'My Australian cousins,' said Sheila, who'd never herself been there.

With Ted and Sue, and sometimes Robert, and occasionally Sheila if she felt brave or sober enough to leave her house, the girl sat in the *Chelsea Potter* or the gay pubs of West London. The *Queen's Head* in Tryon Street, the *Markham Arms*, in the King's Road, or the *Colherne* in Earl's Court where jazz was played on Sunday lunchtimes.

Through Robert the girl met a vainglorious man called Desmond who appeared to know everyone in any pub, party or the afternoon session in the *Picasso Coffee*

Bar. He would know them but few knew him. A bit like Nat, he was another mysterious man. He often wore a dark blue velvet smoking jacket with a silk scarf casually draped over one shoulder or a spotted cravat tucked into a pink silk shirt. His trousers were always immaculate and his shoes shone like a mirror. 'Hello,' said the girl when introduced, extending her hand to shake his. A dry hand with papery thin skin.

Later, when she asked him what he did, he replied, 'Now my dear girl, you must not be interested in an old man like me, my goodness no, no, no. Now do tell me about you. Robert tells me you sing? How lovely, I must hear you one of these days.' To the host of a party he said on another breath, 'that's an interesting painting you have there. Is it a new acquisition? How absolutely beautiful.' And then, with a shrug of a slim shoulder he artfully deflected the attention on himself, and nothing more was gleaned about the perfect guest. He was an oh so jolly man, with old fashioned manners and sweet smelling breath.

'He's a homosexual you know,' a woman whispered behind a discreet hand to Robert of the rippling muscles, 'you never see him with a woman. And no man I know wears clothes like he does.' All the women flirted with Robert. And Robert would wink at the girl over a shoulder here and there. When Desmond took his leave he did so with a minimum of fuss, unlike like his flamboyant arrivals. He disappeared like birdsong after dusk. He simply wasn't there anymore. The girl liked this. She hated goodbyes and took this way of departure into her own life. It was rumoured he was a retired diplomat but none knew where he'd been posted. Or perhaps he was the last of a long line of aristocrats. If so, which family and from where? The truth was that once he'd gone no one thought much about him until he popped up at another gathering. Then people were pleased to see him.

In the mid-1960s like abortion, being a homosexual was still unlawful. And away from swinging Chelsea and oh so degenerate Soho, it was something you had to be very careful about, who you knew and who knew you. The girl was meeting different people. She was drawn to those who didn't fit, didn't lead the prescribed so-called normal life. She listened and learned. She had a bit part in Sheila and Robert's opera. She was an extra in the scene around Chelsea and Earl's Court. She learned from those who lived on the edge and was in awe of the brave people who weren't allowed to openly love. They loved in secret behind closed doors if they were lucky.

One night after a gig Richard introduced the girl to a man called Tony Calder. A mover, shaker and pop star maker who'd worked with Marianne Faithful and

Andrew Loog Oldham. He said he could help her career. It sounded good so off she went one Sunday afternoon to a flat near Baker Street across the road from Regents Park. He answered the door in his pants. Get out girl. She was learning.

Richard was getting bored with the band. Fame seemed illusive. He disappeared for a while with the beautiful Babette. She missed them. At the jazz sessions on Sunday lunchtime at the *Colherne* pub on the Old Brompton Road, she met Louis and Pat. They lived in a basement flat just off the Earl's Court Road.

From Mauritius, Louis was a small and elegant man with ebony skin, dark warm eyes warm and a voice that lilted with the French language of his country. If the words in English failed to come he used French. He was delicate in his movements and his dancing was of another time. It was an old other worldly African dance.

Louis was an enthralling and extraordinary man. He had arrived in London a while ago though he never actually said when. He was a pastry cook and he prepared fragrant food from his homeland. He was also a drummer and his flat was full of drums and records. A tree trunk stood beside the door to his flat. There were leaves and twigs in vases, a stone from a sea shore, a chipped but beautiful cup and saucer on a shelf, no matter they didn't match. It was the beauty of the design, the oldness of the porcelain that he loved. She learned much from Louis and later wrote a poem in his memory. All of her homes from then on would contain an essence of Louis. He died when she was in America, much later.

Pat was from London's East End. Her long dark hair was pulled severely back in a pony tail. A chain smoking, tough talking woman, she had a beautiful strong face and liked the girl, didn't see her as a threat. One night Louis, Pat and the girl dropped a tab of acid. This time the trip was safe. Though she was terrified at first, she didn't want to appear cowardly.

The girl's room, with its colour and warmth, the rice fragrant in a pot on the stove, the incense drifting in the air and the music, was a gentle experience compared to the one before. They found her a record player. 'How much?' she asked. 'No, no, it's cool. It came to us, and now it comes to you,' they laughed, 'it's the way of the world.'

Pat put on some Ska music, *Don't call me Scarface*. She rolled a joint and produced three bottles of beer. The girl bought two records that week. Bobby Blue Bland *Two steps from the Blues* (1961) and Nina Simone *Broadway-Blues-Ballads* (1964). She played them so much she almost wore the grooves out. 'Oh Lord please don't let me be misunderstood.'

At the Sunday *Colherne* sessions with Beat, the girl hooked up with a crowd. Amongst them, Ozzie from Jamaica, Sarah from Maidstone and Keith from the Isle of Wight. Odd thing was, they were all the children of prison governors. They became the cooking posse. It was Ozzie's idea, 'We take it in turns to cook a Sunday dinner.' The young women shrank into their clothes. What to cook? The most sophisticated dish she'd ever produced was a garlic-less bolognese. She begged to go last. They all agreed. There was a roast chicken at Sarah's flat in Fulham, with roast potatoes, stuffing and gravy. Oh how the girl loved gravy. And then Ozzie cooked ackee and salt fish, okra, rice and peas, and plantain, served with white rum and coke. Keith made a beef stew with dumplings, heavy on the red wine. It was suspected that his girlfriend did the cooking and he stole the glory. It was fun. So, what would the she cook?

'Right,' said Sheila. This was her idea of a good time. Lots of young people, food and drink, the whole house would have to be involved. The Japanese butler must have a uniform. 'Let's plan our menu.' Oh God, would Sheila stay sober? When she was on a bender nobody could predict the outcome. The memory of Tony and Peta on the steps as the girl arrived was always at the back of the her mind and she never fully unpacked her bags.

Sheila took over and the girl was the cook's assistant. She chopped, slopped and helped to make the crumble. Avocado salad, mounds of chilli and plenty of garlic on tons of white rice, apple crumble and cream, and of course the booze. There was barely room for the gathering and they all squashed around the table in the basement kitchen. Robert was marvellous. He fetched, carried and flirted. Sue and Ted made everyone laugh and Sheila drank.

The cooking posse ate every crumb. The girl had taken her turn. She'd made her first crumble. She remembered her days in the kitchens in *St Christopher's*. For the first time in her life she felt she was part of a family. She almost mattered in the great scheme of things.

One evening the girl went with Robert and Richard to a Party at Dana Gillespie's beautiful cottage in Knightsbridge. It was rumoured her mother was an Austrian countess and that she'd been a champion skier, but she was singing when the girl first met her. There she met Hilton Valentine, the guitar player from the Animals with their big hit, *House of the Rising Sun*.

After Richard's departure, David wanted to start a blues band and Hilton wanted to manage the girl. So The Race was formed. David Circuit on guitar, Chris on the

Singing with The Race at The Marquee,
Wardour Street, London in 1966.

harmonica, Peter Kester from Brixton on the drums, another Peter, Poole, on six string bass and Roger D'elia on the second guitar.

Roger lived at home with his family in a flat in Colherne Court. His grandmother, a grey wild halo of hair sprouting from her head, wasn't really herself. She would often escape at night in her night dress and be found wandering alone. She'd known Tessie O'Shea and gave the girl a fabulous black velvet dress covered in glittering jet beads which the great lady had worn on stage. The garment would have wrapped the girl three or even four times over and she vowed to make three costumes to wear on stage, all from the one dress.

They usually rehearsed at Roger's place. Huddie Ledbetter blues and Sonny Boy Williamson's *Help me* (1963) Robert Johnson's *Judgment Day* (1936). The girl shouted the blues. No matter that the songs were written by black American men. Songs about love and struggle, guns and running, devils and crossroads. She was a' hollerin and it was the best feeling she'd ever had. Singing with wild abandon over wailing guitars and harmonica. Harmonica Chris' friend Bo was from a family of Battersea rag and bone merchants. Sometimes they drew up with the horse and cart at 16 Oakley Street to take the girl to a rehearsal or gig. Chris and Bo were both very tall and wore moleskin trousers, big coats and big boots. They looked a strange trio in the cart. The two tall men in their long coats and a small young woman in jeans and black velvet.

Although the cleaning agency was still a source of income and her rent was cheap, it still wasn't enough to get by on. The girl wanted clothes and she was out and about in the pubs and the clubs. She needed more money. She found another job in a tiny tobacconist in South Kensington. The shop was on a corner plot and the stock was kept downstairs. Boxes of cigarettes papers, cigars and sweets in jars. The man was warm-hearted, a good boss. To the girl he seemed pretty old. She was to work four days a week and she walked to the shop from Oakley Street. She loved to explore the streets, seeing more and more of this extraordinary London.

All was well at first. Then the flotsam from her life crept up on her. Word was out. The girl was in a tobacconist. First this guy and then another, 'Slip us a pack, go on. He won't notice.' She knew, oh yes she knew this was wrong. She did it once, then twice. Tilly Tea Leaf hovered in the wings. 'Don't come in.' But Miss 'so eager to please', the girl would say, 'I'll bring them to the pub tonight.' Quick, up came the wooden flap, down the ladder she went and slipped two packets of twenty into her pocket. 'I have to sack you,' said the kindly man, 'I won't report you. Go and sort yourself out. You're a nice girl really. You just have some bad friends.' And with that she was gone. Out the door and walking blindly back to Oakley Street, eyes tearful, head hanging in shame. The voice hurt her ears, her head hammered and her heart pounded.

THE BOSS 'Well, come on. Why did you do it? Thief, tea leaf, nasty bit of work.'

The disconnected head had no answer. The disconnected legs walked back to the little green room. A disconnected body crawled into the brass bed and slept, dreaming of vagabonds, thieves and hustlers. In and out the slug man loomed and then disappeared completely, to be replaced by dead foxes in a house with doors creaking in the dead of night. When the girl awoke it was still night time and the house was quiet. She lay looking at the pool of light on the ceiling, cast from the street light on the road beyond the window. She stared at the shadows in the corners of the room.

GUILTY GERTIE 'Murderer, thief, liar. You're guilty, guilty. Your life isn't a dream, it's a bloody nightmare. Rat tails and snail snot trails, that's you.'

The words bounced to the rhythm of her heartbeat. A beating loud, loud, loud in her chest. So loud she thought the whole house would hear it. Keith was there, his girl friend had chucked him out. He was sharing Paul the Japanese butler's room and stayed three or four times a week. Most weekends they were both away.

One nondescript morning before get up o'clock, there was loud banging on the front door. The knocker, the bell and then the police. Three of them came into the house, up the stairs and in the room next to the girl's. She stood in doorway. What the fuck was happening? One of the coppers threw a large pink rubber object across the room and it landed at her feet. 'Know who this belongs to?' he asked. They all laughed. She retreated. 'Excuse me young lady, where do you think you're going? Come on, where's your boyfriend?'

Sheila was downstairs on the telephone in the hall. She sounded agitated. Magazines, photographs, film canisters, sex toys. It would seem that Keith and Paul were involved, running a pawn film business from the Japanese butler's room. Most weekends they were in a rented cottage somewhere in Sussex making films for the dirty mac brigade. A few more phone calls and Sheila's daughter and son-in-law arrived. More words and threats, then the coppers left, taking boxes of evidence. The girl lay in her room, shaking. Paul and Keith went off the radar for a while.

Nina accused Beat of nicking her lipstick and left a lipstick smeared message on the mirror, 'you've stolen my lipstick. I want you to leave.' This was the beginning of a slow decent into the emotional inbalance that was to drive Nina into very dark places, ending in her death at the age of 60 in a tiny house on an island in Greece. She was alone and lay undiscovered for three days.

Beat came to Oakley Street and lived for a while in the room of large pink rubber cocks and seedy films. Beat and the girl began to spread out over the two rooms. The room of sleaze became a room of music. They'd sit for hours around the red and white *Dansette*, eyes closed, adoring Bobby Big Blue Bland and Nina Simone, Billy Holiday, James Brown and Marvin Gaye, the blues and the grooves.

NASTY NELLIE 'A miss, little miss singing bird is as good as a fucking mile.' The girl was confused. 'But I love to sing the blues.' She loved the blues. She loved the old songs.

NASTY NELLIE 'Yea oh yea.'

BETTY BLUES BELTER 'I heard Ray Charles on a Juke Box in 1959.'

NASTY NELLIE 'He was Ray Charles. And you are? What gives you the right to sing the blues?'

When the girl sang she was free. Free from the silly Mouse and the one who wanted to please so badly. When she wasn't singing she lost all sense of reason. Wanted to be bad, to thrash out at whoever she wanted to hurt. Mainly herself. When she thought about the man in the tobacco shop she wanted to bury herself.

The band was changing. Chris moved on because they were becoming too electric. Cecil from Nigeria took over the harmonica and they added a *Hammond* organ player, Tony. The girl fell in love with the organ's big rolling sounds. She found Brother Jack McDuff and bought *The Honey dripper* (1961) with tenor saxophonist Jimmy Forrest and guitarist Grant Green. Then *Brother Jack Meets the Boss* (1962). She listened to Jimmy Smith and Shirley Scott, a woman on the mighty organ.

THE BOSS 'Wow oh wow. Listen and learn girl. Listen and learn.'

They recorded *The Rolling Sea*. David wrote the music and the girl wrote the words. The band began to get some attention and played the *Marquee* for a second time. Then they played at *Klooks Kleek* and the *100 Club*. The Race was supporting bands like John Mayall's Bluesbreakers. Alexis Korner and Eric Clapton were being proclaimed as gods on the walls of the city. There was a review in a prestigious magazine for jazz and blues enthusiasts. Her first review and her very first time with a photo of the band.

> '*Possesses the finest voice I have heard for a long time and with the right opportunities could well become a successor to an all time great like Otilie Patterson.*'

She read and re-read. Maybe? Barely daring to hope.

Nasty Nellie 'Who do you think you're kidding?'

Misery Ivy 'Am I good enough?'

'Oh shut up.' And so on. And turn and turn about. The one inside said 'yes', 'no' and 'yes' again until the girl was dizzy with it all.

She stood on stages, eyes closed and feet firmly planted on the floor with Cecil on one side and David the other, and hollered her blues. Alexis Korner, elder statesman of the British blues boom, had seen them all. Eric Clapton, several Rolling Stones, Long John Baldry, Graham Bond and Dick Heckstall-Smith, the man on the sax she'd seen at her first ever live modern jazz gig in Cambridge.

Alexis was a good man and he meant it to be helpful when he said to her one night after a gig at the *100 Club*, 'You know, the blues, it's all about sex. You got to put the sex in it. You got to move.' Oh she loved to move but somehow out there on a stage in front of an audience she froze. All she could do was stand stock still and sing with every muscle she had, feet planted on the ground. She was afraid that if she moved, she'd tumble head over heels into the audience. And she sang with her eyes closed because she felt too transparent if she kept them open.

'*She does not let her audience in.*' Wrote a man reviewing a gig. '*She needs to open her eyes and come out from behind her hair. You can't see her face.*' He did like her singing though, and Betty Blues Belter began to take hold of the girl. Betty was flame haired, afraid of nothing and nobody, and sang with a loud and gritty voice. Totally the opposite of the small, nervous and insecure girl. Betty appeared only when she sang and disappeared as soon as the girl left the stage.

CLARA THE CLOWN 'Do let me persuade you to stay a while. Promise I'll never mislay this smile. I'll be comical musical. Be my friend and we'll all join the carnival.'

PP lurked annoyingly,

> **PROCRASTINATING PATSY** 'I'm in two minds or is it three? I've been invited to a party but I feel I want to stay at home. You see I can't make up my mind. Seems to me I'm nothing more than a deck of cards on the floor. A game of chance this music, impossible to play.'
>
> **THE BOSS** 'Make up your mind girl.'

Hilton took the band back to the studios in Denmark Street where they cut the Buffy Sainte-Marie song, *You're gonna need somebody on your bond.* He took the girl to clubs like *Blaise's, The Scotch of St James, The Bag 'O Nails* and *The Cromwellian.* She saw pop stars, models, photographers and actors. The new generation taking over the fashion pages, the music scene and the headlines. All the glossy people on the glossy pages. Sitting in nightclubs under low lights, eating steak and fries, drinking *Champagne* or a whisky and coke on ice, watching girls who walked tall and dressed cool. Rock stars, young working class men making money and fame, wanted the daughters of doctors, lawyers and the aristocracy, and bought their mock Tudor pile in Surrey. Not like the parents' generation. No make do and mend, and who do you think you are.

Designer shops were sprouting all over London, feeding the new trade in hip clothes for a generation with cash to splash. No longer did you buy an outfit for Sunday best and a coat that would last a decade. Young lovers of clothes in London went up west to Carnaby Street and the King's Road, to *Kleptomania, Quorum* and *I Was Lord Kitchener's Valet.*

Peta had a scam kiting cheques and organising people to go shopping. It seemed easy. You'd go into *Fenwick's of Bond Street* at a busy time, stand in line at the cash desk, sign the cheque and take the goods in the oh so sophisticated bags. The girl loved Bond Street. No one seemed to look at signatures too closely in those days before we had store and credit cards. Peta's flat contained suitcases stuffed with clothes, shoes and cosmetics. The clothes went to Peta and the pay off was the odd dress, perfume or lipstick. The girl was seduced.

Tilly Tea Leaf rose to the challenge,

> 'Bigger fry than *Pick 'n Mix* and pink lipstick in *Woolworths* or ten *Silk Cut.*'

Peta gave the girl a navy blue woollen pea jacket from *Fenwick's* who then splashed out on a very short pink and grey dress from *Granny Takes a Trip,* the new shop in the Worlds End. Native American chiefs, 'Low Dog' and 'Kicking Bear' were resplendently large in the shop window. Groovy. At a party later that week some guy called her a little 'Dolly Bird' and patted her on the bottom. Not a compliment.

The girl returned to her beatnik look, her ragbag clothes. No way could she turn herself into a tall, cool, long-legged 1960s diva. No way.

The Race was booked to play a blues and folk festival in Brussels. Julie Felix was topping the bill, a couple of American Blues artists and some local bands. They took the boat train from London to Folkestone harbour, then across the Channel. The only water she'd crossed before was the river Thames, and certainly never been abroad. They watched the huge *Hammond* organ and its two *Leslie* speakers swinging out from the dock, down into the hold, making Tony nervous. Then the drums, the amps and band, the van and equipment were all aboard. She was so excited, she may as well be travelling to the Moon.

Someone said the girl looked too young to sing the blues, too young and too white. She started to feel that the only time she felt really alive was on stage. She tried to ignore the comments by putting a cloak of gold over Betty's shoulders, a cloak with hidden wings so she could fly away in her mind's eye.

After the show, food for the bands. A red mess on a dish called steak tartare. Raw cow. Oh God. She took a tentative bite and smiled at the guy in the next seat as he loaded more onto his plate. Lovely.

People said there was a party on the other side of town, so they crowded into a little blue 2CV and drove through the cobbled squares and side streets of old Brussels. The next day she learned you didn't have to pass a driving test in Belgium. Just get a car and go. It felt good to be alive. She was alive and singing the blues at the tail end of the blues boom, on the cusp of psychedelia when everything would change. She seemed to be one step behind all that was trendy, hip and very, very cool. If she wanted fame she'd have to change her tune.

In1966 the girl met Larry. One Saturday morning in July, Keith called her on the phone in the hall in Oakley Street, 'Fancy a drive out to Blackheath with me and Paul?' They had surfaced in Notting Hill Gate after the raid. She met them in the *Six Bells* on the King's Road. Going over the river, she was taken back to the place of her infanthood in southeast London It felt strange. It had been a long and circuitous route. Halina was in the pub and there was a, 'Well hello.' As if her taking of Wally had never happened. Actually it was a very good thing, only she hadn't seen it like that at the time. Halina worked as a live-in mother's help in Blackheath. What is it with so many lost girls working as mother's helps? In another age it was called being 'in service.' Halina was with a bunch of people, one of whom was Larry.

Larry, flirtatious and friendly, had just left Croydon Arts College and before the girl knew it they were hooked up together. She would hear him tell his friends, 'Yeah, a singer and she lives in Chelsea.' He took her to an art house movie, *Woman in the Dunes* (1964, directed by Hiroshi Teshigahara). She was enchanted by the film and by Larry. To her he seemed so nice and clean. Untainted somehow. She took Larry back to Oakley Street. He moved into the little green room and they became a couple.

He took her to galleries and to places she'd visited before but always alone. They held hands and she was loved. She was wanted. Larry found himself a job working as fairground boy at *Battersea Funfair*. Larry's mother was Roma, going back many generations and he had those connections. He'd been sent to an obscure school in north Wales when Iraq, where his father worked, was spiraling into war. Later his parents returned to the UK and they lived in Croyden for a short while Larry went to Croyden Art College.

The girl loved meeting Larry at the fun fair, seeing him on the rides. And she loved the old rock and roll music. They'd ride the bumper cars and eat hot dogs, like the 1950s. She found another job, this time through Sheila, as a lunchtime barmaid in the *Six Bells*. Perfect. Just two minutes from her door, and she had time with the band in the later hours of the day. They had another gig at the *Marquee* in early October, supporting John Mayall again. They were getting to play there once a month.

Early one evening she sat, half buried in a large sagging brown corduroy beanbag pockmarked with tiny round burn holes, in a room above a Chinese gift shop and tobacconist's on Gerard Street in London's *China Town*. It was the premises of Mike Jeffrey's, manager of the Animals. He was living in a tax haven somewhere and this building opposite the *Tin Luk* Chinese restaurant had become rehearsal space and a hang out for bands associated with Anim, the Animals management company.

Sucking on a tin of cold beer, she waited for the guys to appear. After another sip she put the beer down. She felt sick. An hour ago Hilton Valentine had disappeared over the road to fetch something. She wondered the hell people could eat so fast. They were in and out of that *Tin Luk* with hardly a moment to gobble a fortune cookie, let alone a steaming bowl of fried rice and a cup of jasmine tea. Hilton returned looking more than a little spaced out. 'What's happening man?' 'Chas is due with this amazing guitarist from the States he's taken on; Jimi Hendrix. When's your lot due?' 'Dunno,' she said, as she hauled herself off beanbag, 'I thought we said six. They're probably in the pub. I'll go and look.' 'No, just hang out here and wait for Chas, you gotta meet this guy. He's far out.' He gazed at the packet in his hand, 'I got some amazing draw here. He's gonna love it. Blow his mind man.' 'Where did you get that then?' she asked. She sort of guessed but then again, what did she know. 'You don't wanna know,' he winked.

When she later found out that all things drug came from the *Tin Luk*, she wondered why they never told her stuff. Was it all meant to be secret? Man Club? Didn't she smoke it with them, for christ sakes? She'd been out there on the street when they were still Geordie boys living at home, hanging round their mums' skirts in Newcastle. Did they think she was naive or what? No, she was just a chick, a girl. That was it.

She heard the sound of six men exploding with laughter echo up the stairwell. It was The Race turning up for the rehearsal. Various musicians dragged everything up the stairs from a transit van. Black cases, bags of wires and microphone stands, all piled into the once immaculate Anim office. Hilton was still their manager though most of the time he couldn't organise a barn dance in a farmyard. That last mad weekend he'd dropped a tab of acid and attempted to climb *Marble Arch*, unsuccessfully.

Suddenly Chas appeared in the midst of the chaos followed by the most mysterious looking guy the girl had ever seen. Black, whistle thin with brown eyes, wild hair and a voluptuous mouth, he spoke softly with a voice that seemed at odds with his outrageously exotic appearance. Everything seemed to flow and float about him. London wasn't quite into the full on dressing up box of late 1960s California. This was the time of mini skirts, sharp suits and geometric haircuts inspired by Vidal Sassoon. Jimi was a man from Mars.

They all went to see him play that evening in the *Manor House* pub, north London. This was surely music from outer space. His guitar made sounds she couldn't believe. It was blues but blues remade in ways only Jimi could make. Her mind was well and truly blown.

The girl crept into the *Six Bells* the following day and promptly ran into the bathroom, barely making it before she threw up. The landlady said, 'You're pregnant, my girl.' 'Nah, I'm just a bit hung over,' she said, thinking oh my God, what now? Yes, she was pregnant. Gone six weeks or so, well and truly up the duff, in the club. She put it all at the back of her mind and carried on as if nothing was happening inside that small belly, nothing at all. They were playing *Winchester Cathedral* by the New Vaudeville Band on the juke box and she felt sick. Thereafter, she felt sick whenever she caught a snatch of that track.

WICKED WILL O'MINA 'Steady as she goes. Mind the gap mind, the hole in the road. Never mind the hole, mind the mind. Belay the last word. Steady the ship. A rudderless mind is bound to drown, around and around and down she goes.'

A week later she was with The Race back in Gerard Street for a rehearsal. The room was full when she arrived. It was the oddest collection of men she'd ever seen, tall and dressed in a long black cloak, small and fair with the most extraordinary drum kit, held together with gaffer tape and string. Long haired and wild looking, they were posh and rather stand offish with the exception of the lovely drummer. He was Robert Wyatt.

This was the beginning of her tenuous link with the so-called 'Canterbury Scene'. When she realised how small the music scene really was. Though she never felt in any 'scene'. She didn't get that. On 15th October she went to London's first ever all night rave, the *International Times* launch party at the *Roundhouse*. Her eyes nearly popped at the sight of this costume, masque, fantasy, loon, blowout drag ball. In the gloom the crowds mingled with Yoko Ono, Paul McCartney, John Lennon, Jane Asher, Marianne Faithful, Monica Vitti and Antonioni.

Pink Floyd played their first *Roundhouse* gig that night. Public school boys playing blues and R&B. Soft Machine played and 2000 people turned up, all offered sugar cubes as they came through the door. LSD? No, it was an urban myth. Imagine all the people imagining. There was plenty on offer inside, though. Handed out by the new street pharmacists near the steel pillars.

A party meant jelly of course and someone made one in a bathtub. Pink Floyd's van ran into it while they were setting up, so hardly anyone saw its original wobbling glory. There was psychedelic palm reading in a tent and Marianne Faithful in a nun's habit you wouldn't expect, won a fancy dress competition. She was the sexiest woman around. The girl felt spaced out, at a distance from it all, like looking through crazed glass.

It was October and winter was just around the corner. She wondered where she and Larry would be in a year, or even six months. Well into the eighth week, she decided to tell Larry the news. 'Wow.' Was all he could muster, as he gazed into the middle distance and then back at the girl. 'Wow. Really? Wow.' He grinned. She thought oh well, he must be pleased.

She wrote to Beryl, not telling her but enclosing a letter to her mother in New Zealand, asking Beryl if she'd send it on. A month or so later she found a letter on the mat addressed to Carol Freeman. The mother wrote,

'If you want to make a mess of your life, then go ahead. You made your bed now lay in it. I wash my hands of you.'

So that was the end of all of that.

The girl told Tony, the *Hammond* organ player and he said, 'I'll lend you the money for an abortion if that's what you want. Look, the band is taking off. You'd be mad to give it all up. I'll help.' She was still reeling, the pain just below the surface. She remembered the woman, the soapy water, the aluminium basin and the vomit on her chest. One morning a few days later she was on the Northern Line to Elephant and Castle, to a doctor's surgery where, through this word and that, she'd made an appointment. Abortion was not to be made legal in the UK until late the following year.

She sat in the waiting room, fidgeting on a hard backed chair. There were dogeared magazines on a side table. Needing the lavatory, she went to a dismal little room on the landing with a crusty towel on a hook on the door and shiny toilet paper in a puddle on the floor. She couldn't wee.

Back to the waiting room and her name was called. The doctor, his face impassive and yet judgemental, sat behind a desk like it was the counter of a bank or police station. He stated the cost of the abortion, and where and when. She then knew what she was going to do. Keep the baby. She stuttered and stammered. He said, 'you're wasting my time. No, not that way.' He inclined his head towards a door behind a faded blue curtain. She scuttled across the room like a mouse with its skinny tail hung low. She went out and down to the street, stood underneath a railway bridge and listened to the rumble of a train overhead. Now that was a comforting sound, an echo of the very recent past. She was in life and soon a child would be in life with her. She swore she felt a quickening and wanted this baby more than anything.

The Race's first record, *You're Gonna Need Somebody On your Bond*, was coming out in the New Year on *Polydor Records*. That's a fact, she did. Sheila told her many times, especially when drunk, 'Larry's a silly boy and not a man. If you want to spend your life with a fluffy teddy bear, that's it, you're out.' Leaving Oakley Street was like leaving home, leaving an erratic but adorable adopted mother and a mad but loveable dysfunctional family. David Circuit said, 'come to us, stay until you find a place.' A makeshift bed was put together on the floor of their front room. The girl would lay awake in the early mornings, ginger cat hairs everywhere and fleas, hopping, skipping, leaping. Then one morning the cat came in with a pigeon in its mouth, wings limp, eyes glazed and bloody. What a present and what an effect on the pregnant girl. She threw up.

The girl and Larry found a bed-sit in Earl's Court, not far from Pat and Louis. Guests were not allowed on the premises. There was a gas fire with a very hungry meter and no cooking in the room. They spent a lot of time with their friends. The band did gigs and she carried on growing her baby. Louis made cakes, cooked rice and fish, and played his drum. The basement was a cave of warmth. She craved tinned lychees, gobbling them up whenever and wherever she could, sitting in a Chinese restaurant ordering bowlfuls. Yum yum, fragrant fruits, pearly translucent white flesh wrapped around satin smooth stones. When lychees weren't available she ate *Heinz* baked beans straight from the tin. That's how she liked them.

A Bridge from the past to the future: towards motherhood

The girl was in turn, fearful, astounded, excited and benumbed. How was she going to cope?

> PROCRASTINATING PATSY 'I'm in two minds, or is it three? Or four, five, six, seven...stop! I'm going to be a mother! Mother. Yes, me! A mother. I'll be 23 when he or she is born in May. What a lovely month. Cherry blossom and green parks. I will be a mother and Larry will be a father. We've nothing. No home and no money. But we'll be a family. Time to be? Time for change? How? How will I be this mother?'

> THE BOSS 'You'll know what to do. You're in love with this infant already.'

John, a friend from the Richmond days hanging with the beat and the musicians in the *Imperial* pub, offered them space in his flat in Swinbrooke Road, North Kensington, just off Golborne Road at the top end of Portobello Road. Christmas 1966 was looming. The years in Earl's Court and Chelsea were left behind and the years in The Grove began. She didn't leave Beat or Louis. They too would end up in The Grove.

VERSE 16

Larry and Sam

White Rabbit Jefferson Airplane 1967

1967: The Grove, St Stephen's Gardens and Portobello Road. A wedding and name number three. Exploding Galaxy. The 14 hour technicolour dream. Turn on, tune in, drop out. A baby is born.

The new roof above their heads was the front room settee of John's small first floor flat in a terraced house in North Kensington. John was an aspiring guitar player, that's if he could ever lift his backside from his favourite seat at home or in the pub. A man not given to bursts of energy, he was happy talking music and smoking in convivial company. A small time dealer in hashish and grass, and friend to many of the new generation of folk singers and blues guitarists, those to who smoked the weed or popped the pills. John would sell just enough to fund his own habit, living his life in the night hours, strumming his guitar, listening to records, nodding, smiling and rolling endless joints, saying, 'You gotta listen to this track man, heavy.' The needle scraped across the circle of black vinyl, 'Pass the skins man. This is good shit.'

John was in need of money to help with the rent and pleased to have them stay. On the bathroom floor was a mound of festering clothes waiting to be taken to the launderette. The lavatory was stained a nasty brown streaked mess. Had it ever been white? It made her retch. And as for the kitchen.

> **NERVY NORA** 'Cook on that and it will endanger life. You'll catch a deadly serious disease.'
> **MISERY IVY** 'It's a living and ancient fungus and a health hazard'.
> **NERVY NORA** 'Ooh, we'll die, the baby will die. I want to go back to Oakley Street.'
> **SENSIBLE MA SADIE** 'Just get going. You know what to do.'

The girl attempted to clean the cooker. The grease was surely vintage 1937. Feeling sick, she gave up. There was a table covered in a pile of papers, old cigarette packets and skins, neat little oblongs torn from the packets in order to make a roach for the joints, reefers or spiffs, depending on what the roller called them. The kitchen sink was a pool of slime and old tea leaves, and every cup was chipped and stained a dark tannin brown.

203

The girl felt a pang of missing Sheila's house and the tiny green room in Oakley Street. It was too late now. She'd taken her teddy bear and fled. Outside in the street below the window every weekday morning when it was still dark, she heard an engine, vroom, vroom as a neighbour attempted a cold start. 'Bloody hell, come on damn you.' Finally the engine would shudder into life and the car turned the corner at Golborne Road, leaving silence at least for a while. She tried to sleep again but it was no good. She curled up on her slither of settee and thought, 'Is this it?'

Her mother's letter had said, 'you made your bed now you lay in it'. She wasn't even lying in a bed. She re-read the letter in her mind, trying to hear her mother's voice, see her face. She struggled and then looked at the sleeping Larry and pondered the question of love. Did she love him? She curled herself around his back and thought, 'I think so.' She picked a daisy in her mind and petal by petal, she loves him, she loves him not, she loves him. 'If you want to be with a fluffy teddy bear for the rest of your life...' Sheila's voice. The girl tried to sleep.

She went out and about with the band doing a bit of press. *NME*, *Melody Maker*, *Record Mirror*. The single was coming out soon. A photographer came round to Swinbrooke Road and she pulled in her belly in a pathetic attempt to not look pregnant. 'Look sexy,' he said, 'come on, give me sexy.' She felt far from sexy. Her breasts were sore and her clothes were becoming tighter around her middle. But her face and limbs were as skinny as ever.

The Race played at the *Marquee* on a cold dark Sunday night in January, supporting John Mayall's Blues Breakers. She tried hard to enjoy the moment. This was what she wanted, wasn't it? Eric Clapton on guitar? 'Look at me now,' she thought, talking to... her mother, the Lowestoft music teacher, the world.

The band were playing the same gigs as many blues bands of the day, sharing the same cramped dressing rooms. She was pregnant, virtually homeless if you don't consider a settee a home, and with not a pot to piss in. This wasn't a good place to be. On the stage in front of the familiar stripes she and Betty hollered the blues. Two electric guitars, a bass, the drums, the girl and the mighty *Hammond* organ, a one, a two, a one two three four.

BETTY BLUES BELTER 'I can't do it all by myself. You got to help me, baby.'
She sang the Sonny Boy Williamson blues and meant every word of it. The audience witnessed a small white girl belting out those songs she'd learned as she huddled around a record in the basement rehearsal rooms, Cecil standing alongside, blowing the hell out of his harp, bending the notes just like she did with her voice. The

audience may have been waiting for Eric Clapton, god on guitar, but they listened and even asked for an encore. A storming *Stormy Monday Blues*.

BETTY BLUES BELTER 'Call it Stormy Monday and Tuesday's just as bad...'

Where was the Mercy? Where was The Lord? She was expecting no mercy from the invisible man in heaven.

WICKED WILL O'MINA 'The Lord is my Shepherd, I shall not want. Want? Who is to provide? Ah the Lord, come on then, show me your face, give me a sign.'

In February that year 240 helicopters flew over Tay Ninh province in Vietnam. War? My god, new life coming in to the world and the world never stops fighting. God? 'Oh Lord, please have mercy on me' The Race was no more. It was their last gig. Her baby belly was more prominent and the band moved on and away.

In Swinbrooke Road John had his amazing record collection and a constant supply of hash and grass. Larry loved it, she did not. Something was missing and she'd no idea what. Larry acquired a striped tabby cat from his parents who were off to Trinidad. He named him Mustafa. She held the purring cat close to her and whispered into a fluffy twitching ear, 'Get me somewhere over the fucking rainbow, any rainbow. Meow.' She hoped she wouldn't turn into the measly mouse of yesteryear and end up being gobbled up by Larry's cat.

SENSIBLE MA SADIE 'A home, yes a place to be, to rest. A nest.'

NASTY NELLIE 'What's that inside you? A bun, a rabbit, a baby?'

THE BOSS 'Get out and look. No one else gonna do it for you.'

They looked at the *Standard* 'for rent' section every day and trailed around from Putney to Earl's Court, Paddington to Shepherds Bush, Kilburn, Hammersmith and Ladbroke Grove to Maida Vale. A landlady in Shepherds Bush sneered. She took one look at the pregnant girl and slammed the door as they stood on the front steps. 'I told Snell, no Irish, no children, no coloured's, no pets.' London was still in the grip of East End criminal gangs, bent landlords and bigotry. A man in his shirtsleeves opened a door in Cambridge Gardens, 'Why don't yer go 'ome to yer mum?' he laughed, 'looks like you two should 'ave be'aved yourselves.' For God's sake, she thought, I'm 22 years old. She looked more like 15 and Larry not much older.

The immigrants were coming to the motherland, looking for work and a new life. They paid the rent and a few, though not many, would drift into the underbelly. The Krays and their like were still around and Soho was a no-go area for some.

The area often referred to as 'The Grove' was Ladbroke Grove, eastwards towards Westbourne Grove, across towards Paddington. By the end of the Second World War it was partly derelict. The London suburbs were filling up with families wanting nice leafy green homes, away from the bomb sites and the filth. This meant that cheap rooms were more available in Notting Hill and it's surrounding area, in Peter Rachman's old territory. Sadness and despair dwelt in a lot of those basement flats, tenement houses and in the tower blocks thrown up in post-war Britain.

Facades of once grand terraced houses were unkempt and the rooms in these crumbling edifices were some of the cheapest in London. Slums stood cheek by jowl with big white stucco dwellings just a few streets away. Holland Park nuzzled close to the top of Ladbroke Grove. Down the hill past the convent it was a very different scene on the streets around Ladbroke Grove station. It had been less than a decade since the teddy boys and the African Caribbeans fought on the streets of The Grove and Notting Hill. White people were still saying, 'No blacks and no Irish.' And still called out, 'spics and spades', 'micks and yids,' 'wogs and wops'.

The disenfranchised, the unemployed, the down and nearly out would turn the blame for their lot on whoever they could, particularly in the slum areas. Wary, angry or both, they viewed Johnny foreigner as less than human, suspicious at the very least, 'Nicking our jobs, our women, our homes.' The community from the Caribbean were now well established, as were the Portugese, the Italians and the Irish. The Grove would've been a greyer, duller war-sore place without them. A pale place of over boiled cabbage and spiceless food, devoid of the energies of new and vibrant cultures from outside this small island.

In the 1960s, girls who 'gave it away', who were an 'easy lay' were sometimes treated with less respect than prostitutes. Especially the high class Mayfair girls. At least they made good money. The new wave of feminism was about to emerge but in those days men ran the world, ran the show and ran the women. In the '60s and the early '70s, if you mentioned that some radio DJ or record company man had groped your tits or pinched your arse, you were laughed at. 'A harmless bit of fun, don't be so uptight.' 'Oh, men will be men.' 'You a lesbian then?' 'Well, you was asking for it, gagging for it in that skirt.'

A Bridge of rampant sexism

She's a slag, a slapper, a scrubber, a slut a bimbo, a bitch, a bint. She's a cunt, a cow, a minga, she's a dead ringer for a dog, a trollop, a tart. She's up and down like a whore's drawers. She's all fur coat and no knickers. At best she's a bird, a babe, the old lady, a doll, a chick, a crumpet, or a sex kitten. 'Lets cop a feel.'

Past it and she's a cougar, a crone, an old tit, a dragon, a hag and a bag. A girl who didn't put out is a prude, she's frigid, an uptight mare with a face like smacked arse, a dyke, a fag hag or a prick-teaser. Back in the day men paid a brass, a moll, a strumpet, a streetwalker, a tail, a harlot, a tom tart, a whore, a hooker, or a lady of the night. She's on the game. Game? A thrupenny-upright, a knee trembler or a trick. An angel? A male who pays for sexual acts. 'You big girl's blouse, you old woman.' A man or a boy who behaves in ways other men think womanly.

NASTY NELLIE 'Got that lot off yer chest then?'

The girl found two unfurnished rooms at 113 St Stephen's Gardens, W2. Freshly wallpapered with a pale and indistinct floral pattern, the doors and window frames were painted gloss white, all looking fairly clean. The front room had a fireplace with a marble mantelpiece. A smaller room in the back had a cooker and a sink. As far as she was concerned, it was heaven. They paid a month's rent in advance and moved in with their bags, records and not much else.

Three families shared the bathroom on the landing two floors down. The girl hated that and felt vulnerable as she lay naked in the stained tub of tepid water. She would stare up at the cracked ceiling, mindful of the sliding door with its warped wood and flimsy bolts, and shivered barefoot on the cold cracked linoleum as she tried to pull clothes onto her still damp skin. The kids from downstairs would sometimes stand outside and giggle, vying for a peek through the small crack in the door. She'd yell at them to go away but street sharp and tough as nuts, they took no shit from a dippy looking pregnant girl. They'd laugh louder and half skip, half run down the stairs when she pulled the bolt and made the dash up to her room.

The older girl who was tall for her age had red hair and sharp suspicious brown eyes set in a beautiful but often sullen olive skinned face. Of the the two boys, one was small, stocky and boisterous and the other, the elder, was slow and quiet. He was the calmest of all three, willing to plod along in the wake of his smarter sister. He would fetch and carry for them all. They were the children of the couple on the first floor. An English woman from Yorkshire and Joe, her Jamaican husband.

The mother was thin and seemingly boneless. She had pale blue eyes and her hair was dyed blonde, revealing her mousy brown roots in a thick strip on top. She had a flat face, wore thick glasses and most of the time her lips were set in a firm tight line of discontent. She'd left Leeds to find a new life and met Joe in a pub near Leicester Square one Saturday night. Joe was a tall, slow speaking thickset man. He'd been a boxer, crushed in defeat a few times too many. Punch drunk, his shoulders were now hunched. He ended up in London, a less proud man, almost broken and far from home. Their rooms smelled of stale piss, cheap cooking fat and over boiled vegetables. There never was the warm smell of Caribbean home cooking.

The children had never seen the parks only a mile or so away. Their lives were crushed into two rooms and the kitchen, the launderette, the local shop, the chippy, the post office on Westbourne Park Road and the pub on the corner of Talbot and Ledbury Road near Powis Square, where mother would drink a rum and coke and Joe his bottles of *Special Brew* or the odd nip of rum.

On the ground floor lived two ancient ladies who kept themselves to themselves, wrapped up in hats, coats and thick *Lyle* stockings from January to December. In the basement lived a large Irish family with five red haired rollicking children and their red haired harum-scarum parents. They laughed, they argued, they drank and partied, sharing their lives with the street. When they moved on, it was suddenly and terribly quiet on that corner of the street. In the top flat underneath the eaves lived a family from Trinidad. A quiet couple with two boys, one around four and a teenager of 13. The mother worked as a nurse and was often on the night shift. The father worked the days as an electrician. A beautiful and dignified woman, she kept a tight ship. They deserved better than they had.

There they all were, living at 113 St Stephen's Gardens. The girl and the artist, the boxer, his wife and three children, the two old ladies, the family in the attic and the huge family in the basement. They had their own ablution area out in the back yard, down below the girl's kitchen window. She'd often hear a frantic shout for the paper as bums were wiped with *The Mirror* or *The News of The World*.

John and Larry found a wooden rocking chair in the street and dragged it back to number 113. She rocked and stroked her baby belly. She loved being near the Portobello Road and was as happy as a hog in a truffle filled wood. She adored the market, the fresh fruit and vegetables, orange, green and yellow, piled high on the stalls. New potatoes, bunches of mint and parsley, exotic sweet potatoes and yams, grapes and garlic, mounds of nuts, lemons and limes. She found rice, pasta and soft cheese. The food here was so much better than a fatty chop and two vegetables swimming in brown *Bisto* or waxy yellow mousetrap cheese and margarine on *Mothers Pride* bread.

The girl cooked almost every day in the cramped little kitchen overlooking the rooftops and backyards. She'd learned a little in her Oakley Street days with the merry band of jazz loving Sunday cooks and Sheila's insistence on teaching her how to make a salad and dressing. *Heinz Salad Cream?* 'Oh no. You'll ruin the salad.' Sheila taught her how to mix olive oil, lemon juice, vinegar, a little sugar, and a pinch of dry mustard. The girl experimented with pastry and pies, nut roasts and rice. The folk who lived in The Grove persuaded them to become vegetarians. A guy she'd known in the old Earl's Court days showed up. Colin Wilson, not *the* Wilson, came round with a book, *Zen Macrobiotics* by Georges Ohsawa, the new bible for the hippies and the counter culture people. Colin got it from Craig Sams and was a zealous convert.

From speed and weed to Yin and Yang and LSD. From eggs, sausages, chips, *HP Sauce* and pies to brown rice, seaweed and Mu tea. Colin preached with the same blazing energy he had for jazz and speed. Larry and the girl listened and were converted. She wanted a healthy baby, to clean up her polluted insides. At least that was what Colin said, 'We're all polluted with the shit we eat and the air we breathe.' Pause for dramatic effect... 'Brothers, we must obey the rules of the universe and look to the brothers in the Orient.' 'What about the sisters?' she thought, rocking in her chair and thinking how she should cut her carrots in the correct Zen fashion. 'There is nothing intolerable in this world,' said George from Kyoto, 'a life without fear or anxiety, a life of freedom, happiness and justice. The realisation of self. This is the medicine of the mind, the body and the soul.' 'That's a big promise,' thought the girl, 'all this in a bowl of brown rice and a pot of Mu tea?'

She learned how to make wholemeal pastry and baked leeks and carrots in a béchamel sauce in a pie. She cooked rice in a pot on the gas stove. One day as she bent down to light the oven and boom, blue flames shot out and singed her hair and her eye lashes. The smell was horrible and the girl was in shock. The next day she cut her hair, or rather hacked at it and then people said she looked like an elf. She had a permanent surprised look on her face until her lashes grew back. Beat thought the look suited her and said, 'You can't hide behind your hair now when you sing.' 'Huh?' said the girl, 'what singing? It's all over.' But Betty hadn't gone away. She was waiting in the wings, though the girl didn't know that at the time. The baby was due in late May and a wedding was booked for February.

The wedding day was so cold that the silver foil on the milk bottle outside on the window sill had been forced an inch from the bottle by a stump of frozen

milk and the slab of butter in the little yellow bowl was rock hard. Larry and the girl made their way to the Kensington registry office in an old transit van driven by a friend of John's. Larry wore a purple striped *Granny Takes a Trip* jacket with pink trousers and a silk shirt. She wore a short cream and brown striped dress with a hood. The hood was the bride's headgear. She'd seen a pair of turquoise and white shoes in the window of the shop on the corner of Chepstow Road and Westbourne Grove. She splashed more or less the last of her cash on cream lacy tights and a black velvet coat with a dusty pink lining, a find from the Portobello Road Market.

Arriving for the wedding with Larry, and (*below*) with Beat and Richard.

Her wedding outfit was complete. She had no bouquet of flowers, so on the way she bought four pink carnations for Larry, Richard, Beat, and herself.

(Front row, l to r) Richard, Babette, Marion, Larry, Carol, Rita, Beat and John. *(Back row, l to r)* Nina, Jan and Tony.

She held a little body in her womb. Could she, would she, love? Richard was the best man with Babette looking as ethereal as ever, her long golden hair flowing down the back of a brown velvet coat, like a women in a Rossetti painting. Beat was the bridesmaid, wearing *Biba* clothes and a wonderful hat. Also in attendance were Beat's friend Rita, John from Swinbrooke Road, and Tony with Jan, his new girlfriend. And even Marion, Larry's girlfriend from his art school days, who managed to stand next to him on the steps outside after the ceremony,

An official took some pictures. Marion stood so close to Larry she looked like the bride. They had a wedding breakfast in *Mike's Café* in Blenheim Crescent. Egg and chips with cups of tea. They were now Mr and Mrs Smart. She was no longer Carol Freeman, she was on to name number three. Higgs, Freeman and now Smart.

Mike beamed, Larry beamed, the people in the café beamed. They all thought it very lovely. There were shouts of congratulations and, 'Hey man, well done man.' The girl dipped her fat golden chips into the yolk and wondered how the baby was doing inside her. She thought if she could keep this moment for ever, it would all be fine. All three would be fine.

There had been no proud parent at the wedding to celebrate the union. No relatives stood beside the bride and groom. No tears from a loving mother wearing an over-the-top hat. No father in a mothball smelling dark suit, smiling with paternal pride. No wedding presents. No romantic first dance. And certainly no honeymoon. The bride and groom went home to St Stephen's Gardens and the bed that was a mattress on the floor, in the room that was a studio, a bedroom, a sitting room and soon to be a nursery. She waited for her baby on the street that was infamous for its residents from the community of lost souls, dealers, pimps, prostitutes and people passing through. Lucky Gordon, a player in the drama that was the Profumo Affair, lived three doors away. The single recorded with the now defunct Race had a polar bear's chance of survival in the iceless deserts of Arabia.

But this was 1967 and change seemed possible. *Middle Earth*, *The Arts Lab*, the *Roundhouse*, the *Electric Cinema*. Hey, it's all happening round here man. The San Francisco scene in London. And in London, The Grove was happening most of all. Or so said the folk in The Grove. It was to be the summer of flower power, free love and macrobiotic food. Brown rice, brown nut loaf, brown lentils. All things Indian. Hallucinogenic drugs, beads, baubles and joss sticks. Pungent Afghan Coats that smelled of camel piss. The age of Aquarius and Janis Joplin, the Doors, Jimi Hendrix and Happenings. Larry would paint, she would sing, the baby would gurgle, and they would suck it and see. Hippies were tripping up and down the Portobello Road, in and out of the bed-sits, flats and artist studios. The Saturday parade.

WICKED WILL O'MINA 'I've been everywhere man. Just back from India. Off to Afghanistan, man. Catch me if you can, man. See me in California, or see me in Ibiza, or Goa or Deià. Hey, who knows where man? I'm a groovy traveller, man.'

THE BOSS 'So you, I assume, don't want to travel?'

PROCRASTINATING PATSY 'Well of course. Maybe, perhaps later, when the baby is older. Oh I don't know. I want to be at home. I want to sing. I want to see the world. I want..?'

Weekend tourists, cameras around their necks, would amble down from Notting Hill Gate. Past the *Sun in Splendour* on the left hand side, then a pretty Victorian terrace on the right. One house blue, another pink, the next primrose yellow. Red, white and pink geraniums grew on window sills. Daffodils and tulips in the spring. The girl so wanted a pretty house with a front door and a little garden out the back. A warm bathroom with white fluffy towels on a radiator and *Pears* soap on a dish. She'd have a kitchen with a pine table and a dresser where she could display the bits and pieces found on the market. A blue and white dish, a green jug, the pretty cups and saucers. In her mind she was making a pretty cherry tree Kensington home.

NASTY NELLIE 'You need money for one of those. You need a proper job for a home like that. How are you ever going to achieve that? Only nice people get to live in one of those.'

At the Westbourne Grove crossroad stood *Hennekeys* pub with its beer garden. After that the market really began. Antiques stalls, *Alice's Emporium* and all the little arcades. Nooks and crannies where dealers sat for hours, willing you to choose that perfect piece of silver. On past Elgin Crescent and Colville Terrace where the *Midland Bank* and the *Duke of Wellington* stood on each corner. Here the stalls were piled high with fruit and vegetables. And the *Colville* pub on the corner of Talbot Road where men from Trinidad and Jamaica and other far away islands far away, gathered to place their bets. 'You never know your luck, man.' Gold teeth glinting, hopes high. Ska or calypso records were playing on the jukebox and kids hung around outside waiting for crisps or a coin or two for sweets.

Kensington Park Hotel, the *KPH* on the corner of Ladbroke Grove and Lancaster Road, where young musicians and old men gathered, and junkies pedalled *Mandrax* and *Speed*. Where down and out Irish guys from Dublin and Donegal, from the bogs and small towns beyond, gathered to talk of the old country, drinking *Special Brew* or *Guinness* and waiting for the winning horse to romp home. With their purple noses and shaking hands they were too far gone for the IRA. Irish or Jamaican, Trinidadian or Greek, Portuguese and the old white families from the area, the market trader families, butchers, bakers and candle stick makers. London W10 and W11 in the 1960s with its imprint of many years. The girl loved it. It was home.

The tourists didn't wander much beyond Elgin or Blenheim Crescents. They turned around and found one of the old pubs back up towards Notting Hill Gate or Holland Park. A pub lunch and a fascinating bargain, a memento of London. They took photographs of the hippies in their finery or the man with the parrot and the wind-up gramophone, tap dancers and guitar players. A wispy boy blowing a flute, his wispy girl trailing behind him blowing bubbles, the blind man playing his

The blind accordion player.

accordion and the onion man on his bicycle. Locals would wander further on, past Blenheim Crescent and Cambridge and Oxford Gardens, past the old cinema, on past *Woolworths* and *Tesco*, and past the building works for the *Westway*.

On past the *Mountain Grill* and the *Monastery*, turn right onto Goldbourne Road. This was rag and bone man land. In 1967 you could furnish two rooms for very little money. Dead man's furniture. Larry and the girl bought a little pine table for a pound and two chairs for less, a mattress, sheets, a pair of blankets and a cot for the baby. She was making her nest. Beat had taken a live-in job with a family in Campden Hill Square, Notting Hill. Tony and Jan split up. Jan was with a new man called Steve in a flat on Ladbroke Grove, opposite the *Convent of the Poor Clares*. Jan asked, 'Have you got anything for the baby?' 'Ah, well. I've got no money but I'm looking around the market for stuff. We got a cot.'

Larry had been sent some money from his parents. She managed to extract some from his tight pockets but it was like trying to scoop the mud from underneath a comfortable and sleeping Piglet. He seemed to imagine they were living on fresh air and good vibes. He bought a hi-fi system. Stereo, wonder of wonders. As long as there were records, dope for the pipe and money for canvas and paint, what the hell! Once a week he took whatever from the welfare state over the counter at the post office. The rest, when it came, was cash in hand. She never did find out how much his parents had sent him.

She was off to Oxford Street with Jan, to *John Lewis* to buy for the baby. This was her first vist. Oh, the nice ordinariness of it. The smell of teacakes and coffee on the fourth floor, the pretty baby layettes, shiny new cots and prams, little booties, snow white nappies, little girl dresses and little boy shorts. She bought two soft towelling babygrows in blue and white, nappies, talcum powder and a mobile. The most money she'd ever spent in one shop. She set up the mobile as soon as she got home, hanging it over the cot which they'd painted primrose yellow. It tinkled Brahms lullaby as the wooden sheep twirled around. A surge of love for the little person flooded through her innards. The colourful mobile somehow made it real. She gathered in baby ribbon-edged cot sheets and a pram that was rather the worse for wear. With a through clean it would be perfect. She leaned into the cot and wondered who he or she would be. Would he or she love her? The more the baby grew inside, the more she wanted the love. *Love, love me do.*

Another friend brought a little knitted blanket in all the colours of the rainbow, and some baby clothes she'd made herself for her own child, now a toddler. A purple velvet matinee jacket, some tie-dyed vests, a striped jumper and a purple and pink knitted hat. The baby wouldn't be naked.

THE BOSS 'Yes, you can do this. You'll love this baby and this baby will love you.'

They found a bundle of Hessian, dyed it a beautiful burnt orange and hung it in the windows over a long stick of Bamboo. They had curtains. They filled a buttercup yellow vase with flowers and placed on the mantelpiece. She stood back and admired it with pleasure. She sewed glass beads onto the rim of a lampshade and the room danced with rainbow prisms when the sun shone.

She collected old cups and plates, mismatched but wonderful. Rabbit and duck shaped eggcups and a brown *Betty* teapot. She bought wooden stirring spoons. Many spoons and rolling pins, saucepans, cutlery and Indian bedspreads. She had a treasure trove on her doorstep. They had no television, car or telephone but they had a cream and brown *Bakelite* valve radio radio that had belonged to Larry's parents. It sat on the mantelpiece next to the vase and kept the girl company as she craved normality. She and Sensible Sadie loved to listen when alone, the voices a comforting sound.

215

The skirting boards, windows and doors were painted purple. Larry was doing a lot of painting. Bridget Riley had been his tutor at art school and the walls were soon covered with enormous canvases of red and green stripes. They shimmered and shook and were just the thing to sit and look at as you dived into a trip. Around the canvases the clean wallpaper became splattered with colours from Larry's many tubes of acrylic paint. He was obsessed with the Grateful Dead, a 'Dead Head' man. They bought John Coltrane's *Kulu Se Mama* (1967) on white vinyl, imprinted with a red design. Then someone took it one day. It was gone. They listened to Captain Beefheart and Janis Joplin, Dr. John the Night Tripper, Frank Zappa and the Doors, Miles Davis and Ray Charles. You can never be lonely with good music, thought the girl. The rooms, flats and crash pads of The Grove were revving up, high on LSD and weed, hashish and speed. Everyone was wired, catatonic or simply plain old high on life and the music. All except the girl. Like her home, she was clean. Marc Bolan and Steve Took formed Tyrannosaurus Rex and the Edgar Broughton Band, and then came along Quintessence, Juniors Eyes, The Pink Fairies and The Deviants.

Paul, the Japanese butler from Oakley Street, was living with a gentle long haired girl called Linda just off Goldbourne Road. He would sit cross-legged on a large paisley covered cushion, smoking endless pipes of peace with Larry, talking Buddhism, Hinduism, macrobiotics and the best dope to smoke. The pornography business had been exchanged for the spiritual journey. Peace and Love. Much better.

If you went out walking out around The Grove you might bump into Lemmy or Michael Moorcock, Barney Bubbles or Nik Turner. The place rippled with musicians, artists and photographers, dreamers and schemers. Julie Driscoll had sung with the Steampacket, with Long John Baldry and Rod Stewart, and then with Brian Auger, *Wheels on Fire* in 1968. The hippest chick in London with a beautiful voice. But she moved out and over to Keith Tippett and free jazz. She married out of rock and *Top of The Pops*, into experimental jazz.

The girl loved the sweet honey voice of Dusty Springfield but Dusty did the television Saturday night family shows and was ridiculed by the purveyors of the new cool. Dusty was old school, in her unhip clothes with her sprayed candy floss hair and thick old fashioned make-up of heavy black eyes, heavy with false lashes. Lulu and Dusty had big voices but they were last year and mainstream. In with the new, out with the old. Music was a cruel business. 'Power to the people, man.' As ever there was little power in the hands of women. Those in bands and visible at this time were Julie Driscoll and Beverley Martyn. John grabbed the fame and

Beverley was held in the wings, out on the edges. Sandy Denny, Jacqui McShee and Maddy Prior were emerging from the folk club scene, all going amplified and electric. Christine McVie, to step into Fleetwood Mac in 1970, married John Graham 'Mac' McVie, who played with John Mayall & the Bluesbreakers.

The rock stars would buy the massive white stucco houses up the hill, then mansions in the shires and apartments overlooking Central Park in Manhattan. From revolution to manor houses, penthouse apartments, private planes and swimming pools. The bands that were taken and promoted into the big time were not the bands from the London of the 1950s and the mid '60s with black and white musicians together, a representation of the cities they all lived in. Great bands to see live in hot basement clubs and the back rooms of pubs. No. These were deemed far to risky to promote to the general public. Musicians who'd learned their chops and paid their dues with those groups, learned from the African American artists. They played their blues and jazz with a lilt of the Caribbean, with those that came to the motherland on the *Empire Windrush*. Those who walked down that gang plank in Tilbury in 1948, just as the girl was beginning her school days in Lewisham, meeting children from far away. And as children will, they played together. What a pity about the bigotry of the previous generation.

These musicians would spread out around Britain, bringing Calypso with Lord Kitchener, a star in his native Trinidad, welcomed with open arms by those who were already here and homesick. *London is the place for me.* Although too often it felt such a hollow lyric given the treatment some of those people endured. Joe Harriott, 'Jiver' Hutchinson, his daughter and jazz vocalist Elaine Delmar, Ernest Ranglin, the St Vincent-born trumpeter Shake Keane, Harry Beckett here since 1954, and Root and Jenny Jackson. Music making the sound of London.

Crucial to the mix and ignored by the mainstream were the Africans, often fleeing from poverty or wars. Mike Falana, the trumpet player that the girl had watched with Graham Bond. Gasper Lawal, Speedy Acquaye and many more would arrive in the following years. Major record companies signed up Led Zeppelin, Status Quo, Spencer Davis and Free. Bands fresh out of the British blues boom. The record companies were taking no risks. Bob Dylan, who'd moved it all along then took it into the 1970s. The Race had been a band with black and white musicians and a white chick singer. No one would rush to sign them.

Larry had moved on from bouncing stripes and was painting the trip, *Exploding Galaxy*. An artist called David Medalla turned up at 113 one day. A lithe and

217

smiling man, he ran a dance troupe of blooming flower children. Larry, a dancer? They called the troupe 'The Exploding Galaxy' after Larry's painting of the same name. He then gave the painting to Lol Coxhill.

The girl would rock in her chair with the Tessie O'Shea black velvet dress wrapped around her, or she'd wear a beautiful long blue lace dress she'd found in Goldbourne Road. She held her baby in her belly whilst the hippy life whirled around her. She was Larry's 'old lady.' Exploding Galaxy would often gather at 113 but she felt removed, looking on through her own painted windows.

The former members of The Race were joining bands or beginning the long slide to obscurity. A life on the margins of the music business. Some would do well and others disappeared into the quicksand. She would be singing lullabies, not the blues.

BETTY BLUES BELTER 'Rock a bye baby on the treetop, when the wind blows the cradle will rock.'

NASTY NELLIE 'And down will come baby, cradle and all.'

SENSIBLE MA SADIE 'No, no, no, it will not break, not this bough, not with my baby.'

She had a check up at the hospital and found herself laying on a narrow hospital bed surrounded by a blue plastic curtain, waiting to be seen. She heard a doctor talking in the next cubicle, 'If you have any more pregnancies, you might very well lose the baby. It could endanger your own life.' There was a loud silence and then he said, 'A nurse will come and talk to you about the ways in which you could avoid another pregnancy.' The woman, Irish and pregnant with her sixth child, then began to sob. A priest, with the woman in her cubicle, began intoning with his deep male Irish voice, 'Contraception is a mortal sin. Artificial birth control is evil, an offence against the law of God and of nature. And those who indulge in such are branded with the guilt of a grave sin. She must honour her faith.'

The doctor and the priest were then gone and the woman left alone with her sobbing and guilt. The girl lay on the bed and thought about sex, love and religion. And then the memory of the christening in the cliff top church in Lowestoft. She remembered the house on the Avenue and then her own tears came. This life, this bloody life. It wasn't easy. She remembered her own lost baby as he lay in an aluminium dish in a hospital on the Fulham Road. Her tiny dead blue baby.

7th April 1967 was her 23rd birthday and Syrian gunners fired from the Golan Heights onto an Israeli tractor farming in the demilitarised zone. Israel later siezed control of the stolen land. 'When will we ever learn, when will we ever learn?'

NERVY NORA 'Do you exist, God?'

CLARA THE CLOWN 'What's that got to do with the price of fish?'

Here was another picture, another snapshot a month before the baby was due. 29th April 1967 at Alexandra Palace. The *UFO Club*. One massive happening. *The 14 hour technicolour dream*. Word went out to all the London hippies and groovers. Beat and Velma were there dancing their butts off. The girl, now so close to her time was given a wide berth. One of the Exploding Galaxy asked, 'Where will you be? Where will you sit? You need a place to sit down.' John 'Hoppy' Hopkins, photographer and founder of the *International Times* and *BIT*, man of heart, soul and courage, took her up onto the platform with the lighting rig and the cameras. 'Hey man, is she gonna give birth up here?' joked one to another. 'Far out man,' Hoppy said, 'just ask someone to find me if you need me. I wont be far away.' The men then went back to their manly pursuits of tripping the light fantastic.

She noticed a beautiful dark haired girl on the stage, wearing her blue lace dress, arms waving, weaving and whirling. Writhing on the floor, she was at one with the dance and it seemed with Larry also. The dress was ripped to shreds. Larry, the sweet artist had given away the blue lace. The girl discovered later that he'd given more than lace.

The night wore on and the hallucinogens pumped through the painted bodies. She wondered and prayed to whoever may be listening, that her waters wouldn't break. The waves of her womb could easily flood the platform and wash away the oh so groovy film makers, the light riggers and hangers. Larry was down there amongst it all on the biggest trip of his life. She felt like a voyeur, watching from above, out of reach, out of mind, nurturing her baby egg.

That year *Release* was founded by Caroline Coon. Larry was involved in the early days and would hang out at number 50 Princedale Road when the defence of the right to smoke cannabis was being discussed. A 24-hour telephone help line was set up and run by volunteers.

They were invited to Jan and Steve's for dinner. It was a Sunday evening on the 28th May. She felt like an enormous waddling creature, constantly getting out of her seat and heading to the lavatory. A baby sitting on a bladder is not a good recipe for dinner with friends. Richard turned up with Babette. It seemed it would be a long night and she didn't feel like toddling back up to St Stephen's Gardens on her own. Then without warning, oh the pain. And another, followed by more and more increasing in intensity.

THE BOSS 'This is it.'

They all piled into Steve's car and went up the road to the St Mary's Hospital, the maternity wing just off Ladbroke Grove. Oh my God how it all suddenly seemed too much. She wanted it to stop, to slow down.

> **MISERY IVY** 'Wait, wait. I'm not ready. I can't do this now. Oh no, it hurts. I can't to do it, I can't.'

And then the one who speaks with barbed tongue.

> **NASTY NELLIE** 'That face of yours. Misery on legs. Oh dear, such a fuss girl. You have no choice. And where's your voice now?'

A quake surged through her body.

> **NASTY NELLIE** 'It's enough to raise the dead. Yes, your baby is on the way.'

The voice came from a sour place, way down in her guts.

> **WICKED WILL O'MINA** 'Hello Mudda, Hello Faddar, here I am in Cape Granada?'

She went into A&E and then up to a ward. Bright lights in her face. Pant, and pant some more. An enema, a shave, more pain, more hours and then an epidural. This wasn't what she wanted. A long labour and her baby scooped out by forceps. Weighing seven and a half pounds, he was yellow, like an egg sunny side up with a bruised and pointed head where the forceps had gripped. She held him and wept. Sam, born on Monday 29th May 1967, took almost 13 hours to arrive. 'My little baby Sam,' she said, 'my tiny one.' That was the moment she knew what love was. A love supreme. And in America, Aretha Franklin sang *Respect*.

It was said on this day in 1967,

'Now, eleven years after 1956, we are restoring things to what they were in 1956... The issue now at hand is not the Gulf of Aqaba, the Straits of Tiran or the withdrawal of UNEF, but the rights of the Palestinian people.' (*Nasser speech to the Egyptian National Assembly in Cairo, 29th May 1967*).

P. F. Sloan at the tender age of 19, wrote, 'The Eastern world it is exploding, Violent flares and bullets loading,' sung by Barry McGuire.

> **GUILTY GERTIE** 'Yes indeed, there will always be war, and what of the baby you murdered? Would you have loved that baby?'

She held her baby close to her. 'No, no, please stop and be silent.'

> **THE BOSS** 'Scumbag, get back in your box.'

Larry had wanted to call him Frodo. Frodo for heaven's sake. He was a Sam. They were all reading *Lord of the Rings* that year. Love, that's what she felt. Love for this tiny creature, so frail and frankly not a pretty sight. His birth had been a tricky one. They took him away to the nursery, wrapped him up in a hospital blanket and put him in a cot along a row with many other babies. She lay in the hospital bed, fretting. 'I want my baby.' She could hear his cry. She knew for certain the loudest cry was hers. 'You must let us bottle feed him,' they said. 'No,' she said, 'no, no, no. I want to feed him.' They were impatient. 'You will disturb the rest of the ward.' They brought the baby to her, closed the curtains and left her to it. She tried so hard to feed him. He couldn't latch on. She struggled, he struggled and no one helped. The night nurse stood with her arms folded across her white uniformed chest, crackling with starch and indignation, 'I told you so. You can't do it and you're wasting my time.' She took him back to the cot in the other room.

The next morning a nurse took the drips and tubes from the girl's arms so she could hold her baby properly. She set to and the second day he was feeding. The look on the nurses faces said it all. 'Bloody nuisance, that's what you are. Breast feeding and a vegetarian.' They didn't encourage breast feeding in 1967 and spoke to her in the same way they did to a young Indian woman who was also vegetarian. She sat with the woman at lunch that day, eating soggy overcooked cabbage and carrots, giggling over the white lumpy rice.

Larry arrived at visiting time wearing a silk flowered shirt and pink trousers. Beat also came and seemed to have no interest in the jaundiced baby. 'I've come to see *you*,' she said, as the girl bent painfully forward to show Beat the new born boy, 'not...' Beat faltered, barely looking at the baby. It didn't occur to the girl that perhaps Beat saw this as the end of the closeness they'd shared. The girl was falling in love with her tiny boy and simply didn't notice.

The following day came beads, bells and the smells of exotic oils. It was Larry and the girl who'd worn the blue lace dress. Then Jan, Steve and Richard. 'What's that on your finger?' said Jan. Her finger was green. The brass wedding ring that Larry had bought had been tarnished by the sweat of childbirth and stained her finger. 'Take it off,' they all said, 'nasty. It looks like your finger's going to drop off. Looks like it's rotting.' It took her weeks to get rid of the brass mark. She was married but now without a ring.

It took less time for the scratching to stop where they'd shaved her. She was reminded of the moment she discovered the crabs in a toilet behind the

International Stores in Lowestoft. This wasn't a good memory as she'd scratched herself almost raw.

'Did you bring me a nightdress? And I need toothpaste and stuff,' she said. 'Ah.' Larry said, 'nightdress.' Then, 'what's wrong with the one you're wearing?' 'Too short,' she said, 'I have to borrow a dressing gown at meal times and they told me off for not having slippers.' She wanted the soft, warm and pretty nightdress from the children's home in Lewisham all those years ago. She thought of the tiled bathroom and warm gown on her small cold body on a dark winter's afternoon. She didn't cry though her eyes felt hot. She certainly didn't cry for her mother.

You have too many visitors,' said the nurse, 'you're only allowed three visitors at a time.' Some were amused and others affronted at the spectacle of hippies gathering around the girl's bed. As they left, the smell of incense lingered. She looked into the cot beside her bed and whispered, 'It's all change now, tiny one.' Jan brought her a kimono and said, 'keep it, it suits you.' The girl wrapped herself inside the silky gown, blue with a print of tiny red blossoms. 'Lovely,' she said, 'really lovely, thank you.' Her eyes filled with tears and she didn't know why.

The girl began to see that the tall Nigerian sister, although fierce at first, had a good heart. The nurses were all keen to clean, make beds and keep sister and matron happy. The ward was spotless. 'Oh,' the sister said one day, 'look, you have a white hair.' She plucked it from the girl's head. 'But I'm only 22, no I'm 23 now.' The sister laughed one of her rare laughs and said, 'you certainly don't look it.' She'd given up asking the girl where the grandparents were. 'Where's your mother?' she would ask, 'your parents, where are they? Don't they live in this country? What about your husband? A child needs grandparents.' After no response she'd click her tongue, signalling her displeasure. The girl had a feeling the sister didn't think much of English family life. And that she didn't hold out much hope for the girl's parenting skills. She certainly didn't like the hippies.

Ten days later Larry arrived to take them back to St Stephen's Gardens. 'Where's the pram?' said the girl, when they pushed through the doors and out onto the street. The light of that early June day hurt her eyes. She blinked. Tears and sunlight. It felt as if she'd been in the hospital much longer than 10 days. She wanted to go back. She wanted the order of the ward, the safety and the sister. 'Oh,' he said, as if she'd been speaking in outlandish tongues, 'pram?' He smiled and nodded, 'it's over at John's place. We'll go and fetch it tomorrow.'

At the bus stop she held the baby and he carried the bag. A woman stopped and tried to push a silver coin into Sam's tiny palm, 'Good luck for the baby. Your mum must be beside herself, dearie. Are you going home? She chucked you out has she?' 'Yes, we're going home.' She was 23 years old, and one month, but looked 16 and rather weary with dark shadows under her eyes and a face as pale as a hospital pillowcase. She reckoned the old dear had her down as a schoolgirl mum.

The bus arrived and on they climbed, all three. They went around from the hospital, down Ladbroke Grove, around the corner and got off in Kensington Park Road. At St

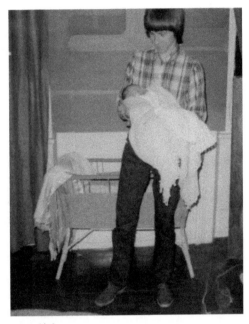

Larry with Sam.

Stephen's Gardens they climbed the linoleum covered stairs. The door on the second floor opened a crack and a thin flat-faced pale woman glared out. 'There's too much fucking noise,' she said, 'I'll call the police if you don't shut the fuck up.' Her man called her back into the room. As the door closed, the sweet smell of rum drifted onto the landing.

On the third floor they opened the door and what was to be life at 113 was revealed. A small group of smiling people sat cross-legged on the floor, waiting to greet the artist's baby. *Sergeant Peppers Lonely Hearts Club Band*, recently released, was playing on the deck and a celebratory joint was doing the rounds. Larry set up his *Hubble* water pipe. *Lucy in the sky with diamonds*. All the girl wanted was to lay down on the bed with her baby. She was a mum and Larry, a dad. Sheila's voice came to her through the smoke and the Beatles, if you want to spend your life with a fluffy little teddy bear.'

'Hey, great pad you got here man,' said a friend of a friend as he lay sprawled on the bed, his bare feet dangling, his head propped up by her treasured purple cushion. She saw his brown leather sandals on the floor beside a denim jacket and a large battered canvas bag, and her heart sank. This guy was pitching to crash down at their place. She just knew it. She'd never seen him before, 'What's happening man?' These weren't the words she really wanted to say.

THE BOSS 'Say it, Say it. Why can't you just say it.'

She prepared the speech.

THE BOSS 'I'll tell you what's happening man. I've just had a baby and I'm shit scared. I want to go to sleep and you're on my bed with your dirty feet. Go away all of you. Go, go, go!'

She began, and faltered, too exhausted to continue.

THE BOSS 'Come on girl, spit it out, say it. Say what you mean to say.'

She stood there with a stupid grin. The moment had passed and the man on the bed skinned up another joint. There's a mouse in the house, squeak, squeak.

WICKED WILL O'MINA 'If you don't say what's on your mind, the words will gather like puss in your ulcers, and one day they'll explode, making a nasty, yellow mess.'

'Larry. I feel a bit sick and I need to lie down. The baby will wake soon and I'll have to feed him.' She felt the tears welling up again. What had started as a ploy to get rid of the free loader on the bed suddenly became very real. She was crying for the mother who wasn't there, for the baby she had to care for. She felt overwhelmed and frightened, like a little girl. How would she manage?

NASTY NELLIE 'No good crying for your mum. Mum? There's no point in looking for your dad. Dad? You made your bed, now lay in it. If you can find your bed that is. It's one thing having a bun in the oven. Now the bun is a real live baby.'

The baby began to stir. 'Shush, shush my little one, shush,' she cooed, rocking him in her arms, 'sleepy one, go to sleep.' Sam began to wail. Nothing wrong with his vocal cords. 'I'm gonna split, man.' The man with dirty toenails left. She took Sam into the back room, sat in the rocking chair and gazed at the tiny boy cradled in her arms. She'd never known love until this moment. An all consuming, down in her guts love. She looked for the baby that she'd once been. Looked for her own mother. For a way to be with this baby, with motherhood. 'How mummy, how?' Her pleas would spin out into silence, save for the sound of her breathing and the breathing of the infant. The air around them was heavy with absence. She held Sam close and put the thoughts away in the old place. She looked down at his face and for the first time in her 23 years and one month felt a sense of peace and purpose. The singing would have to wait.

Down the end of a long dark tunnel she heard the Platters singing *Only you*. There was an echo far away in a front room on a council estate in Lowestoft from a long time ago. The hopes, the wishes and the maybes. She had a feeling that the world, her world, wasn't going to be bright unless she made it so herself. 'Only you can make my dreams come true.'

Larry with Sam, and the first Jimi Hendrix poster.

VERSE 17

Deptford

Who Know Where the Time goes? Sandy Denny 1967,
sung by Carol Grimes on *Mother* 2003

2007: looking back from Soul Britannia. 1967 to 1968: Apple, a 'beautiful place, where beautiful people can buy beautiful things', Christmas on Earth Continued, a Space Odyssey, Zappa, Joplin, wholemeal bread and miso spread.

My older eyes saw the time that had passed, looking into my younger eyes. No, my mind wasn't playing tricks. I was 63 and getting old. I listened to the radio and those over 60 were called 'old people' or 'pensioners'. I didn't feel like an 'OAP'. I didn't feel old.

Time is an illusion. Ten, nine, six or seven years, eons or seconds pass slowly or quickly, depending on what you're doing. Sitting and waiting. Waiting for decrepitude. Now that takes an age. Age, or the feelings of age, are dependant on the mind. Was this a trick of the mind? I saw the years etched into my skin but my energy, my desires and needs, were still running at full pelt.

Shaking my head up on the roof in Deptford, I watched a gaggle of Great Tits. Coffee mug in one hand, a slice of toast in the other, I watched their little wings flitting from a honeysuckle to a prickly pink rose. Now I see them, now I don't. A pair of blackbirds. A brown and industrious female collecting shreds from a hanging basket for her nest. A glamorous male, glossy black feathers, bright yellow beak, flapping away at the rustle of my arrival. One little coal tit feeding from seeds on the table. I tried not to breath too loudly. A plump little robin, beady black eyes, stepped brazenly over the threshold to peck at the pot just inside the door. All of this on a concrete flat roof above Deptford high street.

This was my mind. This was what it felt like in 2007, and still does. All my recollections are like fluttering birds, darting, diving and searching for that girl. Now you see her, now you don't. I see her, smell her, almost touch her and then she vanishes. The memories would appear as words on the screen as my fingers pecked at the keyboard. A sketch, a snatch of melody, a half forgotten song. A smell, a taste, a touch. Faint, then clear and determined, as if she were here by my side telling me her story. I have to be quick to catch her before she flies back to the place behind the locked doors, inside the labyrinth that lies within.

Carol with Soul Britannia performers in 2009.

I had recently performed at the *Barbican* in London with a cast of characters like me. The Barbican announcement read:

'*Soul Britannia All-Stars brings together a stellar cast to celebrate the huge diversity of sounds emerging from the UK during the '70s. The unmistakable vocals of Linda Lewis and Blue Mink's Madeline Bell, feature alongside the powerhouse grooves of Gonzalez and the yearning blues of Carol Grimes. The show also brings together original members of Caribbean Brixton funk band Cymande, now playing together for the first time in over twenty years. An event for all lovers of real soul music.*'

I'm still performing in 2017 and loving the music, year after year.

Also with Root Jackson, TJ Johnson, Spy, Alison Evelyn and Flo Harrison. Televised for posterity on BBC 4, the concerts had been advertised as a celebration of black music in Britain circa '70s. I felt like an impostor, even when the audience gave me a roaring welcome. When was I going to feel in the right place? The band kicked in and I was there in the music, in the company of musicians, many the children of immigrants or immigrants themselves. Apart from one song, *Uphill Piece of Mind*, a song I'd recorded in Memphis, I sang words and melodies I'd written myself. *Cool Fire*.

I remembered my early days with The Race and the problems we experienced in finding our place in musical history. Had things changed for the better, for immigrants and their children, for women? For older musicians? I wished this could happen more. Putting my voice where it felt so good to be. In the middle of the sound, hanging on the beat, slip sliding around the rhythms, dancing with the words, rolling the songs around in my belly.

Click

The eyelid is a camera shutter. Blink, click and catch it quick. Memory doesn't run in a smooth line. It starts and stutters. It has gaps. Memories are lost. Maybe it was the acid? The tabloids wrote that LSD fried your brains though never with any exact medical proof. It was said that if you remembered it all, you weren't there. I was. But some of that being there had disappeared. I see Sam in a cot waving his arms, practicing his many faces, his eyes forever shifting with his mood. 'Feed me, cuddle me, change my nappies, and play with me.' All conveyed in the language of infant to mother. I remember all that. I remember the two rooms in St Stephen's Gardens, a gathering place for assorted movers and shakers, poets and painters, musicians and clowns, dancers and thieves, dealers and wasters. All sitting around smiling and giggling as Larry painted.

They received an invitation to the opening of the Beatles' *Apple Boutique*, advertised as 'A beautiful place, where beautiful people can buy beautiful things.' 5th December 1967. Twiggy, George Harrison and John Lennon invited guests to, 'Come at 7.46. Fashion Show at 8.16.' During the evening, where models and rock stars mingled, drinking apple juice and already talking about where they were going onto afterwards, the girl slipped downstairs. The baby was restless. She sat amongst the coats and hats, the bags and parcels and caught the familiar aroma of good grass. She parted the coats and there was John Lennon. 'Hi,' he said, 'what's happening?' 'I came down here to feed the baby,' she stuttered. What do you say to John Lennon? 'Hi.' He nodded and asked, 'a boy?' She nodded and grinned stupidly. He peered through the coats at the baby in her arms. She smiled back at him. His eyes looked weary and wary, as if he wasn't sure whether to talk to her or not. What should she say? She wanted to talk, not to the rock god but to the man. Sam gave a toothless smile.

She thought about those take it easy, what's mine is yours oh so cool people she barely knew. She grinned and said nothing. The big rip off was happening. The Fool and their psychedelic circus trousers, posters, hats and rainbow shirts, silks and satins, all gone. It was said they treated the shop like a personal dressing up box, a bottomless cupboard of goodies. Help yourself, and they did. Then, with a smile John was gone. Gone to find Yoko?

The shop went bust in only eight months. Eight months of chaotic hippy business mayhem. *Apple* had lost almost £200,000. Jon Lyndon, the new manager, threatened to ban The Fool from the store if they charged any more debts to Apple. Who was fooling who? Something tickled.

There was a gig in the cavernous and cold Kensington Olympia, promoted as an 'All night Christmas dream party'. *Christmas on Earth Continued*. It was Friday 22nd December 1967. The Jimi Hendrix Experience, Eric Burdon and the New Animals, Soft Machine, the Move and Pink Floyd. It was Syd Barrett's last appearance before he flipped out and disappeared into mind chaos. Also on the bill were the Graham Bond Organisation, Sam Gopal's Dream, and DJs John Peel and Jeff Dexter.

Sam was seven months old. The girl wrapped him up, put a woollen Tibetan hat on his head, popped him into the papoose baby sling, and off they went. Most of The Grove community were there. It was one of those nights people talked about way into the future. A transcendental, psychedelic experience. Strangely, the attendance was sparse. The fears she'd always had about huge crowds and not being able to see were unfounded.

They were coming up to their first family Christmas. She bought Sam a brown bear with little button black eyes and fat paws, a rattle, a blue and white striped hat and a yellow duck to float in the sink. Downstairs in 113 they drank peach brandy and opened tinned fruit and condensed milk. The smell of roast fatty pork drifted through the house. Occasionally they were friendly and at other times, hostile. On bad days friends ran the gauntlet of yelps and curses. 'Fucking hippies.' On other days it was all smiles. 'Have a drink.' 'Eat some crisps.' And Sam was cuddled and admired. She never knew what to expect. She made a nut roast for Christmas dinner from a Marguerite Pattern recipe book. She made dishes of carrots, jerusalem artichokes and parsnips, and even managed a vegetarian gravy. When friends or neighbours asked, 'Are you going home for Christmas?' She replied, 'I am home.'

CLARA THE CLOWN 'But you could fly me to the moon.'

She invited Beat and Richard and whoever else was around. It became the first of many 'waifs and strays' Christmases. They played the new Jimi Hendrix, *Axis Bold*

Guy Cross at St Stephen's Gardens, Christmas 1969.

as Love (1967). The next year they listened to *Cheap Thrills* (1968) by Big Brother and The Holding Company. She shivered, as if Janis was the embodiment of the singer she wanted to be, out there and roaring. And she had missed the bus. Also, Van Morrison's *Astral Weeks* (1968), and there was The Grove immortalised in song, 'Saw you walking down by the Ladbroke Grove this morning.'

Larry was painting a *Mini Cooper* for Terry, who worked for George Harrison as his main man. Driver, arranger of appointments and protector. A myriad of colours. Paul Templeman was drafted in as his partner in painting.

On the sweet spring and summer days she pushed Sam in his buggy up to Holland Park, to the adventure playground to see the gorgeous peacocks. She hoped the male would strut, his tail feathers fanning out in fantastic display. Naturally psychedelic, she thought. No need for LSD. She shopped at the stalls on Portobello Road for a little wedge of cheese, a sweet or an apple for the boy. She cooked meals for friends and even made her first garden by planting tomato plants and flowers on two window sills. She read stories to Sam. *Paddington Bear*. 'Oh look it's Portobello Road and Paddington Station,' Sam would say, 'we live there.' And, 'Sam I am, Green Eggs and Ham.' Oh how she and Sam loved *Where The Wild Things Are*. 'Let the rumpus start!'

Larry and the girl went to gigs in underground spaces around the old Covent Garden, *Middle Earth* in King Street. Rotten fruit lay around the cobbled streets in the early morning as pubs opened for the night time traders who wanted a beer and a chat before going home to catch some shut-eye. The last dregs of that wonderful old market. The venues were tatty and worn in daylight but at night they glowed with Barney Bubbles blowing globs of light across worn white walls. There was smell of hashish and incense, and dancing underneath strobe lights. She tripped the light fantastic in a gold paper dress she loved. You could screw it into a little ball and shake it out for another dance night.

Words were nuzzling her inside head, disturbing the thistles.

THE BOSS 'Write your words, sing your songs.'

MISERY IVY 'But I can't. I don't know how.'

THE BOSS 'What the hell do you think all those words inside say? Are they not your words?'

The girl cooked and the baby gurgled. She washed him in a little bowl in the kitchen sink, not wanting to take him down to the draughty bathroom on the landing. She had two buckets under the sink for soaking nappies, then took them round to the launderette for drying. Jiggling Sam on her knee, she watched the washes going round and around.

The ceiling quivered in the occasional breeze in that hot so called 'Summer of love' in The Grove. A wriggle of silver balls, mobiles, glass prisms and Larry's paints and brushes in old jam jars filled with paint muddy water. All on the little pine table. All this as war raged in the far away East. And Country Joe and The Fish wrote the song that made a generation sing about Vietnam. He stole the melody, *Muskrat Ramble*, from Orleans jazz trombone player Kid Ory, recorded by Louis Armstrong and his Hot Five in 1926. It went to court much later and Country Joe won. Give with one hand and take with the other. Peace and love man? Don't think so.

An old Irish prostitute called Mary lived across the street. She would shuffle over to see the girl with the baby, her calloused feet in her *Tartan Bata* slippers. Mary, with her smiling face, cheap whiskey breath and cigarettes, peered into the pram and gazed with her watery blue eyes. She chuckled and crooned, a little unsteady on her feet. Once every few weeks, usually around 11 o'clock after the pubs had shut, she would stand on her front doorstep, shouting and hurling milk bottles one by on into the street. Crash, the bottles shattered, shards strewn across the pavement and into the street. She'd save them for weeks in her dark hallway for those moments of rage and frustration. In the morning she would carefully and slowly sweep up every last bit of glass, and then disappear back into her basement. The girl in her room was alert, her body taut with sympathy.

Money was short and the girl found a job as a waitress at Craig and Greg Sams' *Café Seed*, not far away in Paddington. It was just for a few hours a week and it was a good place to work. It got her out of the rooms in St Stephen's Gardens. Gave her a little air for a few hours. In the tiny kitchen out the back she helped herself to a couple of plumbs from the fridge that were marinading in juice. Tilly Tea Leaf opened her mouth and put in the plum. It was an avocado pear moment. Not what she expected at all. Oh dear, oh dear, where to spit it out, salty horrid Umeboshi plum. Aside from dishing up muesli, bean stew and brown rice at hippy festivals, the Sams family were also whole food suppliers to the Lennons. Whole food and tabs of LSD. Craig did time but didn't speak of it. He came out and the following year he and Anne had a little baby girl called Rima.

One day the artist from the flat above the bakery in Richmond walked in, wearing his customary leather and arm in arm with a man who wore a silk scarf thrown casually around his neck over a paisley shirt and dark velvet trousers. 'A couple,' the girl thought, if ever she saw one. The penny dropped. He smiled, she smiled and that was it. From July 1967 being gay, being a homosexual, was no longer against the law.

The weekend 'parade' on Portobello Road was attended by many, including those who'd just returned from India or Afghanistan, or who were leaving in a day or so for Ibiza. You'd see the obligatory Ibiza straw bag draped casually over one shoulder, filled with carrots and incense, *Tamari* sauce and black seaweed. India talk, drug talk, West Coast bands talk. The hippies in The Grove wore Indian shirts, long skirts, old hats and Afghan coats. The white people had smooth, tanned skin and wore flowing exotic clothes on their lean and languorous bodies. Everyone gathered round the bongo drummers and guitarists. They used to say you could get busted for smiling. If 'PC Filth' or 'Detective Fuzz' saw you grin, he assumed you were out of it and would search that big 'ole straw bag, or ask you to take off your new leather boots from *Gohills* in Camden Town.

One Saturday Larry and the girl met Terry and Renate, photographer and model, just back from the Balearics. They lived in a small flat off the Edgware Road, near Seymour Place. Renate was beautiful. Tall and slender with a long sheet of white blonde hair and warm green eyes. The girl liked her immediately but was a little in awe though she couldn't explain why. In her head everyone else seemed more beautiful, more interesting than she could ever hope to be.

CLARA THE CLOWN 'You silly, silly girl.'

They were invited to dinner one evening and met a couple from Germany who lived in Hampstead. It was at that time they also met Simon Postuma and Marijke Koger, the Dutch designers who called themselves 'The Fool'. On a Saturday the German couple would drive over to Portobello Road in their brand new VW van, dropping in on Larry and his old lady at 113. She was cooking as usual. Dressed beautifully, wearing paisley shirts and velvet capes, pantaloons and boots of Spanish leather, they'd leave their bags of fruit and vegetables, brown rice and wild apricots, sweet smelling teas and bottles of juices in the shiny van down in the scruffy street below, covered over with an Indian bedspread. They didn't entirely trust the street and its residents. Out with the smoke, on with The Dead. Grateful that is. There were countless Saturdays in The Grove with the Hampstead homestead a convenient drive away, and never digging into those bags in the van in the street. The girl was relieved when they pissed off to India for a while with their gorgeous clothes and address book of convenient numbers.

Paul's girlfriend Linda was looking after Sam. 'Come on man, everyone's gonna trip tonight.' Expand your mind, take a dip. Come on, just a little trip. The edge of a square of blotting paper. Good Swiss acid, man. Larry was already high, his eyes flashing, his mind zapping. She was losing him. She hung back. She wouldn't do a whole tab. Barely licked it. She'd seen people lose their minds in a morass of paranoia and was scared. So called acid casualties. She'd become more fearful since the baby was born.

An artist who dropped by to talk and smoke with Larry said one day, 'that cover on the baby's bed, it's evil. Get rid of it. Burn it.' He wore a silver ring. In place of a stone was a silver coffin and in the coffin was a skeleton. He talked of Aleister Crowley. A lot of people did. 'Hey man, it's heavy man, really heavy. It's a death, an omen man.' Grace Slick sang, 'tell 'em a hookah-smoking caterpillar. Has given you the call. Call Alice. When she was just small'.

In 1968 they went with Hoppy and Suzy Creamcheese to see the film of the year, *2001: a Space Odyssey*. She'd never seen anything like it. Wonderful. Kettle drums, boom, boom, the first brass chords, da da... The notes pulled at her hair follicles. Delicious music, awe inspiring majesty.

She fed Sam in the dark quiet hours of the night, his fingers clasped tightly around hers, his serious and direct gaze. Serious business this feeding. She would lay with him next to her, afraid to sleep in case she squashed him but not wanting to put him down. She loved his warm little body next to hers.

He started teething, couldn't sleep and she seemed to be constantly feeding him. She was at her wits end. Someone said go to the doctor and get some *Valium*, that'll help you. The doctor said, 'Go away and don't bother me. You've had a baby and babies don't sleep. Get on with it. You think you're the only woman to have given birth?' No sympathy there then. Out she slunk. She'd no strategy for dealing with those in authority, the doctors the teachers, the police. All were to be feared.

One dark early morning when she was sitting with the crying baby there was a soft knock on the door. It was the woman from upstairs, home from her night shift. 'I think you're running out of milk, your milk's dried up.' The woman gave her a bottle filled with milk. 'I put a little bit a rum in it,' she said, 'You too, have a milky drink. Then you'll get you some sleep.' And so it was. Her milk was gone. Sam soon got used to the taste and texture of the rubber teat. He suckled and slept. Thank god for the gentle women from Jamaica.

The next evening when she put Sam down after his bottle, she felt something snap. Their first bond was severed and her baby needed her less. He was six months old. She fed him goats milk, as Colin said it was the nearest to mother's milk. She stuck a sticker on his cot. *Safe as milk* (1967). From Captain Beefheart's new album.

She called her son at the age of one a 'Silver Bombshell', with his cloud of silver hair, shining blue eyes and flashing energy he only let go of in sleep. She had loved him even when her skinny legs could barely support the huge roundness that was the baby in her belly.

Frank Zappa and Janis Joplin performed at the Albert Hall. Sitting there was almost unbearable as she found herself spinning far away from all she'd hope to be, from her dreams of singing. But she was now clean. She ate her brown rice and hard wholemeal bread with *Miso* spread, drank *Mu Tea* and cooked vegetables by the ton. She washed her face at night, rubbing in the cream she'd bought in the Notting Hill Gate health food store, *Holland and Barrett*. She loved the smell and the feel of it on her skin and she was ulcer free.

BETTY BLUES BELTER 'I want sing the blues again, with a shit kicking, funky blues band. I want to smoke fags and down a pint of Guinness after the gig. I want to hang out with the band in a warm red velvet faded bar somewhere.'

Carol and Sam in front of *The Exploding Galaxy* painting.

THE BOSS 'Hey, if Janis is doing it, why not you in London W11?'
The girl wavered in her wispy willed Procrastinating Patsy 'I don't know who I am'
sort of way. She wore her beads but resisted the bells. 'I'm not a cat,' she thought,
as she wondered if she'd ever sing again.

VERSE 18

Formentera

Safe as Milk Captain Beefheart 1967

1968: a first flight, a month in the sun then back to Notting Hill Carnival and Portobello Road.

They were off to Formentera in the Balearics, to stay with Terry and Renate who had moved out of London to make a home on a sunny island. The flight from Heathrow was the girl's first. She loved being above the clouds, closer to the moon. At take off the baby cried. His ears were popping and the air hostess, beautiful in her smart navy blue suit, took him to her seat for a little while. They landed in Ibiza on a very small airstrip and walked with the baby and bags to what was little more than a shed. A box of *Froment* (wheatgerm) was of interest to the customs men. They shook it, sniffed it and looked at the little family suspiciously. They then set them free to roam their islands.

Terry and Renate picked them up in a Spanish car and the drove to the port, taking the ferry to La Savina on Formentera. She'd never been south, to the blue skies and sea under the hot Mediterranean sun. The blue so bright it hurt her eyes. She was used to northern skies, often tempestuous grey over dark grey seas.

The house was small and away from the town of Sant Francesc de Formentera. The car rattled over a track that could never be described as a road. Apprehensive and excited, she held Sam firmly in her arms. Here was west meeting an ancient Moorish world, as close to North Africa as it was to Spain. Local women wore dark scarves on their heads and aprons around their waists. They fetched water from ancient wells and picked olives and figs, growing what they could in the sun parched earth. To the girl's untravelled eyes it looked like a scene from a bible story, like the pictures on the wall at Sunday school in Lowestoft.

The new residents from the wealthy countries in the west lived a separate life alongside the Moorish ways, laying naked on the beaches, smoking weed and taking LSD. Sometimes the girl felt uncomfortable about that. They bought food in the little small town shops. There was a limited selection compared with the abundant choice from around the world you'd find in London markets. They drank beer in a bar and met the island hippy community. Germans, Americans, British and Dutch, all

236

golden tanned, brown feet in leather sandals, Indian beads around necks and silver bracelets on wrists.

At Terry and Renate's place she asked for the bathroom. 'Here you are,' said Renate, handing the girl a toilet roll as she opened the door to where the sky was the colour of soft black ink. Out into the cactus patch she went,

Renata in her Formentera home. *photo: Terry Seymour*

afraid at first. As her eyes became accustomed to the night sky she marvelled at the brilliance of the milky way. *The Plough* straddled the universe and star light seemed so much nearer than in the north. Shitting under the stars was a wonderful thing she said to herself, as she placed a stone on the ground over where she'd been.

Renate looked up from the oven as she took out a brown terracotta dish filled with a bubbling vegetarian stew. 'How's that?' 'Great,' said the girl, 'really great, and do you always go to the same place?' 'Well, I suppose yes, around the same place. I love it outside at night.' The girl agreed and could see why the island had enchanted those who'd settled from the chaotic cities. Renata gave the girl a hug.

People remarked on how pale the girl and Larry looked, as if it were a sin to be so or at the very least funny. Ha, ha, look at you, city faces from the north.

NASTY NELLIE 'Was it a sun tanning competition?'

The white people were browning themselves while brown and black people were treated as lessor beings. 'We're all a bit skewed,' she thought, 'it makes no sense.'

One day their hosts announced with great pleasure, 'We'll take care of the baby and you two can go off for the day.' With great ceremony, they were presented with a hit of acid. Larry was up and ready, the girl was wary. But they were off. He led the way across cactus and rock, down the dry dirt track to the sea. They found a small cove and lay naked in the sand. She watched in wonderment as a lizard crawled right up to her chin and she was face-to-face with a creature that looked a million years old. They swam a little, made love and then the girl needed to be back with her baby. They returned to a frosty vibe. Terry had been annoyed at

237

their sudden departure, 'We wanted to share some of your trip with you. You left so quickly. You're so speedy man, so London speedy.' The girl was embarrassed. More rules she'd failed to understand. Still buzzing with the acid, she buried her head into her child's neck and took refuge in the familiar smell. Suddenly she wanted to be back in London, in her own home however shabby that may be.

There was to be party a few miles away. 'Everyone will be there. You can leave the baby here. He'll be safe. He'll sleep. Don't be so uptight. This isn't London and nothing's gonna happen. Relax. We all watch out for each other here.'

The men's hands were on the drums, guitars were being strummed, pipes and joints were doing the rounds. The women bustled between oven and table. Rice, beans, carrots and onions, golden olive oil and tomatoes, all infused with island herbs. Eating flaó and thyme, and drinking frigola. She stayed for an hour. A storm was brewing, rattling around the Balearic islands. The baby was sound asleep when they left but she knew he'd wake up. The wind or thunder would disturbed him. She found him laying in a different way and spent the rest of the night curled up next to him. She vowed she'd never leave him alone again however much people mocked and called her uptight.

It was early days for the ferries from Ibiza and salt water still ran in the taps. A legacy of a once thriving salt industry at Las Salinas. The island was flat and the soil poor. It was a dry, windy and desolate place in many ways. But many who visited decided to stay, falling under its spell. There were fish in the sea and land was cheap. She loved the smells. The pine and fig trees, vines, olives and junipers. And feeling the sun warming her northern bones. She loved watching the goats and sheep sheltering in the lea of a bent and twisted fig tree. Lizards scattering at the sound of human footfall. In the last years of the nineteenth century the economy failed and the menfolk emigrated to the Americas, Argentina, Uruguay and Cuba, returning every few years. Formentera became known as 'women island'.

The girl and her family stayed a month. The baby's skin browning and his hair was almost white. Word was out that Taj Mahal was on the island and the hippies were buzzing. Everyone wanted to hang with Taj. Men who'd made a pile of money selling grass and hashish to the visiting musicians and their hangers on, were buying the humble fincas and filling them with sound systems and rugs from Morocco, cooking pots from India, and drums from Africa. Others bought plots of land, started free schools and opened bars.

Across the water, the same was happening in Ibiza. Only more so, with new boutiques selling hand made clothes and ethnic jewellery in the Old Town. Clubs were opening and the tiny narrow lanes were beginning to throb with drums and guitars as young western people wandered around in flowing clothes and jingle jangle jewels. The seeds were sown for what was to become the big party town.

The girl wanted to go home and find herself a band and songs she could sing. Terry had played an Umm Kulthum album for her in London. What a gift. Egyptian blues, Egyptian soul singing. She loved the way the musicians and singer would hit notes she'd never heard before. Bending and weaving, half notes and quarter notes. She kept the sound locked up inside her with all the other voices she'd encountered. Ray Charles and Sam Cooke on the jukeboxes in Lowestoft, Ottille Patterson and Miles Davis in Cambridge, Bobby Blue Bland, Edith Piaf, Nina Simone and Oscar Brown Jnr in Oakley Street. The voices that touched her heart, the secret heart that nobody ever had access to. All areas barred. Except for her Sam and Larry.

One morning Sam sat in the sun on a step outside the kitchen door, gurgling and giggling. She looked closer and saw a row of red ants marching across his feet, and as they marched they tickled his toes. She picked him up gently and walked over to see the goats in the cactus patch. The month was up. They were returning on the boat to Ibiza Old Town, to the airport and then back to The Grove. She was a tanned and freckled girl with an Ibiza straw basket slung across her chest.

Back home she turned on the tap at 113 and was astounded. Instant water and no salty tang. In the market buying the fruit and vegetables, she was struck by the city and its delights for those who had the money to buy. Life on a small southern island was very different in 1967. She would never take drinkable water and fresh food for granted ever again.

One day the boy bounced high in his cot and dislodged the bottom. From then on she put him to sleep in a bed in the kitchen, a bed that had served as a sofa in the daytime. He looked so small. She stroked his head and hoped she could be a good mum. She loved him so much it made her afraid. Tucked up and kissed, he said, 'I'm a big boy now.' They placed a screen around the bed. Another step away. First the feeding and now the sleeping. She sang him a song, 'There's a worm at the bottom of the garden and his name is Wiggly Woo.' She sang it softly. And then when she thought he was asleep, he said sleepily, 'Sing it again mummy, sing it again.' She did, three times.

Later on that summer was Notting Hill Carnival. A small local affair in those days, it had initially been established by Trinidadian born activist and journalist, Claudia Jones, née Claudia Vera Cumberbatch, the 'Mother of Caribbean Carnival'. Claudia Jones lived a life that was short but passionate, packed to the very rafters. Hounded out of the USA for her communist connections, she founded Britain's first major black newspaper, the *West Indian Gazette*. In her 1949 paper *An End to the Neglect of the Problems of the Negro Woman!* She wrote, 'The bourgeoisie is fearful of the militancy of the negro woman.' A woman of substance and courage, Jones had arrived in Britain to placards and attitudes. 'No Irish, No Coloured, No Dogs.' The first Mardi-Gras-based carnival had been held at St Pancras Town Hall in January 1959. Performing were the Boscoe Holder dance troupe, jazz guitarist Fitzroy Coleman and Cleo Laine.

Dancing through the streets in 1968 with Sam on her hip, she met Dee, with his woman Ronnie and Tarquin their baby boy. It was said that when Dee was up before the magistrate for a small amount of grass and hashish, he held his fingers up behind the magistrate's back, like a small boy playing cowboys. In London in the mid '60s, the joke wasn't regarded as very funny, though some did laugh. Dee was given a ridiculous sentence of three months. When he died he was buried with his old and legal name, Ruben Hollingsworth.

Dee was from Trinidad. The girl heard it said, 'You can taken the man out of Trinidad, but you can't take Trinidad out of the man.' Absolutely true in Dee's case. He cooked in the *Mangrove* on All Saints Road and made a carrot juice that was nectar, using a recipe that was his mother's, and her mother's before that. He had the energy of a much younger man and loved his food and his music, taking in life with enormous pleasure. He was to become a very dear friend to the girl.

Portobello Road on a Saturday would find them promenading, just as they'd done so in Spain. They'd bump into Bicycle John or Honk, Paul and Linda, or Dee on a break from his cooking. They'd hang out out in *Mick's Café*, wondering about the two men who always sat together, faces distorted by some sort of birth condition. Some people called them the 'elephant twins'.

After hunting out a record, they would go into *Ceres* for rice and beans, and *Hawkins* on the corner of Portobello and Blenheim Crescent for cheese, where the proprietor was a friendly man. Always resplendent in his clean white grocer's coat, he presided over the marble slab where he sliced cheeses and hams. Round cheeses cut into triangles like a cake. He gave the little boy in the buggy a lump of cheese or a biscuit, but not the ham. Never the ham as the little one wouldn't eat the animals. Carrie and her husband, who always wore a battered brown hat and a brown overall, ran the girl's favourite fruite and veg stall. They'd buy a Saturday present for a good boy in *Barnetts*, the toyshop on the corner of Elgin Crescent and Kensington Park Road. Together with *Woolworths*, it was a place of magic for children in The Grove.

This was before the days of fine food from *Mr Christian's*, which didn't open until 1974, and *Books for Cooks*, which began after the girl had moved east to Bethnal Green. The older market traders called it 'The Lane' from the old days when that part of London was a collection of villages. Portobello had been a farm named after the Caribbean town of Puerto Bello, in memory of the British captain responsible for capturing it. That would explain the *Admiral Vernon* antiques arcade. It's interesting, a colonial history followed by a call from the motherland for bus drivers, nurses, cleaners and cooks.

Terry and Renate were in London for a few days and came over. One evening as the girl prepared a meal they heard screaming from the family on the same floor next door. The man constantly shouted, the woman sobbed and the children cried. It was always so. But that day they heard the terrible sound of glass shattering. He'd pushed her out the window. She landed on the roof of the kitchen two floors down. The police were in the street. The man was taken to the station, the woman to a hospital and the children to who knows where.

On 17th March 1968, Larry and the girl went up to Grosvenor Square, taking the bus from Notting Hill Gate to the US Embassy. They joined the protest against the continuing war in Vietnam, dodging police cordons and flying hooves as the horses charged into the unarmed marchers. She was becoming more aware of the unequal world and saw how wealth was divided, or not. Little went to the workers, the engine drivers in every sense of the word. The streets of North Kensington were the perfect place to witness this as the Holland Park mansions sat close to the peeling poor streets around the Portobello Road. None of the wealth and privilege came her way. Opportunities for a poorly educated woman with no money were scarce.

The music now playing in the underground clubs and on the stereos in The Grove was no longer the charged, edgy blues that had so captivated the girl in the Chelsea, Soho and Earl's Court days. She had the new Etta James album *Tell Mama* (1968), with *I'd Rather go Blind*. 'Now there's a sound, there's a singer,' she

241

thought, 'gimme more of that.' God knows she could have done with a holler. She'd better find her way and fast because she knew for certain that the boil of desire, if not lanced, would burst in pain and misery.

Larry was up and far away. Free love and other shenanigans. The times they were a'changing. A German film crew came along to film the hippy family, the artist and his family in his garret. She didn't feel like a wife, she felt like an extra in a film. Like an onlooker, watching the people who tripped in and out of the colourful cave. Some are still frozen in 1968. Some moved on and out, scattered all over the world, doing this or that. Some died too early.

NERVY NORA 'I'm fearful of the past, the present and the future.'

THE BOSS 'You and the rest of the world, mate.'

Larry went to Formentera again, without the girl and the baby. He went to paint. She'd better get singing. What did she think Larry was doing on the island? Looking at the stars alone? Of course not.

On April 4th 1968, Martin Luther King Junior was shot and killed by James Earl Ray, sparking race riots in Washington D.C., Chicago, Baltimore, Louisville, Kentucky and Kansas City. That year, Eddy Grant and the Equals were the first multi-racial group to reach number one in the UK charts, with *Baby Come Back*.

Paul Templeman (*left*) and Larry.

VERSE 19
Babylon and Blind Faith

Fools Meeting Delivery 1970

1969: Bablyon, Blind Faith, name number four and an invitation from Steve Miller.

Larry had returned from the Balearics and was painting mandalas. He smelled different. His eyes were seeing the girl but he wasn't looking at her. Their lives continued almost as if he'd not been away, and they didn't talk about his trip. She bought a copy of *Melody Maker* and looked down the adverts for singers. Before Larry and baby, the music was all happenstance.

 THE BOSS 'Calling Betty Blues Belter!'

 CLARA THE CLOWN 'I'm not over yet you know.'

The girl attempted to execute a *Flamenco* dancer's stance and smiled as she picked up a multicoloured hat, far too big for her small head and gestured towards her bizarre ensemble.

 NASTY NELLIE 'You know, this is all make up and make believe. This
 goes into a wardrobe when I get home, until the next performance.'

The *Flamenco* dancer didn't answer; she didn't speak English.

  An advert caught her eye, 'Girl singer wanted for soul and blues band.' Auditions were to be held in a room above the *Rising Sun* pub on Tottenham Court Road. She took Sam over to Jan's and off she went with no thought as to what she would sing. Fred, a Jamaican man who played the tenor sax, met her. She sat with a group of girls, feeling strangely shaky. Fred said, 'Come and sing.' She was the last to do so, 'A blues in E,' she said, a chorus in and there she was roaring *Stormy Monday Blues* once more. Fred smiled. The band was called Babylon.

  Fred had played with various bands; Herbie Goins and the Nightimers, and Jimmy James's Vagabonds. He now wanted to start his own and recruited keyboards and drums, guitar and the bass. Fred said, 'We get rehearsing and I'll set up the gigs. In a month or so we'll be on the road.' And they were.

  Back in St Stephen's Gardens she told Larry the news. 'It's great, I got the gig.' 'I got the gig Larry, I got the gig.' It was like going for a job and getting it. Weird. She took no exams and gave no references. She'd just opened her mouth and they liked it, well Fred did. He picked her up in his old red jag and they rehearsed in a room above a bingo hall in Kilburn.

So, Larry would have to be a dad. A dad who did. At first he struggled. He wanted to be free to paint, smoke his pipes and go out and about wherever and whenever. The Formentera trip had taken the last of his parents' money and the girl asked, 'What do we do now. Starve?' Where was the bread, the dough? The Doh Ray Me? Do we live on air and fantasy? They resorted to picking up fruit and vegetables from the street after the market had packed up for the day.

The press lumped the counter culture and the hippies all together, naming them 'Flower Children'. Cartoons would appear with long-haired men and women smoking themselves to oblivion. Stories of pot heads, hippies, flower children and the beautiful people, usually accompanied by photographs of pretty girls dancing topless in floaty skirts with ethereal abandonment. As ever, the reality was very different. It was a cover for the more active on the scene. *King Mob* and the *London Squatters Campaign* had opened the lid on the squatters movement, making lists of empty properties, sussing out the legalities and rights. The girl knew that not everyone sat in a blue haze of pot.

July 20th 1969, the Apollo 11 mission. Neil Armstrong walked upon the moon followed by Buzz Aldrin. People without a television crowded outside electrical shop windows. It was an unbelievable event, magical,and even a little frightening. What would they find out there? Sam was two years old. The two rooms in St Stephen's gardens had seemed to her a paradise, even though they had no bathroom and she was hauling her baby, the buggy, her shopping and the washing up and down three flights of stairs. Surely if you worked hard enough, things would change. She was singing at the *100 Club* on Oxford Street, supporting Long John Baldry and Steampacket, with Rod Stewart, Graham Bond and Alexis Korner. Back on the circuit and far from the moon, she'd loved 'I see the moon and the moon sees me.'

She would get up at seven, feed the little one, clean and prepare for the hours when she'd be away from home. If the gig was out of town the van would arrive with the boys who, of course, had risen at noon for a late breakfast. They drove to student unions, clubs and pubs. They were taken on by the Gunnells' agency and then Robert Stigwood, the manager who'd had the Bee Gees and Eric Clapton, in Cream and then Blind Faith, the first so called 'super group'. Things seemed to be moving on.

NERVY NORA 'What if we have to tour, what if we go abroad, what do I do?'

'Rock a 'bye baby on the tree top, when the wind blows...'

THE BOSS 'Don't rock it, don't drop it.'

Sensible Ma Sadie cooked and cleaned the two rooms, arranged the flowers picked up at the end of market days, plumped up the cushions, shook the rugs, swept the floor and baked a loaf. It was her own two-roomed palace in the slums. Larry was painting portraits using acrylic on wood. Jimi Hendrix, John Lennon and Bob Dylan. A guy called Rupert who ran a shop

Larry's portrait of Bob Dylan, © Sam Smart.

in Blenheim Crescent, the *Dog Shop*, took the originals except for the Dylan which Larry gave to Richard as his 21st birthday present. Rupert had them silk screen printed and began to sell them. They adorned many a wall in many a room, in The Grove and beyond. They sold well but Larry didn't seem to see much of the money. The girl certainly didn't.

Gigs came in, Larry painted and played with Sam and life began to be more fractured. They were drifting apart. She knew that Fred liked her. He'd give her love hungry looks. They added a male singer, Lou Rich. She remembered him singing at the *Café des Artistes* in 1965. He wasn't from the hippy scene. He was more old school, eager for fame and money. The Gunnells bought in a brass section. They were going for a British version of Delaney and Bonnie. The girl could tell it was being manufactured. This was indeed the music business. 'Business' being the main word. 'What about your name, Smart? They said, 'What were you before? Freeman? Ha, ha, ha *Freeman, Hardy and Willis*, not a good name for you.' 'How very original,' thought the girl. Standing in a queue in the post office on Westbourne Park Road one day, Grimes came into her head, she chose Grimes. Why, she didn't know. Name number four. Higgs, Freeman, Smart, and now Grimes.

Carol in Babylon.

The management paid for some clothes from *Browns* in South Molton Street, a very smart shop indeed. Dresses with cleavage space and a long dark brown wig. She was encouraged to hang out at *The Bag O'Nails*, a Stigwood owned club, and at that time one of the places where the hip and happening crowd went. Trouble was, she had a baby at home. How could she be a rock chick and a mother all at the same time?

She loved the big brass sound of the new horn section, with Fred, Dick Cuthell on trumpet and Dave Quincy playing tenor or soprano saxophone. It was like singing on a big brass bed. Stab, stab, in with the rhythm section. The horn solo sounded fruity and dirty. The girl wore her boutique frocks and Lou looked like he should be in Las Vegas. They were renamed Rich, Grimes & Babylon. They were being played and moved away from the band that Fred had put together. Subtle changes were made to the repertoire, to how they looked on stage and in press photographs.

THE BOSS 'Speak up you fool, you mangy fool. You know you don't like this.'

MISERY IVY 'It's doing my head in. It's rustling my cobwebs and disturbing my thistles.'

She pleaded and wheedled.

Nasty Nellie 'Yeah, yeah, you just don't know how to do this. And they're bigger than you, tougher than you. They're the business and you're just a little thing. You're dispensable.'

A bridge of hysteria

The Boss 'You're neurotic. Get a grip, or it's crash landings for you.'
Nasty Nellie 'You're equidistant between the guy with horns and a pitchfork, and the deep tumultuous sea.'
Clara The Clown 'Hold onto your wigs and gather your wits about you girls, here we go, wheeh!'

She thought about her singing and what she'd been told over the years. It was a chorus of chaos. What was she to do? 'You got great tits, let's see 'em a bit more!' 'What about a bit of leg?' And 'You're not as good as...' 'Hasn't she got piggy little eyes!' 'Slut, prick teaser.' 'You made your bed, now lay...' 'If you want to live with a teddy bear.' Around this time the girl was beginning to see that for every one arsehole there were many lovely people. But what should she do do if the arse hole mixed with the lovelies, if a whole gang of arseholes should gather around her?

Two days before Sam's second birthday in 1969, the band had a gig at the *Marquee*. The first of a few. They were playing on the bill with a band called Taste. She sang her numbers and Lou did *Spinning Wheel*, the crowd pleaser and big hit for Blood Sweat and Tears. Were they to become a covers band, a crowd pleaser? She had a pint of *Guinness* before the gig in the *The Ship* down the road in Wardour Street. Once in the music she was tippy toe high, flying her singing kite in the skies. Afterwards she felt overwhelmed and tired. 'I want to go home,' she wailed, 'I want to see my baby.' Her head was in turmoil. She had one foot in the band, microphone in hand, and another in her room in The Grove.

What to do and who to be? This didn't feel right. Someone was pulling those ropes again. Do this, wear that, sing this, say that, fuck him, and go there, please, please me. Please, please who? John Gee, who managed the *Marquee*, put her in a cab. At home, she staggered up the stairs to find Larry and a girl with Dr John, *The Night Tripper* (1968) on the hi-fi player. The girl had black curly hair and dark eyes that seemed to be mocking her. It was the girl who'd ripped her blue lace dress to shreds. *Walk on gilded splinters*. Voodoo Funk from New Orleans. Larry took her down to the front door and when he returned the girl hid in the bed with the blankets over her head.

Blind Faith was booked to tour, with the great god Clapton, Ginger Baker, Stevie Winwood and Ric Grech. A group of men who didn't get on at all. Babylon were booked as the support band. In late June the band departed, going to places she'd never dreamed of. Helsinki, Oslo, Stockholm, Göteborg and ending in København. Blind Faith had performed a pre-tour free concert in Hyde Park, on a sunny Saturday 7th June 1969, with Julie Driscoll and Long John Baldry, The Third Ear Band, Edgar Broughton, Richie Havens, and a solo performance from Donovan.

Babylon travelled by van to Newcastle and then took a ferry to Sweden. She spent many hours sitting in back of the van, watching the Scandinavian pine trees and log cabins beside fjords. All so clean and crisp. She'd stupidly sneaked a lump of Moroccan hashish into the collar of her velvet coat. She did it for the guitar player who told her she wouldn't be searched. They got out of the van at the customs dock.

FRANK PALE MOUSE 'Oh shit!'

The customs men were searching the bags and instrument cases. The drums and guitars were put out out on a bench, and there was her coat drapped over the back of her seat. Heart racing, she thought, 'Clang, clang, it's in here. The dope, it's in the girls coat.'

FRANK PALE MOUSE 'Oh shit, shit!'

They didn't find it. It was a miracle. 'You can get ten years for that,' said one of the guys in the band, laughing. She thought of her boy at home and once again shook her head in shame. Where the hell was Sensible Ma Sadie?

They stocked up on cheese and bread, cans of Coke, papers and cigarettes. The guitar player rolled a very long fat joint as they wound their way out of the port and onto the freeway. 'Good draw, man,' he said, 'a packet of skins cost an arm and a leg. They really don't want you to roll your own here, do they. And as for a bottle of bloody lager, well forget it, man. You could spend the whole of your gig money just getting high, man.' On the ferry over to Finland she stood on the deck, the first class deck where she shouldn't have been, and watched as the sun didn't sink, but met the moon in a fantastic play for superiority in the kingdom of the sky. She loved the stars and was enchanted by the midnight sun.

The girl was both lonely and happy. At this point she realised that being alone was good. Lonely was another thing altogether. She enjoyed solitude. Sometimes she hungered for intimacy and yet was wary of getting too close to another human. She thought of her beloved boy so far away. She may as well have been sitting on that slither of a moon. What was she doing so far away? She thought about Larry.

NERVY NORA 'Hubble-bubble, toil and trouble.'

She imagined him with the beautiful dark haired girl and was anxious. It was a two week trip. She was indeed making money and building a future but did she need to be so far away to do it?

Blind Faith and entourage, including Stigwood, would arrive fresh from flights and good hotels. The Babylon crew would pour out of the van, stiff and sweaty, and onto stages facing crowds who were waiting for the main event. Eric! Eric! She loved the vastness of the venues after the small clubs and pubs back home. It felt good to sing out in such big spaces. Less intimidating because you couldn't see the whites of their eyes. She could barely see from beyond the first few rows of people. She remembered Alexis Korner's words and tried to free up her body. She even danced a little, a tiny *Flamenco* stomp here, a flick of an arm there.

On the road at the motorway stops, the main fodder was meatballs and potatoes. Still vegetarian, she had to eat eggs. Omelettes, more bloody omelettes. And cheese, cheese, cheese. One night in Stockholm after the concert and a meal in a café with the band, she stepped out onto a crossing and was suddenly confronted by police with guns in holsters. 'My God,' she thought, 'this is a turn up'. All she'd done was a jay walk after midnight. Fierce. Normally she'd wait for the road crew to pack up and then they'd seek out a small bar wherever they were, a jazz club or maybe some blues. Robert Stigwood gave her a ticking off and said, 'You must go out to the right clubs, not those cellar dives with the roadies. Why do you think we bought you those clothes?' She hung her head, felt her cheeks flush red. She felt angry. Didn't she own a voice or have a choice of her own? What they were actually saying was, be seen. Find a rock star boyfriend, do the right thing and court the press. Play the game girl, play the game.

Babylon recorded *Into The Promised Land* and *Nobody's fault but mine*, released on *Polydor* Records. The sax player would take the piss. He made her feel she wasn't good enough. He was into jazz and kept talking about a wonderful singer, a real jazz singer called Norma Winstone. 'You're not in her league,' he said, 'now there's a real jazz singer.' He ran a weekly jazz night in the *Three Tuns*, a pub in Beckenham, Kent,

booking top British jazzmen like Ronnie Scott, Tubby Hayes and Phil Seamen. He was doing a gig he didn't care for. It was a money gig. 'I never said I was a jazz singer,' she said, just out of earshot, downing another beer.

> **NASTY NELLIE** 'Let's face it girl. You're crap, crap. Go home girl. Go home because you're never gonna make it.'

It was a hard world, this music world, like being shot at from all sides. Bang, bang the girl is dead. Up she gets for another round. Say hello to Clara the Clown. Fred left Babylon. Did he jump or was he pushed? The Grove heads were dancing, arms raised, waving above their acid heads, at one with the universe. Cool man, cool Barney Bubbles, a mass of colour, weaving, flowing, the smell of incense, hashish, Krishna, Buddha, patchouli oils. She played more gigs in underground rooms around the old Covent Garden market. Arthur Brown and the Exploding Galaxy.

A Bridge of questions

Who wears the hippy cloak? Who owns the cosmic clam of cool? Who's in and who's out? Who pays when the music makes it? Makes what? Money, you got to make the money. Art? Don't make me laugh.

> **NASTY NELLIE** 'There has to be rubber necking. Brown nosing and arse licking. The product isn't playing the game.'
>
> **THE BOSS** 'I'd rather fly a paper plane to Mars or sit down in a bed of stinging nettles than give up on the singing. But not this way.'

There was more to this music than an expensive frock from South Molton Street. And what was it with the wig? What was the matter with her own hair? Betty Blues Belter had found her voice. The resonance of her singing flowed through her body, through her veins, pumping her heart. Without it she would die. Lou was a good soul. He got on with the job, always the trouper. But she knew he'd prefer her not to be there, so he could front the band himself. He was probably right. It was a man's band. Misery Ivy followed in her wake like a depressed apostle denied the *Valium*.

> **MISERY IVY** 'Away from the rotting, damp, the flaking ceilings and leaking lavatories and scampering mice, where landlords send round hard-nosed bullies to collect the rent.'
>
> **THE BOSS** 'A stepping stone. Sing up, sing up.'

She felt like an inadequate 'girl singer as band eye candy.' They weren't interested in her song wishes and writing desires. She ditched the wig, the dress and the attempts to glamourise her. She began to play with the songs. Stretching and bending them. This didn't go down well with the band or the management. Simon Stable wrote good things about her in the *International Times*, the paper that Hoppy had set up along with Jim Haynes and others. Babylon bit the dust. She missed Fred. He was out on the road with Jimmy James and the Vagabonds.

Larry was busy with his mandala world and silkscreen portraits. Their room span with concentric patterns of many colours. She filled the mantelpiece with fir cones and dried flowers plucked from the parks and the market after six on a Saturday, before the dustbin crews arrived to clear the streets. She found a log when visiting new friends called Reg and Jane who lived on Elgin Crescent with access to a garden square. They rolled it back across the Portobello Road and up Talbot Road to St Stephen's Gardens, up the stairs where they placed it next to the fireplace. She found an old mirror on a skip, painted the wood surround purple and propped it up behind the mattress on the floor, which also served as a settee covered with an Indian bedspread and a few cushions.

Louis moved into a flat in Trellick Tower, the Goldfinger designed block that you could see for miles around. He was near the top and when it was windy the building moved gently. It made the girl feel queasy and that made Louis laugh. He would pass by St Stephen's Gardens, often with a cake, and would sit and spin his stories, smiling at the growing boy, doing the *Hubble Bubble* pipe with Larry and whoever else was around. All was not perfect in St Stephen's Gardens.

One morning there was a loud knock on the door downstairs. A woman, together with a man holding a camera, stood on the steps, 'Hello, sorry to disturb you. We're setting up a business and we've seen you out in the area with your beautiful baby. Let us take a picture. We'll do it cheap for you, as we're just starting out.' She was a sweet smiling woman and he a big silent grinning man. They seemed friendly and the girl let them in. Young Paget from the family upstairs wanted to be a photographer. He'd taken lots of photos and thanks to him, she had her baby held for all time in those early days of his life.

A week later and it was time to pay up. The charge was high, too high. Way more than they'd said. She had no money, not enough for them anyway. The woman wasn't on the doorstep this time, just the big man with a menacing leer as he handed over three badly developed prints. He returned the next day and the following days until she paid up.

Another day and another knock on the door. November 1969. On the doorstep was Steve Miller with his younger brother Phil, from a band called Delivery. She'd shared the bill with them a couple of times in Steve's *Ramblin' Jacks Blues Club* and the *Speakeasy*. They wanted to expand, add a singer, was she interested? Was she ever? They had almost hooked Robert Plant, a Midlands based blues singer and friend of blues player Victor Brox. Robert was then seduced by a better offer, a band with Jimmy Page, which of course became a little combo called Led Zeppelin.

Those that had played the city clubs, Steve's club, then became the mainstream of the British rock blues scene, followed by worldwide fame across the Atlantic. Fleetwood Mac, Chicken Shack, Savoy Brown and Free. By the end of 1968, the band had replaced the singer Dez Fisher with Simon Leigh, who also didn't stay long but he did introduce the band to the saxophonist Lol Coxhill. Perhaps that was why some members weren't so welcoming. She wasn't the first choice or even second. And she was a woman.

Bruno's Blues Band became Steve Miller's Delivery, later shortened to Delivery. They had supported blues artists such as Lowell Fulson, Eddie Boyd and Otis Spann, and had regular bookings at Ronnie Scott's in Frith Street. The brothers lived in a flat on the Upper Richmond Road, together with Pip and a friend called Bengy who drove the band around. They were a tight knit group. She found her own way by bus and train across Barnes Common. It was blues but with a very different vibe. Phil's playing was more fluid than the players she'd worked with previously. She missed the solid simple grooves of The Race and Babylon. These guys had a new sound. This was, as Steve Miller was to say later, a learning band for him. It was the same for the girl. She sensed that Pip wasn't keen on her being pulled into the band by the brothers Miller. Who knows, with Pip and Steve both gone, she'd never have that conversation.

VERSE 20

Delivery and Uncle Dog

A Change Is Gonna Come Sam Cooke 1964

1970 to 1971: Delivery, John Peel approves, Guy and Elizabeth, Uncle Dog and Glastonbury. Time to pack her bags.

On 28th July 1970, the Westway, running between White City and Paddington, was opened. Although an eyesore and a concrete divide over the Portobello Road, it did provide spaces underneath for performance and for people to pedal their wares. In The Grove there was more unrest. A demonstration virtually every other day, protesting about police persecution of the *Mangrove* Caribbean restaurant on All Saints Road.

A march made its way up the Great Western Road. The police tried to direct it away from the old Paddington Green Station, which then provoked a riot on Portnall Road with seventeen demonstrators arrested. What followed was a long trial of the Mangrove Nine, including Frank Crichlow and Darcus Howe. The Street was raided regularly with police turning up unannounced at one door bell or another. The girl was in an area that was about to explode once again. The last time was in the 1950s. White teddy boys from the White City estate up against newly arrived Caribbean immigrants in The Grove.

The girl was still hanging onto the blues and wanting to fly, to

(*Above*) Sam.
photo: Guy Cross
(*Right*) Outside Carol's St Stephen's Gardens window one day.

253

improvise, to let loose, flap her jazz wings. From the moment she'd first heard Miles Davis, the voices of Umm Kulthum, Oscar Brown Jr and Etta James and, all those years ago, the queen who was Ella Fitzgerald. Her voice sang of life, humour, love and, with a twist and a turn, deep anger at injustice and cruelty. Benefit Bertha began to emerge and Delivery were playing gigs on her patch at places like All Saints hall. They played benefits for local issues, like play space for children in Powis Square. They played in the reopened *Electric Cinema*. A man called Dr Sam Hutt was involved, with a new manager Peter Howden, who'd installed Winston Churchill's old projectors. Hutt later became country singer Hank Wangford. The cinema had originally opened in February 1910, and had been called the *Imperial* or the *Bug Hole*. Christie had worked at there, adding to the story. One night as she watched a film with Larry, a wasp crawled up the sleeve of her velvet coat and she began to feel very odd indeed.

Delivery had a gig in Cambridge and the girl was picked up in an old Bedford van, the horn beeping down in the street. She'd rushed her day, settling Sam, making sure dinner was ready on the table by the oven, milk on the window sill keeping cool, apples and bananas in the fruit bowl. 'You're only going for a few hours,' Larry said, as she worried, fretted and finally left.

The van parked up by the tube stairs at Marble Arch. 'We're picking up Lol,' they said. She was in the front seat. Steve was driving. 'Budge up.' Lol Coxhill, saxophone player extraordinaire, climbed in beside her, stuffed his sax case on the floor and within moments had fallen asleep on her shoulder. He had a big bald head. He busked most days and was a single father. He'd worked as a bookbinder and lived with his kids in Aylesbury. Larry liked Lol. He gave him the *Exploding Galaxy* painting. After a year Lol left Delivery to join the Kevin Ayres' band but still did the odd gig and recorded with them.

The girl did what she always did when life became confusing. Don't look too closely and the brothers Miller will run the band. It'll be all right. It's got to be. There was meeting with a man called Wilf in a Mayfair Office. He wanted to act as the band's agent. He had a habit of cracking his tattooed knuckles. Love and hate. 'Now then lads,' he said. He never addressed the girl and always spoke directly to the Millers. He talked of big cars, a Rolls Royce, 'Each,' he said. He talked of world-wide fame, of recording contracts and selling a million. The band was dropped by Stigwood, who had the girl under contract, and signed to the progressive label, *B&C Records*. They were due in the studio in April and she had to write lyrics for four of the tracks. She was terrified. Where would the words come from? She found them from her own life. Onto paper, then out of her mouth and into the air.

She liked moments of solitude when writing. With Sam asleep and Larry who knows where. The album would be released on the *Charisma* label, *Blind to Your Light*, *Miserable Man*, *The Wrong Time*, and *Fools Meeting*. Her words. She was more thrilled by that than by the recording which was rushed and uncomfortable. Pip barely spoke to her. The bass player, Jack Monk, had left and was replaced by double bass player Roy Babbington. Steve Miller was a wonderful man. Family. That's what she was looking for. The band as family. But some of her adopted family just didn't want her there. Maybe it was the singer thing. She was beginning to realise that some instrumental musicians were wary of singers, didn't consider them real musicians.

The band was given the services of Max Needham, publicist for *B&C*. He was known as Waxie Maxie, a man devoted to '50s rock and roll. He got the girl a session singing on a track with the Red Price Combo. Red Price, a tenor sax player, had backed Frankie Vaughan, Shirley Bassey, Eartha Kitt, Louis Armstrong and many others during residencies at the *Batley Variety Club*. There was Gene Vincent and the Houseshakers and Shakin' Stevens and the Sunsets. The Studio was littered with half-eaten sandwiches, empty beer glasses, and full ash trays. A studio full of musicians she'd never met. This was the session player's world.

The recorded track is long gone and forgotten. Show business rock and roll, a blast from Lowestoft and the jukeboxes. What was Marion doing now? Did she still jive on a Saturday night on the south pier? And Bridget? Where was Bridget? It was the first time in a very long time she'd thought about Lowestoft. It felt like another country. Pink socks, tight jeans, pink lips, *Outdoor Girl*, sooty black mascara, ponytail swinging. 1958. Fourteen years old. Where have the dreams gone?

NERVY NORA 'I'm doing it. I am, look at me.'

THE BOSS 'Please watch your step and do speak up.'

Click

Another picture. A hippy happening in Holland Park. Drums drumming, guitars strumming, joints being rolled, hippy chicks wafting under trees, dancing. Like *A Midsummer Night's Dream* but with no Bottom. Just peacocks, babies, puppy dogs, 'hash' brownies and bubbles. The police appeared and it was all reported in the underground paper *Frendz*.

'A large crowd of so called freaks were gathered, quietly smoking dope and playing guitars, when a bunch of pigs (Policemen), cunningly disguised as bushes and shrubs, leapt out and busted part of the crowd.'

That caused a laugh.

Delivery was advertised on the outside of the venue. Delivery, Deep Purple and DJ John Peel who liked the band and wrote about them in his *Disc and Music Echo* column on 14th November 1970.

'Her singing was at times like a funky Eartha Kitt and at others she reminded me of Grack Slick.... the intensity and power... '

Delivery in 1970: Pip Pyle, Roy Babbington, Carol, Phil and Steve Miller. *photo: Guy Cross*

Oh, she thought, 'Eartha Kitt, he said I was like Eartha Kitt,' 'I'm just an old fashioned girl with an old...' She was whirled back once more to Lowestoft. She imagined herself as the beautiful Eartha. Life seemed to come around in circles, meeting in the most unexpected places. For a moment she believed what John Peel had written. It was John Peel after all. She bought a copy and sat in secret in the cold St Stephen's Gardens bathroom, gazing at the words. 'Wow' she thought, 'Well, you never know, maybe, just maybe, it's not all over. I still have a chance.' Her time with Babylon had shown her what the industry was really like. It took you in and spat you out. That's no problem. There was no looking back. Play the game or get the big heave ho.

Just four days to the recording in *Morgan Studios*. At the session she did her best. She couldn't hear herself very well and, thinking the cans were called tins, she asked for more level in her tins. This caused much laughter and a red face. She sang her words and meant everything she'd written. In the end it was a thin sort of sound, tinny and hysterical. Hurry, hurry, said the record company.

They put a single out, *Harry Lucky*. Waxie Maxie wrote an article in the *New Musical Express*, set out like an interview. Lies, all lies. He said her friends called her Cherry Ripe or Little Bessie. That she ate gravel and had a handbag full of miniature bottles of booze. That she'd worked topless in a Moroccan bar. Morocco? It was embarrassing. She'd written about lost love and the end of the world and the album was called *Fools Meeting*.

Blind to your light. 'Groping in the dark, trying to find the switch to the light.'

Fools Meeting 'It was a fools meeting last night now I sit here on my own.'

Carol performing at Sussex University.
photo: Nando

257

The Wrong Time. 'It's the wrong time to feel as I do now.'

MISERY IVY 'Oh woe, woe is me.'

THE BOSS 'Totally daft. Who's gonna believe all that?'

Long before she knew the word catharsis, she was getting it all up and out. Lol Coxhill blew his soprano sax, taking it into an improvised section and then in came the girl, screaming, fit to bust her ribs, scraping her voice to shreds, a cry from the guts. Was it about Larry? A little of their broken down marriage maybe but actually it was more to do with all that had been before. The dark dreams of her loveless childhood, though she wasn't aware of that at the time. She was living in the moment. It's best that way. The stuff of all the blues she'd heard was about lost love and being mistreated by some man or woman. Songs mimicking life. Her life was in the songs. It may all have been heard before but these were her words, from her life.

Listening back to that girl's young and strained voice, I want to stretch out a long hand, back down the years, to say, 'Hey it's ok, you're killing yourself and why? Relax girl, relax, chill out girl. What are you trying to prove? Who are trying to impress?'

B&C rushed the band through the recording sessions, delayed the release for months and then promoted the girl as a solo act, the English equivalent of Janis Joplin. The band wasn't best pleased even though in every interview she said over and over to every journalist, 'It's a band, it's not my band. I'm just the singer in the band.' It became her mantra, 'it's a band, it's a band.' But the damage was done. Those members who'd never wanted her had their amunition.

One weekend they were playing a gig in Plymouth's town hall. It was winter and the drive was long and cold. Shown into a dressing room, they had a sandwich or two, then went on stage. Who were they supporting? Long gone. The promoter said, 'Lads there's no money.' The bass player made a quick dash, grabbed the cash and ran out the door. The snow got worse and drifted across the roads. They were stuck in the van all night, huddled together for warmth. Early the next morning they they set off for the next gig at Leicester University. Then finally, a gig in Birmingham. Out the van and into another dressing room. It was a tough way to pay the rent.

CLARA THE CLOWN 'I wandered lonely as a cloud but the cloud was full of lightning. I was fried alive and kicking.'

WICKED WILL O'MINA 'Give her the pills, please.'

CLARA THE CLOWN 'Here we go round the mulberry bush, one more time.'

They set off for London after the last gig and the van broke down. This time the engine spluttered and gave up the ghost on the M1. They got a lift in a coach to the *Blue Boar* where she found another band stoking up on all day fry-ups and cups of brown tea. It was a band from The Grove. She arrived home three days later, cold and stiff. Did she make any money? Barely. They were out selling the album, promoting their wares.

It went from bad to worse. The Delivery family was unsettled. Bass players shifted and the drummer left to join a band called Gong, a spin off from Soft Machine, led by Daevid Allen. Lol was still playing with Kevin Ayers, and she felt it were all her doing. If only Maxie hadn't written that article. If she hadn't had those pictures in the papers. Hippy chick singer from The Grove fronts Delivery, sexy girl singer and more.

GUILTY GERTIE 'I'm a bad smell, a dark cloud, an omen that's murky.'
She sat on an amp in the back of the van. Last night it was Newcastle and tomorrow it would be Birmingham again. They lost an hour setting off and were nearly too late for the sound check. The drummer had overslept.

MISERY IVY 'I'm splitting. Is this gonna break me? Is this a real day? Is this a nightmare?'
Musicians were preaching revolution and power to the people. Though it didn't happen back stage at the big university gigs, in the town halls, clubs and college campuses. Glimpsed behind the blockade of denim clad roadies, huge sets of keys jangling on leather belts, were minders guarding the main band dressing rooms filled with bottles of wine and vodka, cheese, bread rolls, bowls of sweeties and the rest.

CLARA THE CLOWN 'Ooh loverly, I'm starving.'
NASTY NELLIE 'Not for you. You're small fry, a maybe, a not very likely contender.'
Often the smell of a cooked meal would waft down the corridor. The support bands were given half a dozen cans of warm cheap ale and a curling cheese sandwich or two, if they were lucky. It was the pink and the blue uniforms all over again. On stage with an empty belly and tired through lack of sleep, the girl tried to be both a rock chick and a mother.

NASTY NELLIE 'What do you want? Jam on it?'
Part of the deal for the support band was the use of the main acts PA but did you get a decent sound? Oh no, you're a pain in the arse for the engineer, unless you get a good one, not yet burnt out and cynical with life on the road. They're there

to serve, honour and obey the main band of the day. Thing is, they often made the support act sound inferior, keeping the volume down. But she found her own the power from her days of busking with Nat. She had to or she'd be drowned out by the wall of sound, the guitars, drums and bass, the marshall stacks floor to ceiling, and Pip with his brand new double bass drumkit.

CLARA THE CLOWN 'Sitting on an amp in the back of a van, turn right, no left, oh fuck, round we go again.'

Another gig and there she was, roaring the blues and the songs of love and betrayal, songs of anger and of joy, bashing a tambourine on her thigh until the skin bruised and her voice cracked. Her belly often lurched with nerves. Sitting in the van with Delivery, her voice singing in time to throb of the engine, the wheels turning and burning the miles. The words were there. Her voice crackling along the wires of her body, remembering the poem, the cloud, the lonely cloud. And then she was elsewhere. Wordsworth forgotten.

WICKED WILL O' MINA 'I wandered lonely as a cloud, but the cloud was...'

NASTY NELLIE '...full of wind, wind and water.'

MISERY IVY 'Is this in my dream? Somebody wake me. I'm taking a high dive. I'm splitting. Is this gonna break me? Is this a real day? Is this a nightmare?'

THE BOSS 'Will you please leave. Catch your mouth on the way out and zip it up.'

Jimi Hendricks died. The rock and jazz loving western world, the world that worshiped Jimi couldn't believe it. The man who'd played the guitar like no other. The magic man with the face of a warrior painted by Larry. The gentle soul who metamorphosed himself into the fiery god of the electric guitar on stage. He'd played with baby Sam, helped the girl put him to bed and then chatted over joints about music and life. He was gone and the music would be forever diminished without him.

Delivery played a gig in St Katherine Docks. People were squatting in the now disused docks and putting on wild and wacky events. A magical but poignant place that signalled the end of the London *Thames* of her childhood. She wandered around the waterside, past the old council block that had housed the dockers, men and their families for generations. This was before they built the giant brown turd of a hotel beside *Tower Bridge*. The sonorous sounds of tug boats would lesson as trade moved down to Tilbury.

They did a gig at *Brighton Art College* with Roy Harper. He played so long there was no chance to plug in, let alone perform. Roy was apologetic as Delivery climbed back in the van at the end of the night. 'Hi man,' he said, and pushed a handful of ready-made joints in the front window of the van. 'Oh cheers, mate,' thought the girl. All that time waiting to sing, always nervous but knowing the singing would take the pain away, thinking about the complicated arrangements she'd made so eveything was fine with Sam.

The *Sunday Times* came round to interview her, taking pictures. She was a name? A face on the scene? It didn't feel like it. She felt adrift without a lifeline, a kite that's lost its string.

One day in the early spring she pushed Sam in the buggy up to the park. She'd decided on Kensington Gardens and, taking a short cut past Pembridge Gardens, she saw Guy, Elizabeth and Jason sitting on a balcony outside their window. 'Hi there, lovely day, lovely sun, lovely girl with lovely child.' The woman on the balcony laughed and smiled. Her teeth were perfect. The little boy had a mass of curly hair. The girl blushed, smiled and waved. She was charmed. On the way back she took the same route. 'Hi.' They were still at home, inside their room but the window was open and a white cotton curtain flapped in the light breeze. 'Come in and meet Jason, our little boy,' they said. And that was the beginning of a new friendship.

Jason was the same age as Sam. The two little ones played warily at first but in time, as children do, they got on with the game. Jason brought out his precious toys for inspection. A small tricycle, a ball. Guy was an American photographer, a very good one indeed. Elizabeth was English and blond with the most luscious mouth the girl had ever seen, like Marilyn Monroe. She oozed sensuality. Guy was known as daddy Guy and Elizabeth was always Elizabeth, never Liz.

Delivery were booked to play on *Eel Pie Island*. The girl was thrilled. She remembered her trips out there with Beat in the Earl's Court days and how she'd longed to sing on that stage. Guy came along with his cameras, over the little bridge across the *Thames*. The gig was good. The crowd enjoyed it but the girl knew she was sitting precariously on a pinhead. They then recorded a live *John Peel Show* for the BBC in the Paris Theatre. It was exiting. She was on the radio. The radio that had been the backdrop to her life.

Jan had a baby. A girl. They could go to the park together. Beat was working with her family in Campden Hill Square, but would sometimes come around at the weekend and they'd potter around the Portobello Road. Beat was coming round to Sam. She softened. Whatever happened, she and the girl were in it for the long haul. They didn't voice it at the time but they were sisters under the skin. They'd be there for each other, though with the girl being a mother, she'd drifted slightly away, as if motherhood had put her into another camp, the mum camp. Unlike the childless, she could no longer swing out to a club or a pub in that spontaneous way.

On her way to Jan's one morning, with Sam toddling along beside her, they saw a nun walking towards them. 'Who's that?' he asked. 'A nun,' she replied, 'a nun from the convent.' Holding his hand tightly, they crossed Ladbroke Grove. The little boy was quiet. An hour or so later, in Jan's flat, he piped up, 'but I saw her mummy, I did, she was there.' He was a confused little boy and the girl began to laugh. She told Jan and they all split their sides. He thought she'd said. 'None.' Out the window they watched the big brown knickers flapping on the line in the Convent Garden and waited for a nun to appear to take down the washing.

Jan told the girl about a very good nursery school the other side of Ladbroke Grove. Sam needed other children to play with and she needed some time to rehearse, to pull her working life together. Her earnings were on the up. Sam had a few hours each morning in the nursery school up near Holland Park. He loved it. At first he would cry and cling to her but then he loved playing with other little people. She had a bike with a child's seat and they cycled over each morning just before nine.

She did an all night gig at Leeds University with Delivery, Stone the Crows, Free and Status Quo. They performed after Stone the Crows sometime after two in the morning, singing to a sea of beer and plastic beakers. Most of the crowd were students, drunk on cheap university beer. She loved it and was also scared. The fear of being seen and judged was greater than ambition but the need to sing was greater than the fear. She hardly dared speak to Maggie Bell, though Maggie was a fine and friendly woman. The girl admired her and felt humble in her wake. But she did make a connection with Paul Kossoff, the guitarist in Free. He appeared as shy as her, displaced in a bold, bad, mad world, while trying to strut the guitar rock god.

Two other musicians arrived on the doorstep of 113 St Stephen's Gardens. A pair of Johns. John Pearson, a drummer from the Babylon days and John Porter. 'Hi, we're getting a band together, so how about it?' said John Pearson, or words to that effect. She said yes. After all, why not. She'd been unhappy and unsure with Delivery. They said she wasn't jazz enough, that she couldn't improvise. This wasn't true. She loved it and felt she could fly. But she'd always sensed that jazz was seen as an educated musicians music. Though deep down she knew this wasn't strictly true. After all, Billie Holiday and Ella weren't college girls.

PROCRASTINATING PATSY 'No, no that's not it. I mean I'm no way as good. I mean I can sing. They weren't at any school for jazz singers, blues singers. I meant to say... No, I know I'm not a Billie or... I'm. I'm... Oh what the hell.'

THE BOSS 'Get a grip girl, what do you mean?'

So yes, she said yes. And that was Uncle Dog. The blues and the jazz dreams were tucked away. *Uncle Dog and Other Poems* by Robert Sward (1962). That was where they found the inspiration for the name. John Pearson, John Porter, Phil Crooks and Honk, a tall bumbling Welshman who lived in The Grove. Guitar, bass guitar and drums, and now the girl. It was a new band so she was in from the beginning, like she'd been in The Race.

It felt good, like they were from the same tribe. Phil Crooks was from Sheffield. He knew Tommy Eyre and that became the beginning of another line of music links. John Pearson and his American wife lived in a flat down near Worlds End, Chelsea. John Porter seemed to be the one with the contacts and the where-with-all for the hustle. You had to hustle, be seen, know the right people and hang out on the scene. And he did just that.

In May the band were booked into a mill cottage in Cambridgeshire to rehearse, then to be out and about and, hopefully, record. The girl who had Sam with her,

Sam with Carol and Uncle Dog
in Soho, London.
photo: Guy Cross

stayed in a room looking out over water, the huge wheel and the countryside beyond. On the second day David Skinner arrived. He knew John Pearson. He was a keyboard player and songwriter, and had been with a band called Twice As Much with a couple of records out on Andrew Loog Oldham's label, *Immediate*.

Guy came up one day with Elizabeth and Jason, and took some photographs in a furrowed field. Larry was back in The Grove, painting and hanging out. The band found a manager and was signed to *Island* through Lionel Conway. They renamed him 'Nylon Contract'. Things seemed good and the girl felt very welcome. She wasn't stepping on eggshells as with some of the Delivery people. John appeared to know a lot of women on the scene from aristocratic and wealthy families such as Arabella Churchill, an organiser of the first free festival on Worthy Farm near Glastonbury, with many of The Grove bands. The Pink Fairies, Quintessence and Hawkwind. It would be the beginning of the modern music festival era. Eventually the Glastonbury Festival as it is today, the size of a small town with fancy yurts and bands jostling to play the main stages.

Uncle Dog managed to get themselves on the bill for the second year in 1971. They were added at the last minute alongside Melanie, Quintessence, The Edgar Broughton Band, the Pink Fairies, Terry Reid with David Lindley from Little Feat, Linda Lewis, Gong, David Bowie, Hawkwind, Arthur Brown, Brinsley Schwarz, Fairport Convention, Family and Traffic. It was a wonderful line up but as Uncle Dog were a last minute add on, there was no sign of them ever being there. Remembered as the 'Mystical Festival', the 1971 Glastonbury event was all about the summer solstice and Worthy Farm's connection with Stonehenge in a ley-line sort of way.

They didn't use her name for this gig. She didn't want a repeat of the damaged Delivery egos and had had enough of dealing with the moody pissed off musicians. They were billed and introduced as Uncle Dog. It was the Johns' band and she just wanted to sing. Admission to the festival was £1, including free milk from the farm. Craig Sams from the macrobiotic café and some of his friends produced the food. Muesli, brown rice, red bean stew, porridge, unleavened bread, tahini and miso spread, but no salty plums. Larry came down with Sam, then aged four. Larry was in heaven. Pretty women, skip skippy, skip in the green grass, weed in the pipe and non-stop music. Uncle Dog performed in the afternoon on the first pyramid stage built with scaffolding and metal covered with plastic sheeting on a site above the Glastonbury Stonehenge ley-line.

Sally Anne McKelvie Paine was then aged 20 and about to come into a fortune. Her uncle, Peter Shand Kydd, was heir to the family wallpaper fortune. He was later to marry Lady Diana Spencer's mother, making Sally a step cousin to Diana, the future princess. From the very first gatherings, Glastonbury was a magnet for rich girls. The girl and Sam named her 'Sally Sparkle' because she loved sequins, sparkles and dancing. She had her eye on John Porter. He had his eye on many cool and wealthy girls. Girls that would hang around the bands. Posh groupies, lost rich girls looking for love. Rock Stars, from the suburbs or beyond, loved to trade up and live in manor houses with trophy women.

At the side of the stage Uncle Dog waited for their afternoon slot. Sally Sparkle danced up to the girl just before they were getting ready to play. 'I'll look after Sam,' she said, and the girl was grateful, though the little boy was used to standing on stages and hanging about in dressing rooms. The back stage was a field with thousands of heads, freaks, hippies, and assorted aristocrats in their finery. Ossie Clarke dresses, floating scarves, velvet trousers, and paisley silk shirts, denim, silk, satin, or bare butt naked. Freak out. There were faces that would appear at any gathering, like the dancing man who called himself Jesus, various drummers, and flute players and assorted music lovers, hangers on and locals looking on in bemusement.

THE BOSS 'It's not what, it's who. Got it? Connections. Talk, flirt. Ok?'

NASTY NELLIE 'She's seeking the cosmic clam of cool.'

WICKED WILL O'MINA 'No, it's tightly closed. Snap, you can't enter.'

Why?

WICKED WILL O'MINA 'Because you're not cool.'

Why?

NASTY NELLIE 'Your face doesn't fit.'

Why?

NASTY NELLIE 'If you don't know, you're not cool.'

What is cool?

NASTY NELLIE 'Not you.'

Why?

Larry was out in the fields, communing with nature. The girl knew he was gone. Although they were living together, neither could talk about it. People observing them would never have known.

The band did well. It was easy music. Perfect for a summer afternoon in a field in the west country. Most of the songs were written by Dave Skinner or were covers of those they loved. It was wonderful, singing under a tarpaulin pyramid, looking out at the Tor and the fields. So very different from the urban places she was used to. She sang for the sky, the birds and the hills beyond and wondered whether this would be the magic band. It had none of the edge of Delivery and she knew it. But she was looking for family, though she wasn't aware of that at the time. John the drummer and his wife were wonderfully warm and welcoming, and David was becoming a good friend who made her laugh a lot. He was married to a German woman who eyed her with suspicion, a woman who worked for the television show Beat Club. One of those shows you had to appear on in order to break out into the big time in Europe. She had power. Honk was eccentric. Solid as a rock on the bass guitar when he could prop himself in an upright position, which over the months was less and less. John Porter was a mystery. She didn't read him well.

The van engine was running and they were heading back to The Grove. History would leave the band out, as if they were never really there. The rooms in London seemed to be more cramped, the street more scruffy, and the people looked more desperate. The comparison to the west country idyll appeared more intense. Downstairs their doorbell buzzed and on the step stood a policeman. Larry was on edge. Oh my God she thought, a raid. But no. 'We came to this address on Saturday evening 'But.' The policeman shrugged his shoulders, 'there was a complaint over the weekend, about the noise.' The girl looked confused, 'but we were away,' she said, 'at the festival. I mean a holiday in the west country. I...' As if being in a band was illegal, as if they were about to busted.

The woman downstairs had made a complaint. 'We weren't here,' she said again. 'I know,' he said, 'I'm following it up because we have to. I won't trouble you again.' He closed his notebook and left. Larry was furious. He'd flushed his last bit of Moroccan Red down the lavatory. 'What a drag, man,' he said, 'what a fucking drag. That was really good draw.' She laughed with a profound sense of relief, dressed the little boy, took him downstairs and out to the market to find food.

As she walked with her shopping bags hanging from her shoulders and Sam in his buggy, she saw the girl with dark curls and mocking eyes, wearing a dress. It was one of hers. Her head span. She wanted to shout up and down the market, in and out the houses and cafés, shout at the Exploding Galaxy girl wearing her clothes. Seething with anger, she pushed the buggy back to St Stephen's Gardens. She simmered and sang the words in her head, to the beat and clang of the trains clattering under London. Words morphed as they moved in her mind to the gun shot rhythms. Spit it out.

    PROCRASTINATING PATSY 'Got to, gotta got to go. Can't stay. I can't stay. Shall I stay? Do you want me? Do you? Do you? Say something, anything. Talk to me! Do you, do, do, do you?'

She began to pack her bags.

    PROCRASTINATING PATSY 'Shall I stay or shall I go? Shall I stand by the door? So tell me. Do you want me? Do you? Lickety-split, I quit. I wasn't here. Near but not here.'

At the *Roundhouse*, London, Sam on tambourine!

VERSE 21
All Saints Road and Island Studios

Old Hat Uncle Dog 1972

1971 to 1972: 8a All Saints Road, the Mangrove, Larry paints a mural, recording at Island Studios, the demise of Uncle Dog. Chilli Willi and the Red Hot Peppers, an invitation to Nashville. Time passing ever faster. Three strikes and you're out.

She'd been in five bands and was the wrong side of 25. It was no age at all but in the business called music, if your luck wasn't in by the time you were 23, forget it. The seconds, minutes, hours and days retreated in her wake, into the past.

NASTY NELLIE 'For crissakes, keep up. It's now or never.'

The Sams brothers, Craig and Greg, who'd founded *Whole Earth Foods*, hired Larry to design cornflake packets and peanut butter labels. In 1970 the Paddington macrobiotic café moved to 8a All Saints Road and was called *Green Genes*. Above the café was a small empty flat. She took it. The rent was reasonable. The place was

the size of a dolls house, painted yellow on the outside. She loved that. It was sparsely furnished, not that there was much room for much. A settee, a dark wooden sideboard in the sitting room, two single beds and a chair or two. Just as well. All she possessed were their clothes, Sam's toys, some pots and pans and a few records.

You went up a narrow flight of stairs to a kitchen with doors to all three rooms. This meant there was little wall space for cupboards and certainly no room for a table. It had a sink, a cooker, the smallest of work surfaces and a shower in the corner. Blue and white gingham curtains hid some shelves underneath the worktop. The draining board

Carol in the doorway of 8a All Saints Road. *photo: Guy Cross*

268

was so small that the tiniest amount of washing up would collect in the sink and the shower would become an overflow. At night the choice was to wash up or have a shower. You'd better keep up with the dishes and if you wanted to clean your teeth, the sink had better be empty. Otherwise, the pots would be covered in a sticky white paste in the morning. It was like living on a small ship. A ship on the ocean Grove. The lavatory was downstairs beside the front door and was used by the café customers. It had a little window next to the door of the *Mangrove*. She heard some very interesting conversations sitting in that small room.

> **Sensible Ma Sadie** 'Well, well. No room to swing the cat or cook a meal and now the boy has to learn to like a shower.'
>
> **The Boss** 'There are worse places to live. At least you don't share the shower.'
>
> **Nervy Nora** 'Send Clara out. She's the social one. The one who can make 'em laugh, make 'em smile, make 'em dance.'
>
> **Procrastinating Patsy** 'Give me a chance to take a breather will you?'
>
> **Clara The Clown** 'You gotta admit you need me now.'

The *Mangrove* was the African Caribbean restaurant run by Frank Critchlow, a man with a smile that could light the world. And the world needed lighting up. The three-day week, the strikes and power cuts were just beginning. Out of candles? Quick, down to *Woolworths*. All sold out. Try the hardware store. Yes, she had light.

A Polish man ran the launderette opposite, and Pat ran the dairy on the other side of St Lukes Mews. Very convenient for pints of milk and loaves of bread. Rice was stored in a cupboard in the corridor. Mice lurked in dark corners, hoping for a grain or two. The first night as she lay awake in her tiny room in All Saints Road, she listened to the folk gathered outside the *Mangrove*. Only a few feet away from where she lay on her mattress on the floor.

She missed Larry. They were no longer that twosome, Larry 'n Carol. Like Terry 'n Renata, Paul 'n Linda. A woman is defined by her old man, the husband. Larry eventually moved out of St Stephen's Gardens into a place on Westbourne Grove with Christian, the dark eyed girl.

The band came over. She made tea and coffee, and they planned and plotted. Soon they'd be in *Island Studios*, which luckily for her was a just a spit away, down the mews in Basing Street. Friends dropped by and she was glad to see them. Paul Kossofff and Archie Legget, Honk, Beat and Dee, Louis. There were so many musicians in the area and she was slap dab in the middle of it all. In the *Speakeasy* one night, she met Henry McCullough with Alan Spenner. They'd both played in the Grease band with Joe Cocker and also knew Tommy Eyre. She met a bunch of singers down from Liverpool. Dyan Birch, Paddy McHugh, Frank Collins and Neil Hubbard, another Grease band member. Grease band meets Arrival and on into Kokomo.

Larry and Christian were then no more. Larry moved over to a flat near Queensway. He often dropped in and she was glad of that. He didn't help out with money but he did what he called his 'baby sitting'. Was Sam not his baby too? In spite of this, she knew Larry loved his son.

'Snazzy' Sammy Mitchell arrived on the scene, another lad from Liverpool. A wonderful bottleneck guitar player who'd worked with Long John Baldry and Alexis Korner. He was the girl's link with the blues scene, which she still held close to her heart. Uncle Dog took him in with open arms. She was thrilled. A sound was developing and with Sammy it was heading towards the eccentric blues she'd had in her head, the blues that Betty Blues Belter really wanted to sing. The girl wanted to sing of her life, the London blues. She wasn't an African American man from the deep south. She was a London girl and wanted to be true to her roots.

WICKED WILL O'MINA 'Roots?'

Larry was asked to paint a mural in George Harrison's house at Friar Park in Henley. It was a huge mansion with keepers' cottages in the grounds, walled gardens and lakes. Larry wanted the girl and Sam to come along. A huge car picked them up, posh and shiny with a driver wearing a peaked cap.

It was a huge rambling house with a grand hall, fireplaces as large as one of the girl's rooms, and grounds as far as her eyes could see. The Harrisons had large dogs that Sam rode like ponies. The first evening was spent in the kitchen. George's wife Patti cooked a meal and they chatted. Then Larry handed over the Umm Kulthum records. Oh no, gone! Larry painted his mural, and the

Larry in George Harrison's bathroom.

girl and Sam slept in a four poster bed. She found the old house very strange. She was scared when she had to creep down the oak panelled corridor to the bathroom. What was she doing here in this palace?

The next morning George put the kettle on. 'Tea or coffee?' he asked, 'Milk?' An ordinary question asked in an ordinary way, like you do in when people come to stay. But he wasn't ordinary. His face and voice were so familiar and yet she, like millions all over the world, didn't know him at all. Patti drifted in, tall and slender with wonderful flaxen hair and an enchanting smile. Patti showed the girl around the garden and one of the tiny coach houses where a friend was living. It was all extraordinary. What a place to be. The epitome of success. This was living paradise, wasn't it?

Back in All Saints Road the car purred to a halt and there was Dee. 'Worr'appened man?' The girl giggled, 'My chauffeur,' she said 'he'll be around tomorrow to take me to *Tescos*.' There was much merriment, and the story was told over a cuppa.

There were people who cared for her and who loved the band. The journalist Steve Peacock, a gentle man who came to gigs, wrote lovely things and seemed to enjoy the music. His wife was called Jenny. She loved gnomes and Steve called her Gnome. The girl liked that. Mr and Mrs Gnome. His friend Penny Valentine was the first woman the girl had met who was in the rock and roll business. She was a journalist and a good one. A respected woman holding her own with the men and the office politics.

Honk went before they began recording. A sign of the shifting scene that was The Grove. He did massive amounts of drugs and would hang out with Paul Kossoff who was heading for a sad decent into oblivion. Sammy played slide guitar and dobro, with Phil on rhythm. John Porter switched to bass and they still had a band. John Porter and Lionel had fixed Trevor Lucas to produce. He was living with Sandy Denny, the wonderful singer from Fairport Convention and in 1970 they formed a band called Fotheringay. It began well. The girl was again determined not to make the same mistakes she'd made with Delivery. She wanted to get it right, to know who she was and what she could do. She wanted to make music that spoke of herself and not simply drift wherever the days would take her. But David Skinner was the songwriter, so her songs were tucked away once more.

THE BOSS 'Come on coward, speak up girl, speak up. You're a mouse, a frickin' mouse.'

Trouble was, she feared that if she did speak up and say what she really wanted, she'd be replaced. The Grove was full of other singers waiting in the wings. So the cowardly girl kept silent and the battle of words raged on in her head. She and Dave shared the vocals. A young man called Bob Potter, all bright eyed and full of nervous energy, was the tape operative. She could tell he was up for this job in a big, big way. She held her breath when the 16 track tapes were edited, reel to reel. Zip, zip, the strange mix of weird sounds as the real music time was distorted backwards, forwards, fast and slow. Locate the precise place in the track, slowly does it, there it is and slice with the razor. Ouch, that could've been a note or breath!

Trevor Lucas didn't like the girl and as the sessions went on he became more and more dismissive. 'You're too emotional,' he said. He gave not a smile but a smirk in a moment of transferred power from behind the glass in the control room. She sang. He listened and said, 'Sing it this way, no, sing it like...' Did he want her to sound like Sandy? She opened her mouth and what came out wasn't what he wanted to hear. She tried not to cry as that would just prove his point. Yes, she was too emotional. And why? What was wrong with that?

He then got rid of John Pearson, the drummer. Said he wasn't cutting it. True, he did slip the odd beat. Terry Stannard replaced him and the girl lost a good friend. John Porter was with Lucas all the way. She and Dave were unhappy.

> **Nasty Nellie** 'This is a business girl, a business. No time for sentiment. If you're looking for family, this isn't the place to find it. Do as they say.'
>
> **Wicked Will O'Mina** 'Please deposit your feelings in the bin provided. Any sign of weakness, such as tears or deep sighing is punishable and a fine will be levied. Any protestations will be punishable by the withdrawal of your mouth.'

The girl would scuttle up the road to collect Sam or to fetch something, getting away from the tension. Larry was often around. They were still in each other's pockets and she thought that perhaps they should've simply been friends. Was Sam the only reason they married? Though shaken by the events in the studio, she found David and Sammy firmly behind her and Lucas lost the fight. Bob Potter was then in the producers seat. This was his opportunity.

Paul Kossoff dropped in one night and played a solo as the girl recorded her vocal *We got time*. John 'Rabbit' Bundrick played some keyboards and then the horn section from The Average White Band. She began to enjoy the whole process of making a record. She watched and learned. So that's how a desk works.

She came in from recording another vocal to find the control room packed to the rafters. Party, party. Long white lines on the desk. 'Hi,' she said, 'how was that?' Half the lines disappeared, blown away by her breath. There were more where those came from. She was putting down the basic tracks of her life.

NASTY NELLIE 'Too emotional, reign it all in.'

CLARA THE CLOWN 'Now this is a saucepan of shit and no mistake. How are we getting out of this?'

The 1970s was a time of unrest. The worst since the Great Depression. Many homes and businesses during this decade would be without power for up to nine hours a day. The Miners would picket power stations and a three-day week would be imposed. Army generators would provide electricity. In Kent an ice cream firm at Deal would send four vans with generators to hospitals in Canterbury and Margate. The big London hospitals would struggle and uncollected rubbish would pile up in the streets, attracting rats. The angry brigade was active with bombing by the IRA and unrest in the Middle East. Then, as now, people were protesting. 'When will we ever learn, when will we ever learn?' Peace and love rolled into anti-war demonstrations and then, as now, life seemed to be teetering on a brink of disaster. Such a mix, the '70s would feature *Red Barrel* beer, *Action Man*, *The Six Million Dollar Man*, *Wonder Woman*, *Charlie's Angels*, Roger Moore as James Bond, Bruce and Anthea in *The Generation Game*, and *Chopper* bikes.

The *Apollo* pub, a few doors down All Saints Road, became the girl's favourite. Musicians would call in on their way to and from *Island Studios*. She was rarely alone and the street bustled right underneath her windows. Guy Cross took some photographs and designed the sleeve. The band had roadies, Denny and Fran, and they had gigs. 'Oh,' she said at night in her bed, 'oh please let this be, let this happen.' Hoping against hope, she knew she was already too old for the machine that determines the fate of would be rock stars. Especially girls. They had to be young and malleable.

The girl bought Sam a pair of blue and white *Oshkosh* dungarees and little striped sweaters from *Tiger Motts*, a shop devoted entirely to children's clothes for modern kids. She loved him with a fierce passion but often worried. Was he really happy? How had the split from Larry affected him?

Summer slipped into autumn and Sam began his school years just off Queensway, near where Alexis lived. On the first day she took him to a new photo booth. 'Sam, smile, it's a special day. Let's have a picture.' Her little boy was now a schoolboy.

Twice a day, to and fro past the nursery where she'd briefly worked when living on Cromwell Road. How had it all affected him? Her friends would say, 'You had to leave.' Larry would always be the man with the twinkling eyes, and his eyes were for lots of girls. He'd never be able to support her and could barely support himself. But she still wanted him as a friend. She wanted to talk to someone about her child and the one person who loved him as she did was Larry.

The last mixes on the album were done and she sat in the *Apollo* drinking *Guinness* and brandy. Sam was with Larry. He'd be back in an hour or two, so this was an unexpected time to drink and talk. No gig, no rehearsal, simply hanging. Sammy came in. 'Drink?' he said, waving his hands in a 'Want a drink?' sort of way. 'Oh, a brandy. Thanks, that's great.' She knew she was drinking too fast and smoking too much. It was one of those nights. Get it while you can. Her nights out were limited and she used a baby-sitter only when she really had to. The conversations swam around as she slipped under the table. 'Come on,' someone said, 'I'll see you home.'

A Bridge of many brandies

She's in her cups, she's pissed, she's sloshed, she's bladdered, she's hammered, she's three sheets to the wind, she's wasted and drunk as a lord, she's smashed, plastered, legless and she can't stand on her own two feet. She went to bed to mend her head with gallons of water. And then what? This is your liver speaking, give me a break.

CLARA THE CLOWN 'What the flapping frogs are you doing?'

THE BOSS 'You can't kid a kidder.'

MISERY IVY 'I need to sleep. Let me sleep. Shut your head off.'

From the windows of her flat the girl witnessed first hand the police persecution of the *Mangrove* and its regular clientele. And of anyone with a black skin on the street or in the vicinity. The unrest was palpable. Guy and Elizabeth went to America to live in New York. She was sad to see them go though other friends would drop by. Beat was still up in Campden Hill Square, Notting Hill Gate but the cooks posse had disappeared. Ozzy returned to Jamaica and dropped out of university. Oh boy was he gonna get it. She lost touch with David Circutt and Hilton Valentine, and Keith was who knows where. So many from the days of madness, speed and too much of everything else.

An American musician had invited Uncle Dog to play in Germany. They were to be a backing band after a stint playing the US bases and anywhere he could get.

After the first gig the man who'd been all charm and gold teeth announced, 'She can't sing with the band.' The girl was being made redundant and things looked bad. There was nothing up front and threats were made. A gun appeared under a table when David and John asked for money. So they made a plan to escape. They'd play the next gig and act like it's all cool. She'd stay out of the way. Then they'd creep out of the guesthouse at a very late hour and onto the train, the sleeper to Calais. This they did and on the train they slid into unoccupied bunks until the ticket inspector disappeared down the corridor. Then finally, home sweet home.

She met a beautiful tall brown girl with a devastating smile called Susie. Susie was a 'penthouse pet' and worked at the *Hilton Hotel* club, wearing a satin corset with a bow around her neck and a little puff tail on her very lovely bottom. She'd been a competitive runner at county level. Susie wanted more than being a good girl and eventually went to Italy to be a dancer in a club. A few months later she returned with infected breasts, the result of a bad breast enhancement operation. Oh my God, why? The girl tried to understand why Susie did such a terrible thing to her body. Nothing was wrong with that perfect young woman's body. Another lost girl, she eventually healed and went back to her rich man in Milan, never to be seen again.

The girl bought herself a secondhand television from the electrical shop down on Westbourne Grove. All television programs ended at ten-thirty and the little boy loved it. *Star Trek* and *Dr Who*, *The Two Ronnies*, *Happy Days*, and the IRA bombing campaigns on the six o'clock news. They watched *The Sweeney* being filmed in the street one day and saw John Thaw coming out of the newsagents. Oh that was really exciting.

Sam wanted trousers with flares from *Tesco*. Brown and horrible, they shrank in the first wash but he loved them more than the dungarees and *Levis* jeans she'd previously bought him. He wanted trainers and cheap flared trousers. Kids no longer wore plimsoles. The trainer revolution had arrived from the US and parents would have to dig deep into their pockets. Sam had his own ideas about what a kid in The Grove should wear and it wasn't hippy. A new generation was brewing.

Signpost, a label attached to EMI Records, released Uncle Dog's single, *River Road* with John and Yoko's drummer, Alan White. He replaced the out of time original drum track that John Porter and Trevor Lucas had objected to. Dave Skinner had written the song which made the American charts. As it climbed, the A&R (artists and repertoire) man at the record company was head hunted for another label. The next man in cleared the desk and the single plummeted. Like a game of snakes and ladders.

Uncle dog became a shifting band of musicians. Mainly players who lived around The Grove. Mighty Baby guitarist Martin Stone, then with Chilli Willi and the Red Hot Peppers, played a few gigs. Martin, a long time friend of Michael Moorcock, was also a rare book dealer and famously turned down the Rolling Stones as a replacement for Brian Jones. He was one of the most interesting men the girl knew at that time. George Butler replaced Terry who went off to play with Kokomo. Paul Rudolph from the Pink Fairies replaced Archie Legget, who went on to play with Kevin Ayers. Uncle Dog went the way of many bands and it was only her dogged refusal to stop that kept it all going. What else could she do?

At a gig in Birmingham the promoter leered at the girl's chest and said, 'I'm disappointed. I thought all you women libbers burned your bras.' A review for a *Speakeasy* gig commented on her 'mobile chest.' Going braless seemed to be as sexually titillating to the men as the pointed cones of the 1950s. The red tops loved to run stories of braless girls, free love and drug fuelled orgies, acompanied by photos of scantily dressed women. The girl's men friends were friends in every way. But the music industry and the rest of the world, it would seem, regarded woman as the lesser sex. Men dictated what she should wear, what she should sing and how. Men ran the business and they were in control. She reflected on this and remembered the hippy girls at the stove, watching the brown rice and serving the men with their joints. She thought about the beautiful girls and the newly rich rock gods. Looking beautiful, thats what's required.

Portobello Road was the spine of The Grove. The head shops still sold Chillums, Kandahar shirts, incense, natural oils, Moroccan leather bags, Afghan coats, Tibetan prints, and rock posters, including Larry's Dylan and Hendrix. They sold books by Jack Kerouac, Herman Hesse and Aleister Crowley, and studies of Buddhism, Hinduism and Taoism. Sam wanted a drum kit from *Woolworths* and there it was that Christmas, under a tiny tree. Sally Sparkle was around. She sometimes stayed in the flat and seemed live on a tightwire, dancing in Paris with her guru of the dance, Matt Mattox, freestyling, then back to London to train with yet another new leader. Dreams she possessed for many years.

Life at 8a became more difficult. John Porter had asked if he could stay for a bit and then his new girlfriend, a model from New Mexico called Shadow, joined him. In the mornings the tiny floor was littered with takeaways and over flowing ashtrays. Out most evenings, they never cleared away their bed or washed up. It was a disaster, and she'd no idea how long they were staying.

One day John returned with a tall man accompanied by an even taller woman. It was Bryan Ferry and Jerry Hall. Brian and John had been together at art school in Newcastle. The girl didn't like their music at all. That will never sell, she thought. How very wrong was she. The soon to be rock star not only barely acknowledged her presence but asked John if he would get the girl to make a tea or a coffee, or something. And John played the part, like it was his home. John and Shadow eventually moved out, much to her relief. Their lives remained in parallel and she never met him again.

The band was still upright. Sammy and the girl became close in a gentle way. They were together through the music and a mutual need for a warm body to curl up with at night. Then Sammy became really ill. He set fire to the altar in All Saints Church one afternoon as he ran wild, claiming there were devils were in 8a. 'We must light the fire.' He brandished the poker, 'devils out, out, out.' He would sometimes disappear for days. She was terrified.

Dee and Frank came to help. The girl may not have had the pleasure of knowing her father but there were lovely men close by who had her back. 'You have to get help,' they said, 'you got to protect the boy.' They decided to talk to Sammy's ma, bring her down from Liverpool. It turned out to be hepatitis that had been ignored for so long that he ended up raging, his skin orange and his liver shot. 'My lovely Sammy.' The girl was so sad. He was the best blues guitarist she'd ever sung with and he was a lover. But hey, she always knew they'd never be able to support each other. He would always be lovely. A brief and beautiful light that was in her life.

They had to leave 8a. The Sams were expanding the business and needed the flat. Sally Sparkle came too and they ended up on the Portobello Road in two empty floors above a shop, almost opposite *Ceres*. They made a home, though why Sally was there was a mystery. She had her own reasons for not taking up her birthright. The wealth, a mother, father and brother.

They met another Sally. Sally Beauchamp, another weathy and well connected girl. Descendants of Lord Beauchamp, Sally's family lived in a grand house on Harley Street. So why wasn't Sally in the bosom of her family? The girl was finding out that money doesn't' make you happy. They were right, 'money can't buy you love.'

One Saturday, a French couple asked if they could set up shop in the front porch and make crepes. Delicious crepes for all. The rooms in the new place were bigger than 8a but she had no furniture. Sally Beauchamp gave her a chest of drawers and a bed. It seemed the girl and her little one had guardian angels.

David had split up from his wife and visited one evening with his new girlfriend, Clare. On the way back to Fulham a truck pulled out, killing the beautiful Clare. David still did their next gig at the *Tally Ho* in Kentish Town the following week. 'What else can I do?' he said, 'it won't bring her back.' It was a strange gig with George Butler on drums, David and Paul Rudolph from The Pink Fairies, and the girl.

The hammer seemed to be coming down on Uncle Dog. Four down and where do you go now? A group of people came back to the house on Portobello Road for Clare's wake. In the evening David's ex-wife appeared and made a terrible scene. It was a dark end to a wonderful adventure.

Clare's parents were artists and lived in Ibiza. David wanted to see them and so the girl contacted Terry and Renate. 'Come,' they said, 'come and stay, and bring David with you.' They booked a flight, and eventually they were standing outside a bar in the Old Town where Clare's father used to sit and talk with friends. The barman wouldn't serve them and appeared to be angry. In the street later that night, a man who'd witnessed the exchange told them. 'You cannot walk the streets with a child. I have a room in a hotel.' Initially they needed to stay in the Old Town, so the man gave them a bed. Angels in unexpected places.

The next day David hired a car and they drove out to where Clare's family lived. The house was empty. The girl wouldn't go to Formentera until David was settled. They found an empty hut and decided to sit it out. They spent a day there and bedded down for the night. In the morning an old man stood staring at them. It was his hut. He was the goat man. The amazing thing was that he spoke English, and with an American accent. He'd been out in the west building roads and rail tracks. It was all the work he could get though he decided he didn't like America and returned home to his beautiful island. An old man now, he was happy with his goats. 'Stay,' he said, 'stay as long as you need to.' His kind eyes were almost invisible, shrouded in the folds of a face worn by years of labouring under the sun. He played with Sam and introduced him to the goats. Unlike the barman, he had compassion. They waited four or five days and David said tearfully, 'We should leave. They're not going to come here to meet me are they.'

Terry and Renate had moved to a little house out near the Cap on Formentera and Terry was renovating a large house on Ibiza. The girl missed Larry. He was still her friend, no matter what had gone on between them. Larry had missed her too when he was last here. They loved each other but couldn't be together. Terry and Renate had had a baby and named her Astra Space Seymour. Now three years

Sam and the goat man.

old, she was beautiful like her mother. The girl never forgot what Renate said to her, 'You know, I now understand what was going on with you, when you came that first time with little Sam. I'm so sorry. I see now what being a mother is and what it makes you feel.' Renate was a woman of truth and she was grateful for that.

One day as she and Renate wandered back from the shop in the town laden with bread and vegetables, they met Shelly, a Welsh woman with a small boy called Teifion in a sling on her back. They also met Maxine with her daughter, Afra though it was with Shelly who really connected with the girl. Shelly wasn't the usual well schooled, wealthy type of hippy, so ubiquitous on the scene, both here and in The Grove. She was probably one of the most 'up front in your face' women the girl had ever met.

The sunshine brought out the girl's freckles on her nose, her cheeks, forearms and shoulders. Sam turned a warm brown, just like his father. They shared the legacy of their Roma blood. Sam scampered about the place with the agility of a goat, even climbing a steep rocky outcrop as they all sat on the beach one day. She had her heart in her mouth as she watched David sprint over to the top, encouraging Sam upwards.

After two weeks she was to return to The Grove to pick up the pieces. Compared with the bright Mediterranean light, London seemed grey, overcrowded and very noisy. Sally was still in the place on Portobello Road. The news was that the Sams had changed things. The flat was empty again. Did she want to move back in? She did. The squatting thing had been too insecure. She never knew when the door would be forced and they'd be out on their backsides. She found herself back in the flat, next door to the *Mangrove*, with her bits and pieces, and an earthenware dish carefully carried back from Ibiza.

One day she noticed a man standing across the road, looming up at the window. She waved and he crossed over. He was a nice man. 'My family had the shop here for years,' he said, 'oh it's changed around here, I can tell you. We were here before the war. Now we're all out in Watford.' He chatted and she made him a cup of tea. A link with old London she thought. He reminded her of the Saltz family. A soft and distant memory.

Uncle Dog was still hanging on and getting around in the strange old Japanese orange bus bought by Denny and Fran. They went up and down the motorways of Great Britain and over the sea again to Germany, France, Denmark, Holland, Belgium and beyond. These were always short trips and Larry would come to 8a for a week or two. He was on his own again, though there was always a girl in the wings.

Uncle Dog had a few gigs in Northern Ireland. They went to Belfast on the ferry from Liverpool. A beautiful city surrounded by hills. On arrival the orange bus seemed all wrong. They were in the country of the Orange Order, at war with republican Ireland. Those with a London accent may be viewed as the enemy. Though the reality was very different. The crowds were wonderful. They yelled, 'more, more!' As if every gig was the last gig, every song the last song. She loved it. The passion, the smiles and the offers to stay. 'Stay, stay longer,' they said, 'don't go home just yet. Let's go visit this... we want to show you...' Bands from elsewhere didn't go to Northern Ireland much during the troubles. And yet Uncle Dog were made more than welcome, in spite of the orange bus. She would love to have stayed a little longer but had to go back to her boy who was more than life to her.

They had a small tour of five gigs in Wales, the country where women had to sit in women's bars in the small valley towns. Shelly had said, 'call round when you're in Wales.' On a day off between gigs they made their way to Portis. She also said, 'it's hard to get stuff down here. Bring us something good from London.' Of course they were stopped, and as they were searched and interrogated at Carmarthen police station, the gift tucked in the girls' knickers grew damp inside the greaseproof wrapper. But once again the angels protected her. A little late than planned, she, Fran, David and George bounced down a dirt track to Portis. There was Shelly with Teifion and a dark and tall man called Mick Coakley, who lived in a cottage a short distance away over the hill. He was an Irish man from County Kilburn. The boys called him spaceman and Mick told them the pylon on the hill was his spaceship. They liked that story.

Portis was a small cottage owned by Owen, the local farmer. Shelly had a field, a barn, a yard and a stream outside the back door. The cottage had one large room with a Rayburn range in the corner, and a kitchen out the back in a small lean to which held what was once the outside lavatory. Upstairs were three bedrooms. It was remote. You had to go off the A478 and down a winding narrow lane, looking out for a herd of cows or a tractor as you took a left hand turn down a dirt track to Portis. In the nearby village of Glandwr there was a school, a garage, a post office cum local store, and that was it. Shelly didn't drive but Mick had a beat up old wreck of a car and drove her wherever she needed to go.

'Come down with Sam., Shelly said, 'stay for a while. There's a whole scene going on down here. You'd have gigs and Sam will love the country life. It's great for kids.' She had returned from Formentera as her mother was very ill. When her mother had died, Shelly decided to stay. A wild Welsh woman with a voice like a foghorn and a temper to match, Shelley was also funny, warm and much stronger than the girl. Raised with two sisters and two brothers, she had to fight for her place in the family hierarchy.

David's estranged wife Agatha had committed suicide and he needed to get away. He would move to Brighton, eventually marry again and have a daughter. The girl missed him. He was a good and loyal friend but moving was absolutely the right thing for him to do.

The last Uncle Dog gig took place under the Westway. The great concrete road that had split The Grove in two. The gig was with David, Martin Stone, George Butler and Paul Rudolph. Eno from Roxy Music was there and shortly after that David joined Bryan Ferry's crew, along with John Porter when Ferry toured. He then he joined a band called Clancy with Dave Vasco, another friend. It was a small world. The girl had sung in all those places she'd been to. Places she never dreamt she would sing in. The *Roundhouse*, *Implosion* and *UFO*, the *Arts Lab* under strobe lights, *Eel Pie Island*, the *Marquee*, the *Lyceum*, and *Middle Earth*. Maybe this was the end.

Beat was pregnant. She gave birth to a beautiful boy with green eyes and auburn hair, and named him Robin. The live-in job with the family in Campden Hill Square came to an end and she was homeless. 8a became very crowded. Beat and Robin in one room, the girl and Sam in the other. 'Two women and two small boys in a pint pot,' Frank Critchlow said, 'you know you have to say you've no room for

281

Beat. She has to be homeless to get re-housed.' 'No, no,' The girl said, 'I can't do it. She'll be housed in a shitty bed-sit or worse, a hostel,' he said, 'she won't have to stay in it all the time but you've got to do it. It's the only way to really help. She needs her own place.' The girl hesitated and then she and Beat, with Frank for support, went to speak to the housing people and Beat was placed in a bedsit just off Ladbroke Road. The girl insisted that Beat kept her keys to 8a and eventually she was allocated a flat in Earl's Court. Two bedrooms, a sitting room and a small kitchen and bathroom, just around the corner from the flat on Cromwell Road West. Beat was back on the patch where she'd cut her London teeth and felt at home. She was an Earl's Court girl. 8a felt empty but it was good Sam got his own room back. He was into hats. Policeman's hats, army hats, sailor hats. They'd trawl the market and friends would look out for them. The box for hats was filling up. At one time much later, Sam was destined for the American Navy. 'American?' 'Well, whatever, it'll be a big huge navy with big, big ships,' he said.

In the winter of 1973, Chilli Willi and The Red Hot Peppers were recording down in Cornwall, using the Ronnie Lane mobile at *Lucky Abattoir Studios*. The girl was invited by guitarist Martin Stone to sing harmony backing vocals alongside Jo Ann Kelly and Jacqui McShee. The *Bongos over Balham* album was later released in 1974. She drove down on a cold winters day with Keith Morris, the photographer and Jo Ann. They were half way there and darkness fell, closely followed by snow and Keith's windscreen wipers weren't working. It was a hellish journey with lovely people. On arrival she was allotted a bunk bed in the kitchen. The band were already assembled and after greetings, tea and beer, she was hoping for a beautiful sleep and no nasty dreams.

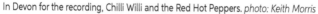

In Devon for the recording, Chilli Willi and the Red Hot Peppers. *photo: Keith Morris*

What she didn't say, because she was too embarrassed, was that she suffered from vertigo. Yes, going up a small ladder to bed was tricky, though going up was slightly easier than coming down. The next morning, as the bleary eyed people arrived in the kitchen looking for breakfast, she sat with her legs dangling over the edge, trying to appear nonchalant. Jo Ann asked, 'You coming down, you wanna coffee, Carol?' 'Yes,' she said, 'I'm just looking for my socks.' That was a lie. Her socks were on her feet. Martin, 'had a good sleep Carol?' 'Yes.' The toast was on and smelling divinely toasty. Jo Ann rumbled her and Martin helped her down. 'I can't climb it backwards and I can't climb facing the front. I'll slip.' They laughed and down she came, legs trembling, to toast, coffee and plans for the day. What a wonderful job it was, singing. The three of us in Devon on a winter's day. She loved singing with others, especially Jo Ann. She was her hero.

Bob Potter called by one day and asked, 'Do you want to come out and record in Nashville?' He'd been out there working for the producer Bob Johnson who had produced Bob Dylan, Leonard Cohen and more. The girl was gob smacked. Who was going to pay? It was for an offshoot of a new Label, *Virgin*, called *Caroline*, managed by Simon Draper who believed in her. Oh goodness. She was one year away from being 30 years old. Nashville? Why not! In Britain it was all strikes and IRA bombs. Though she did have her child, her music and a roof over her head. She had Dee, David, Louis and Beat. Frank was there on the doorstep in the *Mangrove*. She had tasted the best carrot juice in the world and had a gig next week. What's wrong with all of that? Live for now. The future can wait. The long future, the one beyond the week after next. Nashville, now that was scary. That was exciting!

She was living in The Grove and she knew the groovy people. Or maybe not. She looked back at all the off shoots when musical differences reared. Quiver, the Deviants and Junior's Eyes. The men were The Grove's icons. Men who ruled the counter culture. Were there women in those bands? Very few. Black faces in those bands? Very few. It wasn't an equal world.

It's doubtful many could say they knew her, nor she them. It was so rough around the edges. Friends and neighbours really cared but everyone else, the duckers and divers, the hopers and the hopeless? How could they care? She'd overhear in the pub. 'He trashed the place.' 'Blew my stash man.' Wars between dealers, wars between users and the pigs, the filth so called. Crash landings, falling out. People overdosed. People went crazy. Amidst all this she was putting down the tracks of her life. Over and over, never enough, never good enough. Pin prick pupils, lazy talk or gabbing like a comets tail.

Nasty Nellie 'Too emotional. You need to cool it.'

Auntie BBC 'Hey, you down there with the glasses, ta, da, da, da, da, dah'.

She needed glasses. She squinted when waiting for the bus. 'What's that, a 31 or a 28?' The grey hair noticed by the ward sister when Sam was born had mulitplied and she started to use henna. She could feel the passing of time accelerating. An hour seemed to last less than an hour. And more and more she felt the lack of a significant other in her life. Her need lessened when she held her child close.

The girl had to earn money, and not just to fund a roof and food. She needed to make something of herself, prove herself. Is she this or is she that? She may be poorly uneducated but she could read. That had saved her. She would side with the oppressed and the underdog but she didn't belong there either. Neither did she fit in with the rich. Becoming detached as soon as she was born, and having no experience of being loved, she found making attachments difficult. On her passport she had no distinguishing feature. She wanted one. She craved a tribe. She'd no idea who her father was and her mother had spent 15 years trying to disown her. 'Return to sender, address unknown.' Flipping the line for a fish, casting her mind back, she could see herself inside a sheath, a thin membrane covered in wispy spider weavings. She rolled from one situation to another, easy come easy go. Don't think too much, don't dwell and never plan. Look at the hour to come and not the ones that have gone. Time is only the next tick of a clock, always moving forwards.

Clara the Clown 'Once bitten twice shy, here's mud in yer eye, fly me to the moon, why don't cha?'

Nasty Nellie 'Hey you're walking like a wonky wheeled supermarket trolley, a spent condom on the tideline at Brighton beach.'

The Boss 'Now then, chop, chop. All hands on deck. Get a grip girl. Gird your loins. Grit your teeth and get on with the show.'

The Bridge between the war and 'you've never had it so...'

She'd been brought up on *Spam* sandwiches with a scraping of *Echo* margarine and a cup of hot *Bovril*. At a time when a settee wasn't a sofa, and dinner was at lunchtime. Tea was at six and bedtime when they told you to go. Jam was for Sundays and if you were lucky, tinned peaches or mandarin segments in syrup served from a cut glass bowl, maybe even with *Birds* custard or sticky sweet condensed milk.

It was a time when the front room was shut away from the sunlight to protect the soft furnishings and the 'pictures' was a Saturday night out. A time when you were tricked into believing that Rock Hudson was a 'ladies man', and Doris Day the girl next door. Hiding always hiding, lying always lying. Those were heady days when the dreams and aspirations for a girl were expected to be a hubby, a mock Tudor semi in the suburbs and a couple of chubby babies. Teenagers in the 1950s exploded when they heard the call of Little Richard, Elvis and Chuck Berry. Those war babies were changing things, demanding things. The peasants were revolting. Yes indeed. And the establishment was afraid, very afraid.

The girl would listen to Little Feat and Stevie Wonder, Weather Report, and Aretha and Joni. Sly and the Family Stone, Captain Beefheart, Etta James, and Van Morrsison. Winter's darkest nights after a meal, warm around the tiny fireplace, a log or two for the flames and being with people she felt safe with. That was good. The Caribbean community in The Grove gave her friendship and support. They were some of the most generous people she would ever meet. Foraging for treasures up past Cambridge Gardens, up to Golborne Road. A pretty plate, a picture that caught the eye, a pot or an old dress that would be perfect for a gig under club lights. Maybe a black velvet hat. She loved all that. She held it all in her heart to remind her that life could be good, very good. She just had to hold on to it.

THE BOSS 'Hold onto it. Hold very tightly. Ding, ding, mind the gap.'

VERSE 22

Warm Blood

Taxes on the Farmer Feeds Us All (traditional) on Warm Blood 1974

1973 to 1974: Nashville, New York, Woodstock and a caravan in Wales.

Calling from Nashville, Bob said, 'Hey girl, its all cool. I've got the musicians, the studio's booked and I've sorted the songs.' 'Songs?' she thought, 'don't I get to choose?'

    THE BOSS 'Your songs. Where are *your* songs?'

All that was forgotten and she had to get ready. She received a small advance and bought an old showman's van. Painted green, it had a stable door with a small window, a bluebird in stained glass. It slept four and was warm and snug, complete with a wood burning stove, a little galley kitchen, cupboards, and a tiny room with a bed for the boy. And it could be towed down to the field on Owens' land next to Shelly's cottage. This was to be the girl's first owned home. She'd be back from Nashville at the beginning of August, before Sam returned to school. Apart from the odd days here and there, the most time she'd been away had been the Scandinavian trip. This would be longer. Excited and anxious, she felt she must take this risk, to see whether she had a chance of making it in the great big America. Was it a job? Or was she simply addicted to the thrill of singing?

    Mick from Kilburn took the flat while she was away. He needed to be in London for a while. Perfect. She bought a beautiful straw hat down on the market and pinned pink fabric roses to the brim. A hat for the hot Tennessee summer sun.

    NERVY NORA 'I need to feel tall. I need to look elegant.'

    NASTY NELLIE 'You need to be not you.'

Leaving for Nashville in the middle of July, she took her first flight across the Atlantic. Flying to the land of the music she loved. The home of blues and jazz, Louis Armstrong and Ray Charles, Ella Fitzgerald and Billie Holiday, Nina Simone and Miles Davis. Oh my God. And she'd be singing in this America! She passed through customs having learned her lesson. With nothing tucked away, she wasn't going for third time lucky. Her legs shook as she dragged her suitcase into the ladies restroom. Sitting on the white plastic lavatory seat, she put her head in her hands and thought of Sam on another planet, across the universe, down in that valley in the shadows of the Preseli Mountains. What was he doing, she wondered.

She found the domestic flights and when settled on the next plane gratefully took up the offer of dry peanuts and a can of coke. She was tired, hungry and very thirsty. It was the best Coke she'd ever drunk. Maybe they made it differently here, or maybe America was the simply the right place to drink it. The plane landed and the hot summer air of the American south drifted over her as she waited for Bob. He drove a low slung red car of some sort. She was never good at naming cars and she'd never learn to drive. The car had no air-conditioning and by the time they'd driven out of Nashville, she was sweating, in need of a 'washing and a 'sleeping'.

Bob lived in a bungalow about 20 miles out of town, with a front porch and a swinging seat. It was America just how she'd imagined. He shared it with the pianist, Bob Wilson. 'This,' he said, 'is your room while you're here. It's got a water bed, you'll love it.' And then he said, 'me and Wilson have a session tonight. Sort yourself out. The kitchen with food in the fridge is over there. The shower there, and the television works like this.' He punched a few buttons and the screen flickered into life. American life. The huge fridge, full to the brim, was almost as big as her kitchen in All Saints Road. Cartons of processed milk, blocks of *Monterey Jack* cheese that felt like wax and tasted of nothing, vast tubs of ice cream and jars of peanut butter. Frozen for a moment, her body still throbbing as if she was still in the air, she thought about that shower curtain scene in *Psycho* all those years ago, and remembered running

Carol on the porch, Nashville.

down a country lane with her feet on fire. Here she was now, in scary America. They all had guns, didn't they?

She sat on the bed for a while. A nap, she thought. She felt seasick as the motion of the water in the rubber mattress rolled underneath her. She must have slept but a galloping cast gathered in her dreams. The *Lone Ranger*, a stabbing knife, red blood, a drowning man. The slug man? She woke up suddenly, feeling utterly lost.

The plan was to have a week rehearsing in the house, record the album the following week and then back to London for overdubs and mixing. The next day she met the band. Kenny Buttrey who was in Neil Young's band and had played on all the Nashville Bob Dylan sessions, and with Joan Baez and many of America and Canada's finest. Mac Gayden, song writer and guitarist with J.J. Cale and Dylan. Tommy Cogbill who'd recorded with Elvis and had arranged some tracks for Aretha Franklin. Ron Cornelius and Bob Wilson, who'd worked with Earl Scruggs and Slim Harpo.

And here they all were, setting up in the room just outside her bedroom. Little bitty one-skin American grass joints were being rolled, coffee was brewing on the hob, and in moment, in a very small moment, she'd have to open her mouth and sing in front of a man who'd played bass for Elvis. Should she run now? It was fine, all the songs were good. Bob had chosen one of Dave Skinner's and the rest were from the Nashville guys, including Bob Johnson, JJ Walker and Bill Withers. First up was *Taxes on the Farmer feeds us all*, a traditional song. 'Well, the banker says he's broke and the merchant stops and smoke. But they forget that it's the farmer that feeds them all. It would put them to the test if the farmer took a rest.'

The girl's child may well have been on Mars, so far away was Glandwr in the farming valleys of the Tywi, Cothi, Teifi, Gwendraeth and Taf in Southwest Wales. All names from an ancient world. Worlds away from a city of neon lights and diners with red banquets and silver chrome. She ate eggs, grits, biscuits, gravy and pecan pie. She watched the guys tucking into ribs and pancakes and discovered the glorious taste that was maple syrup, prompting memories of the malt jar and a tiny room at the top of a house beside Blackheath Station in Southeast London.

One evening in *TJ Fridays* she drank large gin and tonics and became maudlin for her boy. It hurt her inside her belly, she missed him so much. Someone gave her a Quaalude. She wobbled and they took her home, back to the bed that was a rolling sea. She threw up and then slept.

THE BOSS 'Oh dear. Stay clean, stay dry.'
Bob decided the girl performed best in a live studio. So she was to sing along when the tracks were going down. If anything needed changing, she could redo sections. The band kicked in an eight bar intro to *You're the only one* and in that tiny amount of time she looked down on herself and the musicians, heads down and focused on the music. Then she was in. Everything she'd learned on the hoof fell into place. She had to be in the music or nothing would work.

THE BOSS 'Focus, don't think about anything, just this moment in this room with these musicians. It won't happen again like this.'
Kenny Buttery's timing was impeccable. It came so easily to these guys. That expression 'sit on it' was here in real time. She rode on the bass lines, tucked in with the drums inside her headphones.

A wild boy, Bob Potter wasn't given to soft hearts and sentiment. He was on the road to do whatever it was he wanted. After producing Uncle Dog he'd got himself out to Nashville to work as Bob Johnson's right-hand man. It was clear he wanted whatever Johnson had, which made for an uneasy atmosphere in the studio

Carol with Bob Potter (*left*), Bob Johnson on keyboard and Tommy Cogbill (*right*).

289

whenever Johnson was around. In Nashville, Johnson was king. The man who'd recorded Dylan and Cohen, Patti Page and Burl Ives, Simon and Garfunkel, and the rest. His word was law and Bob Potter was his studio man. The girl never really figured out the history.

THE BOSS 'Life girl, life. There's always history and some of it stinks. Sing the songs and get home to your boy. You'll always be outside of what's gone on before.'

She made a friend. A journalist called Patrick who would hang out with the Johnson crowd. He had a genuine warmth and wrote for Rolling Stone, CREEM and the local Tennessee music papers. He used to ask her, 'Jeez, how do you keep up with them?' It was Patrick who dubbed Bob 'the Potter Monster.' On the second evening after the rehearsal they went to a club, the *Exit/In*, on Elliston Place near Vanderbilt. They said this was the place, with the new music, not the establishment *Grand Ole Opry* scene. The so called 'Outlaw Movement'. Bobby Bare, Waylon Jennings and Willie Nelson, wanting their own scene, their way of doing the business and the music. She heard the musicians' talk of country music, of old school and of the new bands that were breaking the rules, taking control. She listened and learned, realising they'd committed to the life. Sometimes their families paid a heavy price for what they did.

She was indeed that autumn leaf once more, blowing along with Procrastinating Patsy. The truth was, she loved all the music she heard and sang. When she wasn't in the studio she loved to sit on the swing seat in front of the house. The motion soothed her and she could smell the grips and gravy from the little café just down the road. She wondered if she could do this 'America' she had thought, 'we speak the same language.' Wrong, so very wrong. When she said she'd get 'pissed', they thought she meant angry and they collapsed with laughter at the word 'fortnight'. It was so medieval, they said. People didn't walk, they drove. Cars 'eased out' onto the highway, out to the mall, to the little 'burbs' outside Nashville. And Route 66, hey, what trip, the iconic highway that had become a song. 'If you ever plan to motor west, travel my way, take the highway that is best. Get your kicks on Route 66.' Chuck Berry motoring from St.Louis.

One day the studio session was cancelled. Bob Johnson wanted to use it and what Johnson wanted he got. A picnic was planned and this was to be one of Bob Potters amazing moments. Ron Cornelius, Bob and the girl went to the woods just outside

Nashville. Ron pointed out the signs for the whiskey stills. Crudely written in red paint, in code on slats of wood nailed onto tree trunks. Arrows pointing to even rougher tracks. 'All illegal of course, but out here it's wild, crazy country, hillbilly country. The stills have been around ever since human beings have been here,' said Ron.

Driving deeper into the wooded foothills, they stopped for a while and climbed a few smallish rocks where they cracked open a couple of beers. 'There are bears here,' said Bob, 'big brown bears.' He howled with laughter. She moved in a little closer, looking over her shoulder, a city girl. Their destination was one of the fire towers that were scattered all around the national park. Vertigo. Up is bad and coming down is a leg shaking, tummy churning nightmare. This was worse than the bed up the ladder in the Cornish farmhouse.

THE BOSS 'Steady yer legs. This is going to be your first and last picnic in such a place. Go for it.'

Up, up, up and what a view for the girl from England's green and pleasant tiny fields and copses, hedgerows, streams and villages. As the song goes, 'I can see for miles and miles and miles.' Tree tops spreading as far she could see. Huge horizons and the curve of the earth. In the cool bag there were chopped hard-boiled eggs, slivers of celery and cucumber, chopped onion and her very first ever beluga caviar, dark and glistening like tiny pearls. A taste sensation like nothing she'd experienced before. She had a cold beer to wash it down with, slowly sipping, holding on tightly to the only defence between her and a very long way down.

One afternoon, hanging out around the pool before a studio session, she noticed the women looking at her. She knew they were judging her. Her pale skin and unshaved armpits. Feeling self-conscious, she pulled on her t-shirt and took another sip of gin and tonic. She felt like a hairy bear. These were blonde and well groomed women, married to successful musicians, music business moguls and promotors. Willowy women with perfectly manicured hands and feet, smooth legs, well toned, well groomed, sun-kissed caramel skin, pretty pink toes, big blown blonde hair, clean blue denim and white teeth smiles. Nashville girls in zippy little air-conditioned sports cars. She felt frowzy and homesick. The beauty queen from Norwich would've fitted in much better here.

In the studios, back stage at gigs, in the hotel rooms and in the toilets at clubs, drugs were on the menu, like ice cream or a tiramisu after a pizza at *Pizza Express* today. And if you refused you were 'weird man', not rock and roll, not playing the game.

NERVY NORA 'I gotta have a drink, gotta have a smoke, gotta take a pill. I'm feeling ill. I can't do this.'

In the Tennessee summer the ice and the tonic slid down her throat far too easily. Management and record company moguls fed their rock stars whatever they wanted. White powders and pills. Rock stars fed their energy banks, dealers fed their money banks. And the press and the public gorged on the feast that was the music business.

The 'Potter monster' was out with his high-octane energy flashes of madness one Sunday afternoon and the girl was invited to the Johnson home for lunch. She noticed a crackle in the air, an atmosphere, a laugh too maniacal, a glance behind and a barbed comment. She felt nervous and knocked back another large gin and tonic, struggling to steady the glass in her hand. She laughed a little too loudly.

THE BOSS 'Down Clara, down.'

She fell into Bob Johnson's pool. Fall is perhaps the wrong word. She attempted to dive in and hit her head on the bottom. She'd pay for that later. She tried to cool it but here she was, a girl in a southern man's world with that squeaking mouse in her head. She had to prove her rock and roll stripes. She remembered the incoherent asides and then the brittle ecstasy that had been the white powder. Was that a joke? A dig? Was it me? Was it Potter?' What did she know. Chaos was looming but the album was sounding good, really good.

The musicians were keen and gave her plenty of support. She liked them. Bob Wilson was edgy and she overheard him mouthing off with Potter about Johnson.Oh dear, here we go again. In and out, and shake it all about. Why didn't she pack up, go home and become a gardener? Lead a quiet and calm life. Oh no. These guys had worked with the best and they were treating her like one of them. She gave herself a hug, hoped and prayed to whoever was listening. Please let it be a success. Please make them step away and let me do this. Please stop the rows, the bad feelings, the temper tantrums and the bad words. What the fuck was going on?

The final day recording was the next day, earlier than planned. She had a week or so before her return flight. She was to fly to New York where Guy and Elizabeth had persuaded her to stay for a few days. The day of departure was 23rd July. She was packed, ready and wanting to leave Nashville. Potter popped his head around her bedroom door. 'Back soon' he said. And seeing her face, 'don't panic. I'll be back to get you on that plane.' He leapt into his red car and took off down the road, tires spinning. He didn't come back. She rang Mac and he and his wife got her there just in time.

She caught her flight to New York. 'Potter,' he said, 'is a mad man. Crazy. I hope it wasn't too bad for you? But hey, we made a great record.' A voice of reason in a tricky moment. She had her tracks as rough mixes and a cassette to play to her friends. The album would be completed back in London at *Island Studios* the following month.

Guy and Elizabeth had said, 'Take a flight at...' They gave a time. 'We won't be there to meet you. This is what you do, trust us.' Instructions were given as to where she should take the bus into Manhattan. Oh, she thought, that's weird. At least she was leaving the chaos that had been Nashville. She found the bus and as it chugged from LGA Airport over the Queens Borough Bridge at sunset, there it was, Manhattan. Taller and more city than any she'd ever seen. She immediately fell love with it. It had an energy, like London only more so. After almost an hour they were there, Grand Central Terminal, 125 Park Avenue. 'You would've been talking, we all would've been talking,' said Guy and Elizabeth, 'we wanted you to see the city for the first time as the sun set over Manhattan Island.' And indeed it was an enchanting moment. They lived in Greenwich Village in a loft that was both a home and a studio. They also had a house in Woodstock. Things seemed to be going well.

The girl was in shock. Nashville and now New York. She shivered and it wasn't from the cold. It was all so thrilling. They wandered the streets, in and out the cafés and bars of Guy's hometown. They took her to *CBGB* and to see Iggy Pop at *Max's Kansas City* rolling around in broken glass, his hand down the front of his very tight jeans. She watched, wondered why and remembered the cold linoleum in the

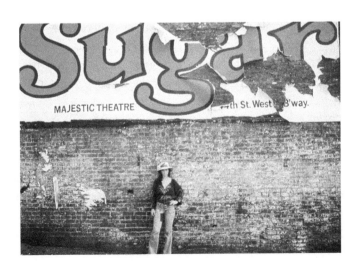

Carol in New York.
photo: Guy Cross

293

Lowestoft bathroom. She wondered, has he? Did he? She just want to sing. It was weird and her mind was in chaos. What was this business, this music business? What did you have to do? What were the rules?

The Summer Jam, 28th July 1973 at Watkins Glen. Six hundred thousand rock fans watched the Grateful Dead, the Band and the Allman Brothers. The Dead played two long sets. They opened with *Bertha*. She wished Larry was there. He and Guy had spent hours in St Stephen's Gardens, Dead Head bobbing, out of it, toking the weed. The Band followed the Dead with one two-hour set, interrupted by a thunderstorm. The Allman Brothers did three hours and there was an hour encore jam featuring musicians from all three bands. *Not Fade Away* and *Johnny B. Goode*. Her legs were beginning to twitch with fatigue and she wanted to sleep during the Grateful Dead. She was glad of Elizabeth and Guy's reassuring confidence. They knew everyone and had the right passes, the right places to hang out. Big crowds were not for her. Being only five feet bugger all, in among thousands of people. The tall American people submerged her.

Guy and Elizabeth drove her out to Woodstock, to a delightful wooden house with a garden. There was Jason, other friends and almost normality, with little shops, a bakery and a deli. The next evening they took her to a club. She, clutching her newly hatched tapes. Guy wanted her to sit in but the girl wasn't sure. 'Wad 'ya mean? He said, 'You've just been recording with legends man, legends. Wad 'ya mean, they won't want you to sit in? Tell 'em who you've been recording with. Woodstock is a small town. You're from London, the big city. The Stones, the Beatles, Floyd, the scene man.' He was selling her to herself.

THE BOSS 'Get a grip, strut your stuff. What are you? A mouse?'

FRANK PALE MOUSE 'Yes, I am, I am. Squeak, see my whiskers. They're twitching, you get it? I'm scuppered. Take me to the river and drown me,'

During the second set he edged her up onto the low stage. 'Now,' he said, 'now, go for it, girl.' One of the guys in the band, the bass player, nodded at her with a smile. It was fine. She opened her mouth as a blues kicked in, a slow blues in C. The man who fronted the band, the lead guitar player, was certainly not pleased. He ripped out the lead to her microphone. She fled after two choruses. 'Don't worry,' they said, 'it's cool, it's him. If he's threatened by a skinny little English woman, it's his problem. You wiped the floor with him in two minutes flat.' She didn't want to wipe the floor with anyone. She had been an incident.

The next day she was out and people came up to her saying, 'hey, that was great. Just ignore those arse-holes. They're just guys with big egos and little pricks.' As they walked out of the liquor store, another woman approached, 'hey man, great voice, you staying here? You need to get a band together.' A man revving up a bike outside the store said, 'hey, Janis, go girl.' 'Janis.' she thought, 'I'm not myself?'

Guy and Elizabeth said, 'they won't forget you. We'll get you your own gig next year, you'll see. They'll eat their cowboy hats when your album comes out, man.' They were among the most generous people she'd ever met. Back in Greenwich in the studio, Guy took some photos and then they went out and about in New York. It was soon time to go home. She'd been away for nearly three weeks.

All Saints Road, home. And there was Dee leaning against the *Mangrove* door in the sunshine, having a chat with Frank Critchlow. Hugged to the point of breathlessness, they asked. 'Where's the boy?' She was always with the boy when not away singing. Reg and Pat came out the dairy four doors down. 'Hey Pat, Reg,' he called, 'she's back from America.' Pat beamed and wiped her hands on her very clean overalls, 'you'll need your milk and bread.' Compared to Nashville, the road and the tiny yellow house was shabby. She'd been in homes with swimming pools, manicured lawns, swivelling sprinklers, sofas as large as her own front room, refrigerators as wide as her kitchen, and brown shag pile carpets in which you sank up to your ankles. Homes with chrome and marble topped tables and rooms used only for playing pool, with a bar in one corner. Guys pouring drinks, rolling weed and watching a television the size of a small cinema screen.

Compared to Manhattan, her corner of London felt like a toy village. But it was hers. All Saints Road was a street in miniature, built for the horse and cart. The mews that ran beside 8a were once the stables and storage for carts and barrows from the market. Compared to the lofts she'd seen in New York, her flat was a shoebox. A dusty dolls house that didn't smell like her home but of man and man's boots and socks. Mick had gone back to his cottage in the Login valley.

She suddenly felt all consumingly exhausted, and yet sleep wasn't even remotely what she wanted. She wanted to see her son. Her back was beginning to ache. Ever since the dive headfirst into Bob Johnson's pool, she had twinges in her back. Make that call to Portis now. She'd set the phone line up before she left for Nashville. A caravan in a field and a telephone in the cottage. She had a drink in the *Apollo* with Dee, then to sleep, unpack and plan the rest of her life. Her mattress bed felt so low on the floor but at least it didn't wobble with water.

She could sleep without feeling seasick. The street underneath the window sounded impossibly close but the dialects of Trinidad and Jamaica, of London and Ireland, sounded reassuringly familiar. She was home.

In the morning she wondered where she was. New York? Nashville? Woodstock? No. Up, up, get up. Her back still ached but her heart beat fast in anticipation. Larry was coming to London with the little one.

The cupboards were almost empty. Aside from the loaf, butter and milk she'd collected from the dairy, there was a tin of *Heinz* tomato soup, one of beans, a half finished packet of *Quaker* porridge oats, a pot of *Marmite* and a half finished packet of *Macvities* chocolate digestive biscuits, soft and past the sell-by-date by months. She remembered the *Cadburys* flake and the maggots back in the rooms in Brompton Road and tossed everything into the bin under the sink. It smelt sour and she found six empty milk bottles waiting to go downstairs, each containing a dead mouse.

The shopping could wait until tomorrow. They'd go to *Pizza Hut* in Islington for supper. The boy loved pizza. She had to talk to Beat and Sally, and catch up with Louis. Maybe all of that could wait too. The homecoming from America was overwhelming. Had it all been worth it? Was the record a good one? Had it been worth leaving her beloved boy? More questions. Her head was spinning.

At two-thirty the next day she stood at the Paddington barrier waiting for Larry and her son. She was half an hour early and each second felt like an hour, waiting, waiting. At last, wearing his *Osh Kosh* dungarees, he smiled and dropped his little tousled head, as if he couldn't bear to look. Was he angry? She held his little body to her like she'd never let him go. They took the tube to King's Cross and one hop on the Northern Line to The Angel Islington for pizza and a *Coca-Cola*. All the things that were forbidden in the macrobiotic world of serious food balancing. Today was for treats and eats of the kind that a small boy wanted. Ice cream, pizza and cuddles. It was one of the best meals of her life.

She'd bought gifts for friends. Cigarette lighters that played the Tennessee Waltz. Great, she thought, beautifully kitsch. She gave one to give Beat, who lit a cigarette and noticed it said 'Made in China.' on the bottom of the box. Blimey, so much for made in Nashville gifts. She bought some records and two bottles of *Southern Comfort*. She knew that Louis and Dee had a sweet tooth. It tasted like syrupy cough mixture.

A letter arrived from Patrick, the journalist from Nashville. He wrote about the rows that had erupted between Johnson and Potter after she'd left. Old arguments, things she knew nothing about. Power struggles, politics, male egos set on a major collision. Potter was sacked. All change. Deals were lost and the album was shelved. Everything was in the air again. It all seemed so far away. She was more than happy not to be in Nashville but the songs she'd sung there were still in her head. The stories the musicians had told her, of sessions with Elvis and Bob Dylan, of Johnny Cash's legendary prison recordings, of Dylan's *Blonde on Blonde* (1966) of Simon & Garfunkel's *Parsley Sage, Rosemary and Thyme* (1966) and many more.

It was always the business side of things that seemed to create madness and mayhem. The terrible twins, money and egos. There were meetings with Simon Draper at the new *Virgin* record company offices in Vernon's Yard off the Portobello Road. They were planning some overdubs, then the mixes, the sleeve design and release date. She wanted to get down to Wales, to the caravan. She'd only slept in it for a week before she left for Nashville. Sam was to go to the village school in Glyndwr in September. They walked to the market and bought vegetables and fruit. Her home began to smell the way she remembered. Garlic, apples and a bunch of flowers on the dresser in the tiny living room, the smell of her own perfume and the skin of her child.

She would try and juggle her life, and work in the city only when she had to. They had a week in London where she caught up with friends, and then headed to the fresh air for the boy's lungs in the green fields of Wales. It was almost dark as the train creaked and groaned its way past Swansea, on towards Port Talbot. The tall chimneys of the steel works were spitting flames into the dark sky. Red flames, grey smoke and no stars. 'Mum, mum,' said her son, 'it's hell. The devil's in there. Look at the fires.' She held him close and told him all she knew about steel, which wasn't a lot. She talked about how they made trains and tracks, and that the devil was nowhere. Where has he heard about devils and hell? Who has spoken to him of such terrible things?

From Clunderwen Station, through Llandissilio and Efailwen, on the road to Crymych and then a left turn down a narrow lane down towards Glandwr. Past fields of sheep, the donkey sanctuary and then a sharp left turn beside the milk churns from Owens' Farm, up the track to Portis. They arrived at Portis in the taxi, heavy with bags of fruit, organic oats and runny golden honey, brown rice and soy sauce from the Sams' shop in Portobello Road, a slab of Cheese from Mr Hawkins and two bottles of wine from the off-license in Notting Hill Gate. In the muddy yard stood Sally Sparkle's old car, dirty now from driving the winding tracks and lanes of rural Carmarthenshire. A hermaphrodite goat called Meirwyn bleated and

Carol's caravan in Wales.

Shelly's dog barked. Shelly and Teifion stood at the door. The cottage was smoky with the Rayburn door open on a damp Welsh day. The girl shivered, unused to the chill. Tea was on the hob. She ran out to her caravan, the van she'd barely used. She couldn't wait to sleep in it, with the boy in his cozy room at one end. Back in the cottage they talked for hours and drank the wine. Mick called in from Login, his car held together with rope and industrial black tape. She played a track or two from her new album but didn't really listen, and then drifted over to the van to unpack her bag.

One day she noticed the boy rubbing his eyes. He said he'd been cuddling the goat. It was crabs. He had crabs. The crabs from Lowestoft were on the march. The doctor in the village who'd been drinking said, 'It's an eye infection. I'll give you a prescription for some drops.' He winked at her and she smelt the whisky behind the peppermint on his tongue. She washed Sam's hair with a special shampoo for

Carol in the caravan.

the annihilation of lice and other such tiny beasts. Carefully, one by one, she picked the crabs from his eyelashes and hairline and said, 'Don't hug the goat any more.' The crab culling was just about the worse thing he had to endure.

Willie, a Canadian and a good man who worked on a farm not far away with retired police horses, would ride over sometimes when she had a nasty chest infection. He rubbed her back with horse lineament and told her to wait. She'd be smelly for days but the infection

298

disappeared. He would say, 'what's good for the horse is good for you.'

The school term began just a few days after the crabs. There was a phone call from the school, 'Can you come and collect your goat. He's in the playground eating the sunflowers.' Trouble was, the he/she goat had an insatiable and peculiar appetite, helping him/herself to cabbages, and more, from the gardens on his/her way down to the village, following the boy to school. Oh dear, what to do? She had bought herself a chamois leather skirt in a Nashville thrift shop. One day, she cleaned some dirty marks with a wet sponge and hung it out in the yard to dry. Meirwyn chewed his/her way around the hem until it hung in shreds. A goat with culinary imagination.

Teifion and Sam.

It was autumn and the water was high in the stream that ran behind the cottage. On the way over the fields to Owens', to fetch the milk and eggs with the two boys, one of her boots was sucked into the sticky mud. She fell flat on her arse holding the milk aloft as the boys laughed. 'Very funny,' she said, as she withdrew one muddy bootless foot and slurped back to Portis, sopping wet from the waist down. She warmed her chilled bones beside the Rayburn.

She needed to go to London for a few days to the studio and then hopefully, to the Nashville *Warm Blood* album release. It was another wet day. Water was pouring down the lane, rendering it a stream as she sloshed her way up to the road at the top. She wore Shelly's wellington boots, a size too big. She had a bag in her hand, a *Sou'wester* on her head and a wish in her heart for a lift soon, soon. The goat followed and she bellowed, 'Go Meirwyn, go home!' She was less in love with the goat since he/she had chewed the skirt. He/she stopped at the hedgerow for a munch, and as she set off once more for the road at the top in order to hitch a lift to Carmarthen, he/she walked behind her once more. Who is going to take a girl and a goat to London? Standing in the lane with water dripping down her neck, she kicked out in the general direction of the goat who'd begun munching something juicy in the ditch. One boot flew over the hedge and she sat on a gate not knowing whether to laugh or cry.

CLARA THE CLOWN 'Oh the glamour of it all.'

NASTY NELLIE 'If those Guys could see you now, life in the fast lane, ay?'

Then a miracle happened. The goat set off back down the lane towards Portis. The girl retrieved a pair of unsuitable shoes from her bag, left the solitary boot in the ditch and reached the top road. A few minutes later she had a lift to Whitland and caught a train to Carmarthen.

She was back in the studio and the music sounded strange. Created in Nashville, they were now putting the London stamp on it. Her voice and the songs bounced back to her from Tennessee to *Island studios* in Basing Street. The horn section included Malcolm 'Molly' Duncan and Roger Ball from the Average White Band, with the wonderful Henry Lowther playing trumpet.

Sammy Mitchell was on the sessions. He was well once more. The following day with Gasper Lawal, he came in to play congas. The girl had really wanted Sammy to come with her to Nashville but sadly the budget wouldn't run to it. Jess Roden and Graham Bell sang some harmonies, and John 'Rabbit' Bundrick added some *Hammond* organ. Sammy was on blistering form and it was great to have the horns. Even Bob Potter was in good spirits that day. Nothing was said about her exit from Nashville, the way he left her packed and ready to go, never coming back. She remembered a night when they'd met up with friends in the *Finch's* pub on Fulham Road, leaving after closing time in the rain. They danced and sang *Singing in the Rain* all the way up Redcliffe Gardens, on up Earl's Court Road to Kensington High Street, up Kensington Church Street into Notting Hill Gate, down into Portobello Road and on to All Saint's Road.

Five days later she was on the train from Paddington with two pairs of wellington boots, a jar of *Marmite*, dried fruit, oats, cheese and wine. Back to the caravan in the field. Shelly took a trip for a few days and the girl was there alone with the two boys. She'd never lived in such an isolated place before. She loved her caravan, especially at night with the glow of the stove, the flicker of candlelight and the cosiness of the rugs and cushions, carried down from London.

Shelly knew all the incomers. The hippies had settled in communes and occupied cottages and houses around the Carmarthen and Narberth area. At a party in one of the big houses owned by a man called Giles, a woman laughingly called the girl a pasty faced Londoner. The woman herself wasn't Welsh and had sprung from the suburban lanes of Surrey. Some of these people were from very wealthy families, wearing their hand knitted jumpers and hats, growing vegetables and cooking vegetarian dinners. Dogs, donkeys and often a beat up old van in the yard. A son of Elizabeth Taylor here, a daughter of a lord there, musicians buying farms and land, converting barns into studios and building homes.

Back in London, Jan had died one night in her flat opposite the convent on Ladbroke Grove. She took her own life and that of her baby girl. What had happened? Tony was in prison and she'd split from Steve. Oh that beautiful woman and her child were gone.

The man with dark eyes and the coffin ring also died. The Grove was going insane, its fragile inhabitants crazy with amphetamines. A grass hit had been replaced by a psychotic trip and the drinking had become more manic. Cheek to face to arse in The Grove.

Tenements and poverty. Turn a corner and the white stucco houses are too close. Rich neighbouring poor. Anger was brewing. This time around, those who would've doffed a cap or tugged a forelock in another era, were saying, 'No. I want some of that.' Saying, 'Pay a decent wage.' Saying, 'Provide affordable homes.'

Speed was at the gatherings. Up noses, in the clubs and the basement flats of London, from Brixton to The Grove, Camden Town to Earl's Court, Ealing to Bethnal Green. She'd known that scene before. Long before the hippies, before the psychedelic days. It was like taking a step back but with brown rice and lentils for some.

The girl's debut *Warm Blood* album was finally released in 1974, with a small fanfare and some ads in the music press for the label *Caroline Records*. Her album, amongst the first for that label, was never going to be a major announcement. There was some airplay. Coverage

on the John Peel Show, an interview and some very good reviews. Reviews don't necessarily make money. Simon Draper believed in her but the record company had bigger fish to fry. A new music was bubbling up behind her. She was roots and blues. And the *Caroline* disk label? It was an image of two very young girls sitting naked, shoulder to shoulder. A dirty old mans dream? She mentioned it and was laughed at. Those were the times.

Life became the rail track and the roads in between South Wales and London. On the train or a lift from someone going to London or Bristol, or a hitch for a few miles. It was an odd life, neither one thing nor another. But she'd kept her little home above the shop in All Saints Road. She'd sung in America and now she was back with one foot in a field in Wales and the other in a dolls house in The Grove.

That winter the dark clouds lay low over the Preselli Hills and the wind at night kept her awake as she listened for the bark of a fox, maybe the one that had frightened the boys on the track as they walked home after dusk from the village. Mr Fox, eyes glittering in the light from the torch she held in her hand, bushy tail swishing behind him as he ran behind the hedge, back to his lair or maybe a night hunt for chickens. She felt estranged from this land where people switched languages in the villages, and in the pub when an English person walked in. Where the hippy incomers had called her a white faced Londoner. She felt the 'hiraeth,' a great longing for her home, her river and her own hometown.

Being a Londoner was a multifarious thing. Everyone from everywhere and devil may care, sink or swim. It was a city that had existed for many centuries in spite of those who hold bigotry and fear at their hearts. A city built because of its river, built on trade and immigration, bringing everyone from everywhere. A city settled in a valley where forests once grew, where some trees survived. Some of the girl's favourite trees live in Brunswick Square and Coram Fields, in Greenwich Park, Victoria Park, and on Hampstead Heath. Through clay and brick in parks and squares, crescent, avenue and cul-de-sac, trees would sometimes break free, their roots thrusting into the city from the earth below.

Buying some food in Crymych, the nearest large village one day, the talk everywhere was of a hippy burial. A baby had died, maybe a cot death? Or an infection? They buried the baby with unknown rituals in a land devoted to God and chapel. They hadn't obtained a doctors certificate. 'Duw, duw. Shocking.' The women whispered in shops, on the buses, in the streets and on doorsteps, over garden fences and at the school gate. The men sucked their teeth while sipping pints of beer. 'Twll din pob sais!', translated as 'All English people are arseholes!'. It was a bad time to be English in that corner of Wales. It was never a very good thing to be.

She'd been accepted by some at the village school. She was even told by the teacher that word had reached her. Word that the girl wasn't as bad as some, that she kept a clean caravan, the child was well fed, all be it with no meat, that, 'she wasn't hoity toity like some of them.' Still, there was no 'croeso', no welcome for an English person. Man or woman. Her cheery 'bore da.' or 'prynhawn da' remained unanswered for weeks, as if she'd been stained by the terrible events up in the Preseli mountains above Glyndwr. The divide felt similar to the Formentera stay. A total lack of common ground, a lack of sensitivity to the local ways and rules.

NASTY NELLIE 'You hate rules.'

THE BOSS 'Take it slowly. Bulls, china shops. Get it?'

SENSIBLE MA SADIE 'What it needs is less bloody arrogance.'

The days became shorter and the fields muddier on the way to Owens' for milk. The wind seemed sharper, the clouds more menacing and the mist more dense in the valley below, hanging low over the stream behind Portis. For winter it was, and she was 31. Far too old to be a singing sensation on *Top of the Pops*. She began to think that maybe life in a field wasn't such a good idea. So back to London it was going to be, seven weeks before Christmas. This was home. This was where she belonged and she didn't care if the air was sour, the roads were busy or pavements were thronging with people on a Saturday down in the market.

But The Grove had changed. Weed was smoked but harder dope was on the streets. Harder faces, and harder times. Thing was, where was it good? Where could home be? Home must have a kitchen where she could cook their vegetarian food. Cauliflower cheese, rice and vegetables, her pies and nut roasts. She resisted the current television adverts, 'For mash get *Smash*' though occasionally she desired an *Angel Delight* but only the chocolate one.

Years later she found that long letter from Patrick, written in 1974. No, she wasn't crazy. It was a crazy time. Patrick wrote,

> *'It took me a that long [a few weeks] to figure out that Potter was in trouble with your album...I do not mean to depress you with all this information. It was just a depressing situation, and in the long run, it will help you to know how it came out.Johnson cut Potter and Wilson from his roster after your sessions...*
>
> *Those tapes you cut with Potter and your reputation with Uncle Dog will make bookers take you seriously, I'm sure of it. Of course I would be happy to help promote you... reputation is a very perishable thing and you should act immediately The Uncle Dog album is only six months old in this country and it is not at all impossible that you could push MCA into releasing your Nashville album this year, if you were only here to be seen and heard...*
>
> *I've got a lot of faith in you Carol. I don't know you very well, but I like you a lot, and you became one of my favourite singer's the first time I heard you. Otherwise, I wouldn't be writing you in such an authoritative manner. I'll be goddamned if I can stand by and see you get such a screwing by those corporate numbskulls...*
>
> *If you have the proper management you could blow down the walls... but if you fuck one person here you have to fuck them all. It's a bad town for a woman in that respect. It's also a town that you have to leave about every two months in order to be taken seriously'*

Transition

Let's Get It On Marvin Gaye 1973

1974: back to The Grove, Henry and Sheila, an invitation from Stuart Lyon. The London Boogie Band.

Junk Etta and Piss Pot Polly were dancing a dangerous duet.

'Take this pill and you'll grow. Take this for Betty and she'll holler. She'll sing for your suppers. Inside this small packet the brown powder will sooth your head and silence the jabbing and jostling chatterers. This line of smooth white will make you shine. Go and Score.'

WICKED WILL O'MINA 'Put that in your pipe and smoke it.'

The 1970s, oh dear, oh dear. Her head was in a muddle and as for Guilty Gertie and Nasty Nellie? Marvellous moments aside, it was a terrible time. She treasured the times being mum, being with Sam, her little silver bombshell. And performing in wild singing flight on a good night. One moment she would look out the window onto All Saints Road, see the orange urban lights, wave and say, 'How you doing man?' Another moment brought harassment and fear. Fear on the streets of The Grove and havoc in her head. We don't think in packets of time, placed neatly line by line, by day, by year, one after the other. No, in the mind time travels erratically. In remembering, the clicks are exactly that. Click. Held up for review.

What can you do? You can't change it, re-live it, go back and erase it. Time plays tricks. Was that really 30 years ago? Did this happen before that? Clara the Clown to the rescue, and Betty rides again.

NASTY NELLIE 'So what did you do in the 1970s?'

A potent pause.

NASTY NELLIE 'Come on, what did you do? You must have some idea. You losing your mind or what?'

Now where was she.

NASTY NELLIE 'You blew it, that's what happened.'

FRANK PALE MOUSE 'Squeak.'

THE BOSS 'Ok let's sit down and think this thing through. Let's bat it back and forth, toss it around.'

NASTY NELLIE 'Yeah, you spent too much time dreaming your life. Instead of taking control, you dreamed away the bad bits, relived it in your mind the way you wanted it to have been.'

MISERY IVY 'I can't remember. Don't prod me, don't poke me, it hurts.'

THE BOSS 'Hush you tormenters!'

CLARA THE CLOWN 'Oh, come on now, we all had some fun.'

NASTY NELLIE 'A plague of worms, toads and cockroaches on yer head.'

She was torn between wanting the country air and a quiet life for her and the boy, and the need to earn, to sing.

NASTY NELLIE 'Skin side out, your skin is inside out.'

NASTY NELLIE AND WICKED WILL O'MINA 'Outside in, we can impale your heart, break your heart. Inside lies the unborn. Outside is dying. Outside is confusion and hullabaloo. Skin side out, your skin is inside out.'

There were two men outside the window. Raised voices, a bottle smashed on the ground. 'Don't fuck with me man.' A drawl mouth, barely moving eyes, pinprick pupils dilated, snow caked on nostrils. The words that in themselves meant nothing, were repeated. Words were not enough. Outside, the small pool of local dealers and local takers lurked in shadows, and the back rooms of run down pubs. Deals were done over pool tables or packets passed in toilets. It's a dangerous dance.

NASTY NELLIE 'Nobody gets you. You don't get yourself. Charlie and Henry got you. The dealer gets you. Life gets you. Veins blown, head blown, mind blown.'

Sammy Mitchell came round to 8a with Nicky Barclay one day, a keyboard player from LA with a band called Fanny, an all women rock band. The first the girl had ever met. She was impressed. Nicky was a very good pianist and the band rocked. She said she wasn't set on this earth to be a novelty girl act. She was serious and Fanny was doing well. They were talked about. They were on the road selling the music, selling the idea that women do it. They can do it and not just as singers. They can front the band. In the seventies it was still very much a man's world. James Brown was so right there. Nicky and the girl became close friends. When Fanny were in London, it was to the girl's house Nicky came. She had a love of all things Sammy and all things *Peter Rabbit* or *Liberty* in Regent Street. 'So English,' she said. The girl took her to Knightsbridge and to *Harrods* where she bought a *Peter Rabbit* plate and a cup for the boy, and a set to take home to her apartment in Hollywood.

On one of the nights that Larry had Sam, the girl was in the *Speakeasy* just off Oxford Circus with Dave Skinner and Dave Vasco, the guitarist. This was the place musicians hung out. Any night of the week you'd find the rock glitterati eating steak and fries and downing bubbly in the restaurant. In all the gigs she played, she'd never once sat in the restaurant. She would sit just inside the door on a red leather bench, waiting for the guys to collect a round of drinks, until one night when a man with dark blond hair and a soft Northern Irish voice came up and said, 'Hi, I'm Henry and you shouldn't sit there, that's the meat rack.' She learned it was where the groupies sat out on the pull, hoping for a rock star for the night and maybe longer.

Henry McCullough the guitarist, was with Alan Spenner, bass player. Both played in the Grease Band with Joe Cocker. They'd played at Woodstock and hung out with Jim Morrison and Janis Joplin in The Chelsea Hotel bar in Manhattan. The girl met a bunch of singers down from Liverpool. Dyan, Paddy and Frank from a band called Arrival. Then they all joined Kokomo with Alan and Neil Hubbard, another Grease band member. Grease meeting Arrival and being Kokomo with Mel Collins, Jim Mullen and Tony O'Malley. Henry was working with Paul and Linda McCarney in Wings.

Henry came up one day up for a gig at *Dingwalls*, bringing Sheila his wife who came from Ballinamallard in County Fermanagh, Northern Island. 'I'm from the back of beyond,' she said, as if born of the bogs. In fact, she went off to Dublin University to study English and French. 'I escaped,' she said. She and Henry had first met when she was still in school aged 13. They didn't share a bed until she was away in the big city aged 18, old enough for sex and voting. Henry came to England with a band called Eire Apparent managed by Chas Chandler from the Animals, who'd also managed Jimi Hendrix and the girl's first band, The Race. They were all destined to meet. There were the boys in the band over from Ireland in the Big Smoke, broke and sleeping in the band van, parked up for the night under the railway bridge beside Camden Town station.

Sheila came with money from Dublin. Flying into Heathrow on a £6 student ticket, she then took the bus to Gloucester Road Bus Station. She'd never been to London in her life and took a taxi from there, saying, 'I need to find a bridge in Camden Town.' Camden Town! Charles Pratt, 1st Earl of Camden, began to creat the town in 1791. London stank in those days, especially Camden Town. As well as rivers above ground, the river Fleet flowed beneath St Pancras Old Church and Jonathan Swift, writing in 1710, describes the scene following a storm,

> '*Filth of all hues and odour, seem to tell*
> *What street they sail'd from, by their sight and smell.*
> *They, as each torrent drives with rapid force,*
> *From Smithfield to St. Pulchre's shape their course,*
> *And in huge confluence join'd at Snowhill ridge,*
> *Fall from the conduit prone to Holborn bridge.*
> *Sweeping from butchers' stalls, dung, guts, and blood,*
> *Drown'd puppies, stinking sprats, all drench'd in mud,*
> *Dead cats, and turnip-tops, come tumbling down the flood.*'

The rivers Kilburn and Tyburn also flowed underground, all three now incorporated into London's sewerage system, partly because they were so polluted.

The original Euston rail terminus, opened in 1837, was followed by a giant cats cradle of tracks, strung out from stations, criss-crossing up through Camden Town towards Birmingham and beyond. The first station hotels were built, with their red brick turrets and Victorian grandeur. The King's Cross terminus opened in 1852, and St Pancras in 1868, with all their attendant bridges, locks, engine sheds, tunnels, goods yards and sidings. The *Roundhouse*, never actually used as a roundhouse for locomotives, had the winding gear for pulling the trains up the hill from Euston Station and later became redundant. *Gilbey's Gin* had it as a store before the Second World War. In 1964 it became a cultural venue, for the works of playwright Arnold Wesker, the Trade Unions and the Centre 42 movement. A soot-stained run-down place, it was an attraction for artists who couldn't afford leafy, hilly Hampstead and Highgate, from where the rivers flowed.

In that place of many bridges, Sheila found her man, guided maybe by her ancerstors who helped to build the railways and bridges in Camden Town. The Bass Player, Chrissie Stewart, was the first to open the back door at Sheila's knocking. His jaw almost landed on Camden Road. She'd had found them. Henry and Sheila walked and talked all night, ending up in a Wimpy bar in Oxford Street. Now that's a love story.

Many musicians married models and posh pretty girls. Sheila was a small, bright and feisty gal. She could rustle up food for a crowd at a moment's notice, roll the joints and make money when it was in short supply. But most liked a trophy girl. Sheila said later, much later, that she'd been surprised, meeting the girl in an orange *Guinness* oilcloth apron. 'Well,' she said, 'I expected a rock chick in black leather.' The girl laughed, 'Hard to do that every day. Leather isn't cheap.'

The girl had a call from Stuart Lyon who worked with Nigel Thomas, once manager of Joe Cocker and others who'd been unfortunately caught in that particular knotty net. 'We got some tracks,' he said, 'great tracks. We want you to come and put the vocals on.' Tim Hinckley, Boz Burrell and various guys had been laying down tracks in between gigs with other bands. She said, 'Yes, why not.' Off she went to *Olympic Studios* in Barnes. It was the usual party. Bob Potter was there, everyone knew everyone. *Give It Everything You've Got* and *Let's Do It Again*. They called it The London Boogie Band and she didn't even ask about the money. It was never meant to be a permanent thing and they'd record with other singers. People she knew. The tracks were bluesy, easy kind of songs. Then she was asked if she'd sign a contract. 'Take you to America,' they said, 'record you in Memphis. That's where you belong.'

THE BOSS 'Don't sign it, don't do it. Check the small print, get a lawyer.'

Did she? No, she was getting older. The breaks would be gone.

NASTY NELLIE 'The product isn't playing the game.'

MISERY IVY 'Can't win. I give it some welly and you yell at me.'

FRANK THE PALE MOUSE 'I squeak and you mock.'

Memphis ... and More

Birdland Joe Zawinul 1977

1975-1979: Don Nix calls a one-to-one, laying tracks in Memphis in esteemed company. Nigel Thomas shenanigans. Living in a shack in Crockett. Singing with Dick and the Firemen. Rock Against Racism, benefit gigs, a death, a move from west to east and new beginnings.

She was now part of the Nigel Thomas set up. At the time she'd no idea just how many connections there were. Just how many on the scene he had signed. Another headlong rush into the wind tunnel. He managed Joe Cocker and the Grease Band, Gerry Lockran, one of the artists she and Beat had seen a lot on the Folk club circuit, Spooky Tooth, Boxer, with Mike Patto and Ollie Halsall, Juicy Lucy, and the American singer Viola Wills. The first visit to Memphis was to be in September, then she'd return to record the following May.

In the band, put together by Don Nix, would be Donald 'Duck' Dunn, and Al Jackson Jnr playing drums. They'd been the so-solid rhythm section behind Otis Redding, the Staple Singers, Sam and Dave, Delaney and Bonnie, Albert King, Steve Cropper and more. Christ, back in those all night cellar gigs she'd danced her butt off to 'Duck's' bass on *Walking the Dog* and *Soul Man*. They were a major groove team. Steve Cropper, 'Duck' Dunn and Al Jackson in a multi racial band in the segregated land that was the deep south. Also, Frederick Knight, who'd written songs for the goddess of gospel and soul, Aretha Franklin, on the piano and keyboards.

The Nigel and Stuart team had lined it all up with Potter on the desk. But strangely, Don Nix was producing. Don Nix and his Hot Licks. Don had played saxophone for the Mar-keys which later morphed into Booker T and The MG's, along with Steve Cropper, 'Duck' Dunn and Wayne Jackson. The girl would be in illustrious company. She'd go anywhere and do almost anything to sing with these musicians. Any moment she'd wake up and it would all be a dream. But it wasn't and she flew once more to America.

Don Nix called a meeting. A meeting for what?' 'Talk around tracks and shit,' he said. A drink or two later he pulled out a gun, and then his hands were in his jeans and out it came. The girl shrank. He laughed 'Hey stay cool.' he said, 'suck it and see. Go down on me, girl.' She backed off, edging away from the bed that shook with his intentions. Guns and pricks in Tennessee. 'Stay cool, you'll keep.' She could hear his laughter as he walked back down the long corridor to the lift. Women were regarded as easy meat. A screw, a fuck, nothing at all. And if you refused, you were frigid, a lesbian, as if that was an insult. She didn't sleep much that night, keeping one eye on her hotel room door. Later in the studio, three or four days into the sessions, Nix leaned back in the chair in front of the mixing desk, his head full of quaaludes. The chair tipped, he fell and broke his arm. The sessions were over.

Back in London there were talks. Plan B, 1975. Re-group in Memphis with Bob Potter once again in the driving seat. She checked into the Holiday Inn by the Mississippi. One day Tim Hinkley was in town and the white powders came out, causing chaos. Things then got better. Frederick Knight and his wife came over. And Bob's new girlfriend, who'd been in the London cast of *Hair*, and was the epitome of African American beautiful black woman. She lived in Luke's Mews, which runs across All Saints Road, home to *Island Studios* in Basing Street. Home over the years of Lemmy of Motörhead, Screaming Lord Sutch, Chet Baker, Joe Cocker and Joan Armatrading. It was good to have another woman in the camp. No longer was the girl in a gaggle of joshing men. For a while things seemed almost calm.

Well, well she was singing with those guys, 'Uphill, Lord, I got to climb. Uphill baby, Lord have mercy. I have got to climb. I got to find myself a little piece of mind. I got to find myself a little piece of mind.' Oh yes, Frederick Knight, she could sing that one. Way ahead in the millennium years she'd be singing that same song at the *Barbican* in London for the show, *Soul Britannia*, with some of the guys from The Grove and Brixton, from the days when they were young. Then on the tour bus from Plymouth to Edinburgh. The show also featured Madeline Bell and Linda Lewis, Root Jackson, Sam Kelly and the guys from Cymande.

At the Holiday Inn she met an English singer called Claire Hamill. The lift doors opened into the foyer and a young English woman said hello. She learned that Claire had had some dealings with the Nix man. The girl wasn't the first and wouldn't be the last.

They cut the tracks with the Memphis guys and then Potter shipped in Ron Cornelius from Nashville, with his Richmond California crew. She met Jon Sagen, their trombone player from the Bay Area, California. She didn't see too much of Memphis beyond the studio, the hotel and the bars. She didn't even get to Graceland. They lay down *Uphill Peace of mind*, bass and drums kicking in.

311

CLARA THE CLOWN 'Oh holy rhythm, oh holy groove, oh holy dance. Uphill you know I have got to climb, I got to find myself a little peace of mind.' Al Jackson died. A murder, an enraged wife, a robbery? Willie Mitchell replaced him. Another great soul, blues and funk drummer, of all time.

Again, Bob asked her to sing as the tracks were laid down. She was in a strange heaven in a town where some of the greatest soul tracks had been created, with the Memphis horns playing right in front of her. When she had been in London, working with The Race in the 1960s, these musicians had made music together against unthinkable odds. Black and white together in the segregated southern states of the US, amidst lynchings, where white women were called ladies and black women were directed to separate rest rooms and the back of the Bus. 'Duck' told her stories about the early days with Otis Redding in the south. Towns where no hotels would take them, so they parked the travelling truck on a beach and yes, the tide came in and they got their feet wet.

One evening they went to a bar after the session and she realised she was the only white woman there. Needing the toilet, she was met by some heavily made up and wigged women. 'Hello,' she said with her London accent, and the mood warmed. 'Oh You'all from England?'

On another occasion, with Frederick Knight and Willie Hall, she spoke about the fears she had, taking on another culture, 'Coals to Newcastle, black American music'. Frederick talked about the movement of music around the World. Africa, Europe, Russia. 'It's all in the melting pot,' he said, 'you sing it with truth and it's yours. Music travels and we travel with it.' He also believed that not so many years ago in Britain, the poor were slaves. Children in factories and down the mines. *The Boy I love is up in the Gallery* and *Oh Mr Porter!* in the music hall. 'London roots,' she acknowledged, singing the songs, to their surprise and amusement.

The warnings were there. Nigel Thomas shenanigans were looming. He returned to London without paying the girl's hotel bill. Bob managed to sort that. And then back in London for the mixes, Nigel said to Bob and anyone else in the room that was listening, 'We'll get a decent singer in. Haw, haw.' Was he joking? He seemed to have a plan and it wasn't a good one. One of the guys pissed in the fish tank in the reception area. More shenanigans. 'Haw, haw, haw.' Nigel didn't pay the musicians or the American. The Musicians Union were on his back. He offered Viola Wills the Memphis tracks. Two albums for the price of one. Uwe Tessnow from *Line Records* in Germany would take the girl's version and Nigel would sell version number two with Viola in the US. Once she knew where the tracks were from, Viola declined. There was honour amongst some singers. 'Nigel, can you hear me? No, because you're dead.' Rap tap, tapping inside her scull.

'Come out to The Bay.' Ron Cornelius was calling from California, 'I'm back in Crockett,' he said, 'left Nashville. Got the old band together again. Come over and sing with us. It'll be great to have you in the band.

PROCRASTINATING PATSY 'Oh, oh, what to do?'

Ron said, 'Hey, and bring the kid. Move out here. Come on girl, what's stopping you? I hear Nigel Thomas turned out to be a crock of shit. Get over here.'

Maybe all was not. She'd signed a ridiculous contract with Nigel and was advised to go for Legal Aid, which would drag on for years. She had no money, no recording company and no management. She was stuffed. Dave Vasco, Barry Ford and Dave Skinner had joined a band called Clancy, with Colin Bass and Gasper Lawal. All the musicians she knew were busy trying to make a living. The only thing she had going was The London Boogie Band and that wasn't regular.

So once again she left the little house in All Saints Road and once again Mick said he'd take care of the place. She was off to California with Sam, maybe for good this time. Mick was needing a bit more of his hometown. He and Shelly drove her to the airport in the Sally Sparkle car. She wore her beloved straw hat with the pink rose. She was never to see the car or the hat again. The hat was lost in the rush to catch the flight. Shelly was always running late. The van and the car were taken

Carol in the straw hat.

The shack on the Sacramento river.

over by Shelly's life, though the girl didn't know it at the time. Her place in Wales, her van, would be gone.

Her first meal in the Bay Area was sliced turkey, mashed potato, gravy, and red current jelly with Tequila shots. Later on in Crockett, she drank beers at the *U&I* bar opposite the *Tate & Lyle* sugar factory. A little dazed and more than a little jet lagged, she and Sam eventually slid down the bank and over the train tracks to the house that was a shack on the Sacramento river. The river on one side, the railway tracks on the other. It was like living on a boat, a shack or a railway car, depending which window you looked out of.

Gladys Knight singing *Midnight Train To Georgia* and Otis Redding *Dock of the Bay* were never so poignant. Mother and boy shared a little room. Two single beds, a cupboard and a chair. 'You can stay here,' said Ron, 'I'm in and out. We've got some gigs. You'll see, it'll be cool, girl. Hang on in there.' Ron had a girlfriend, Jo Anne, who lived in Santa Cruz down the coast. It wasn't cool. She didn't know why. Ron said, 'Hey, come and meet Jo Anne in Santa Cruz.'

What he didn't say was that he was leaving them, sink or swim, in Santa Cruz. Jo Anne and her friends assumed she was Ron's English slag. So there she was, with no friends, no smiles, and a moment in the bar when they seeemed to be talking about her behind their hands. They laughed at the hat she'd bought. The straw hat to replace her lost one. It was just a hat to keep the sun off and she knew it wasn't a patch on the other one. It was the sort that tourists would buy.

314

She met a friendly and crazy girl known around town as 'Treetop Patti'. Reputed to have lived in tree for a while, Patti was also a dealer in good grass. She had a son the same age as Sam and a house with rooms to spare. A few weeks passed and Jon Sagin became the girl's lifeline, with his friend Red Baldwin and the cats (not the tom cat that sprayed her boots). She was in California, she wore a tourist straw hat and boots that stunk, and she lived with a woman so crazy that people avoided her unless they needed dope.

Out walking with Jon in the California hills, the girl would forget her troubles for a while. She noticed the signs, 'Do not Litter', 'Do not build Fires'. Do not, do not, do not. They ruined the majesty of the landscape. Jon formed what he called the 'Why Botha Club' there. She was member number two of what would be a very exclusive club. He had stickers made, 'Why Botha' and 'Ignore Alien Orders'.

A month passed and Ron appeared, swinging up in his car as if nothing had happened.'Hey we're on,' he said, 'we got gigs at the *Fillmore West*.' Back to Crockett they went. And that was the time she introduced Jon Sagin to Karen Da Voto who lived in Crockett, up the hill from Ron's place. Karen had a beautiful smile and a wonderful lived-in laugh. Karen came along to the gigs and fell in love with Jon, and he with her. They had a daughter together. The girl and the boy stayed with Karen for a while as it become strange at Ron's after the time in Santa Cruz. She'd been blamed for the crime of stealing another other woman's man, and she wasn't guilty.

The girl wanted something. Anything. A hand, a hug, a friend. There was a guy called Dorwin who was said to only eat bread and peanut butter. It was true. His hair was the same colour. In the strange chaos which was life, he would meet up years later with one of the girl's half sisters in New Zealand whilst travelling.

Ron had another friend called Billy Maclin, who sometimes hung out with the Oakland Chapter of Angels. He drank six packs for breakfast and *Jack Daniels* on into the night. In a trailer park outside Fresno, Billy's mother and his older brother cooked speed to make some cash. Billy kept a gun under the driving seat of a low-slung wreck of a car. With the roof down when the sun was out, he'd scrap around the bends in Crockett and Santa Rosa, burning rubber. The radio would be on as loud as it could be, tuned to KSAM Radio. Billy couldn't really imagine Ladbroke Grove.

He heard the girl's English accent. To Billy's ears the girl must surely be an English lady. Billy, with a grin that can't begin to tell you of a life that swung out to the edges of the sun; Billy with a gun; Billy on the run; Billy who rolled skinny reefers with one hand and laughed at the moon when the moon was high;

Billy who saw the hellholes, saw the fire, his voice was like a chainsaw on the Redwoods; Billy with dark tattoos, who wore black t-shirts, blue jeans, a bandana and a heavy silver earring in one ear.

He took young Sam and his ma to the movies. 'A kids cartoon,' they said. It was sex, drugs, rock and roll and digging Fritz the Cat. One day, in a particularly good mood, Billy gun shot holes through the car roof. He died before he reached the age of 35. Billy's mother sent the girl a photo of the memorial service held by the Oakland Chapter of Angels, and a photo of Billy a month before he died, pegged by his t-shirt to a washing line. He had a big grin on his far too early wizened face, standing on his tip toes. Hanging Billy out to dry, the mother had written in a child like hand. 'That's the worse thing. She said, 'when your kids go before you...it's fucked, girl. You take care of that boy of yours.' Billy may be gone but the girl can still see him, grinning and hanging out to dry.

She found herself on stage at The *Fillmore West* in San Fransisco. The same stage graced by Janis Joplin, Grace Slick, Jim Morrison and most of all, Aretha Franklin. Singers and bands she'd listened to in the two rooms in St Stephen's Gardens. The band kicked into a blues. She was with Betty Blues Belter, singing her state of mind and looking straight ahead. Words began to form and she sang her own blues. What had she got to lose? It's not just about singing the blues, playing the blues, it's about *knowing* the blues. The blues isn't pop, it's not even rock. It's folk music, African American folk music. She originally wanted to sing because she heard the blues on a juke box in 1958. Ray Charles, 'Night time is the right time, to be with the one you love.'

After the US trip, most of which was a blur, she arrived back in her little world on the All Saints Road. Fiends came in paper packets, little wraps, Charles and Henry. Wraps of speed, of the numbness, the melting, shrinking into herself more and more. One white, one brown, one to bring you up, the other down, the wine and the beer and the joints and the endless meaningless chatter.

The *Warm Blood* album had come and gone, and even received good reviews. She did gigs with whoever she could find. She may have had an album out but she had no solid band. The gigs were a shifting mix of the same people, in and out of the London Boogie Band, mainly through Neil and Henry who seemed to know them all. Paul Carrack was around following the demise of Ace, his song *How Long?* on every juke box all over the world. Tim Hinkley was on keyboards and Henry McCullough joined them not long after leaving Paul McCartney and Wings.

The girl wore her *Guinness* apron, made tea for all and gathered her kit. A change of clothes for the gigs brought out the lipstick, mascara, money, keys and high heels. Sam would be with Larry for the night. Off to *Dingwalls* or the *Roundhouse*, the *Speakeasy*, *Half Moon* Putney, the *Hope & Anchor* on Upper Street, or out of town, to Brighton, Birmingham, York, Newcastle, Glasgow or Liverpool and across the Channel to mainland Europe. Out on the road.

In All Saints Road she carried on living on the front line of the black community's struggle with the police. Ever since the *Mangrove* move from the *Rio* café at 127 Westbourne Park, the girl and her son were right in the heart of that action. The *Mangrove* was always busy in those 1970s days. The girl often spotted the police peering through the windows. She heard the harassment outside on the street at night as she lay in her bed, and sometimes sat in the dark, watching from behind the windows in her front room. PC Pulley and his merry men kept an open warfare with the *Mangrove* and Frank in the All Saints Road community.

In the *Mangrove*, Frank and Dee had served food to Sammy Davis Junior, Marvin Gaye, Jimi Hendrix, Diana Ross and the Supremes, the Four Tops, Nina Simone, Sarah Vaughan, Vanessa Redgrave, and the cast of The Avengers. One day Marvin Gaye came in and Sam, wearing a Policeman's helmet from *Woolworths* much to the amusement of all, sat with the great man who signed a copy of *What's Going On?*

The girl wallowed in her marvellous moments. Sunny days in Holland Park or Kensington Gardens with the boy, buying fruit and vegetables down the market and cooking in her tiny kitchen. There were lazy Sundays round at Dee's place on Westbourne Park Road. She'd introduced him to all her friends and he cooked them his hot and spicy chicken wings with rice and peas, served with a cold beer to the sound of Trinidadian music. Steel pans, hot calypso songs and reggae remain in her head to this day and will always make her smile. *Hot, hot, hot* by Arrow aways signalled the oncoming summer season.

> *What to do on a night like this*
> *music sweet I can't resist*
> *we need a party song*
> *so with a rum bum bum*
> *let me rum bum bum bum.*

Dee and most of the Caribbean guys were only into weed. It was the musician's who seemed to be taking the dark substances, going to a deeply difficult place.

The girl was seeing Neil. He lived in a rented basement flat in Queensgate, not far from the *Albert Hall*. The house was dusty with black iron railings and steep stairs down to his front door. Neil was spending more and more time in All Saints Road. They were becoming a couple. Was the girl in love? She thought about it a lot and decided she had no idea what this love was, what she was supposed to feel.

The only love as certain as the sky drops rain from grey clouds, was the love for her little one. All other love put her into a spin. As for the real thing. 'Don't know,' she said to herself. Most of the time she slipped thorough the days, doing whatever needed to be done. Kokomo members were paired up. Dyan with Tony O'Malley, and Paddy and Frank had their lovers. Mel Collins and Terry Stannard had wives. She knew deep inside that Neil didn't really love her. She accepted it, fool that she was. He'd bought a *Sony* colour television. It was a Christmas present. Christmas in The Grove.

She sang with Dick and the Fireman in 1976. With Mel Collins, Neil Hubbard and Alan Spenner from the Grease Band and Kokomo. Also, Mike Patto, Bob Tench, Henry McCullough, Tim Hinkley, Boz Burrell, Simon Kirke and John Halsey.

Mike Patto needed an operation. The doctors in America had recently diagnosed cancer. Dick and the Firemen played at the *Crystal Palace Bowl* show to raise money towards Patto's treatment and a recuperation family holiday. Some of the other acts included the Chieftains, Eric Clapton and Freddie King, with guests Larry Coryell and Ronnie Wood. There had been a rehearsal at the *Union Jack*, just off Blackfriars Road on a Friday evening before, and another at the *Tunnel*, a small practice studio underneath a railway arch. Dim lights, hot damp air smelling of beer, tobacco and sweat. Simon and Boz flew in from France after working an all night session for a new Bad Company album. 'Mine's a hose-pipe!' 'A large brandy, a barley wine and half a *Guinness*.' 'Hosepipes all round.'

By two on the Saturday morning all the songs had been rehearsed, and the following weekend young Sam strolled onto the stage of the *Crystal Palace Bowl* just before noon, to grandly introduce the entertainment for the ninth Garden Party. 'Ladiz and gents, pleeze welcome Dick And The Firemen!'

The white powder was taken with others. Chat, chat, she'd known that one. A snort before the gig, a snort afterwards, keep up the energy, don't let go. 'The Brown was a new experience. After the initial sickness she wanted that more than the speedy one. It was something to have in secret, alone at night when the boy was in bed safe and asleep. She would silently open the little packet and then float in a state of warm limbo. Her hands, as she lifted them for inspection were?

JUNK-ETTA 'I don't recognise this hand. Numb my mind. Fill my veins with a smoke screen. Drip, drip, and feed me. My body was in pain, now my mind is indifferent. I don't care where I am. I'm warm. I taste no tears. I feel nothing.'

As she watched an Eric Clapton gig in 1976, Caryl Phillips wrote down some of what he said.

> 'Vote for Enoch Powell, stop Britain becoming a black colony. Get the foreigners out. I used to be into dope, then a foreigner pinched my missus' bum. Now I'm into racism. It's much heavier, man.'

Photographer Red Saunders then wrote a letter in September 1976 for *NME*, *Sounds* and *Socialist Worker*:

> 'You've got to fight the racist poison, otherwise you degenerate into the sewer with the rats and the money men who ripped off rock culture with their cheque books and plastic crap.'

Red came around to the little flat in All Saints Road. They talked. She let him know what it was like living with the harassment towards the black community. The *Mangrove*, opened in 1968, was repeatedly raided by police, on so-called evidence of drugs on the premises but Frank Critchlow kept a clean house. She'd been around the corner in St Stephen's Gardens in 1970, when the trail of the *Mangrove Nine* took place. They were cleared of the most serious charge of rioting.

In November 1976, *Rock Against Racism* held its first ever gig, set up by Steve Cedar. The gig featured the girl and a troupe of musicians and friends from The Grove. Reggae and rhythm and blues. A posse came over to the East End, to the

Princess Alice pub, National Front territory. The pub was packed. Owing to the possibly dangerous location for a bunch of writers, musicians, photographers and activists with slogans, the Royal Group Of Docks

Carol singing for RAR at the Roundhouse, London.

shop stewards committee did the security. The pub landlord was pissed off because someone gave the band a few beers. She did two more gigs for RAR, at the *Royal College of Art* and the *Roundhouse*.

Men would once more intervene. Big careers would be made for some who rode the RAR and then the Red Wedge Wagon in 1985. The girl was was ousted. Neither punk nor reggae, she was old school. So she was out.

There was an all night student sit in at the South London Polytechnic, at the Elephant and Castle, and with the 101ers, a benefit gig for ASS, the Advisory Service for Squatters. Groups of musicians were signing up left and right to play RAR benefits. Roots, reggae bands, Steel Pulse, Aswad and Misty in Roots. The vanguard of the punk movement, including the Clash, Buzzcocks and Sham 69. Punk, reggae, rock, blues, funk. Whatever it was, it all came in from black Americans in the early twentieth century. From blues then R&B, from the Caribbean, from Ska, from Calypso. A lot of the white musicians were on pay back time.

They were all there, with Henry and Sheila, in Dymchurch on the sea edge of Romney Marsh for Christmas 1976. The sky was so clear, you could almost touch the coast of France. Dee was there, the girl and Neil and the two boys, Jesse and Sam. Paul Carrack also arrived with his family.

The smell of Sheila's soda bread would waft across in the morning. It was chaos with the wayward children and even more wayward adults. All in the mix, along with the smell of weed, and the beers cracked open as a snifter before lunch. The children were placated with this and that, chocolate and tangerines, cheese and soda bread. All rather wonderful. The girl felt at home and not alone.

The girl had another invitation from Ron to do some gigs with his band. She travelled with Neil and Kokomo to the south, to Atlanta and other places, then to LA and up to the Bay Area. The boy had been promised strawberries and ice cream on arrival. They went to the *Sunset Marquis* on Alta Loma Road, West Hollywood, down a side street, a block west of La Cienega Boulevard, just below the Sunset Strip. Here you had the *Whisky A Go Go*, the *Roxy* and *Barney's Beanery*. The music world had played here, lived here, partied here.

In the reception she exclaimed, 'It's Colombo, it is!' As the actor with the glass eye sauntered by with a good looking woman and a man in a cream linen suit and black *Ray-bans*, carrying a smart brief case. This was a rock and roll hotel. Luscious and red, the strawberries were watery and tasteless. but the boy didn't care.

The girl was a hanger on with Kokomo and the Average White band. The west coast leg of a tour was beginning in a few days. They were all meeting in a Japanese restaurant the following evening and the hotel could arrange a baby sitter. She'd never eaten Japanese food, and the thought of leaving her child in a hotel was worrying. 'What if? Supposing?' The boy was fine. The hotel didn't burn down and the girl tasted Japanese food for the first time.

Kokomo singer Dyan Birch and the girl had to get dollars from the bank. They went down Rodeo Drive in Beverly Hills, to banks with acres of marble floors, deep black leather sofas and chairs, flowers on glass tables and glittering chrome. All for a measly handful of buck. That was hilarious. Kokomo were playing a gig in San Francisco. Jon Sagin invited the band and friends over for dinner. He was a wonderful cook and knew how to rustle up a meal for a crowd, using the glorious bounty of Northern California.

One Saturday night she was in an Irish bar in San Francisco with Ron and 'dirty little' Billy. 'Three pints of *Guinness*, please.' It was the girl's round. She smiled at the bartender and in the moment of eye to eye she was facing disgust. Bobby Sands, after 14 years in the Maze Prison, was sleeping on boards. She tried to explain to Irish Americans, who were born and bred in the New World, who watched the `Troubles' on big screens from the safety of American bars, that not all the English supported the Brit's claim on Ireland. The bar was hushed. She said, 'Look I'm a singer. I've risked my head doing gigs for 'Troops Out', had bricks and cabbages thrown at me.' She needed that drink. 'I don't give a shit,' said the barman, 'I ain't serving *Guinness* to no filthy Brit.' It was time to go home.

The wrangles went on and on with the Memphis album, *Carol Grimes*, released in 1975 on the Nigel Thomas label, *Goodear.* She lost touch with it, lost faith in it all. Even the reviews didn't convince her. Some gave it incredibly

Carol singing at a benfit gig, Sam on drums (*far left*), Neil Hubbard on guitar, Louis on bongos, Dee on the right.

good reviews, thanks to Steve Peacock and Penny Valentine. Ron? He didn't know the girl, other than the few weeks recording in Nashville, the days in Crockett and Santa Cruz, the mad bad days with Potter as monster and Bob Johnson as the boss of all he surveyed.

Such a move, risking all with a child, was a big thing. Far too big when the toe in the water was so ephemeral, the water so shallow. No one was to blame. She came, she saw, she didn't conquer.

By 1977, the girl was up for benefit gigs, for the right causes. The nowhere girl found her place for a while despite not being a punk or a jazz singer, nor rock nor roll or reggae. She simply hollered and sang as if she and the injustices of the world depended upon it.

Wilf Walker presented the first Notting Hill Carnival stage on Portobello Green beside the Westway. Underneath made a perfect place for music. Aswad topped the bill with Barry Ford from Merger, Sons of Jah, King Sounds and the Israelites, Brimstone, Exodus, and Nik Turner from Hawkwind. On the final evening the unease and anger in The Grove broke loose. Cans and bottles bounced off the riot shields. The girl sang yards from her home and walked back through shards of glass and crushed beer cans. She sang to reclaim the streets and for squatters rights.

Dingwalls in Camden Lock became her home from home with the band. She sang with Henry and with Paul Carrack, managed by Roger and Boss. On a wall outside

8a one day, she saw a poster advertising a gig, 'The entire population of China.' 'Whoa!' she thought, 'what is that?' That was to be discovered when she met Laka Daisical in a band called Soulyard, singing one night, sharing garlic breath together over the microphone on stage. They were a crowd of musicians she would get to know well, all living east of Oxford Street. They became part of the Guest Stars, and Lydia D'Ustebyn's Ladies Swing Orchestra, a feminist swing band of women, with Deirdre Cartwright on guitar, Josphina Cupido on drums, Julia Doyle on double bass and Laka Daisical (Dorota Koc) on piano and vocals. Laka was a wiz at band names.

Mick Oakley appeared one evening at a gig at the *Hope & Anchor* with Sandy Ratcliffe, the actor who played the teenage Psychotic in Ken Loach's *Family Life*. Mick had moved away from his isolated cottage in Login and was living in a squat in Bethnal Green. Sandy was living there with Terry Palmer, a theatre director who'd been in working in Peterborough, along with Howard Dylan and Peter Browne. They were all living in the 'Triangle,' the name for the houses. They were made up of three streets, Bishops Way, Waterloo Gardens and Sewardstone Road, back to back in an elongated triangle. The girl met Karen Douglas, Chloe and Toby Salomon, and actors Frances Lowe and Bobby Mackintosh from Scotland, with his partner, a painting restorer. Also, actors Darlene Johnson and Ken Shorter from Australia, and Harold the kangaroo.

A month or so later she took the Central Line to Bethnal Green for a drink at the local pub, the *Approach Tavern* in Approach Road, and met a bunch of people with those odd connections that life hurls out every so often. Neil had been at Peterborough Cathedral as young chorister and there he heard the legend of an ex-student, Norman Andrews, who burned down the gym block one day. There they were sitting in the bar hearing the story from his son, Simon.

The first time the girl visited Sandy Ratcliffe in her maisonette, she was astounded by the size of the rooms. It was run down but not crumbling like St Stephen's Gardens. The front looked out over the Roman Catholic primary school, and Victoria Park was a one-minute walk away. Neil was working a lot. Kokomo were on a roll, so he decided to buy a flat in Basset Road on the other side of Ladbroke Grove. The girl was wary. 'Oh, you and Sam too,' he said.

THE BOSS 'Watch yourself, don't burn your boats.'

She put a new home together with Neil, using some of her bits from 8a. Neil bought a church pew and a table. It was the first time she had room to sit and eat around a table since her arrival in The Grove. She acquired an old fridge circa

1959 and called it Mildred. She boxed sensibly and kept the rent going on 8a. Once again the Mice took over.

A few months passed and still it didn't feel like her home. It was Neil's. She'd kept in touch with Sandy who'd split up with her husband, Terry. Sandy had decided to buy a terraced house not far away in Brownlow Road, off Broadway market. She wanted to leave the Triangle, which at that time was still short life properties owned by Tower Hamlets Council. 'You want to move into my place in Bishops Way?' she asked the girl, 'I know things are not good for you.'

There was a campaign against the demolition of some East End streets. The Greater London Council had planned an East Way to match the West Way on Portobello Road, taking out some of Victoria Park. The plans were dropped but many of the residents had already been moved on. The original squatters succeeded in saving the area from demolition and a new community was born, eventually becoming a Grand Union Housing Co-Operative, founded by Gary Chamberlin.

The girl bumped into Alan Spenner's Dutch wife, Cici, one day in the market. For once she wasn't asking for anything, like baby sitting. 'Hello,' she said, 'I'm sorry.' The girl smiled and said, 'What for?' 'Well, you know, I think we...' Her words trailed off. They chatted this and that, what Kokomo were doing and that she was thinking of going to Holland to visit family. They went their separate ways. With Frank and Tony from Kokomo, Cici had laughingly called the girl, 'the singing housewife', mocking her for anything they considered uncool. They didn't take her seriously. Behind her back they laughed about her orange *Guiness* apron, her cooking and the hospital corners. But it wasn't behind her back. She knew. She didn't care so much about the apron. She did care that none of them rated her as a singer. When Paddy left the band they didn't ask her to join them. 'Can you have her for an hour?' Cici would say, as she and Alan disappeared for a night, scoring and hanging out somewhere where the drugs were.

Cici died one night, not long after the strange little meet. Her mother was over from Holland, and Sheila and Henry were staying in the coachhouse they'd bought around the corner from 8a. Sheila called Neil and the girl because Alan was out somewhere. Cici had succumbed to asthma and an overdose of heroin. She lay in her bed, waxy skinned on turquoise cotton sheets. The room was heavy with the scent of a vase of freesias on the bedside table and the sickly smell of the deceased. The baby was in a cot in the next room.

THE BOSS 'The needles and the wraps of heroin, flush it all down into the toilet. Out in the bin. Hide it.'

Sheila and the girl got rid. It was decided to get the baby out, so she and Neil wrapped her up in blankets and drove back to Ladbroke Grove in the early hours of the morning. The baby, clearly distressed, had been pulling out her own hair.

THE BOSS 'So, you can see where it will lead. Out cold and stiff on sheets of death.'

The funeral was at Kensal Green Cemetery and the wake at the Alan and Cici's home, the *Coach House* on Lancaster Road. Neil was distraught, saying he'd been in love with Cici. Alan and the girl exchanged glances across the room full of people who were probably thinking. 'There but for the Grace of...' 'Poor Alan, poor Cici.' 'What will happen to the baby?' Here we all stand on the thin line between time past and future unknown.

JUNK-ETTA 'I'm a shell, a kite that's lost it's string, a bell that's lost its ring, a body stinking, sweating. Muscles in pain. Strung out on a line in the wind.'

The days following the funeral were as hazy as old London fog. Cici's mother had returned to Holland, taking the baby with her, to be adopted by Cici's sister. The girl had a gig here and there and attempted to carry on as normal. Sam went to school, she washed their clothes and cooked their meals. But she knew it was the end of life west of Oxford Street. Seeing the place in Bethnal Green had spurred her on towards a new beginning. Her life with Neil was over. Did it ever really mean much? Not when he'd said what he did. He may have been drunk and distraught but his confession of love for Cici was shocking and final. There was no staying now. The girl had lost 8a and Basset Road belonged to Neil.

It was time to move. Kokomo would be off on tour and that would be the time to do it. No fuss, get on with it. She hated goodbyes. She arranged a van, loaded Mildred, her clothes, Sam's things including his drum kit, a few books, records and odds and sods, cups and plates, a kettle and some cooking pots, a rug or two, all trawled during her years living around the Portobello and Golborne Roads. She had the makings of a new home. Apart from a chest of drawers and the little pine table, she owned no furniture but it was enough to start anew. All she needed to do was get rid of the bad medicine and those who ruled her inner airwaves.

The girl's generation had been born into the dark gas lit world of the 1940s. A generation that began life with ration books and austerity, dead fathers, dead uncles, and women clutching at love whose babies were born nine months later if they'd managed to avoid a butcher's knife abortion. If they had money they could buy a clinical procedure, or have the child spirited away. Where's your daughter? Staying with an aunt. A plausible lie during a time of upheavals and absence, death and trauma.

The girl wandered around in a daze most of the time. Living in a bubble with other misfits and outsiders, travellers and tramps.

> **NASTY NELLIE** 'So sad, she lives in a bag. Zips herself up at night. She lives in fear. Afraid to go here or there, never going near the light, unless she has a drink in her hand.'

She was caught in a maelstrom.

> **MISERY IVY** 'I'm drowning. Not waving. Sinking, not thinking about how I can swim. Are my arms frozen? Have I chosen to disappear? I'm drowning, not craving a helping hand, not looking for land beneath my feet.'
>
> **THE BOSS** 'You may as well sling a crock of crap at yourself.'
>
> **MISERY IVY** 'I've tried to be steady, calm and organised but I can't. I'm useless.'
>
> **THE BOSS** 'Ignore them. They're not there, they're nothing.'

She turning on the radio one Sunday evening and the most tender sound poured out. A cello, Pablo Casals *Song of the birds*. It was like hearing Ella for the first time all those years ago. And Miles, and Bobby Blue Bland and Woody. Life was good. Life was beautiful. Life was to live.

So she sat on the bass lines, loving the grooves. She may be too old for *Top of the Pops*, she may be a woman in a man's business, and she may have gone more than three strikes. But no one was going to shut her singing mouth.

> **BETTY BLUES BELTER** 'You gotta have scattitude and attitude, you gotta have the groove. You gotta have swing and you gotta move, so give me those bass lines.'

Donald 'Duck' Dunn rocking *Dock of the Bay*, and *Birdland* with Jaco Pastorius. Miles Davis with Paul Chambers, Marcus Miller, Larry Graham slap-and-pop, Carol Kaye, *You send me*. Sitting on the bass lines, toe tapping with the drums. It was always there, right slap dab in the middle of the band. How she loved the feeling, her voice flying like a kite, held firmly in her belly, whoop, soar, bend and sway. Did she ever have one eye on the big time deal? No, not when she was flying her singing kite.

Betty Blues Belter needed to sing and swing with the band. Bantering with the brass; trombones and saxophones, trumpets and euphoniums, flying flutes and soaring guitars, keyboards and piano. Does she hide away like she only exists when she sings, bringing on Clara the Clown to do the business? Nimble fingers, chunky sexy chords, striding in the middle of it all. Grist to the mill and lead in the pencil.

Procrastinating Patsy wrung her hands, picked at her lip and her nails, and chewed her fingers. Sucking in her belly, she pulled on a pair of jeans one size too small. 'I won't eat today,' she thought.

She went across from the West to the East End of London on the red line, the Central Line. This was a change. So far she'd travelled mainly on the green and yellow District and Circle Lines and on the red buses. It was a fairly busy road, a continuation of Hackney Road over Cambridge Heath Road. She took a few steps up to the red door at 105 Bishops Way. Then up a flight of stairs onto a landing with a glass door that looked onto a small outside space. Plants she thought, that's more than a window sill. 'Pots,' she thought, 'I'll have pots here. I may grow tomatoes and red geraniums. Perhaps have a small table and chair. Such a perfect spot for an evening glass of wine.' Home? Please let it be. She took a second flight of stairs to the first floor. To the left was a back room divided into a tiny bathroom and kitchen. The front room had a high ceiling and long windows. Sandy had stripped back to the brick around the fireplace and the room was full of light from two floor-to-ceiling windows. There was another flight of stairs to the two bedrooms, back and front. The girl took the back and Sam would have the bigger front room. It was a good space for a 10 year-old, his drum kit, his bed and room for more boys to hang out.

The glories of Brick Lane, Columbia Road and the East End markets were all ready and waiting. There was a secondhand shop in a small parade at the end of Bishops Way. She bought a pair of blue and white lined floral curtains. 'From The Savoy,' said the woman who ran the shop. They filled the two big windows and kept out the cold. The house had no central heating, was dusty and shabby, the floorboards creaked, the windows rattled and the roof leaked. But she had a feeling she'd landed in the right place. Then there was the joy of collecting wood from Victoria Park, and sacks of smokeless fuel from Mr Drake, the coal merchant. She'd learned the art of tightly rolling newspapers to kickstart her fire. It was messy cleaning the grate, with dust everywhere and she had to haul the logs in bits and pieces up the stairs. The first Christmas in Bishops Way, she burned the tree on Twelfth Night, turning her home into a Swedish pine forest.

Sam had recently been diagnosed as dyslexic and was attending a weekly clinic at St Bartholomews Hospital near the Barbican. Sandy told her about a fee paying Montessori school called the *Gatehouse* that specialised in dyslexia. The headmistress was married to the Dean of St Paul's. The girl sold some of her swag gathered from years living beside the Portobello Road, the beautiful vintage shawls, the dresses and beads. A month later she saw her beautiful Victorian shawl in a shop window for four times the twenty pounds she'd sold it for. She applied to various charitable trusts in order to pay the school fees for the second term. She had some refusals until she applied succesffully to the *Baden Powell Trust*. Hurrah! Sam could continue at the *Gatehouse*. Life was beginning to settle.

The first night she slept at Sandy's house, she'd dreamed she was trapped on Dogger Bank, or worse, German Bight. She was away from hearth and home, surrounded by a grey and raging sea in a strange northern land with craggy cliffs. In the morning all was blue above, if a little chilly. She often dreamed of water, both fearing and loving the mighty sea.

CLARA THE CLOWN 'What a palaver. Where to next?'

WICKED WILL O'MINA 'You got a stinky, winky look in your eye when you pass by. Oh my, you try so hard. Is the swagger in your jacket? Are the shoes the groove when you move?'

Winkling and winking with the promise of wishes and dreams, she wandered far and wide on the edges of dreams and truth in search of a clue as to who she may be. This girl who nobody seemed to know, exploring the pain and the pleasure of memories. Songs are what she had known. They'd given her life, a voice and structure amidst the chaos. She mustn't piss all the words against the wind. The wind may piss them right back. Certainly dig and delve but rememberings can be tricky. They can turn around and bite you on the bum. She would so often disappear to a place where nobody could find her. Out of her head and away with the fairies, searching for that illusive out of this world place under an old but friendly moon. Off she flew to where the dish ran away with the spoon and the stars were the light and the way.

CLARA THE CLOWN 'Roll up, ladies and gentleman. Roll up girls and boys, and say, 'Hello' to the clown. She'll never go down. Stroll up, walk alongside, watch her fly. A fiddle, a riddle, a diddle de dee, say hello to the clown!'

NERVY NORA AND JUNK ETTA 'There are days when I feel crazy and unbelievably blue, I could throw my life away. Walking around in a perpetual daze, preferring dreams to the real thing.'

THE BOSS 'Please deposit your feelings in the waste paper basket provided. Any sign of weakness such as tears or deep sighing is punishable and a fine will be levied. Any protestations will be punishable by withdrawal of chocolate.'

PISS POT POLLY 'As long as you don't withdraw my glass of wine.'

Songs, melody, words, rhythm and rhyme, she needed to dive deeper. To hold this singing and work on it.

WICKED WILL O'MINA 'Slippy sliding down the street tonight, so what do you want to do? Miss a trick and you don't fly the kite. Who's gonna swing for you?'

MISERY IVY 'I'm sitting on my thumbs, thinking about life every day. Walking into lamp posts, knocking myself out. What can I say? I'm looking for some answers. What's the meaning of life? Oh woe, woe is me.'

She thought about her family, her mother, all so far away, both in time and distance. What did she feel?

NASTY NELLIE 'So who's in your skin? Are you in?'

PISS POT POLLY 'In my youth and young womanhood, so easy to drown it all. Drinking the thoughts to a silent morose, bending the mind into shapes undefined, whatever my Moira. Slip sitting and whistling the days away in my own constructed maze. I'd stay. Go away old feelings, away.'

If she didn't listen to those voices, look at that past, how would she ever understand?

THE BOSS 'Courage is the price that life exacts for granting peace. The soul that knows it not, knows no release from little things. Knows not the livid loneliness of fear or mountain heights where bitter fears can hear the sounds of war.'

CLARA THE CLOWN 'Yes, for the great adventure, take just one more flight. Hold me dark mysterious night, hold me, make me strong and the battle pure.'

Yes, she knew about feelings of love, for her son, for her friends, for life itself.

SENSIBLE MA SADIE 'Put the kettle on! Break out the chocolate *Hobnobs*.'

Her mother had rejected love.

THE BOSS 'Shhhhhh!'

She was the one to be sad and lonely. The one with no mother of her own. The motherless child.

See you around the next corner for the tales into the 1980s and beyond.

Tales in volume number two... kicking the poisons out the window.

From a squat to shortlife housing, then a housing cooperative in Bethnal Green. Back to America, to Texas and California. Poland days, writing songs once more. Finding more women to work with, the GLC days, singing contemporary Opera with The Shout, the *Drill Hall Arts Centre* and more recordings.

Working in South Africa, running choirs for people with Parkinson's disease, multiple sclerosis, cancer and other conditions. Moving to Camden Town NW1 and then south of the river once more, to Deptford SE8. Making a garden on the roof, and finally Folkestone. Another garden to make, this time in the earth with trees. And best of all, a daughter is born.

'I hold a mouses wit not worth a leke, That hath but on hole for to sterten to.'
Canterbury Tales *The Wife of Bathe Prologue*, Line 6154

From Carol's scrapbook

Some pictures from my days living in the Grove, the first community where I came to know happiness and being accepted, warts 'n' all!

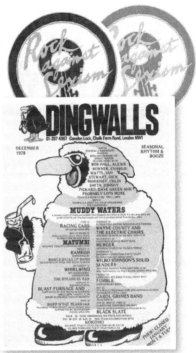

VE MUSIC — HATE RACISM...BLACK AND WHITE UNITE AND FIGHT...CAROL GRIME

1500 came to the
Roundhouse on
Mayday. A music/
politics mix
that worked. Our
music getting back
to the Roots.
Carol Grimes and
Aswad talked to
Temporary Hoarding
after the gig.
Love Music/
Hate Racism.
We've got to chase
those crazy racists
out of town.

Discography

Into The Promised Land, Babylon 1969, Polydor Records

Harry Lucky, Delivery 1970, B&C Records

Fool's Meeting, Delivery 1970, B&C Records, re-released on Cuneiform

Old Hat, Uncle Dog 1972, EMI

Warm Blood, Carol Grimes 1974, Virgin/Caroline

You're The Only One, Carol Grimes 1974, Virgin

Give It Everything You've Got, The London Boogie Band 1974, Goodear Records

Number One In My Heart, Carol Grimes 1975, Goodear Records

I Betcha Didn't Know That, Carol Grimes 1975, Goodear Records

Dynamite / I Betcha Didn't Know That, Carol Grimes 1975, Goodear Records

Carol Grimes, Carol Grimes 1975, Decca

Sweet FA, Carol Grimes 1980, NWM Sweden

Ain't That Peculiar, Carol Grimes 1982, Polydor

Eyes Wide Open, Carol Grimes 1987, Line Records

Daydreams and Danger, Carol Grimes 1988, Line Records

Why Don't They Dance?, Carol Grimes 1989, Line Records

Heart In My Hands, Carol Grimes 1989, Instant Records

Lazy Blue Eyes, Carol Grimes & Ian Shaw 1990, Ace Records Offbeat

Into the Red, Carol Grimes 1992, Distribute by WRPM

Alive at Ronnie Scott's, Carol Grimes & Janette Mason 1994, Jazz House

On Arrival, The Shout February 2001, Shaping the Invisible, Distributed by Carbon 7

Mother, Carol Grimes, recorded in London March & April 2003, released January 2005 on Irregular Records and Proper Music Distribution

Deep Blue, The Shout 2004, Unknown Public

Charybdis, Vortex Foundation Big Band 2004, Babel Records

The Story of UK Funk, Brothers on the Side 2005, Discotheque

Something Secret, Carol Grimes & Giles Perring 2007, Triumphant Records

C.Dawn with Carol Grimes, Dorian Ford, Annie Whitehead, Winston Clifford & Neville Malcolm 2013

Tales of Two Cities, Heath Common & Carol Grimes 2014, Hi 4 Head Records

Press reviews of Carol's work

'It amazes me how she uses her great, bit raw voice to express all the corners of emotion into her music...A fantastic CD, pure, honest and beautiful.' Eelco Schilder *FolkWorld*, Issue 31 1/2000, on *Mother* by Carol Crimes

'Should be regarded as a national treasure.' Trevor Hodgett, *Blues in Britain*, 2003

'Carol's a true "vocalist's vocalist", and sensuous to the last in the Billie Holiday tradition.' David Kidman, *Net Rhythm*, 2003

'Her own compositions, melancholic and reflective without being rambling...and the instrumental arrangements are exemplary, underpinning the attractive, lived-in vocals of a superior English singer.' Colin Randall, *The Telegraph*, 2005

'The show gives many of the group a chance to shine as composers and arrangers. *Song of Work* by Carol Grimes has a vigour and improvised complexity that recalls *The Shouting Fence.*' John L. Walters, *The Guardian*, on The Shout at the Purcell Room, 2005

'These two proms celebrated the singing voice. Getting the afternoon event off to a flying start was an atmospheric opener by Gough called, aptly, *Open*, which featured the mesmerising vocalism of Carol Grimes and Manickam Yogeswaran, among others, ricocheting around the Albert Hall at all levels and from every direction.' George Hall, *The Observer*, on The Shout Proms at the Royal Ablbert Hall, 2006

'Carol Grimes... delivered the evening's most powerful and emotional songs.' Jack Massarik, *Evening Standard,* on The Soul Britannia Allstars, The Barbican London, 2007

'On Saturday this series featured Carol Grimes, and it was a great pleasure to be in right at the very start of such a genuinely promising venture as her Autobiography, an item tucked into her programme of songs...This project has such a strong heart, it really could go anywhere as it develops. It could be a stage play, or radio drama, or album, or any combination of these.' Sebastian Scotney, *London Jazz News*, 2013

'A spine-chillingly powerful singer rooted in the blues who embraces vocal ideas from outside the African-American tradition, Grimes is forthright, moving and imaginative.' John Fordham, *The Guardian*, 2004

'Carol Grimes and her current, beautifully tight band – Dorian Ford (piano), Neville Malcolm (bass), Winston Clifford (drums) and Annie Whitehead (trombone) – put them all together and we had a feast of varied music and a totally sold out venue.' Grimes is a true, charismatic artist.' Carol at Lauderdale House, London Jazz Festival Brian Blain, *London Jazz News*, on Carol at Lauderdale House, London Jazz Festival, 2013

'Carol Grimes, the "Edith Piaf" of British music.' Sebastian Taylor, *Camden Review*, 2015

'Carol Grimes might not include *I Could Write a Book* in her Edinburgh Fringe show, *The Singer's Tale*. The London-born survivor of fifty years in the music business would, however, have every right to sing this Rodgers and Hart standard.' Rob Adams, *Herald Scotland*, 2015

'Carol Grimes needs longer than a Fringe slot to tell her life story.' Rob Adams, *Herald Scotland*, 2015

'The culmination of the Festival for me was Carol Grimes who performed mainly her own creation with a trio accompaniment. There sang everything: voice, facial expression, gestures, motion-she was an artist of a hundred percent. Her lyrics were easy to listen to because of exemplary diction.' *Easti Aeg* (Estonian Times.)

Lightning Source UK Ltd.
Milton Keynes UK
UKHW020635200920
370211UK00007B/355